THE BRITISH DRAMA

A Handbook and Brief Chronicle

THE BRITISH DRAMA

A Handbook and Brief Chronicle

Alan S. Downer
Princeton University

NEW YORK

Appleton-Century-Crofts, Inc.

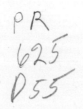

Preface

In more classical days this volume might have been subtitled a *Vademecum,* an accurate description of its purpose and its method. It is intended as a guide and companion to those undertaking for the first time a study of the drama. This in turn accounts for its structure. Although the basic "facts" of literary and stage history have been included, they have been selected and arranged to focus attention on the development of the drama as a form of communication and artistic expression. This will explain the relatively extended treatment of the beginnings and later development of the panoramic drama, the native and unique English form, and of certain plays not usually studied in the classroom. It will also justify and explain the nature of the illustrations which have been chosen not for ornament but for use, to enable the student to visualize in any period the appearance of the drama in its fullest realization as produced on the stage.

For the most part, materials which have no direct bearing on the development of dramatic art have been collected under various entries in the bibliography. They can be easily located by referring to the index.

It is necessary to make a general acknowledgment of my indebtedness to the scholars and critics of the drama on whom I have freely drawn: the amount of my debt may be estimated from the size of the bibliography. I must however, record my particular gratitude to my colleague, Gerald Eades Bentley, for suggesting the book and reading the manuscript, to my former student, Vivian Broman, for executing the illustrations, and to my wife, for criticism, encouragement, and, of course, for the preparation of the index.

A. S. D.

Contents

Illustrations

ix

THE BRITISH DRAMA

A Handbook and Brief Chronicle

━ 1 ━

The Native Dramatic Tradition

In its origin the word *drama* designated something "being done," and the word *theater* designated a place "for seeing." One of the primitive meanings, then, that is associated with the experience of playgoing is the seeing of an action. In a sense this is as good a definition of the drama as any, since it involves the fundamental elements of audience, theater, and action. Such fundamentals, far from being assumed without question, are all too apt to be forgotten in the study of the drama of the past since it exists almost exclusively on the printed page; and the modern reader, if he is to reach anything like a true understanding of that drama, must remind himself that Shakespeare and Marlowe, Dryden and Congreve, Sheridan and Robertson were writing for the stage and not the library.

To be sure, the destroying hand of Time or the creative hand of Mutability have left us with but at best an imperfect record of what, say, the Elizabethan audience actually saw. We know much about the physical aspects of their theater—the scenery, the costuming, the relationship of the audience and the player—but there is much of importance that we can never know, such as the intonation of Burbage's voice in the soliloquies of Hamlet, or the balance of the ugly and attractive in his characterization of Falstaff. And since we are many centuries removed from Burbage and his fellows, perhaps total knowledge is unnecessary. Our *ultimate* concern—for it is a sin of pride to believe that nothing else matters—must be with the meaning of Hamlet to our society, our audiences: his impact on the twentieth century. Only the most thorough analysis of the original to the limits of our knowledge entitles us to make an evaluation with reference to our own world. Such a thorough analysis involves some knowledge of the original conditions under which the plays were produced.

1

For the producing of a play is vastly unlike the printing of a poem or story. Sound, color, and movement, the non-literary elements which the playwright commands and employs freely, differ both in kind and organic importance from paper and binding and even illustration. The physical relationship of players on the stage, the intonation of voices, the pattern and tempo of movement, and conversely the silences and lack of movement, may contribute as much to the total effect of the play as the words of the dialogue. And it must be remembered that these non-literary elements are important tools of the playwright—a word which in itself defines the artist as a play*maker* rather than merely a play*writer*. There is perhaps a partial analogy in the sports columns of our newspapers. The reader learns from them the winner of the baseball game, the score, the errors, the names of the players and what, statistically, transpired. The sports writer is at some pains to make his description "colorful," to use the strongest verbs and the most vivid adjectives in his vocabulary. The result is mere information. But the dramatist is concerned with more than the what, who, why, when, and how of an event. He presents the thing itself, and not as a document, a report to stir those whose receptivity is foreordained, but as a transpiring event whose significance will be made apparent to the observer, prejudiced or not, in the course of the action.

The nature of dramatic action thus becomes of major importance. It is curiously ambivalent: it is real and it is not real; it happens and it does not happen. Hamlet does not really kill King Claudius and Lear does not really go mad—but for the time we are watching the performance we are so persuaded. We in the audience are aware that this is but pretense, that in an hour the blond wig will be stowed in a cupboard and the costume exchanged for a business suit, yet we connive at the cheat and encourage the lie. Nor is this merely that we may escape from the everyday world into a magic fairyland where all the rules are off, for the drama—particularly the modern drama—takes especial delight in portraying the commonplace in all its harsh ugliness. For a true understanding of "drama" and the pleasure we take in it, we must look beyond the simple fairy world of the escapist and deeper into our natures as human beings. The dramatic instinct is universal, knowing no boundaries of race or time, a part of our common humanity. Present in every primitive society, it develops with that society to greater or lesser artistic achievements.

The English drama is in many ways a unique art form, born of a special necessity, developing under peculiar conditions, and—half-way through its history—reaching a climax that was completely *sui generis* in form, subject matter and physical production. The reasons are not far to seek. Until its conquest by the Normans, England had been only intermittently and tenuously connected with the continent of Europe. English arts and crafts, traditions and conventions in "this little world" developed in their own ways with very little guidance or restriction from "less happier lands." This was less true, of course, among the nobility, the clergy and the scholars than among the folk; but the drama of any race or nation begins with the common man and only after many generations is taken over by other classes.

1. THE FOLK PLAY

The English drama arose out of two compulsions; the natural instinct to imitate and the evangelical desire to teach.

The first of these, the instinct of imitation, is the basis of all primitive drama and all popular art. Anthropologists have found curious similarities—and less curious divergences—in the popular drama of many societies; in ancient Greece, in the islands of the South Pacific, among the Amerinds. In England, even today, in such popular festivals as May Day and Christmas, there are survivals of a dramatic tradition centuries old, completely non-literary, and completely conventional.

Like that of other races, the English popular drama seems to have arisen out of the attempts of the primitive mind to grapple with the mystery of dying and being born, which he related to the mystery of the rotation of the seasons and the inevitable succession of spring to winter. Gradually, it is conjectured, the natural event took shape as a myth, the Struggle of Winter and Spring, or of Life and Death, and climactic incidents of the myth were the mock death and revival of the hero. Joined with this "drama," or perhaps preceding it, were the prehistoric ceremonials in which selected members of the community attempted to control the workings of vital spirits by symbolic pantomime or *imitation*. It is difficult to say what these ceremonials or plays may have been like; perhaps in addition to the acting out of the death and resurrection of the hero they involved a procession in which flowers and fruits, symbolizing the fertility spirit, were carried through the community to ensure the equal distribution of the blessings.

This primitive myth became attached to the folk legends of St. George and the Dragon, and Robin Hood, and as such was transmitted orally from generation to generation in versions that vary greatly from one community to another. As their original meaning was forgotten, the plays frequently were made a part of the Christmas festivities, a group of mummers, or amateur actors, going from house to house (the traditional procession) with their own variation.

The St. George plays as they were finally recorded in the nineteenth century show all the signs of corruption which inevitably attends oral transmission over a number of centuries. The folk has a long memory for the ceremonial act and a very short one for the meaning. The mock death and resurrection are here, and St. George under various appellations. Sometimes Father Christmas appears, and sometimes a Turkish Knight who seems to have joined the cast during the crusades. But only the reconstruction by Sir E. K. Chambers makes any sense out of the corruptions and contradictions of the various surviving versions.

The basic pattern consists of a prologue introducing the characters, a fight in which the hero is slain, the resurrection of the hero (usually by a Comic Doctor), a comic scene and a dance, the whole concluding with a passing of the hat—or, in one case, a frying pan—for contributions amongst the audience. Crude and confusing as they are, the mummers' plays are continuing evidence of the folk desire to act, to imitate—the first compulsion in the establishing of drama.

2. LITURGICAL PLAYS

The second compulsion, the desire to teach, is equally universal, though our evidence comes from a later and historic period when the last shadows of what used to be called the Dark Ages were being dispelled by the first glimmerings of the Twelfth Century Renaissance.

Scholars have been at some pains to trace every step in the

origin and development of the English drama. The record is as fascinating, if not quite as pat, as a detective story; but for our purposes a summary alone must suffice. It begins, as such stories must, once upon a time, roughly the ninth century. It begins, somewhat surprisingly (for the church had been the principal opponent of the drama in the late Roman world), in a church. If we do not know what church, or what year, however, we do know the time of year and we can guess at the cause of the church's reversal of its attitude.

To the common man of the early middle ages, churchgoing must have been an experience at once exalting and mystifying. Fond as he was of spectacle, the great cathedrals, with rays of color streaming from stained glass windows to mingle with light from banks of candles, the pervasive odor of incense, the richly embroidered robes of the priests, the inspired voices of the choir, must have filled him with wonder and satisfaction. But he could only, in his ignorance of Latin, have been mystified at the meaning of what was transpiring. It was, perhaps, comparable to attending the performance of an opera in an unknown tongue. You are moved, exalted, perhaps, but you know not why. The exaltation becomes a temporary pleasure and soon passes. To give permanence to the effect of an experience, its *meaning* must be made evident. In this intention lies the birth of the English drama.

An often quoted account of a performance of the earliest of the *Liturgical Plays* survives in a record made between 965 and 975 by the Bishop of Winchester:

While the third lesson is being chanted let four brethren vest themselves. Let one of these, vested in an alb, enter as though to take part in the service, and let him approach the sepulchre without attracting attention and sit there quietly with a palm in his hand; while the third respond is being chanted, let the remaining three follow, and let them all, vested in copes, being in their hands thuribles with incense, and stepping delicately as those who seek something, approach the sepulchre. These things are done in imitation of the angel sitting in the monument, and the women with spices coming to anoint the body of Jesus. When therefore he who sits there beholds the three approach him like folk lost and seeking something, let him begin in a dulcet voice of medium pitch, to sing, *Quem quaeritis* (Whom seek ye?). And when he has sung it to the end, let the three reply in unison *Ihesu Nazarenum*. So he, *Non est hic, surrexit sicut praedixerat* (He is not here, he is risen as was foretold). *Ite, nuntiate quia surrexit a mortuis* (Go, proclaim that he is risen from the dead). At the word of this bidding let those three turn to the choir and say *Allelulia! resurrexit Dominus!* This said, let the one, still sitting there and as if recalling them, say the anthem *Venite et videte locum* (Come and examine the spot). And saying this, let him rise, and lift the veil, and show them the place bare of the cross, but only the cloths laid there in which the cross was wrapped. And when they have seen this, let them set down the thuribles which they bare in that same sepulchre, and take the cloth, and hold it up in the face of the clergy, and as if to demonstrate that the Lord has risen and is no longer wrapped therein, let them sing the anthem *Surrexit Dominus de sepulchro* (The Lord is risen from the tomb), and lay the cloth upon the altar. When the anthem is done, let the [choir], sharing their gladness at the triumph of our King . . ., begin the hymn *Te Deum laudamus.* And this begun, all the bells chime out together.

It should be noted first that the playlet is a part of the service, that the various speeches are chanted and are derived from anthems, and that, in fact, the opening lines of the angel were originally a mere wordless sequence, or vocal elaboration, of the final sustained note of an *allelulia.* Further, although there is some attempt at surprising the audience—the angel is directed to take his place without attracting attention—the actors are dressed in regular priestly garments and employ standard equipment of the church, for example, thuribles, in place of more realistic properties. The whole tends to be symbolic, in fact. The body of Christ is represented by a cross which had been laid in the sepulchre, a small, frequently temporary edifice placed near the altar; the anointing spices are represented by the incense, and so on. But the action is realistic enough. The actors are instructed in detail to step delicately as those who seek something. The actions must speak plainly to all the audience, that the drama may achieve its purpose.

Only a moment of drama to be sure. A few lines of dialogue, taken from the Vulgate Bible and still in Latin, but with a definite attempt to clarify for the congregation by movement and impersonation the meaning of the event. The *Te Deum* of the choir is no longer simply a soul-stirring piece of music—it is the expression of an emotion which grows out of the *allelulia* of the "three women," exultation for the triumph of Christ over the power of evil and of death. Its effect is to transfer the emotion to the spectator. Thus early it becomes the function of the drama to convince men by allowing them to share in the experience of a hero or a group of characters.

That the Church found its new art useful is evident from its rapid development and widespread employment. Copies of the Liturgical Plays—plays which grow directly out of the service of the church, and are employed within it—come to hand from all over Europe and England. The matter is at first confined to the Easter story, adding gradually little "scenes." A Dublin manuscript, for example, develops an opening scene with the Three Marys lamenting, adds business or action to the *Quem Quaeritis* scene as the Marys search the tomb, and follows with two new scenes as the Marys convey the news to John and Peter who race to the tomb to see for themselves. A still later play adds the discovery of Jesus as a Gardener by Mary Magdalene. The next step in the development was the preparation of plays only incidentally connected with the Easter story—the wayfarers to Emmaus for Monday of Passion Week, the Shepherds for Christmas, the Coming of the Magi. The third step, obviously, was the linking of closely related separate plays, as in a "Herod" play, which combines the Shepherds and the Magi and adds for the first time in the title rôle one of the most famous characters of the early drama.

Nor did the liturgical dramatists confine themselves to the story of Christ. They chose such other New Testament subjects as the Conversion of Saul, Herod and John the Baptist, and moving back into the Old Testament, The Prophets (foretelling the birth of Christ). On the continent, particularly, the liturgical dramatists tended to work together great numbers of shorter plays into connected stories of Easter, Christmas, or the Ascension, and even into complete cycles recounting the life of Christ and including the creation story and prophecies of the Old Testament.

The staging of these liturgical plays was, of course, governed by the theater in which they were to be acted. At first, the stage and the setting was a simple representation of a tomb erected at the high altar. When, however, the plays developed many scenes to be acted in rapid sequence, the custom arose of presenting all these settings to the audience at the same time. The tomb was placed at the altar; Herod's court was in one place in the cathedral, the manger in another. These scenes, elevated on boxes or

platforms, were known by various names, the more common being scaffolds or mansions.

Descriptions of some of these scaffolds have come down to us.
A Paradise "is to be placed on a raised spot; curtains and silk
cloths are to be hung about it at such height that persons in
Paradise are visible from the shoulders. Fragrant flowers and

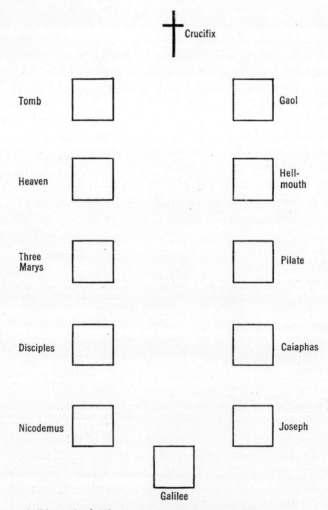

*A Liturgical Play: Arrangement of Scaffolds for a
Performance in a Cathedral*

leaves are scattered there; in it are divers trees with hanging fruit so as to give the impression of a most lovely place." Hell was depicted most realistically. The stage hands are instructed to "make a great smoke arise and they shall shout to each other in Hell in jubilation, and clash their pots and kettles so as to be heard without."

Playwrights became increasingly demanding on their actors. Whereas the early players of the *Quem Quaeritis* were gowned in their ecclesiastical robes and expected to do little more than re- peat the familiar words of the Bible, later players are instructed with all the particularity of a Hamlet: "Adam is to wear a red tunic and Eve a woman's robe of white, with a white silk cloak. . . . And the Adam must be well trained when to reply and to be neither too quick nor too slow in his replies. And not only he, but all the personages must be trained to speak composedly, and to fit convenient gesture to the matter of their speech. Nor must they foist in a syllable or clip one of the verse, but must enounce firmly and repeat what is set down for them in due order."

The liturgical play, to be sure, was only a beginning of an art form. It was too restricted both in subject-matter and conditions of performance to escape the possibility of stagnation. The scaf- folds within the church allowed a certain freedom of movement, of action, yet they prevented any genuine unity of form. This was true also of the construction of the play and its plotting. Even the most elaborate is a succession of scenes, developed by a process of accretion as one incident after another from the Bibli- cal story was tacked on. The subject-matter was likewise re- stricted: the playwright was not free to improvise as he would. His dialogue, in Latin, was quoted from Biblical and other ac- cepted sources. Characterization was thus held to a minimum and realism barely suggested. The players were members of the clergy, and on one or two occasions nuns, whose lives were devoted to the service of the church rather than to the profession of acting. It is clear that if the liturgical drama was to develop, it must break the shackles of reverence. The playwright must be free to alter his source, to add and subtract matter, not simply to re- count, but to interpret events before the drama can become an art. And since the medieval dramatic instinct was powerful, it was not long before the dramatist found a sort of freedom.

In the year 1210, by papal decree, liturgical plays were forbid-

den to be performed within the church building, and the clergy
transferred their playing area to the church porch. The background was still impressive, the massive doors and columns, the
carvings of the saints, the easily available music of the choir
maintaining the religious atmosphere. But the liturgical drama
was not without its difficulties for its sponsors, the churchmen.
Although they tried hard to sustain the gravity of their performances, to foster the serious drama—the frivolous would creep
in. The devils, for example, with their blustering and roaring
became great favorites with the people, and the priests who were
cast as devils were no more able to resist applause than their
successors in the acting profession. They began to fatten their
parts, to appear when they were not strictly called for by the
script—as the author's cautions to Adam indicate. There are also
certain instances of plays written by those Wandering Scholars,
the Goliards, whose exploits contribute so much gaiety and vitality to the middle ages. Rudimentary comic scenes involving
Pilate, or the merchant who sells spices to the Three Marys, as
well as devils, crept into their plays. Herod was well on the way
to becoming the first star part in the history of the modern
drama. In one play, he rages about the church according to the
stage direction *cum maximo furore, cum tanto furore,* and *cum
superadicto furore,* hurling a spear at the choir while his attendants belabor the bishop with inflated bladders.

And if ad libbing actors were not enough, there were the
audiences. They were simple folk in the main, and they delighted
in the crude, the rude, and the boisterous, and they were, some
of them, given to picking pockets. The Abbess of Hohenberg
complained that clergy and laity mingled in disorder at performances, that drunkards and scurrile talkers interrupted the solemnity of the occasion with improper jokes and a clatter of armor.
An English Wycliffite priest declared those who turn the scriptures into "plays and farces" are no better than the "Jews that
scourged Christ." An "open folly" cried William of Waddington,
and Robert Manning quotes, inaccurately but approvingly, St.
Isidore's statement that makers of liturgical plays had forsaken
both God and Christianity. The drama, as it had in Roman days,
found itself at odds with the church and, by the end of the
thirteenth century, cast out even from its dooryard.

The odor of sanctity managed to survive the schism, and the

drama for many years continued to be principally religious in theme and subject-matter. It may well be that the successors of the liturgical playwrights realized they possessed one of the great dramatic stories of all time. At any rate, the story of Christ, embellished with incidents from Old Testament history and later with legends of the Virgin and the Saints is the almost exclusive substance of the pre-Renaissance theater.

3. MIRACLE PLAYS

Fortunately the infant drama, thrust from its original home, found a kindly foster parent in the community itself. In 1264 Pope Urban IV had instituted the feast of Corpus Christi in honor of the transubstantiated sacrament of the Eucharist. Falling on the Thursday after Trinity Sunday, in May or June, it was for England a date friendlier to outdoor activities than either Christmas or Easter, and the principal event of the festival was a procession in which the Host was borne in devotion through the streets of many cities and towns. This procession was under the supervision of the principal religious society of the community, aided by the professional and craft guilds who at first carried symbolic banners and later employed groups of actors to pantomime Biblical scenes.

It was to the Corpus Christi procession that the drama attached itself. The exact process is difficult to trace, but the result is clear. Early in the fourteenth century several series of plays in the vernacular on Biblical subjects were being enacted during the English Corpus Christi festival. Crudely written, in simple piety and superstition, these *miracle plays* or *craft cycles* are nonetheless the recognizable ancestors of the great drama of the Elizabethan era. When the Black Plague weakened or destroyed the religious guilds, control of the plays passed completely into the hands of the trade guilds, and the secular, vernacular drama was free to pursue its own course.

Between the thirteenth and fifteenth centuries, miracle plays were performed at various times and under varying conditions in 125 communities in the British Isles as far north as Edinburgh and as far west as Dublin. More or less complete cycles survive from Chester, York, Coventry, and Wakefield; and single plays or fragments from Norwich, Newcastle-on-Tyne, Croxton, Digby and Shrewsbury. There are in addition several unattached plays, and three cycles peculiar in form and performance, from Cornwall. Information about the plays which have been lost can be traced in town and guild records. The surviving cycles show an understandable similarity in subject-matter and treatment and there are even evidences of borrowing, or at least of common sources, in some of the cycles.

Ultimately, of course, as in the case of the liturgical drama, the craft cycles are derived from the Vulgate Bible and the Apocryphal books of the Old and New Testament. In addition, the playwrights—who must certainly in the beginning have been monks or members of the clergy—drew upon the commentaries of the

Herod and the Priests: A Miracle Play Performed on a Pageant Wagon

church fathers as well as the celebrated pseudo-augustinian *Sermo de Symbolo* and such familiar vernacular pieces as the *Harrowing of Hell,* the *Genesis and Exodus,* and the *Cursor Mundi.* From the Vulgate, from "received history," playwrights drew the story of the Creation, and from medieval tradition the Fall of Lucifer. The story of Cain and Abel and of Noah, deriving originally from the Bible, was colored by the manners of the time. From the Apocryphal Gospels came the domestic life of St. Joseph and the Virgin, of Pilate and his wife, of the harrowing of Hell, and of Veronica. Thus widely and variously derived, the miracles have a unifying didactic purpose and reverence of tone, for the playwrights treated all their materials in the same manner, whether they were legendary or historical, apocryphal or scriptural.

The original authors of the plays are, of course, unknown. Since churchmen almost alone were possessed of the secrets of reading and writing, it is safe to assume that the miracle plays were composed, or perhaps translated from liturgical plays, by members of the clerical orders. And since the number of plays in any one cycle was considerable, it is probably safe to assume also that several authors or translators compiled the original texts. At any rate, the examples which have come down to us show, by their varieties of diction and dialect and rhyme-schemes, and particularly by their theatrical ignorance or sophistication, that many hands have been at work on them, both in their original composition and their periodical revision.

Derived as they were from the liturgical drama, the craft cycles retain and develop many of the traditional methods of staging. Where the older plays, enacted within the cathedral, had employed permanent scaffolds or mansions as acting areas, the outdoor processional cycles substituted the pageant. This was a wagon constructed on two levels and so large that it sometimes required six wheels. Each guild built and maintained its own pageant and the subject-matter of the play determined the use to which the wagon was to be put. Normally the upper level, completely open, was the acting area and the curtained lower level was used for a dressing room. However, if the play demanded scenes on Heaven and Earth, or Earth and Hell, the two levels were available for use. The pageant was as elaborate as the guild could afford, decorated with iron vanes and painted curtains, and drawn either by apprentices of the guild or by horses decked in tassels and braids.

Some days in advance of the actual performance announcers, or waits, read the "Banns" describing with great pomp and ceremony the forthcoming pageantry, announcing the subject-matter of the plays and hinting at the perfection of their realization. Presumably, also, they indicated where the performance would be given, for the craft cycles were presented in a unique manner. The liturgical drama had been performed first at the altar, then at certain fixed spots within the playing area, the cathedral. The miracle plays, associated as they were with the Corpus Christi procession, were moved about the community from one playing place to another.

The playing areas, or stations, were determined at first by the places where the Corpus Christi procession had halted for ceremonial and religious purposes. Later, since outsiders were attracted to the community by the spectacle, merchants bid against one another that the street before their shops might become a station. The records from Chester are typical of this curious mixture of pious tradition and mercantile opportunism: "When the first pageant was played at the Abbey gates, then it was wheeled from thence to the penthouse at the high cross before the Mayor; and before that was done, the second came, and the first went into the Watergate Street, and from thence unto the Bridge Street, and so all, one after another. . . ." The spots, or stations, chosen for performance were by law decorated with banners, flags and garlands, and the fact that a tryout performance was given before the pageant-wagon reached the Mayor is evidence of the care and earnestness of the players.

For, crude as the plays may seem to us, they were taken with great seriousness by their audiences, their sponsors, and their players. Rehearsals were conducted by a specially engaged director who was subject to a severe fine if the performance did not measure up to the standard expected by the town council. The actors, all amateurs and presumably members of the sponsoring guilds, were paid according to the importance of their rôles. The record of a Hull *Noah* play in 1494 is suggestive:

To Thomas Sawyer playing God	10*d*
To Jenkin Smith playing Noah	1*s*
To Noah's wife	8*d*

For a gallon of wine   8*d*
For making Noah's ship   £8/8*s*

And from Coventry comes the record: "8 virgins, 8 pence."

In addition to wages, the actors were well fed during the rehearsal period, at the expense of the guild, and provided with
large quantities of wine and ale. Costumes were made, rented, or
borrowed and were as costly and elaborate as the guild could
afford. There was, of course, no attempt at historical accuracy in
the design of the costume—the splendid was the only wear. What
was good enough for Lady Mayoress of York was good enough for
Pilate's wife, and made immediately clear the status of the
dramatic character to the almost completely uneducated spectators.

Some conventions were observed in costuming, however. Adam
and Eve—always a serious problem to the producer—seem to have
worn "breeks" or flesh-colored tights to suggest nudity. God and
perhaps Christ regularly wore a gilded mask and wig, the Devil
a false head painted black, with a ferocious snout and long horns.
The costume and property list for the Norwich *Creation* play has
come down to us:

> Two coats and a pair of hose for Eve, stained [dyed].
> A coat and hose for Adam, stained.
> A coat with hose and tail for the serpent, with a white hair [wig].
> A face [mask] and hair for the Father.
> Two hairs for Adam and Eve.
> A rib colored red.

Scenery, in the modern sense of the term, hardly existed. The
conditions of performance, if nothing else, would preclude much
realism or spectacle since the playing area must be visible from
all sides. Furthermore, the object of the production was not to
make men see *where* the event took place but to make them understand, intellectually and emotionally, what had occurred.
Locations might be suggested by thrones (for God, for Herod or
Pilate), by trees clamped to the sides of the pageant (to designate
a field), by a spinning wheel or a bed (Mak's house in the *Second
Shepherd's Play*). Noah's Ark was, of course, represented, and on
occasion, rather splendidly. In one performance directions indicate that the ship was brought on the stage in pieces and assembled by Noah during the early part of the play. A standard

machine or "[de]vice" was a pulley-and-windlass combination used for the appearance of angels above the stage, for the ascension of Our Lord, and the hanging of Judas. A smaller vice of the same sort was employed for the flight of the raven and the dove in the Noah plays.

If the method of staging the miracle plays foreshadows the Elizabethan producer's art, the cycles themselves establish many of the conventions which, modified and refined, became the everyday tools of the Elizabethan dramatist. The medieval playwright began with a familiar story which he took to be historically true. But he treated it without any historical sense. The ancient Jews and Romans who figure in the stories become contemporary Englishmen, the soldiers are medieval knights, Noah's wife a recognizably English shrew whose good gossips or friends celebrate in song the virtues of a pottle of Malmsey, a favorite English beverage. Since the Christian world of the time was being invaded by the Saracens, the villains of the plays—Herod, Pilate— become Mohammedans. Cain acquires a plough boy who swears by the Cross and drives seven horses with good English names. The shepherds of the *First Shepherd's Play* present the Infant Christ with a spruce coffer, a ball, and a bottle. And the Magi, as foreigners, speak French.

Such carelessness with historical fact has been customarily labelled anachronism. Yet it was a tenet of medieval philosophy that all things coexist in the mind of God, that yesterday, today, and tomorrow are all one. The medieval dramatist and his audience, therefore, were lacking in a sense of history, a sense of chronological time, and their plays reflect their philosophical position. Noah, for instance, builds his ark on the pageant wagon at Wakefield and announces when he has finished that it has taken him 350 days. In the York play he declares, "a hundred winters away is went, since I began this work," and at Chester 120 years. A similar compression of time occurs in the Chester *Temptation* where the forty days in the wilderness are encompassed in a ten-minute scene. And the Chester play of *The Creation* tells in unbroken sequence of the creation of Adam and Eve, their fall, and expulsion, and the birth and first thirty years of the life of Cain and Abel. Readers familiar with the skillful use of "Freedom of Time" in the later drama will find such medieval instances crude. Yet it must not be forgotten that it is part of an accurate picture of the world as the medieval writer understood it.

So too with the conventional treatment of place, or of the localization of scenes. If more than one "setting" was called for by the particular play, there was no change of scenery. Instead there were erected at the ends of the pageant slightly raised platforms ("sedes") which were identified as Pilate's hall, or a stable, or a peasant's hut by the characters who occupied them. All the "scenes" required in a play were thus presented at once, simultaneously, and the scene was changed by moving the action from one platform to another. A French historian has compared this method of staging to a group of young girls playing in a room, each with a corner which represents her house. The analogy is apt, although it fails to take into account, again, the medieval conception of the world. The staging of the cycle plays conforms to the Ptolemaic universe, presenting Heaven, Middle-earth, and Hell coexistent on appropriate levels and with complete freedom of movement in space for the actors.

The convention of direct address to the audience, a cruder parallel of the Elizabethan soliloquy, presumably is an outgrowth of the didactic origin of the miracle plays although it could be put to other uses. Quite simply and formally the direct address might appear in a prologue (sometimes in character) summarizing the events of earlier plays and indicating the connection with the play to follow. Or, more dramatically, Herod would burst upon the scene roaring for silence among the spectators and threatening dire punishments for those who failed to comply. The audience here is made a participant in the action by being characterized as members of Herod's court. The actual process by which the audience may be drawn into the action is more interestingly illustrated in the Wakefield pageant of *The Prophets,* a subject derived from the celebrated medieval sermon against pagans, atheists and Jews credited to St. Augustine and common to all the cycles. Moses first appears, exhorting the *Israelites* and prophesying the coming of a Saviour. He is followed by David who addresses *his people* on the same subject. Later comes the Sybil who calls upon *all men* to hear her. The play is completely without localization, and the Israelites, David's people, and all men are, of course, the spectators.

The very use of anachronisms, by substituting the familiar for the unfamiliar, increases the reality of the play and enables the audience to participate in the action. When Cain enters, plough-ing, and curses his servant, his horses, and the stubborn earth, he is making his character and position more understandable to the spectators, a large portion of whom must have been farmers. And when the shepherds of the *First Shepherd's Play,* whose names are Gyb, John Home, and Slowpace, complain about the troubles which were besetting English shepherds, and eat and drink to the accompaniment of familiar folk songs, the wonder that the birth of Christ should be first revealed to such humble men—like themselves—must have been strongly impressed upon the audience.

They were simple, pious folk and the plays were carefully addressed to their capacity and interests. The vernacular is strictly adhered to, and Latin tags which creep in are immediately translated. A place is found for slapstick farce—the rough and tumble argument between Noah and his wife is excellent fooling and has many parallels in folk literature—and for violence—the realism of the tormenting and crucifixion of Christ is hardly equalled by the most melodramatic incidents of the Tragedies of Blood—and for homely wisdom and philosophy. And frequent summaries are inserted lest one lose sight of the end.

Such were the conventions and techniques of the medieval dramatist, the instruments he employed to make his play effec-tive. They may be illustrated with remarkable completeness in what is deservedly the most famous and most familiar of all the examples, the Wakefield *Second Shepherd's Play.* There are six "scenes" in the little drama, the first four recounting the common folk-tale of Mak, the sheep-stealer, and the last two the familiar Biblical story of the Nativity. Three localities, or "sedes," are required: a field, Mak's house, and the manger, among which the characters move with the greatest freedom.

The first part of the play, the story of Mak, begins with the introduction of the shepherds who are used for both realism and satire. The first shepherd complains of the oppression of the poor by the gentry, the second of the oppression of husbands by shrew-ish wives, and the third of the oppression of apprentices by their masters. To them enters Mak, pretending to elegance and station by assuming a southern accent. Since they mistrust him, they force him to lie in their midst, but he rises quietly when they are asleep, steals a fat lamb and hastens home.

In the second scene we meet Mak's wife, who like Lady Macbeth is more than a match for her husband. It is her idea to hide the lamb by swaddling him like a "knave child" and tucking him in a cradle beside which she will lie and groan, if the shepherds come searching. Mak returns to his sleeping dupes who awaken in the third scene, discover their loss, and set out to find the lamb, arranging to meet in the evening by the "crooked thorn," a familiar landmark near Wakefield. For it must be apparent that the author is doing everything in his power to make the audience feel thoroughly at home in the situation of the play.

Mak returns to his house and waits for the inevitable arrival of the suspicious shepherds. They come finally in the fourth scene and at first are completely fooled by the circumstantial story of childbirth and the comic irony of the wife's promise to eat the child if she is not telling the truth. The shepherds leave the house; then, remembering that they have made no birthday gift to the child, return and discover the imposture. As a punishment, they toss Mak in a blanket, which so wearies them that they once again lie down to sleep. The whole tone of this action has been farcical, on the level of the folk-tale.

In the fifth scene the tone of the play begins to change. An angel appears in the heavens to announce the birth of Christ. The shepherds awake, discuss the wonder, and—for the comic vein has not been completely eliminated—imitate the angel's song in cracked harmony. They make the conventional journey, by circling the stage, to Bethlehem, and in the final scene greet the Christ Child with their gifts, a bird, a tennis ball, and a bob of cherries. With the Virgin's blessing they arise and depart in great happiness and high spirits.

For all its simplicity, the *Second Shepherd's Play* is an accomplished and daring performance; the author has deliberately begun with an audacious parody of the sacred event. The lamb has been the symbol of Christ from time immemorial and the careful duplication of events (the shepherds' search, the childbirth, the shepherds' gifts) in both stories is hardly coincidental. In this brief play is the seed of what is to become the unique English dramatic form, the double plot, one part of which reflects, parallels, or comments on the other. It is difficult to determine what

the original author's purpose may have been. Sacrilege was far
from his nature, though he makes great use of satire on worldly
matters. Perhaps juxtaposition of burlesque and reverence is a
dramatic analogue of the grotesques found in the holy places of
Gothic cathedrals. More certainly, it seems, the intention is to
involve the audience so deeply in a setting, a story, and characters
of the greatest familiarity, that the transition to the unfamiliar
will be no shock, and that they may comprehend personally the
significance of the nativity. They could hardly fail to notice, for
instance, that the shepherds who had been so bitter about their
oppressed state at the beginning were, at the end, full of joy that
their Saviour had been born.

It is not difficult to find matter to praise in this primitive
comedy. The author displays a real sense of dramatic technique
in finding a common theme—oppression—for the complaints of
the three shepherds, as well as a common event—childbirth—for
the two parts of his play. This parallelism assists the play in
achieving a unity which is all too lacking in medieval drama.
Also, very wisely, he emphasizes not the historical act but the
effect of the historical act on familiar persons, providing an object lesson for his successors who were to follow much the same
tactics in moving from chronicle history to tragedy and comedy.

The dialogue, in a complicated verse form which is handled
with considerable skill, contributes to the general humor of the
play. Since the matter of the first part is from some source other
than the Bible, the author is free to invent. He puns endlessly
(cf. the first shepherd's complaints about the "weders," which
may be either the weather or the sheep), makes great use of comic
irony (one shepherd dreams that he was "full near England"
during the night), and malapropisms (Mak's evening prayer is
addressed to "Poncio Pilato"). The near-success of Mak's scheme
involves suspense, and the discovery of the lamb is excellent
fooling.

THIRD SHEPHERD. Give me leave him to kiss, and lift up the cloth . . .
   What the devil is this? He has a long snout!
FIRST SHEPHERD. He is marked amiss. We wait ill about.
SECOND SHEPHERD. "From an ill-spun woof ever comes foul out."
   Ah, so!
   He is like to our sheep! . . .

THIRD SHEPHERD. . . . . Will ye see how they swaddle
  His four feet in the middle?
  Saw I never in the cradle
  A hornéd lad ere now.
MAK. Peace, bid I! What! Let be your fare!
  I am he that him got, and yon woman him bear.
FIRST SHEPHERD. What the devil shall he be called? "Mak?" Lo, God,
  Mak's heir!

The qualities which set the *Second Shepherd's Play* above the
average miracle play may also be detected in other parts of the
Wakefield cycle. Credited to the "Wakefield master" are *Noah*,
the *First* and *Second Shepherd's Plays, Herod the Great, The
Crucifixion,* portions of three, and odd stanzas in four, other
plays. The unknown master can be traced by his complex stanza,
his freedom in the treatment of the source, and his sharp satire
on the abuses of the times. The stanza, with its internal rhymes
and bobs is sufficiently artificial to seem useless for dramatic purposes, yet the command of the language is such that in performance one ceases to think of the style as a strait-jacket and
begins to take pleasure from the neatness of expression, as in the
euphuistic prose of Lyly, or the epigrammatic wit of Restoration
comedy. The free treatment of his sources has been suggested in
the discussion of his masterpiece. It might also be illustrated from
the domestic quarrels between Noah and his wife which include
several vigorous exchanges of blows, the more lively since Mrs.
Noah was acted by a man. Mrs. Noah announces to the audience
that she wishes she were a widow, Noah advises the young men
to get the upper hand over their wives before it is too late, and
there is a final fight, ending, apparently, with Noah on the
ground and his wife upon him, crying that he has beaten her to
death.

  WIFE. Out, alas, I am gone! Out upon thee, man's wonder!
  NOAH. See how *she* can groan, and *I* lie under!

The playwright is equally free with his satirical attacks on the
abuses of the age. The shepherds' complaints are typical of his
work. In the first play he presents the popular or democratic view
of the disturbed conditions which made the fifteenth century a
harsh world for the common man—money is scarce, the country
is full of bravos. The second play is more specific, with its reference to the Enclosure movement and unjust taxation:

> We are so hammed, [an enclosed pasture]
> Overtaxed and rammed,
> We are made hand-tamed
>　　By these gentry-men.

He is bold enough to attack the perquisites of the crown as he describes the servant, "proud as any peacock," who condemns, on the authority of his badge of office, any property he wishes:

> He can make purveyance,
> With boast and bragance;
> And all is through maintenance
>　　Of men that are greater.

As Chambers has pointed out, his satire is directed against secular authority. Unlike many men of the middle ages he does not attack the corruption of the clergy. He is a faithful son of the church—even in his parody of sacred events—and the devil Tutivillus is deliberately described as belonging to the Lollards, who desired church reforms.

It must not be inferred that many of the miracle plays approach the level of the achievements of the Wakefield master. All too typical are formlessness, lack of proportion, and lengthy, didactic speeches. All too often, though understandably, the source is followed faithfully with a resultant loss of vigor and realism. There are, however, moments of pathos, of humor, and lyric beauty to reward the patient reader. The touching picture of filial devotion in the "Brome" *Abraham and Isaac,* the preposterous bluster of Herod, the simplicity and innocence of the Virgin and the comic suspicion of Joseph that he is a cuckold linger in the mind. So too the simple song introduced into the Chester pageant of the Slaughter of the Innocents. Herod has decreed that it take place, Joseph and Mary escape to Egypt, and two nameless mothers enter, singing, to their children:

> Lully, lulla, thou little tiny child,
> Bye bye, lully lullay, thou little tiny child,
>　　Bye bye, lully lullay!
>
> O sisters two
> How may we do
>　　For to preserve this day
> This poor youngling
> For whom we do sing
>　　Bye bye, lully lullay?

Herod the King,
In his raging
  Charged hath this day
His men of might
In his own sight
  All young children to slay—

That woe is me
Poor child, for thee,
  And ever mourn and may
For thy parting
Neither say nor sing
  Bye bye, lully lullay.

But the average member of the audience was probably less inclined to examine the particulars of the individual plays than to respond to the cycles as a whole. Although they derive from a common source and were intended to serve a common purpose, they vary widely in the number of plays and the subjects chosen for treatment. The Chester cycle, for instance, dates from about 1327, and contains 25 plays in the surviving texts. As the oldest of the cycles it preserves much of the original devotional impulse; it is preoccupied with prophecies and the expounding of such religious formularies as the Ten Commandments and the Circumcision. The plays are, for the most part, simple, suppressing the human element and any suggestion of farce in favor of reverent didacticism.

The York cycle, the longest that has survived, dates from about 1387, and includes forty-eight plays; several more have been lost. Although extensive in conception it is pedestrian in execution; comic elements are developed in Noah and the Shepherds but humanity is somehow kept at a distance. The Wakefield cycle, sometimes called Townley after the former owners of the manuscript, has already been identified as the most satisfactory for the modern reader. Consisting of thirty-two plays, it dates from about 1425. With the York and Chester plays as models, it borrows rather freely some of their better moments, but none of these borrowings is as good as its own original contributions. The Coventry, or N. Towne, plays, the latest group, show the effect of the cult of the Virgin by including a sequence devoted to her, and the development of a sense of unity both in writing and production by definitely grouping other sequences within the whole.

Certain subjects, alone or in combination, are treated by all the cycles:

1) The Fall of Lucifer
2) The Creation and Fall of Adam and Eve
3) Cain and Abel
4) Noah and the Flood
5) Abraham and Isaac
6) The Prophets [except York]
7) The Annunciation
8) The Salutation of Elizabeth
9) The Suspicion of Joseph
10) The Shepherds
11) The Purification
12) The Magi and Herod
13) The Offering of the Magi
14) The Flight into Egypt
15) The Massacre of the Innocents
16) Various Incidents of Christ's Ministry
17) The Raising of Lazarus
18) The Conspiracy of the Jews
19) The Treachery of Judas
20) The Last Supper
21) Gethsemane
22) Jesus and Caiphus
23) Jesus and Herod
24) The Trial of Christ
25) The Bearing of the Cross
26) The Crucifixion
27) Mary's Lament
28) The Death of Jesus
29) Longinus
30) The Descent from the Cross
31) The Harrowing of Hell
32) The Setting of the Watch
33) The Resurrection
34) Quem Quaeritis
35) The Gardener
36) The Travellers to Emmaus
37) Doubting Thomas
38) The Ascension
39) Doomsday

A glance at these subjects indicates that there is an obvious concentration on the events of the life of Christ, in particular his birth and death. Yet a second look shows certain clearly marked divisions within the whole, a conclusion which is confirmed by a consideration of the individual cycles. In the Chester cycle, seven plays are devoted to Old Testament subjects from the Fall of Lucifer to the Prophets, eleven to the events surrounding the Nativity, four to Christ's Ministry, six to Christ's Passion, and three to the Judgement. At York, eleven plays are given to the Old Testament, ten to the Nativity, three to the Ministry, nineteen to the Passion, four to the Virgin, and one to the Judgement. At Wakefield, eight plays are given to the Old Testament, nine to the Nativity, three to the Ministry, six to the Passion, four to the events following the Harrowing of Hell, and one to the Judgement. It is thus possible to discern an Old Testament group, a Nativity group, a Passion group, and one or more plays

about the Last Judgement, with at York and Coventry a group
of plays devoted to legends of the Virgin.

If the cycles may be considered as complete plays made up of
separate units or acts, certain conclusions are apparent which
clearly relate the miracles to the later development of the dramatic form in England. In the first place, the cycles are *panoramic* in structure. That is to say, they move freely in time and
space from the beginning to the end of their story, from the Creation to the Last Judgement, treating those subjects which seem
important, omitting what has no bearing on their ultimate
theme. There is little or no attempt at copying the form of the
classical drama with its intense concentration on the final hours
of an action. The dramatist makes full *use of parallels*. Thus
Lucifer in *The Fall* is the prototype of Pharaoh, Herod and
Pilate, as David is the prototype of Christ. Thus the sacrifice of
Isaac is an anticipation of the greater sacrifice of Christ. There
seems to be a kind of *three part movement* implicit in the selection and arrangement of incidents. Part one, the Old Testament
stories, may be considered a prologue to the whole, the rise of
the spirit of evil in the world, with emphasis on Lucifer, on Cain,
and on Noah's Flood. The second part, Christ's Nativity, Ministry and Passion, may be considered as symbolic of the conflict
between good and evil; the hero, Christ, against the seeker after
revenge, the Devil. In the final movement, with the death of
Judas, The Harrowing of Hell, and Doomsday, good triumphs
over evil and the conflict begun in the first part is resolved. Admittedly such a form is not readily apparent; the leisurely gar-
rulousness of the medieval literary style obscures the dramatic
structure. Yet the later drama was to be distinguished by the
panoramic form, in three movements, with parallels and echoes,
and such a form is inherent in the Biblical story which the craft
cycles chose to recount.

For several centuries the miracle plays successfully held their
own in the country towns and even in London, where professional players provided competition. Their fame was as great as
their popularity. In 1397, Richard II made a royal visit to witness the performance at York, and in 1409 a cycle was played in
London before Henry IV. They began to die out, however, in
the sixteenth century with the gradual weakening of the power
of the Roman church and because of the inability of many

Guilds to meet the increasing cost of production. At length, the populace itself seems to have come to agree with Archbishop Rogers of Chester who wrote about 1595 that he was glad the cycle had been abandoned, "the abomination of desolation, with such a cloud of ignorance to defile with so high a hand the Sacred Scriptures of God." As the poor man's Bible, however, they had served their purpose, to educate men to a knowledge of sacred story and an appreciation of its meaning. They had also laid the groundwork for the triumphant drama to come. Chiefly they were lacking in control, in the sense of balance and proportion so necessary to the art of the theater. In the final analysis, however, they were amateur plays for amateur players and ignorant audiences. What they had initiated, professional players and playwrights would seize upon and perfect.

4. MORALITY PLAYS

In 1639, R. Willis, then seventy-five years old, published a book of devotions and meditations for the benefit of his descendants. Though the modern reader is somewhat surprised to find the theater used as a moral example three years before the Puritans forced the closing of the theaters, one of the chapters is headed "Upon a Stage-Play which I saw when I was a Child." The play described is neither an early farce nor tragedy nor a miracle—to all of these the Puritan might be expected to object. Rather it is a morality, or a moral play, the nature of which will become apparent from Willis' account of *The Cradle of Security* as performed about 1570.

In the city of Gloucester the manner is (as I think it is in other like corporations) that when Players of Enterludes [moralities] come to town, they first attend the Mayor to inform him what nobleman's servants they are, and so to get licence for their public playing; and if the Mayor like the actors, or would show respect to their lord and master, he appoints them to play their first play before himself and the aldermen and Common Council of the city; and that is called the Mayor's play, where every one that will comes in without money, the Mayor giving the players a reward as he thinks fit to show respect unto them. At such a play, my father took me with him and made me stand between his legs, as he sat upon one of the benches where we saw and heard very well.

The play was called *The Cradle of Security*, wherein was personated a King or some great Prince with his courtiers of several kinds, amongst which three ladies were in special grace with him; and they keeping him in delights and pleasures, drew him from his graver counsellors, hearing of sermons, and listening to good counsel and admonitions, that in the end they got him to lie down in a cradle upon the stage, where these three ladies joining in a sweet song rocked him asleep, that he snorted [snored] again, and in the meantime closely [secretly] conveyed under the clothes where withall he was covered a vizard like a swine's snout upon his face, with three wire chains fastened thereunto, the other end whereof being holden severally by those three ladies, who fall to singing again, and then discovered his face, that the spectators might see how they had transformed him, going on with their singing. Whilst all this was acting, there came forth of another door at the farthest end of the stage two old men, the one in blue with a sergeant-at-arms' mace on his shoulder, the other in red with a drawn sword in his hand, and leaning with the other hand upon the other's shoulder. And so they two went along in a soft pace round about by the skirt of the stage till at last they came to the cradle, when all the court was in greatest jollity. And then the foremost old man with his mace struck a fearful blow upon the cradle; whereat all the courtiers with the three ladies and the vizard all vanished; and the desolate Prince, starting up bare-faced and finding himself thus sent for to judgement, made a lamentable complaint of his miserable case, and so was carried away by wicked spirits.

This Prince did personate, in the Moral, the wicked of the world; the three ladies, Pride, Covetousness, and Luxury; the two old men, the end of the world and the last judgement. This sight took such impression in me, that when I came to man's estate it was as fresh in my memory as if I had seen it newly acted.

The earnest Puritan then deplores that the "harmless morals" of his youth have been replaced by plays which are—he has been informed—but little more than "schools of vice."

The Cradle of Security, which he so vividly recalled, was never printed, or if so, no copy has survived; but among the approximately thirty moralities which have survived, dating from the early fifteenth to the early sixteenth century, it would have been completely at home. Like the miracle, the morality began in the church as a dramatized sermon intended to make the ethical teachings of Christianity more impressive for the congregation. As early as 1384 a Wycliffite priest was urging his hearers to attend the performance of the York *Paternoster* play, apparently a pageant of the Seven Deadly Sins, that they might better understand the points he was making.

Since the modern reader is apt to find allegory dull, he is apt to avoid the moralities in so far as he is able. Yet it is an error to pass them by as queer relics of the peculiar medieval taste; as a group, they have much to contribute to a comprehension of the forms and techniques of the later drama, and at least one is a perfect work of art in its kind. For, with all their abundant vitality, the miracle plays leave much to be desired: the great length of the complete cycles and the extreme brevity of the majority of the individual units begs the question of artistic form; their characterization, except for a few types, is rudimentary; they are shackled for the most part to their sources, with the end result that the basic requirement of any play—the conflict— is weakened or even totally lacking. The morality created a form of at once tolerable compass and reasonable magnitude; it discovered the value of a clearly defined conflict and a method of presenting it as a psychological or inner struggle, a contribution to the art of characterization; finally, and perhaps most important, it created its own stories to illustrate its chosen themes. The Morality was a step forward in the liberation of the playwright.

Much of this advance must be credited to the professional actors who, for the first time, figure in the English drama. Although the prohibition of theaters in late Roman times had deprived the players of their conventional means of livelihood, the profession had not ceased to exist. In groups of two or three, the actors had been wandering over the continent and the British Isles, performing skits, singing ballads, presenting magic or acrobatic entertainments or, if they were fortunate, exhibiting the feats of trained bears and dogs. They were quite literally, vagabonds, wanderers, clinging to their profession with a foolish devotion in the face of public diffidence and official distrust. They must have looked with envy upon the success of the amateurs in the craft cycles, the size and splendor of which were beyond their poor means. The Morality was another matter; it was long enough to constitute an entertainment and simple enough to be played by a company of a dozen or less. So the wandering professionals took the Morality for their own, and many of the texts which have survived were printed for their use, with the cast carefully subdivided to indicate how six men may "play at ease" ten or fourteen characters by judicious doubling.

But before the professionals took it up, the form was first developed within the church. The medieval clergy had commonly resorted to fiction to clarify the abstract ethical principles which they were advancing in their sermons. In the fourth century Prudentius in his *Psychomachia* had hit upon the idea of conceiving life in terms of an allegorical combat between the virtues and vices, and in his *Harmatigena* as a siege which the evil forces lay against the soul of mankind. In the twelfth century Bernard of Clairvaux and Hugh of St. Victor elaborated the verse in the 85th psalm, "Mercy and Truth are met together; Righteousness and Peace have kissed," into an elaborate story of the actions of the Four Daughters of God on the day man's soul appears for the Final Judgement. A similar allegorical concept was the Dance of Death, vividly reminding man that death is no respecter of persons and that he strikes without warning.

These were the favored themes of the allegorical homilies; they became the basic themes of the Moralities. Singularly enough they are all illustrated in the *Castle of Perseverance* (1425), the first of the plays to survive in its entirety. It is very long, some 3800 lines, and in other formal ways is not typical. In its subject-matter, however, it is completely typical. It traces the history of man (Humanum Genus) from his birth to the day of judgement. A sort of prologue is spoken by Mundus (the World), and Caro (the Flesh), and Belial (the Devil), each from his own little stage. The first action concerns the birth of man and the struggle for his soul between the Good Angel and the Bad, with the latter victorious. Mundus then grants to Man, as guides, Pleasure, Folly, and Backbiter, to whom soon are attached Belial, Caro, and the Seven Deadly Sins. The Good Angel calls for assistance from Confession, Shrift, and Penitence who rescue Man from his Evil Companions and lodge him in the Castle of Perseverance. In the second movement the Forces of Hell lay siege to the Castle and are opposed by the Forces of Heaven. The evil are defeated, but manage to entice Man (who is now growing old) outside, by the wiles of Avarice. Death strikes Man down, and he dies repentent. In the third movement, the play concludes with a debate among the Four Daughters of God about the disposal of Man's soul, with Mercy holding out successfully for forgiveness as opposed to strict justice. Thus the familiar themes were loosely joined in a single drama.

There is little doubt that it was intended to be performed by the wandering professionals; the speakers of the Banns have a conventional kind of courteous address as they bid the spectators

"welcome be ye when ye come, price for to prove"—or as Hamlet
was to put it, to have a taste of our quality; and a blank appears
in the manuscript at the point where the name of the place of
performance is to be inserted. These are both customary techniques. Unique, on the other hand, is the method of staging—a

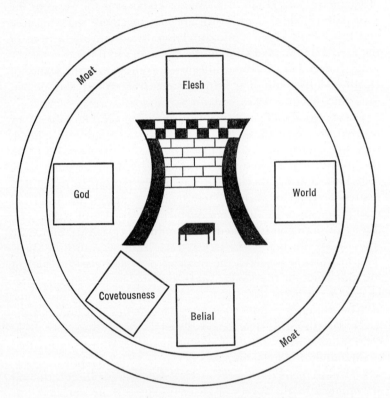

Arrangement of Scaffolds for The Castle of Perseverance

kind of simultaneous outdoor setting for which the stage plan
has been preserved, and which resembles continental rather than
English practice.

It will be seen from the drawing that the playing area was an
open field—"on the green," says the advance man. In the center
of the area was erected the Castle with an open space at the bottom in which Mankind's bed was placed. In a circle about the
castle were erected the scaffolds (like those of the liturgical plays)

of the World, the Flesh, the Devil, Covetousness, and God: and around the whole acting area was dug a moat which was filled with water to keep the spectators from interfering with the action.

While the actual staging is unique it is indirectly related to the English tradition (as developed in the Cycles) of free and frequent change of scene. That it was not copied and used for other plays is probably due to its complexity; few companies were large enough or sufficiently resourceful to perform so long and populous a drama. Quite likely also it proved unsatisfactory from the spectator's standpoint. It is impossible that all the action could be clearly seen by all the audience, and the cautions written into the stage plan suggest the difficulties. Over the drawing of the Castle is noted: "This is the Castle of Perseverance that standeth in the midst of the place: but let no man sit there for letting [hindering] of sight." And in the moat around the playing area: "This is the water about the place: if any ditch be made, there it shall be played; or else that it be strongly barred all about. And let not over many stitelers [constables] be within the place."

As an allegory the play has a very clear meaning on the ethical level: Man lives out his life in a kind of blindness, free to choose evil if it appears to him good, and is subject to the inevitable consequences of his acts. The forces of Good will not lightly let him go over to the forces of Evil, and a last-minute repentance may win forgiveness from a merciful God. The action of the play is frequently symbolic: Belial and his associates are defeated by a shower of roses directed against them by the good forces. The costumes seem also to have been symbolic. The devil appears with pipes of gunpowder exploding from his ears and other parts of his body; Mercy is costumed in white, Righteousness in red, Truth in "sad Green," and Peace in black.

But most important for the development of the art of the drama is the nature of the symbolic conflict. The struggle which the play presents is not really between external forces—Good and Evil do not stand for, say, the English and the French. The struggle is an internal one, within the mind of one hero. The personal subjective forces (Pride, Avarice, Industry, Chastity) within Man are projected into the world and made palpable and visible to the audience. The psychology is not very subtle, perhaps, and the comprehension of the facts of sin not very deep, but the drama is moving closer to the realm of humanity where it will justify its existence as an art.

The most famous of the moralities, *The Summoning of Every-man*, marks a considerable advance over *The Castle of Persever-ance*. It is doubtful that this reverent and often touching play could have been performed by a troupe of wandering vagabonds in the open air; it demands the dignity and peace of the cathe-dral. For this reason many scholars have been happy to declare it a translation of a Dutch play, *Elckerlijk*, though no satisfactory evidence has been produced to determine the priority of either version. Composed before the close of the fifteenth century, it treats with skill the common medieval theme of the Dance of Death. To dramatize this theme the author has happily hit upon an allegorical situation familiar to nearly anyone in the audience. God, presented as a judge, sends his bailiff, Death, with a sum-mons to Everyman to appear in court with his account books that justice may be done him. Confronted with the summons, Every-man searches desperately for someone to accompany him and assist him in his plea. He is forsaken first by his worldly comrades, then by his intellectual and physical powers, and finally even by Knowledge who cannot pass beyond the grave. Good Deeds alone goes with him to the court, although, ironically, he is so weak that he can hardly move.

Stated thus baldly the plot of *Everyman* seems so simple-minded as hardly to be worth consideration. Yet the technique of the anonymous playwright is sufficiently advanced to create a drama of considerable power. For one thing, the play has a unity rare in the pre-Elizabethan theater. The title character is in the center of the action throughout. The focus of the interest is con-stantly upon Everyman and the other characters are held to subsidiary positions. Yet these minor characters are as vivid as the space allotted to them will permit. There is much humor in the little sketch of Fellowship as he rejects Everyman's plea to accompany him:

> EVERYMAN. Why, ye said if ever I had need
>   Ye would me never forsake, quick or dead,
>   Though it were to hell truly!
> FELLOWSHIP. So I said certainly!
>   But such pleasures be set aside, the truth to say.

And Cousin cannot make the journey because of a cramp in his toe!

The playwright proceeds about his business with a refreshing directness. What has to be done is done, what has to be said is said. Since the play is written in couplets there is no need for padding to fill out an elaborate stanzaic pattern as in *The Castle of Perseverance*. Characters unhesitatingly analyze themselves for the audience:

> GOODS. Nay, Everyman, I say no.
> As for a while I was lent thee,
> A season thou hast had me in prosperity.
> My condition is man's soul to kill;
> If I save one, a thousand I do spill.
> Weenest thou that I will follow thee
> From this world? Nay, verily.

This capacity for self-revelation was to become a familiar trait of the Elizabethan *dramatis personae*.

Again, the playwright uses the medieval freedom from a sense of chronological time not as an accepted fact like the authors of the Miracles, but with a sense of its dramatic value. After Death has given his commands and left the scene, Everyman soliloquizes:

> Alas! I may well weep with sighs deep!
> Now have I no manner of company
> To help me in my journey and me to keep;
> And also my writing is full unready. . . . .
> *The time passeth.* Lord, help, that all wrought!
> For though I mourn it availeth nought;
> *The day passeth,* and is almost ago. . . . .

The compression of time here increases the sense of doom, of inevitability, that hangs over the play. It is Everyman, the hero, who gives expression to this sense of doom, however, and not a commentator, a Good Angel, or an abstract virtue. In spite of his allegorical name, Everyman is a recognizable human being as Humanum Genus in *The Castle of Perseverance* was not. He is a gay young man with a human respect for worldly goods, pleasures, and relationships. His terror at the summons of Death thus becomes more dramatic, within the framework of the action and situation of the play, and less abstract didacticism, and is consequently more easily understood and shared by the audience. The

value of this move towards the purely dramatic is doubly attested: *Everyman* was printed at least four times shortly after
1500 and has been repeatedly revived on the modern stage.

Although the Morality was conceived as a serious didactic form
and was intended to convey the highest principles of Christian
Ethics, it bore within it the seed of its own corruption. Not only
Christian virtue was portrayed, but the reverse. The effective
conflict demands that the two opponents must be fairly equally
matched, and the professional playwrights and actors dwelt with
increasing emphasis on the nature of the temptations which confronted the hero. In some of the later examples there is a coarse
realism which reduces the "moral" to a formality; the virtues
are acknowledged with a perfunctory nod, the vices treated *in
extenso.*

Mankind, an anonymous play of about 1475, is an example of
this corruption. Ostensibly it is a dramatization of the debate of
the Four Daughters of God over the ultimate fate of the hero,
but Mercy who is treated as the saviour of man in *The Castle
of Perseverance* is here subjected to every indignity, mocked and
battered, outwitted by the hero and the representatives of the
devil, and permitted his final triumph only as a bow to convention, like the forced happy ending of a modern film. The real
interest of the play is centered in the grotesque comedy of Nought,
Nowadays, and New Guise, and the Vice, Titivillus. The shrewdness with which the players had judged the tastes of their audience is indicated by the fact that, although no admission was
charged for performances, a collection was taken before the entrance of Titivillus who refuses to come on until a generous sum
has been volunteered.

The play is in three parts, reflecting perhaps the natural organization of the miracle cycles and of *The Castle of Perseverance.* In the first movement Mankind resists the temptations of
three minor Vices who beguile him in obscene language and with
a "Christmas song" of surpassing vulgarity: in the second movement, the major Vice, Titivillus, woos Mankind away from
Mercy; and in the third, Mercy—as expected—triumphs over the
forces of evil. It is a simple play, written with some vigor and
intended for a company of six actors, Mercy and Titivillus being
doubled by the same man, while three boys played the minor
Vices.

It is not surprising in medieval art to find the grotesque side by side with the serious; Chaucer's Pardoner jokes with his hearers before delivering his homily. But the emphasis in *Mankind* is so firmly fixed on the comic and the worldly that the reader must recognize the inevitable degeneration of the ethical allegory in the direction of secular farce.

The Morality has often been considered a kind of by-product of the medieval drama, as aside from the stream of the development of the English form. It is true that the complete allegory did not long survive, but allegorical elements are still to be found in the plays of the seventeenth century. Of greater importance, these were the first professional plays and consequently established many of the conventions of professional production. They were outdoor plays—one prologue concludes:

> Now stand ye still and be courteous
> And pray ye all for the weather.

They employed a minimum of scenery; like the Miracle plays they substituted properties, a spade, a chest, a throne, to suggest location. Costumes, however, were as elaborate as the resources of the company allowed. Wisdom, in the play of that name, is required to wear a robe of "rich purple cloth of gold, with a mantle of the same enermined within, having about his neck a royal hood furred with ermine; upon his head a cheveler [wig] with brows, a beard of gold of Cypress curled, a rich imperial crown thereupon, set with precious stones and pearls. In his left hand a ball of gold with a cross thereupon, and in his right hand a regal sceptre." In the list of costumes for John Rastell's professional company, including one of "green sarcenet lined with red tuke and with roman letters stitched upon it of blue and red sarcenet" suggesting their employment in allegorical plays, are five which were valued at twenty shillings apiece.

The Morality casts were small, with allowance for the doubling of parts, and their action compact. Rare indeed is the morality which requires more than an hour of playing time. The conflict in the action is strengthened and externalized, and frequently involves physical combat, and at the same time a method for dramatizing the psychological conflicts within the leading characters is discovered and developed. All these become a part of the conventions of the Elizabethan stage and its drama.

Most important of all is the Morality scheme of characterization. The Miracle play tended to rather rudimentary characterization. Only in the work of the Wakefield Master is there a successful effort to give a sense of humanity to the rôles; the other plays are filled with puppets bearing Biblical labels. The allegorical drama, the Morality, demanded another sort of characterization—the representation of qualities, or *characteristics,* like pride, wrath, or lust. Refined and somewhat intellectualized, this technique of portrayal by dominant characteristics became so standardized on the English stage that it was not only the starting point for the Elizabethans (and particularly Ben Jonson), but, taken up by the dramatists of the Restoration and Eighteenth Century, was carried over into Victorian comedy, and is not entirely dead today.

The character of the Vice, the devil's deputy, is a major contribution of the Morality. The origin of the type is obscure. It has been suggested that he is the ethical opposite of piety as the Devil is the theological opposite of God, that he is a kind of child of the Devil, that he is a dramatic adaptation of the court fool or jester. Whatever his beginning—allegorical or professional—he soon becomes completely humanized in the morality as a man playing the part of a rogue or mischief-maker. Titivillus is his favorite name, derived from the legendary devil who collected the scraps of words mispronounced during the reading of a holy office and registered them against the offender in Hell, but he appears in the Moralities variously as Iniquity, Nicholas Newfangle, Policy and Sin, and in the later drama he is clearly present in the fools and jesters of romantic comedy, in Autolycus and, perhaps, in the gross, pleasure-loving, and irresponsible Falstaff.

5. INTERLUDES

It is difficult, and perhaps useless to attempt to distinguish between the later Moralities and the earlier Interludes. Interlude, indeed, is a term that has successfully defied definition since it was employed with gay inconsistency by the actors themselves to describe everything from a simple farce to an elaborately allegorical chronicle history. It has been suggested that it was originally applied to a playlet (*ludus*) performed between (*inter*) courses at a banquet. Chambers suggests rather that it began as a playlet between two persons. An equally valid definition is suggested by the documents in a fifteenth century lawsuit where "interlude" seems to mean a play performed indoors in the winter, while "stageplay" designates an outdoor summer performance.

Under the term *interlude* may be grouped those plays of the early Tudor period performed by professional troupes for the edification and amusement of the court and the educated classes. Towards the end of the fifteenth century the acting companies had begun to protect themselves from the laws against vagabonds and players by becoming the "servants" of influential personages in the state. In 1482 there were companies under the patronage of the Earl of Essex and the Duke of Gloucester (later Richard III); by 1538 the account books of Thomas Cromwell show payments to ten different troupes, among them The Queen's [Jane Seymour's], The King's, The Lord Chamberlain's, and the Marquis of Exeter's men.

The conditions of performance have been preserved in a later play, *Sir Thomas More*. A company of actors arrives at More's house seeking employment. He desires to know the plays in their repertory.

> PLAYER. Divers, my Lord: The Cradle of Security,
>   Hit Nail o' th' Head, Impatient Poverty,
>   The Play of Four P's, Dives and Lazarus,
>   Lusty Juventus, and the Marriage of Wit and Wisdom.
> MORE. The Marriage of Wit and Wisdom? That, my lads.
>   I'll have none but the best. The theme is very good
>   And may maintain a liberal argument. . . . .
>   How many are ye?
> PLAYER. Four men and a boy, sir.
> MORE. But one boy? Then I see
>   There's but few women in the play.
> PLAYER. Three, my Lord: Dame Science, Lady Vanity,
>   And Wisdom, she herself.
> MORE. And one boy play them all? by'r Lady, he's laden!

There is more truth than punning in that last exclamation. Not only were the players required to double many rôles in a single play, their repertories were large. In order to live they were forced to play not only for the nobility but for the general public, and plays suitable to both audiences must be kept in readiness. Arriving at a town they would play, as R. Willis recalled, for the Mayor, or perhaps for some important churchman or statesman, and then repair to the Innyard to burlesque their way through a crude morality for the common folk of the community. In the early years of the Tudor period, the nobility might be treated to an allegorical debate, a realistic farce, or a rudimentary romantic comedy. The populace were served with a degraded morality, like *Mankind,* full of vulgar witticism, proverbial philosophy, and knockabout farce. This ambivalence in the tastes of the two audiences was to be a determining factor not only in the Tudor, but the later drama: it explains the "comic relief" injected into serious situations and the appearance cheek by jowl of the sophisticated and the vulgar.

It is during this period also that we can begin to speak of playwrights by name with some confidence. The course of the anonymous drama written by clerics for the glory of God is running out, and its place is taken by the works of men who write for advancement in this world, or as participants in political or intellectual controversies. Such plays as John Skelton's *Magnificence* (1515), Sir David Lyndsay's *Satire of the Three Estates* (1540) and John Bale's *King John* (c. 1540) retain most of the techniques of the morality while dealing with the political education of English and Scots kings, and the Protestant Reformation.

But the chief impetus to the secularization of the *matter* of drama came from a group of playwrights associated with the household of Cardinal Morton, Archbishop of Canterbury: John Rastell, the printer, Thomas More, humanist, lawyer, and statesman, John Heywood, musician, and Henry Medwall, minor cleric and teacher.

Medwall is credited with the authorship of the first wholly secular play in English, the "romantic comedy," *Fulgens and Lucres* (c. 1497). Little is known of the background of the play or the reasons for its writing. Medwall's earlier *Nature* (c. 1486) had been in the old allegorical tradition. Yet *Fulgens* has no trace of allegory either in its characters or its situations. From the opening speeches it is obvious that an actor, who has pretended to be a serving man, is addressing the guests at a banquet, and that the play is to be an interlude between courses.

A. Ah! or God's will,
   What mean ye, sirs, to stand so still?
   Have not ye eaten and your fill,
   And paid nothing therefore?

His fellow, B, announces that the bemused diners will be enter-
tained with a play. Says A,

I trow your own self shall be one
Of them that shall play.
B.   Nay, I am none;
I trow thou speakest in derision
To liken me thereto.
A. Nay, I mock not, wat ye well,
   For I thought verily by your apparel
   That ye had been a player. . . .
   There is so much nice array
   Amongst these gallants nowaday,
   That a man shall not lightly
   Know a player from another man.

B then recites the prologue, a synopsis of the play to come.
Thus intimately the audience and players of an interlude were
associated.

The principal actors now enter one after the other, through the
audience, to the playing area. The play proper is a rather dull
one in spite of the enthusiastic approval of its editors. It demonstrates the growing influence of the Renaissance in its source and
theme. Medwall is dramatizing a Latin treatise, *On True Nobility,* an English translation of which had been published by
Caxton in 1481. His plot involves the earliest appearance in the
English theater of the eternal story of the love triangle. The hand
of Lucretia, daughter of Fulgentio, a Roman senator, is sought
in marriage by two young men, the noble and wealthy Cornelius
and the poor but honest Flaminius. Unable to choose, Lucretia
consults her father who, in the original story, decides to make
a public issue of the matter and takes it up with the senate.
Medwall increases the dramatic value of the plot by allowing the
two men to advance their claims to the lady in a debate, decided
by Lucretia's designation of the virtuous pauper as the possessor
of true nobility, of her person, and her dowry.

The somewhat windy proceedings are considerably lightened
by a humorous sub-plot in which the two serving men, A and B,
burlesque the main plot by becoming rivals for the love of

Lucretia's maid, the "flower of the frying pan." It is important to note the relationship of the two plots, for the sub-plot is not simply comic relief. Like the story of Mak in the *Second Shepherd's Play*, it has a real relation to the central theme. Where Cornelius and Flaminius debate on the subject of true nobility, that is, contest intellectually for Lucretia, their servants are required to demonstrate their mastery "in cookery or in pastry" and finally fall to actual fisticuffs over the maid. Thus early the sub-plot is established as a parallel to the main plot on a lower and more obvious level. But the comic parts are so vigorous and well handled, and full of the plain speaking so characteristic of the period, that Medwall with some difficulty forces his epilogue back to the main subject:

> All the substance of this play
> Was done specially therefore,
> Not only to make folk mirth and game,
> But that such as be gentlemen of name
> May be somewhat moved
> By this example for to eschew
> The way of vice and favor virtue;
> For sin is to be reproved
> More in them, for their degree,
> Than in other persons such as be
> Of poor kin and birth.
> This was the cause principal,
> And also for to do withal
> This company some mirth.

The unpretentiousness about Medwall's stated purposes is typical also of the interludes of John Heywood, the best known author of what a sneering Elizabethan chose to call "vulgar devisings." Heywood's works, both those acknowledged and those assumed to be his, provide convenient illustrations of the development of the interlude from debate to realistic farce. *The Play of Love* and *Witty and Witless* are hardly recognizable as plays but were highly satisfactory as after-dinner entertainments for the new humanists. They share some of the amusing qualities of mock-trials or debates upon fantastic subjects intended to display forensic skill. *The Play of the Weather* (1533?) continues in the convention of the debate—one could hardly imagine a less practical question for discussion than how

> to satisfy and content
> All manner people which have been offended
> By any weather meet to be amended—

but progresses in the direction of drama by giving the characters
a personal, not merely an intellectual, interest in the theme. One
by one the complainants file before Jupiter, each demanding
the kind of weather best suited to his occupation, from the fox-
hunting gentleman who requests "weather pleasant, Dry and not
misty, the wind calm and still," and the water-miller who demands "plenty of rain," to A Boy, "the least that can play," who
begs "a bushell of snow or two. . . . [for] making snowballs and
throwing the same." After everyone has talked about the weather,
Jupiter informs them that of course nobody will do anything
about it.

Heywood displays real deftness in the expansion of so tenuous
a joke into an hour's pastime. He has drawn his type characters
with some skill and the juxtaposition of their totally opposite
demands on Jupiter—which might be expected to wear thin—
remains comic because of the intensity with which each character
insists on his "own sort" of weather; the totally unexpected plea
of the small boy provides a humorous climax to the series of requests. The play is further enlivened by Jupiter's messenger,
Merryreport, who introduces the characters, chafes the audience,
and makes much sport of the situation. He is described in the
cast of characters as "the vice" and demonstrates how that familiar type from the older Morality is being turned to the uses
of the secular drama.

The Play Called the Four P's (c. 1521-25) shows Heywood in-
fusing greater realism into the dramatic debate. The four "P's"
are a palmer (a professional pilgrim), a pardoner, a pothecary
(here, a seller of patent medicines), and a pedlar. Meeting at a
crossroads, the first three decide to join forces but cannot agree
who shall be their leader. The pedlar suggests that they engage in
a contest, the winner to take command of the two losers. He continues,

> And now have I found one mastery [art]
> That ye can do indifferently [equally well]
> And that is neither selling nor buying
> But even only, truly, lying!

The others agree and the lying match commences.

The pothecary begins with a marvellous, and thoroughly ribald, tale of a cure that he wrought on a fair young lady afflicted with the falling sickness. Although the pothecary seems to have told a lie to end all lies, the pardoner, highly skilled in such matters, comes from behind to cap him with the story of his trip to Hell in search of Margery Corson, a neighbor who had died without benefit of extreme unction. His is a highly circumstantial report, the kind a pardoner might be expected to give, and concludes with the rejoicing of Lucifer and the lesser devils,

> For joy how they
> Did roar at her delivery,
> And how the chimes in hell did ring,

to be rid of a shrew whose temper was hotter than the fires in Hell's kitchen. The pardoner concludes by informing his hearers that they may check his veracity by consulting the lady herself, on "Newmarket Heath."

Both these lies are extremely long and detailed and the pedlar is duly impressed. He turns now to the palmer, who merely remarks that he is somewhat taken aback by the pardoner's tale since, travelling over the whole wide world,

> Of all the women that I have seen,
> I never saw, or knew, in my conscience,
> Any one woman out of patience.

Even the other liars are thunderstruck by the magnitude of the little story. "By the mass," says the pothecary, "there is a great lie!" and the issue is determined.

It will be seen from both *The Weather* and *The Four P's* that for Heywood the old jokes were the best. His skill in refurbishing the commonplace is perhaps best illustrated by *A Merry Play Between John John, the Husband, Tyb, his Wife, and Sir John, the Priest,* generally credited to him. The basis of this little farce is a *fabliau,* a French popular anecdote, in matter and action closely related to Chaucer's handling of the same form in *The Miller's Tale.* The characters are familiar types—John the henpecked husband cuckolded by his shrewish wife and the village priest. While many conventions of the earlier interlude are preserved—the characters speak freely to the audience and John at one point asks a spectator to hold his coat—there is a definite change of locale as the action moves between John's and Sir John's house, and a developing plot as the meek husband is finally driven to challenge the priest to physical combat, in which the wife joins. John is obviously defeated, but his spirit is roused and he goes off determined to see to it that he does not end up with "a pig in the worse panier." Further, Heywood's earlier plays had made at least casual acknowledgement of the didactic purpose of the older interlude—the pedlar of the *Four P's* moralizes:

> Where ye doubt the truth, not knowing,
> Believing the best, good may be growing.
> In judging the best, no harm at the least,
> In judging the worst, no good at the best.
> But best in these things, it seemeth to me,
> To take no judgement upon ye;
> But, as the Church doth judge or take them,
> So do ye receive or forsake them;
> And so, be sure, you cannot err,
> But may be a fruitful follower.

John John ends, on the other hand, with no apology, no moral, no statement of didactic purpose. It is pure comedy and its intention is solely to amuse. The satire on the clergy is so conventional that it could hardly have had any sting and the wife and husband were, as has been suggested, standard types. This is realistic popular comedy composed to "pass the time without offense." In it Heywood has finally freed the art of the drama from the shackles of didacticism both religious and secular. Yet it is only a comedy *in posse,* what the modern theater might classify as a sketch for a musical revue. Fully developed comedy must wait upon the comprehension of the secrets of sustained plotting which scholars and teachers were beginning to discover in the classical comedies of Plautus and his imitators.

It should be emphasized that until the time of Heywood in the early sixteenth century, the development of the English drama has been along native, not to say insular, lines. Allowing for the non-national character of the Liturgical Play, the history of the vernacular Miracle, Morality and Interlude is remarkably free from influence from continental drama. While the themes and subject matter may be similar the treatments differ widely. Such literary influence as the writings of the European church fathers is not to be denied, but only in *Everyman* is there clear evidence of translation—and it has never been satisfactorily demonstrated on which side of the English Channel the translator worked.

Even a group of professional plays seemingly derived from classical works was treated completely in the native tradition. It is somewhat startling to come upon an English dramatic version of the familiar Greek myth of Orestes and his mother and find that it owes nothing to Aeschylus. The title of John Pickering's *Interlude of Vice Containing the History of Orestes* (printed 1567) clearly suggests the treatment to which the classical story was to be subjected. In place of intense concentration of time, single locale, and relegation of the action to behind the scenes, Pickering moves about with medieval freedom, relates the entire story in an hour's traffic of the stage, and lards the whole with violent action. The difference between classical tragedy and professional interlude may be suggested by the author's directions to his players: "make your battle lively, and let it be long ere you can win the city." The Vice, who calls himself variously Courage and Revenge, plays a large part in the working out of the plot, and a pair of realistic peasants participate with no apparent feeling, on their part or the audience's, that they are as out of place in prehistoric Greece as Mak was in ancient Palestine.

Similar treatment was dealt to the classical tale of *Appius and Virginia* (printed 1575), and the biblical stories of *Godly Queen Esther* (1561), *The Life and Repentance of Mary Magdalene* (by Lewis Wager, 1566), and *Most Virtuous and Godly Susanna* (by Thomas Garter, 1578). An echo of the medieval, and an anticipation of the Elizabethan, fascination with the romantic East is to be found in *King Darius* (1565) and Thomas Preston's *Cambises* (c. 1569).

The latter play, because it was unmercifully mocked by Falstaff, has had a fame far beyond its artistic or historical deserts. Since all these professional plays are of about equal merit, however, *Cambises* may be chosen as typical. Certainly we approach the descriptive title with a sense of familiarity—*A Lamentable Tragedy Mixed Full of Pleasant Mirth*—for it is after this model that Peter Quince labelled his drama of *Pyramus and Thisbe* "very tragical mirth." The casting is so arranged by the printer that the thirty-eight characters could be managed by a troupe of six men and two boys; and a busy troupe it must have been, for a typical assignment was to play "Councill, Huf, Praxaspes, Murder, Lob, The Third Lord," the whole gamut of rôles from historical persons and realistic clowns to allegorical characters. A sense of penurious pomp is inescapable, for all the doubling, as the King enters in splendor for a council meeting followed by one counsellor and one knight.

His speech, however, leaves nothing to be desired in point of inflation. It is composed in rhyming fourteener couplets, one of the unhappiest measures ever employed for dramatic dialogue. The king begins:

> My council grave and sapient, with lords of legal train,
> Attentive ears to-wards me bend, and mark what shall be sayn;
> So you likewise, my valiant knight, whose manly acts doth fly
> By bruit of Fame, that sounding trump doth pierce the azure sky.
> My sapient words, I say, perpend, and so your skill dilate.

He continues at some length since these early players were nothing if not articulate. A speech of twenty lines is barely sufficient to express the simple affirmative, and the possibilities of reiteration and tautology are thoroughly explored. The Counsellor announces, for example, the arrival of a new character:

> Behold, I see him now agresse and enter into place!

And yet for all this flow of language, Preston is quite unable to convey any sense of genuine passion or feeling. A mother coming upon her murdered child cries out,

> O blissful babe! O joy of womb! Heart's comfort and delight! . . .
> O heavy day and dolefull time, these mourning tunes to make!
> With blubber'd eyes, into mine arms from earth I will thee take,
> And wrap thee in mine apron white. But, oh my heavy heart!
> The spiteful pangs that it sustains would make it in two to part,
> The death of this my son to see! O heavy mother now,
> That from thy sweet and sugar'd joy to sorrow so shouldst bow.

A spectator at another such dramatic expression of grief cynically remarked, "This passion, and the death of a dear friend, would go near to make a man look sad."

Not that the play, for all its concern with speech, is wanting in action. Preston presents a pageant of violence which would hold the attention of the most exacting among the vulgar. Cambises, in the beginning, is a man fully aware of his kingly duties;

later he becomes only too aware of his kingly prerogatives. In the first part of the play he executes what is only justice against a would-be usurper, though the means adopted are prophetically severe: the evil-doer is beheaded and flayed as a warning to his son. Later in a fit of pride he shoots the prime minister's son through the heart with a bow and arrow, kills his own brother in a fit of jealousy, and condemns his Queen to death in a fit of lust for his cousin-german. In each of these displays of princely willfulness he is abetted by the Vice, Ambidexter, who is also involved in several rough-and-tumble scrapes with Huf, Ruf, and Snuff, the low comedians. Figures from allegory and classical mythology add further confusion of tone to this patchwork tapestry, the whole being resolved by an accident intended to prove that a

> Just reward for his misdeeds the God above hath wrought.
> For certainly the life he led was to be counted nought.

A more apt moral might be that divine justice works in mysterious ways, since Cambises meets his end:

> As I on horseback up did leap, my sword from scabbard shot
> And ran me thus into the side—as you right well may see.
> A marvelous chance unfortunate, that in this wise should be!
> I feel myself a-dying now; of life bereft am I;
> And Death hath caught me with his dart, for want of blood I spy.

It was part of the convention, of course, that no want of blood was to be spied by the audience which was at this moment treated to the spectacle of the monarch groveling on the ground, the sword thrust into his side, bleeding profusely. Earlier it had seen Sisamnes flayed, the child's heart pierced by an arrow and cut out, and the king's brother spouting blood as a spear pricked a little bladder of red wine attached to his costume.

Although the play is tolerable today only as a source of laughter, and although Preston was over-zealous in supplying the audience demand for a deal of action and amusement to a pennyworth of tragedy, Cambises is not wholly despicable. There is no unity between the discordant elements of native interlude-morality and historical subject matter, yet the play has a kind of structure, a rising and falling action, which gives it a true place in the development of the English dramatic form. It is divided not

into four acts but three "movements"; in the first, introduced by
the anonymous Prologue, Cambises assumes the Throne of Persia
and sets out to be a worthy king; in the second, introduced by
the allegorical figure of Shame, he attains the full dignity of his
position and commences his willful misbehavior; in the third,
introduced by Venus and Cupid, he commits his final misdeeds
of lust and falls to his doom. This pattern of rise and fall, related
to the medieval concept of "de casibus" tragedy, the wheel of
fortune, will be examined in greater detail in the next chapter.

We have been considering then the development of a native
popular tradition, and, before it becomes contaminated or regularized by external forces, it may be well to pause for a summary
statement of its characteristics. The native drama begins by
drawing on Biblical *history* for its matter and clinging closely to
the source materials for its treatment. Some freedom creeps in
with the fictional plots of the Moralities, but the historical label
—the True Tragedy, the True Chronicle—remains an attractive
one to the audience and partially explains the immense popularity
of the Chronicle play in the sixteenth century. The Biblical matter
is, however, treated with some freedom in the sense that it is
assimilated to the conditions of life in medieval England. Herod,
the feudal ruler with his troop of knights, Mrs. Noah, the recognizable sister of Dame Alice of Bath, and Mak, the English
confidence man, are not anachronisms so much as portraits according to the medieval concept of history; yet the effect is to give
a quality of *realism* to the story which never wholly departs from
the later drama. As the form develops, also, it is evident that
popular taste has declared for *action* as opposed to narration.
The conflicts become increasingly physical, and there is no attempt even to confine the action to a single place—the players
move freely from house to house, town to town, and even country to country within their play. There was little attempt to maintain a *unity of tone;* the comic, the grotesque explodes in the
midst of the most serious situations. Occasionally, perhaps accidentally, there is a close relationship—as in the *Second Shepherd's Play* or *Fulgens and Lucres*—between the serious plot and
the "comic relief" but not until late in the sixteenth century does
a playwright discover how to make a single work of art out of the
chaos of seriousness and burlesque dear to the popular audience.
Finally, it might be recalled that these early plays are populated

~ 2 ~

Panoramic Drama: The First Movement

1. SCHOOL DRAMA

The drama does not anticipate changes in the climate of opinion. In general, it must wait until its audience has been prepared to receive new ideas or ideals before it can employ them with confidence. Special plays may be composed for special audiences, of course, and may in time find wider acceptance; one has only to recall the struggles of various stage societies and little theaters to establish themselves in our own era, and the limited appeal of the early Shaw and the early O'Neill—playwrights who have since been welcomed by the popular theater. Such was the case in the Renaissance of the fifteen century. Until 1500 an English playgoer would hardly have been aware of the revolution in art and philosophy directed by the humanists. By 1600, humanism, though it did not replace the native popular tradition, had been completely absorbed into it.

A brief consideration of the Renaissance will provide a useful introduction to its belated though profound effect on the drama. Literally, *renaissance* means *rebirth;* as applied to cultural history, it means specifically that great awakening of interest in the classical past which began in Italy in the fourteenth century. The causes of the awakening are obscure and complex. Mr. Shaw dramatizes them with telling effect in *St. Joan,* a chronicle history play concerned in part with the efforts of the individual and the nation to break through the confining walls of the medieval world and ways of thinking. Dissatisfied with the old concept of the world and world order, Renaissance, man began to assert his own importance, his dignity as an individual, and the art and literature of the ancient world provided him with a new pattern and inspiration. The renewed emphasis upon man is evident in

49

painting, where the realistic portrait begins to challenge the
supremacy of religious and allegorical themes as suitable subject
matter; it is evident in literature, where the plays of Seneca with
their analysis of psychological conflicts between the rights of men
and their duty to society become models for imitation; it is evident in religion, as men desire to communicate directly with their
God; it is evident in economics, as the feudal system is replaced by
capitalism, as the communal organization described in the familiar parable of the Body and its Members is replaced by the desire
for personal aggrandizement.

The Renaissance touched England early in the fifteenth century as the result of the visits of various Italian schoolmen and
teachers, but it was not until the accession of Henry VII in 1485
that it became established in influential circles. To one of these
groups, the circle of Cardinal Morton, and later of Sir Thomas
More, we have already referred in discussing the Interlude, and
it is in that simple form that humanism first appears in the English drama. The "serious plot" of Medwall's *Fulgens and Lucres*
is just the kind of argument which would be pleasing to the pro-
ponents of the New Learning. True nobility, so runs the argument, is invested in the man who spends his time in study to
"eschew idleness," defends his country when called upon, and
promises his bride not wealth and ease but "moderate riches,
And that sufficient for us both." And the ancestry of the argument, ultimately the *De Vera Nobilitate* of the Italian humanist
Bonaccorse, was impeccable. This early humanist "documentary,"
to be sure, was performed for a special clique at Cardinal Morton's but for even so receptive an audience, the heroine finds
it necessary to add an apologetic word lest she give offense:

> . . . I am fully determined with God's grace
> So that to Gaius I will condescend
> For in this case I do him commend
> As the more noble man, sith he this wise
> By means of his virtue to honor doth arise.
> And for all that I will not despise
> The blood of Cornelius, I pray you think not so:
> God forbid that ye should note me in that wise,
> For truly I shall honor them wheresoever I go,
> And all other that be of like blood also . . .
> I pray you all, sirs, as many as be here
> Take not my words by a sinister way.

The dramatist must not expect too much tolerance, even among the emanicipated.

Later interludes, including Heywood's, show some evidence of humanistic influence. It is also to be marked in what might be designated Secular Moralities, a group of plays of the interlude type but allegorical in style and didactic in intent. Among these should be included John Rastell's *The Nature of the Four Elements* (*c.* 1517), an exposition in dramatic form of recent discoveries in science and geography, the "prodigal youth" plays— such as *Hickscorner* (*c.* 1510), *Youth* (*c.* 1520), *Lusty Juventus* (*ibid.*), *Mundus et Infans* (pr. 1522)—in which foolish youth learns hard lessons in the school of experience where tedious lectures are delivered at frequent intervals by allegorical commentators. Perhaps the best of the lot is John Redford's *Wit and Science* (*c.* 1530) which presents the scholar's life in the terms of a fairly lively allegory. Wit, a student, desires to marry Lady Science whose father Reason sets him certain tasks in the manner of the old romances: Wit must overcome the monster Tediousness and make a pilgrimage to Mount Parnassus. It is obvious that such a play was not of interest to the audiences of the professional companies, and indeed it seems to have been written for performance by the choir boys of St. Paul's either at the Court or before their fellow students. The moral is unimpeachable and the allegory simple, but the play is enlivened by a series of delightful songs, several amusing scenes including a burlesque spelling lesson, and the monster Tediousness is a worthy descendant of Herod, his medieval ancestor. *Wit and Science* must have been a highly entertaining lesson for Redford's pupils.

The drama was employed as an educational tool not only by choir masters, but by the universities, the great public schools, and the Inns-of-Court. The classic Roman plays of Plautus and Terence and Seneca were held up to students as models of literature as well as models for living, and their performance by both schoolboys and their teachers was a pedagogical device for inculcating their moral lessons and literary style. It was but a step to the production of original plays in Latin—for example Nicolas Grimald's *Christus Redivivus* (1543) and *Archipropheta* (1547), and Richard Legge's *Ricardus Tertius* (1579)—and but a step further to original plays in the vernacular, still in imitation of classical models. It is not surprising that comedy should develop first; the comic complexities of Plautus and Terence were obviously more attractive to the young idea than the stoical horrors of Seneca.

It is generally agreed that *Ralph Roister Doister* (1534-41) is the earliest of the extant "regularized" English comedies. It was written by Nicholas Udall, probably while headmaster at Westminster, and at first glance is a thoroughly Romanized affair. As in the *Miles Gloriosus* of Plautus, the title character is a braggart warrior whose bravery is purely verbal and whose love affairs are inspired by an empty pocket rather than a full heart. As in Plautus also, the vainglorious hero is mocked and flouted by a parasite, an amoral rogue who lives by his wits and by flattering the follies of the stupid. The action is divided into the classical five acts, and the conflict is extended and elaborated where Heywood and the earlier native comic writers had been content with a situation or an incident. Udall's plot involves a series of incidents leading to a climax and conclusion. Ralph seeks the hand (and fortune) of the widow Custance in the absence of her truelove Gawain Goodluck. Although the lady spurns him, his own stupidity and the promptings of Merrygreek (the parasite) encourage him to continue his wooing. Before the comic courtship is ended Goodluck returns unexpectedly and suspects Custance of inconstancy. The plot is, of course, unravelled without difficulty in the last act, but simple as it is and in many ways close to Heywood, it is a long step ahead in artistic sophistication.

Even more interesting is the plotting of *Gammer Gurton's Needle*, a comedy produced at Christ's College in Cambridge a few years after *Roister Doister*. It is a nearly anonymous play; the title page credits the authorship to "Mr. S. M[aste]r of Art," variously identified as John Still, William Stevenson, and John Bridges, with perhaps the strongest evidence in favor of the last. The author was, at any rate, a disciple of the New Learning, for he follows the plan of classical comedy with its division into five acts, its intriguing parasite, its complex plotting. Yet the situation which he handles in so classical a manner is a typically native one which might have furnished a half-hour's sport to John Heywood or the farce-writers. The genuine debt of the English drama to classical comedy is nowhere better demonstrated than in the working out of this truly "merry play" in which the mere loss of a needle provides a comic situation expanded over five acts without a moment of padding or dullness. One can imagine the original joke: did you hear about the woman who lost her needle while repairing her man's breeches? And who found it again when he sat down after putting them on? With this as a starting point, Mr. S. introduces the character of Diccon "The Bedlam"—that is, a beggar discharged from the insane hospital. Diccon owes his place in the comedy, no doubt, to the inevitable parasite of Plautus and Terence, as does Matthew Merrygreek in *Roister Doister*. Like Merrygreek, too, there is more than a little of the practical-joking Vice about him. But Diccon, whatever his origins, is a purely English character, a familiar part of the English scene (*cf.* Edgar's disguise in *King Lear*). So too is Hodge, the handyman whose ripped breeches are the cause of all the commotion, and Dame Chat and her neighbor Gammer Gurton, and Doctor Rat, the village curate, whose attempts to separate the brawling ladies end catastrophically for himself. If this play illustrates the regularization of English comedy by classical models, it demonstrates even more vividly the complete naturalization of the models.

Roister Doister as the older and more obviously classical play has generally received more attention from critics and scholars—it is somewhat more dignified, and better fitted to academic purposes, and its moral is plainly stated in the prologue. The end of the dramatist, declares Udall, is to hide virtuous lore under merry comedies, and his own comedy "against the vainglorious doth inveigh." Not that the moral is so obtrusive as to spoil the comedy. There are good situations (and this is neither the first nor the last time that they appear in English comedy) in Ralph's mispunctuated love letter to Dame Custance, in Merrygreek's open insulting of the hero under the guise of reporting a message, and in the pitched battle in which the braggart warrior is trounced by ladies armed with distaff, broom, ladle, and kitchen poker. *Gammer Gurton,* on the other hand, is purely English and pure fun. Its moral, whatever it may be, has successfully escaped detection. Apart from the historical record, there is little in it to suggest a learned or specialized audience. Thus early the form of classical comedy has been totally adapted to the uses of the English popular theater.

The transmutation of the classical tragic form was a longer process. To the English Humanist, tragedy was almost synony-

mous with the works of Seneca, closet dramas intended in part
as documents to advance the Stoic philosophy of resignation.
Seneca's theme was of sure appeal: the conflict of passion, temper,
or appetite with external duties. His subject matter was chosen
from the most violent of the old myths. Murder, adultery, and
incest are the nucleus of his plots. *Thyestes,* a kind of prologue
to the familiar story of Agamemnon, may be considered as typical. It begins with a ghost "dragged from his place among the
shades" to witness the working out of a curse on his descendants.
The plot is divided, rather arbitrarily, into five acts by Choruses
who chant lengthy commentaries without being in any way identified with the action (as in Greek tragedy), the characters speak
at length and almost entirely in rhetorical bombast, and the multiple offstage horrors are reported minutely by long-winded messengers with a passion for detail. Obviously *Thyestes* would be
unrecognizable as tragedy to the audiences of *Cambises.* It is
equally obvious that *Thyestes* would be unsatisfactory as tragedy
to the audiences of *Hamlet.* The serious dramatists of the New
Learning, however, dreamed only of climbing "to the height of
Seneca's style."

The *Ten Tragedies* of Seneca were translated into English and
published between 1559 and 1581, but they had been readily
available in the original for many years before. The Latin plays
of Grimald and Legge were written under their influence in the
1540's. It was not until 1561-2 that a full length Senecan tragedy
in English made its appearance. The occasion was the Christmas
feast of the Inner Temple, one of the "Inns-of-Court" where
young men prepared for the Bar, the play was *Gorboduc, or Ferrex and Porrex,* and the authors were Thomas Sackville and
Thomas Norton, two young lawyers about to embark on promising careers as public servants. *Gorboduc* was received with great
enthusiasm by the Templers, repeated at Court at the command
of Queen Elizabeth, and hailed by Sir Philip Sidney as "full of
stately speeches and well-sounding phrases, climbing to the height
of Seneca's style, and as full of notable morality, which it doth
most delightfully teach, and so obtain the very end of poesy."
The story, as outlined by the printer, is derived from mythical English history: "Gorboduc, king of Britain, divided his realm in his
lifetime to his sons, Ferrex and Porrex; the sons fell to dissension;
the younger killed the elder; the mother, that more dearly loved

the elder, for revenge killed the younger; the people, moved with
the cruelty of the fact, rose in rebellion and slew both the father
and the mother; the nobility assembled and most terribly destroyed the rebels; and afterwards, for want of issue of the prince,
whereby the succession of the crown became uncertain, they fell
to civil war, in which both they and many of their issues were
slain, and the land for a long time almost desolate and miserably
wasted." The moral was particularly directed at the unmarried
queen:

> Hereto it comes when kings will not consent
> To grave advice, but follow wilful will,
> This is the end, when in fond prince's hearts
> Flattery prevails, and safe rede hath no place:
> . . . And this doth grow, when lo, unto the prince,
> Whom death of sudden hap of life bereaves,
> No certain heir remains. . . .

Yet for all the applause of its audiences and the approval of
Sidney, for all the excellence of its moral and its apparent suffi-
ciency of action, *Gorboduc* survives only for its historical interest.
As a play it is surpassingly dull.

Not all the faults of this play are to be attributed to Seneca.
The authors' penchant for a series of orations instead of dramatic
dialogue is not entirely warranted by the practice of their model.
They do, however, follow him in dividing their work into five
acts, each ending with a chorus of "four ancient and sage men
of Britain," whose presence is never explained. Sidney complained that the play broke the classical unities of time and place,
although it might be said that unity of action is established by
the fact that all the action in the play transpires offstage: not
even in Seneca are messengers kept so busy relating horrors to the
audience. And since nothing happens on stage, the characters are
left with nothing to do but talk. This they do in speeches which
run up to 100 lines.

Gorboduc contains another innovation of considerable importance. In 1557 Surrey had published his translation of the *Aeneid*
in blank verse and Sackville and Norton seized upon the new
form as the closest English approximation to the Latin meters
of Seneca. Hitherto English tragedy had been written for the
most part in fourteener-couplets with results ranging—as may be
seen in *Cambises*—from the ridiculous to the appalling. The two

innovators are under the usual disadvantage of having no models, and their success is more frequent in passages of dignity than of passion. There is no hint in their work of the flexible instrument blank verse was to become in the hands of Marlowe and his successors, but it has the gravity wholly suited to a tragic theme and the dignity which should accompany the fall of princes.

One other innovation of great importance makes its appearance in *Gorboduc.* Each act is introduced by a "dumb show" enacted in pantomime to the accompaniment of flutes, violins, and other instruments. It seems likely that these dumb shows trace their origin to the *intermedii* of the contemporary Italian stage. They are, characteristically, allegorical or symbolic and in *Gorboduc* they are intended to be self-explanatory:

> First the music of flutes began to play, during which came in upon the stage a company of mourners all clad in black, betokening death and sorrow to ensue upon the ill-advised misgovernment and dissolution of brethren: as befell upon the murder of Ferrex by his younger brother. After the mourners had passed thrice about the stage, they departed; and then the music ceased.

Until the very end of the panoramic drama, the dumb show continued to be an attractive device, introducing added variety in action, pageantry and color in staging, and appealing to the popular taste for allegory. In later years, however, it was customarily "interpreted" in the subsequent dialogue for those of the audience who failed to comprehend it. All audiences—even the courtly—were not as quick as the young men of the Inns-of-Court; the scholar Hamlet himself complains about the inexplicable dumb show and even a king, on one occasion, seems to have been unaware of what he had seen pantomimed.

The success of *Gorboduc* naturally led to imitations. In 1566 the students at Grey's Inn presented *Jocasta,* also in blank verse, equipped with dumb shows and the standard Senecan apparatus. In the next year came *Gismonde of Salerne,* a thoroughly romantic story recast into the fashionable classical mode, although written in rhyme. As late as 1588, the young lawyers kept their taste for classical tragedy. In that year a whole squadron of authors of whom the chief was Thomas Hughes and the most famous Francis Bacon collaborated to produce *The Misfortunes of Arthur.* The resulting product is a mélange of British legend with echoes from the Oedipus myth. The form, except for the elab-

orate dumb shows, is Senecan and a great many of the speeches
are lifted line by line from his works.

Although neo-classical tragedy seems to survive for a quarter
of a century, it must be remembered that it was in no sense of the
word popular drama. None of these plays stands between the
Roman heritage and the professional stage as *Gammer Gurton*
does in comedy. Only a man who intended to earn his living by
practising law could afford to write such a play as *Gorboduc;* the
taste for the English-Seneca was rarefied, not to say assiduously
cultivated.

2. COURT PLAYS

The adaptations of classical comedy to English tastes by Udall
and Mr. S. were larded with plenty of rough and tumble action
and broad, if not vulgar, jokes. Since the Court of Elizabeth in
the early days was made up of bluff, hearty nobles fresh from the
wars or the country, this combination of farce and bawdry would
seem to be all that it would desire. But it was also a court conscious of the great world, of Italy and Spain particularly, with
which it had to deal, and it was almost pathetically eager to be
taught refinement.

In the theater demand creates supply, and sophistication and
gentlemanliness were taught to the courtiers in two schools; the
theaters of the Inns-of-Court and of the Children of the Chapel.
Their plays were the sugar-coated pills prescribed by Nicholas
Udall, but the center of the pill was etiquette, proper behavior,
a modernization of the medieval ideal of knightly chivalry and
courtly love.

Love in the popular drama had hardly been a romantic subject. When it entered the interludes, it was usually associated
with adultery and the comic cuckold; in *Roister Doister* it was a
perfunctory device to move the plot. The importance, then, of a
series of plays adapted from Italian Renaissance comedy must not
be overlooked, for they provided the Elizabethan theater with its
most common theme, the ideal quality of romantic love, and its
subject matter, the merry tangles which must be resolved before
a happy marriage may crown the end.

Of these plays, George Gascoigne's *The Supposes* (1566) is the
most famous, largely because it furnished the underplot of disguise and intrigue for *The Taming of the Shrew*. Translated

directly from Ariosto's *I Suppositi,* it was first presented at Grey's Inn with such success that several printings were demanded and a production before the scholars of Oxford University. A brave new world was opened to the audience for, although the typical intrigue and stock characters of Plautus were present, the emphasis had shifted from the simple outwitting of old men by young to the elimination of obstacles to the wedding of true hearts. Slapstick and vulgarity are eliminated, and a ragged prose substituted for the verse of native comedy. Puns abound, and what the Elizabethans called "word-catching," playing with semantics and etymology. The prologue toys with the title of the piece: "the very name whereof may peradventure drive into every of your heads a sundry suppose to suppose the meaning of our Supposes."

A greater refinement is evident in the comedies enacted for the edification of the court by the Children of the Chapel Royal. These were a body of choir boys, whose performances were not restricted to religious occasions. When required to provide entertainment for secular festivities they would often present plays or "disguisings." That they were remarkably skillful is attested by their success with the public and their ability at certain times to attract the services of such major playwrights as Jonson and Marston, but their years and training governed the kind of plays which they might present. Their major talent was, of course, in speaking and singing and these are the distinguishing characteristics of their repertory, and their contribution to the refinement of Elizabethan comedy.

In 1561, Richard Edwards was appointed Master of the Children. As a musician and poet he set himself the additional task of providing original comedies interspersed with songs for the training of his charges and for the amusement of the court. In the prologue to one such play, *Damon and Pithias* (c. 1564) he enumerates, after Horace, certain improvements which he feels the English stage still lacks. He will abandon the matter and method of "toying plays," interludes, and will observe proper "decorum" in characterization:

> In comedies the greatest skill is this: rightly to touch
> All things to the quick, and eke to frame each person so
> That by his common talk you may his nature rightly know.
> A roister ought not preach—that were too strange to hear—
> But, as from virtue he doth swerve, so ought his words appear.

The old man is sober; the young man rash; the lover triumphing
  in joys;
The matron grave; the harlot wild, and full of wanton toys:
Which all in one course they no wise do agree,
So correspondent to their kind their speeches ought to be.

Furthermore, the play will be a blend of tragic "history," the
familiar classical story of the two Syracusan friends, with lively
comical matter, a wit combat between Aristippus and Carisophus.
The comic frame lightens the tragic action and makes less un-
likely the happy outcome which Edwards has devised. This was
a new form, as the Prologue recognizes:

Which matter, mixt with mirth and care, a just name to apply
As seems most fit, we have it termed a "tragical comedy."

The mixture of "mirth and care" is to become most typical of
Elizabethan drama and the term *tragicomedy* is to be revived
in the next century to justify another sort of blending. Edwards
is careful that his mixture shall be in good taste. The serious
scenes are touched with a grave dignity, the comic with wit; they
do not intrude upon each other. The result is a somewhat academic play in a loosely rhythmical and occasionally rhyming
prose. Although, like Gascoigne, Edwards follows the pattern of
classical intrigue, the play is not divided into the classical five
acts, and the action moves as freely as in the native three-part
form.

John Lyly is the greatest of the playwright-masters and his contribution to English comedy is of greater importance. Continuing
the refinements in plot and character of such men as Gascoigne
and Edwards, in dialogue he made use of a unique prose style
called Euphuism, after his sensationally successful novel, *Euphues,
The Anatomy of Wit*. To the modern reader, Euphuism quickly
becomes monotonous with its succession of balanced clauses, parallel constructions, antitheses, puns and alliterations. To its original readers, however, it was a revelation: it brought an order,
albeit elaborate, out of the chaos of pre-Tudor prose, created a
better vehicle for wit than the often-strained couplets of earlier
writers. Once Lyly adapted his style to the theater, he established
as the proper medium for comedy a prose that was lively, pithy,
pointed, formal, and—on occasion—concentrated.

The Prologue to *Midas* (1592) furnishes an example of Euphuism, as well as an exposition of Lyly's dramatic intentions:

> Gentlemen, so nice is the world that for apparel there is no fashion,
> for music no instrument, for diet no delicate, for plays no invention,
> but breedeth satiety before noon, and contempt before night. . . .
> At our exercises [entertainments], Soldiers call for tragedies, their ob-
> ject is blood: Courtiers for comedies, their subject is love: Countrymen
> for pastorals, shepherds are their saints. Traffic and travel hath woven
> the nature of all nations into ours, and made this land like Arras
> [tapestry], full of devise, which was Broadcloth, full of workmanship.
> Time hath confounded our minds, our minds the matter; but all
> cometh to this pass, that what heretofore hath been served in several
> dishes for a feast, is now minced in a charger for a gallimaufrey [hash].
> If we present a mingle-mangle, our fault is to be excused, because the
> whole world is become an Hodge-podge.

The typical court comedy provided by Lyly, then, is to be written in stylized dialogue and is to be a mélange of elements, tragic
and comic, romantic and classical. He is careful to divide his
plays into five acts, according to the classical rule, but in complete
disregard of that rule he employs romantic freedom of movement
in time and space. In fact, the old native structure in three movements underlies most of his work, together with the native mingling of comic and "serious" elements.

Endimion (c. 1588) is a good example of his comedy. One plot
concerns the love of Endimion for Cynthia, the woman in the
moon, with Tellus and Dipsas as chief obstacles. Paralleling the
mythological action is the comic story of Sir Tophas, a braggart,
who is not able to effect his romantic goal either. The play is
filled with the trappings of romance: significant dreams, magic
spells, an oracular fountain, a transformation, songs and dances.
In addition to this variety, the play achieves unity in that the
whole action turns about the person of Cynthia, and may be
interpreted (by those acquainted with court intrigue) as a rather
hidden allegory of Queen Elizabeth and the Earl of Leicester.

Apart from the allegory, the theme as usually in Lyly, is love,
specifically unattainable love, and the lovers are Tudor descendants of the courtly lovers of the middle ages. As a concession to
modern notions of what constituted a satisfactory love story, Lyly
does have matters set right by decree in his final scene, but the
whole attitude towards romance is a pose, bloodless, formal, and
idealized. Later playwrights concern themselves with vitalizing

the ideal. Lyly's contribution is to the art of polished expression, intended to mix counsel with wit and to provoke "soft smiling, not loud laughing." In the prologue to *Campaspe* (1583) he defines his own position in the development of the drama, and his fate: "With us it is like to fare as with these torches, which, giving light to others, consume themselves."

3. THE CHRONICLE PLAY & THE PUBLIC THEATER

As has been suggested several times, these Plautine-Senecan-Italianate plays were not intended and had little appeal for the average playgoer. He continued to be supplied by the professional troupes with drama tailored to his measure, drama with plenty of action transpiring on the boards, free movement in time and space, and frequent intrusions of boorish comedy into serious matter. Sir Philip Sidney, in the same famous passage with his (tempered) praise of *Gorboduc*, attacks at some length the unclassical vagaries of the popular drama,

Where you shall have Asia of one side, and Africa of the other, and so many other under-kingdoms, that the player when he cometh in, must ever begin with telling where he is, or else the tale will not be conceived. Now ye shall have three ladies walk to gather flowers, and then we must believe the stage to be a garden. By and by we hear news of shipwreck in the same place, and then we are to blame if we accept it not for a rock. Upon the back of that comes out a hideous monster with fire and smoke, and then the miserable beholders are bound to take it for a cave. While in the meantime two armies fly in, represented with four swords and bucklers, and then what hard heart will not receive it for a pitched field?

Now of time they are much more liberal. For ordinary it is that two young princes fall in love; after many traverses she is got with child, delivered of a fair boy, he is lost, groweth a man, falleth in love, and is ready to get another child,—and all this in two hours' space.

Sir Philip was, of course, arguing for a set of rules based on the principles of classical playwrights as codified by Roman critics. To the man who admired *Gorboduc, Cambises* must seem absurd. To the man who admired *Cambises,* however, *Gorboduc* was equally absurd. The modern reader, who admires neither, while comprehending Sidney's point will nonetheless have some difficulty in sympathizing with it since our own popular drama, the movies, enjoys the same freedom of movement that was basic equipment for popular drama of the sixteenth century. If the common playgoer liked to see anything in an announced title better than "A lamentable tragedy mixed full of pleasant mirth," it was surely "The life and death of ——." And Samuel Johnson was only putting rhymes to a centuries-old truth when he wrote:

> The drama's laws the drama's patrons give,
> And we that live to please must please to live.

Shortly after the middle of the sixteenth century the professional players hit upon a subject of unfailing attractiveness to the citizens of a nation which was just beginning to know its own strength. The *chronicle play* has a long and not entirely honorable history; it was subject to all the excesses of popularity and jingoism; it suffered from a completely uncritical theory of history, failing to attempt a distinction between romantic fiction and chronological fact while posing as the sober truth; it incorporated the worst features in Sidney's bill of complaints. On the other hand, it gave dramatic expression to that awakening of the national spirit evident in the popular historical writings of Stow and Holinshed, in the English legendary and historical poems, in the *Mirror for Magistrates,* and in the early attempts at the biographies of English worthies.

The earliest appearance of English historical matter in the drama may be traced to a curious hybrid, part-history, part-morality, *King Johan* by John Bale. A former Catholic priest who had become a Protestant convert, Bale composed a group of plays to be used by his own touring company as propaganda for the religious reforms of the English church. *King Johan,* surviving only in a manuscript which preserves two or three different revisions of the original seems to date from about 1538 and is in many ways one of the most confusing of Tudor plays. Not the least contributor to this confusion, for the modern reader, is the attitude towards the central figure. John enters alone and announces:

> I have worn the crown and wrought victoriously,
> And now do purpose by practice and by study
> To reform the laws and set men in good order
> That true justice may be had in every border.

Bale is exercising the dramatist's license of making the facts of history serve the purposes of the artist.

The purpose of the artist, obviously, is to establish the authority of the King as supreme in his own kingdom; this order has been decreed by God in his "Scripture evident." Certain other purposes are incidental: a vitriolic attack on the Catholic church, on the venality of priests, on the mingling of church and state, on the retention of Latin in the services at the expense of the common people. The method of the artist is one-third historical and two-thirds allegorical. At the beginning of the play John hears the complaints of a Young Widow, who stands for England. Later he is engaged by Sedition, Nobility, Dissimulation and Usurped Power, abstractions who at appropriate moments become concrete as Steven Langton, Cardinal Pandulphus, Simon of Swynsett, and Pope Innocent III. While this might be a most interesting step in the development of the art of characterization, Bale's system is mysteriously confused and the relationship between the abstract and the historical irregular. The services of the Interpreter and Veritas are wisely provided to keep the main points before the audience, but it is hard to believe that any spectator could follow the play, at least as it survives.

It is not, of course, pure Chronicle History, though in its use of history as a device rather than as a plot it anticipates later developments of the form. For Chronicle History in its unadorned state, we must turn to a genuinely popular anonymous play, *The Famous Victories of Henry the Fifth, containing the honorable battle of Agincourt* (c. 1585) credited on the basis of a rather suspicious joke to the comedian Richard Tarleton. This is genuine work-a-day drama, wholly without pretense or ulterior purpose. It intends to give a "scenic representation of history" and follows the chronicler Raphael Holinshed wherever he leads, with a lack of attention to form and proportion, to structure and emphasis which is made more apparent by the perfection of Shakespeare's reworking of the same material.

The story is the familiar one of the wastrel Prince Hal, reformed in time by his father, Henry IV, and becoming the ideal king who conquers the insulting "Dolphin" of France and weds his sister the Lady Katherine. Inserted into the historical story are the unrelated buffooneries of Derrick, the low comedian (Tarleton's rôle), much jesting with the simple watchmen, and considerable boasting at the expense of the French. The characters are merely outlined—the action is the major interest—yet there is a certain boyish vigor in Henry the Fifth and his wooing of "Kate" is properly brisk:

KATE. How would I love thee, which is my father's enemy?
HENRY. Tut! stand not upon these points. 'Tis you must make us friends.
I know, Kate, thou art not a little proud that I love thee. What, wench, the King of England!

The playwright, it will be observed, has finally escaped from the compulsion to versify and turned to a businesslike prose more than equal to any demands he can make upon it.

The Chronicle History was slow in developing, but after the year of the Spanish Armada it rode the wave of triumphant nationalism into great popularity. From the period before 1590 about a dozen histories survive, in the decade after 1590 nearly eighty were produced. It was always the drama of the people, as the miracle plays had been, and it shared many of their characteristics. Unlike the miracles, however, it fell into the hands of playwrights of genius who remade its sprawling, amorphous, almost epic, structure into drama of enduring power, without sacrificing its patriotic appeal, making full use of the skills and resources developed over a century by the professional companies.

It is a mistake to assume that the professional actors were in the same artistic class with the rude mechanicals who blundered through *Pyramus and Thisbe* in *A Midsummer Night's Dream*. From their predecessors, the minstrels and wandering players, they had inherited a tradition of expertness in singing and dancing, in fencing and tumbling which served them in good stead in the vigorous plots they were called upon to animate. Further, however ridiculous the fourteener rant of King Cambises and his fellows may appear today, a deft reader can make it into something very close to poetry—and the deftness of these players is not to be questioned. When blank verse and Marlowe's mighty line came together to the professional stage, the actors were ready for it, largely because of their training in handling the sustained rant of the fourteener.

As performers, too, they must have been very adaptable, playing without hesitation in any location where an audience could collect, a banquet hall, a village green, or an innyard. The innyard was the most convenient. Conventionally it was an open area surrounded on four sides by the walls of the building. Entrance was possible only through an archway at one end, where a money-taker could be stationed to collect admission fees, obviating the necessity for the strategic interruption of the performance for voluntary contributions. The windows and balconies along the inner walls would provide excellent vantage points for those who could afford higher prices; the commons were content to stand in the yard at the far end of which the players set up their stage. This might be a temporary scaffold or some modification of the pageant wagon; in any case it projected into the audience and seems to have been backed by a curtain behind which the actors dressed. If necessary the inn balcony above the stage could be used as an additional acting area. In such a makeshift theater the later moralities and interludes, *Cambises* and *The Famous Victories of Henry the Fifth* were played by liveried professionals who were permitted to call themselves the Queen's Majesties Servants, or The Earl of Leicester's Men.

The Globe Theatre

It was for this latter company, under the leadership of James Burbage, that the first permanent theater was erected in the fields north of London in 1576. They called it, simply, The Theatre, and the location was chosen as not too far for citizens to walk for entertainment and yet beyond reach of the city fathers who feared that their community might become morally infected. It has been pointed out that behind the moral objections to a public playhouse within the city limits were more practical ones: large gatherings were excellent means for spreading disease, inciting to riot, and creating fire hazards. Whatever the principal motive, however, the public theaters were effectively kept outside the jurisdiction of the city council for several decades.

The Theatre has a double importance, first as a prototype of all Elizabethan public theaters, and second, as the original home of Shakespeare's plays. Pulled down in 1599, it was reconstructed south of the Thames on the Bankside as The Globe. It was a unique auditorium, totally unlike any that we are accustomed to today, and its structure was especially adapted to, and to some extent, influenced, the structure of the Elizabethan plays themselves. It was itself influenced, of course, by the nature of the playing places to which the company was accustomed—the inn-

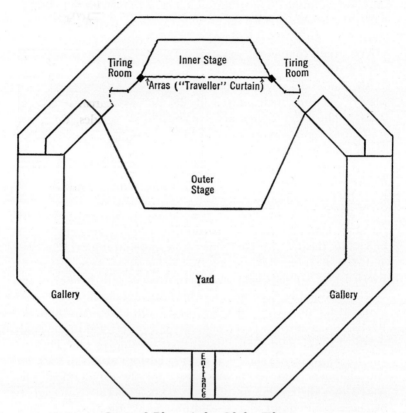

Ground Plan of the Globe Theatre

yards. A secondary influence was the shape of the buildings used for bear-baitings and other public "entertainments." These were circular, or octagonal, as best suited their function. A combination of the bear pit and the innyard, then, resulted in that "wooden O" as the Prologue in *Henry V* describes the auditorium.

Taking the Theatre-Globe as typical, and recognizing that many mutations were possible, it is essential to an understanding

of the drama of the age to establish the principal features of the
Elizabethan public playhouse. It was a large building, nearly a
hundred feet in diameter and three stories in height. It was
topped by a thatched roof, and at one end, above the stage, there
was a cupola from which a flag was flown on the days of performance. The single entrance for the public was through the
wall opposite the stage beside a sign which exhibited the symbol
of the playhouse: Hercules bearing a globe and the words *Totus
mundus agit histrionem,* echoed in Jacques' famous line "All the
world's a stage." Passing through this door, the spectator dropped
his admission-penny into the gatherer's box. He now had the
choice of standing in the yard without further payment, or for
an additional penny or two of renting a seat in one of the three
tiers of galleries which circled the interior.

If he remained in the pit, he found himself facing an enormous
platform some five feet high and built out from the rear wall
nearly forty-five feet into the audience-area. At the back of this
platform was a traverse curtain flanked on each side by a door.
When the traverse was drawn back, an inner stage was revealed.
Above this inner stage was another room, the upper stage, and
above the stage doors were windows. Above the upper stage, projecting over and supported by columns on the main stage was a
roof, sometimes referred to as "The Heavens," under which plays
were performed in all weathers.

Thus it will be seen that the characteristic feature of the
Elizabethan theater was a multiplicity of playing areas. The main
stage, the inner stage, the upper stage, and even the cupola, plus
the upper windows and innumerable trap doors in all the stages
and the Heavens, permitted a constant flow of action without
pause for scene change, an effect which has again become possible
only in late years with the invention of the motion picture.

Scenery, in our sense, there was none. "Barkloughly Castle call
they this at hand?" demands Richard II and the audience knows
where the "scene" is laid. But Sidney's complaint that the actor
must be forever making explicit his present location is not just.
A good many of the descriptive passages in Elizabethan drama
may be attributed to the necessity for orienting the audience
without the use of realistic scenery, but it should be noticed that,
more often than not, there is no desire and hence no attempt on
the part of the dramatist (or the character for him) to locate the

action in any precise sense. Shakespeare, opening *Macbeth,* is most careful to give no indication of time or place; the Three Witches circle their cauldron out of time and out of space. On the other hand, if a knowledge of place is vital to comprehension of the scene, the information is given.

Some scenery was available, mostly suggestive properties, like the "mossy bank" which appears on an early inventory, or the beds in which sick characters are continually "thrust on." The stage itself was well planned to suggest locations without presenting them: the inner stage might be a study, a bedroom, even a tavern. (It seems likely that if the action of a scene did commence on the inner stage, for the sake of better visibility the actors would move forward onto the main stage as soon as the fact of place had been established.) The upper stage continues to function as the city wall, a hilltop, Cleopatra's monument, Juliet's bedroom, or as actual house windows. All in all the Elizabethan theater was an ideal structure for the swiftly moving, widely ranging drama which it presented.

In addition to exciting scripts, the theater specialized in gratifying spectacle. As in certain modern theaters, much more money was regularly expended upon costumes than upon the plays themselves. This was partly due to the spirit of the age—the Elizabethan delight in gaudy display was not limited to stage performances. Non-professional costume was fantastic both in cut and in value, and the professionals were driven to extremes to outshine their audiences. The theater was prepared to offer more than mere dress, of course. The presence of trap doors suggests that much was done with sudden appearances and disappearances. The armies (even of a half-dozen men) put on a brave display with drums and trumpets. Audiences dazzled by the pageantry of dumb shows and the ballet-like interludes of masquing, together with such special features as "the dragon in *Faustus,*" and Tamburlaine in his chariot drawn by Kings would have had little desire for realistic scenery. The actor, after all, was the thing, and the Elizabethan theater allowed him to shine forth with unobstructed brilliance.

On the great platform stage, projecting into the midst of the yard, the actor established a relationship with the audience quite impossible on the later picture-frame stage. Surrounded by spectators, in the focus of every eye he could be sure of a ready re-

A Production of Titus Andronicus *in the Globe Theatre*

sponse. Many of the conventions, so absurd when transported to a realistic stage, where the aside becomes a bellow and the soliloquy a harangue, are understandable when fitted into their proper setting: the aside *is* a quick whisper to the nearest spectator, the soliloquy a sharing of the character's inner thoughts with the audience. The relationship established between the actor and his hearers was, in fact, quite similar to that of the miracle plays in which Herod addressed the assembled citizens as his people.

Such was the Elizabethan public playhouse, a people's theater. For in an era of inflation the admission-penny deducted from a 7-shilling weekly wage was still far cheaper than the cost of any other luxury and indeed of most necessities. Although the larger portion of the audience was made up of the lower income groups, shopkeepers and craftsmen, the other classes were by no means unrepresented. The nobility came, and occasionally rented stools on the stage to the annoyance of the spectators but to the profit of the manager. Respectable ladies were plentiful, as well as the less respectable. Prentices and students mingled freely with the pickpockets and nut-sellers. But in the main, the audience was middle class, young (it required some stamina to stand throughout a play), and respectable. Riots and crimes might occasionally be perpetrated in the theaters, and common vice make its appearance, but with less frequency than in other public gatherings. The children of a violent age, these audiences were pleased with violent delights, yet their taste was catholic. They enjoyed the bloody and bawdy, duelling and tumbler's tricks, but they had also an incomparable ear for verse, an intellectual delight in word play, and a sympathetic reaction to spiritual suffering or exaltation. The many-headed monster in the pit was satirically fleered at by playwrights, and took all insults in good part. The conventional pun on the under*standing* of the "groundlings" is closer to the fact. After all, this heterogeneous, largely uneducated audience recognized the genius of Shakespeare and rewarded him so liberally that he was able to go into gentlemanly retirement. It is probably safe to say that no group of writers of the stature of the Elizabethan dramatists ever had such general recognition from their immediate audience. Since the dramatist is very much the servant of his audience, the variety of backgrounds, of classes, of intellectual levels in the Elizabethan audience was both a challenge to the playwrights and an un-matched opportunity for them.

The Elizabethan playwrights were as mixed a lot as their audiences. One thing they had in common was the desire to earn a living as professional writers. As always, the returns from a fortunate hit in the theater were greater and more quickly realized than from other branches of literature, and men who in other times might have turned to journalism or the writing of popular novels affiliated themselves with the various established troupes as hack writers. They did what they were told, composing new passages to be inserted in old plays, as Ben Jonson did for a revival of *The Spanish Tragedy,* or completely reworking an outworn script as Shakespeare did *The Famous Victories of Henry the Fifth.* If they were sufficiently successful, they might escape from the menial tasks of the hack and betake themselves to the more congenial task of constructing two or three "original" dramas. For the Elizabethan theater as a repertory theater con-sumed a great number of plays in the course of a season and its authors wrote at top speed to supply the demand. The average successful new play might be performed about once a week for twelve weeks before it had exhausted its audience, which might by that time have totalled some 20,000 to 30,000. The average receipts from a performance were £8-10: a reasonably successful play might bring in £96 in the course of its run; a great hit (like *I Henry VI*) as much as £256. These receipts were shared by the manager of the theater and the members of the company on a stock basis, so many parts a week to each according to his invest-ment in the concern. Very little went to the playwright, who normally received about £8 for his work and a share of the re-ceipts of the third performance. In 1599, for example, Thomas Dekker was paid £35 for playwrighting, a good sum; but in ex-change he had entirely written three plays and had contributed portions of six others.

The virtues of the Elizabethan public playhouse are immedi-ately apparent: multiple playing areas, a method of production not cribbed, cabined and confined by realistic scenery, an acting company of skilled craftsmen, and a full and understanding auditory. Its drawbacks are more apparent to us than to its habitués, and the principal drawback is certainly that it was ex-posed to the vagaries of London weather. John Webster found that one of his best plays had not succeeded because it "was acted in so dull a time of winter, presented in so open and black a theatre." The actors, it is true, were somewhat protected from snow and rain by the projecting Heavens, but the larger part of the audience was not, and bad weather must have cut into the receipts. The unfriendly climate, as much as anything else, must have been the motive behind the establishment of the indoor "private" theaters.

The Children of the Chapel Royal and the Choirboys of St. Paul's had, as we have seen, given occasional performances of interludes at their schools within the city limits while the professional actors were relegated to the suburbs. In 1596, James Burbage purchased several rooms in the first Blackfriars building and boldly remodelled them into a theater, following as far as was feasible the structure of the public playhouse. He was prohibited from using his new theater by the city authorities, and his son Richard, the famous tragedian, leased the property to The Children of the Chapel who occupied it until 1608. After this date Burbage's company was permitted to use Blackfriars as a winter home, returning to the larger public theater in the summer. Not much is known of the structure of the private theater. It could not have been very different from the Globe as the same plays were performed at each. Since it was enclosed, however, there must have been provision for artificial lighting, and it is possible that some attempt was made at representational scenery —perhaps a revival of the older simultaneous setting.

Thus, as early as 1575 the essentials for a great dramatic era were present in London. The Theatre was built and equipped and its methods of production standardized. Established professional companies were developing such talented players as the great Edward Alleyn who had been "bred an actor"—for boy actors were apprenticed like any young craftsmen to a master to learn the business, during which period they normally played women's parts—and Tarleton, and Kemp, the celebrated buffoons.

A large percentage of Londoners had become habitual playgoers experienced in following through a complex plot and appreciative of poetic speech. All that was lacking was a group of playwrights—and they were not long in forthcoming.

4. THE UNIVERSITY WITS

The vast body of Elizabethan dramatic literature is as rich and various as the age which gave it birth, and any classification is foredoomed. However, the attempt must be made if a discussion of that literature is not to become a mere chronological record. The classical distinctions between comedy and tragedy will hardly suffice, as will be seen, and something more accurately descriptive must be sought than the Drama of the Court and the Drama of the People. Fortunately a kind of classification suggests itself in the varieties of drama undertaken by the first group of major English playwrights—the University Wits.

The Wits, though they group themselves obligingly, have little in common except a University training, a thorough grounding in the literature of the past and a desire to become men of letters; but the variety of their dramatic interests introduces the major types which the panoramic drama was to develop. The revenge play may be said to begin with Kyd's *Spanish Tragedy,* the *de casibus* drama with Marlowe's *Tamburlaine.* The shaping of chronicle history into genuine drama can be seen in Marlowe's *Edward II,* and romantic comedy is established by Peele's *The Old Wives' Tale* and Greene's *Friar Bacon and Friar Bungay.* While such a division, as has been said, is only partially satisfactory, most of the plays of the period may be classified under one of the headings, or under a combination. What is principally lacking is realistic comedy and domestic tragedy, types ignored by the University Wits but developed gradually by the demands of the audience and the opportunism of lesser dramatists.

It is uncertain whether or not *Tamburlaine* preceded *The Spanish Tragedy* on the public stage but, since it is the simpler play and more closely related to the medieval heritage of the era, it may properly be granted priority of consideration. To the modern reader, it may well not look like a play at all. It seems rather a kind of epic in dialogue recounting the adventures of a ruthless superman who assaults the ear in high astounding terms and drowns the stage in blood. But no maiden work (though it is not established, of course, that Marlowe had not experimented earlier) was ever more typical of its author and its audience. It is intended for those spectators who delighted in the preposterous exploits of Cambises, with the same background of the mysterious East, the same bombast, the same violent action. Yet if this is Cambises-type, it is not Cambises-vein. Marlowe makes this clear at once as the anonymous prologue announces:

> From jigging veins of rhyming mother wits
> And such conceits as clownage keeps in pay,
> We'll lead you to the stately tent of war
> Where you shall hear the Scythian Tamburlaine. . . .

Thomas Preston and his fourteeners and the Vice with his rough-and-tumble slapstick are banished from the tragic scene. What is most pertinent to the Elizabethan age, vaulting ambition, is carefully preserved.

Tamburlaine is a truly panoramic play. In the first part the hero appears as a simple shepherd driven by his nature to embark upon a career of conquest, capturing Zenocrate, joining with Cosroe to defeat Mycetes, then outwitting and defeating his treacherous ally. Following this excellent start, he moves to greater victories over the Turkish Emperor, the Governor of Damascus, and the Sultan of Egypt. In the second part of the play, the hero's triumphant progress continues, only momentarily checked by the death of his queen and the cowardice of one of his sons; but in the end, with nothing left to conquer save the gods themselves, at the hands of Death "The Scourge of God" meets his downfall.

It is immediately apparent that the medieval allegory of the wheel of Fortune has been fully realized in the structure of the ten acts of the two parts of *Tamburlaine*. The hero's humble beginnings, his rise to great heights, and his eventual fall are an exact equivalent of the favorite *de casibus* theme, "the Falls of Princes," so pervasive in the thought of the Middle Ages and almost instinctive in the Renaissance. But Marlowe, in giving it a dramatic form, has also related it closely to the character of his hero—this is not mere didacticism intended to show the futility of worldly ambition, this is the portrait of a man governed by a passion so burning that all considerations, earthly and spiritual, are consumed in its intensity. In the hands of a lesser dramatist, Tamburlaine might have become a ruthless puppet, a figure of a tyrannous dictator, and even here there are moments when the hero seems a creature of rant. But Marlowe's sense of the theater, his ability to employ the physical resources of the stage, as well

as his insight into one of the motivating impulses of his age com-
bine with his poetic gift to make Tamburlaine stand out from
the line of dramatic monsters descended from Herod, as a recognizable man for all his pride and pomp and poetry.

Marlowe humanizes the superman in several ways, by contrasting him with foolish Mycetes and treacherous Cosroe, by treating
his love for Zenocrate with the same intensity as his lust for rule,
by the unforgettable moment of grim humor when Tamburlaine
enters drawn in his chariot by the defeated kings:

> Holla, ye pampered jades of Asia!
> What! can you draw but twenty miles a day
> And have so proud a chariot at your wheels
> And such a coachman as great Tamburlaine?

For Tamburlaine, like his creator, was a poet and something of
an actor. It is in the latter character that he dreams of "the sweet
fruition of an earthly crown"; it is in the former that he gives
voice to the Renaissance worship of unattainable beauty. At the
very moment of climactic victory in the first part of the play, the
Scourge of God can yet pause to soliloquize over his beloved:

> What is beauty, saith my sufferings, then?
> If all the pens that ever poets held
> Had fed the feeling of their master's thoughts,
> And every sweetness that inspired their hearts,
> Their minds, and muses on inspired themes;
> If all the heavenly quintessence they [di]still
> From their immortal flowers of poesy,
> Wherein, as in a mirror, we perceive
> The highest reaches of a human wit;
> If these had made one poem's period,
> And all combined in beauty's worthiness,
> Yet should there hover in their restless heads
> One thought, one grace, one wonder, at the least,
> Which unto words no virtue can digest.

Such passages suggest that not the least of Marlowe's contributions to the drama was a practical lesson in the writing of blank
verse which, while escaping as had the earlier *Gorboduc* from the
jigging vein of *Cambises,* also escaped from the formality, the
stiffness of *Gorboduc* itself. The flexibility, the verbal music of
Marlowe's "mighty line" have been often commented upon. Its
dramatic value lies beyond verbal melody, however, in that the
repetitions which furnish a major part of that melody serve a

second purpose in giving the impression of a mind at work, of humanizing the speaker. It is almost impossible to quote any passage of Marlowe in which the antithetical balance between half-lines, the modulated alliteration, the use of doublets fails to give the effect of grandeur, a reaching outward in the verse to parallel the aspirations of the hero. The dramatic effect of repetition is nowhere better illustrated however, than in the brief speech which follows a long passage of violent rant as Tamburlaine realizes Zenocrate is dead. Theridamas, his friend, tries to quiet him:

> Ah, good my lord, be patient; she is dead,
> And all this raging can not make her live.
> If words might serve, our voice hath rent the air;
> If tears, our eyes have watered all the earth;
> If grief, our murdered hearts have strained forth blood;
> Nothing prevails, for she is dead, my lord.
> TAMBURLAINE. "For she is dead!" Thy words do pierce my soul!
> Ah, sweet Theridamas! say so no more;
> Though she be dead, yet let me think she lives,
> And feed my mind that dies for want of her.

Dr. Faustus (c. 1589), Marlowe's next play for the public stages, retains the special virtues of Tamburlaine while making an advance in dramatic complexity. Where the earlier play had been simply cumulative in its plotting, one scene following upon another in a series of events illustrating the life of a single hero, Faustus approaches the typical Elizabethan form of the double-plot play. Once again the central figure is a man of boundless ambition, this time the more daring ambition for complete intellectual power. To obtain this power the scholarly hero is willing to bind himself to the Devil whose representative, the cynical and philosophical Mephistopheles, is far from the half-comic grotesque familiar to the audiences of the professional troupes. The significance of Faustus' bargain is not lost upon the common audience, however, since—in the scene following the drawing up of the contract between the scholar and Lucifer's emissary—the clown, a country bumpkin, enters into a contract of apprenticeship with Wagner, Faustus' servant. Similar parallels in action are presented throughout the play, a passage of realistic farce echoing the serious business of the main plot.

The discussion of Faustus is complicated by the patchwork

state of the text. An extremely popular play, it was frequently revived "with new additions" by other and less artistic hands, and the various surviving versions are a considerable distance from Marlowe's original. It is probable, however, that no very great alteration has been made in Marlowe's intention, to depict "the form of Faustus' fortunes good or bad," to dramatize the intellectual aspirations of the Renaissance, to present the scholar's life as a *de casibus* tragedy—aspiration, partial achievement, inevitable failure.

Once again the form is panoramic in the fullest sense. The play opens with the first ventures of the hero into the fields of learning, shows his progressive dissatisfaction with philosophy, medicine, the law, and divinity and his turning, as a last resort, to metaphysics. The action of the brief tragedy encompasses the twenty-four years of Faustus' pact with Lucifer, intermingled with passages of clowning. The medieval freedom from a sense of time is here turned to dramatic effect as the early years of Faustus' life are compressed into a speech of some sixty lines and the last hour of his life into fifteen minutes of action. The effect is never naïve or crude; it rather—and particularly in the magnificent final scene—gives a sense of doom, of inevitability, which raises the fate of the hero to tragic heights.

In a sense, *Dr. Faustus* is a Renaissance version of a morality play, with a Good and Bad Angel struggling for the hero's soul and promising him forgiveness or damnation. If the morality was an allegory of a kind of civil war within the individual, Marlowe has turned it to good use in the characterization of his scholar. The psychological struggle becomes objective without ever becoming didactic allegory. When Faustus has completed his cross-questioning of Mephistopheles he has some misgivings about the bargain he has made:

> FAUSTUS. Ay, go, accursed spirit, to ugly hell.
>   'Tis thou hast damned distressed Faustus' soul.
>   Is't not *too late?*
> EVIL ANGEL. *Too late.*
> GOOD ANGEL. Never *too late,* if Faustus can *repent.*
> EVIL ANGEL. If thou *repent,* devils shall tear thee in pieces.
> GOOD ANGEL. *Repent,* and thou shall never raze thy skin.
> FAUSTUS. Ah, Christ my Saviour,
>   Seek to save distressed Faustus' soul.

The repeated words in that passage dramatize the effect of a man thinking; indeed they are a kind of stream-of-consciousness device. Marlowe is attempting to portray the inner drama, not merely the external conflict.

Marlowe's achievements as a dramatic poet are nowhere more clearly indicated than in Faustus' famous and aria-like speech to the apparition of Helen of Troy:

> Was this the face that launched a thousand ships
> And burnt the topless towers of Illium?
> Sweet Helen, make me immortal with a kiss
> Her lips suck forth my soul; see where it flies!—
> Come, Helen, come, give me my soul again.

Any extended discussion of Marlowe's work inevitably must include analysis of verse since the mighty line is his most famous contribution. Yet it is not solely the "mighty line" which distinguishes Marlowe's drama but a general reshaping, or modification of the formal and regularly stressed iambic pentameter, as used in *Gorboduc,* into the flexible dramatic blank verse. The tragic impact of *Dr. Faustus* depends far more upon the hero's expression of his aspiration and defeat than upon the interaction of the forces which bring about his momentary success and eventual fall. Marlowe's own weakness in the *Tamburlaine-Faustus* plays is a weakness in plotting characteristic of his predecessors in the native tradition. The makers of comedy had learned the art of plotting by turning to their Roman predecessors. For the makers of tragedy, however, the resort to classical models was less satisfactory. Charles Lamb once noted that "The Tragic Auditory wants blood," but the ancients provided in the main only narrations of bloody events. Nonetheless, the first skilfully plotted English tragedy is deeply indebted to the Senecan heritage, and its success provided an incentive for later playwrights to study the technique of construction.

Thomas Kyd's *The Spanish Tragedy* was indeed a sensational success. It seems to have been produced about 1586, was reprinted some ten times between 1592 and 1633, and was constantly revived on the stage with additions and revisions by company playwrights. Its speeches were quoted as often and as casually as we today quote Shakespeare, and Hieronimo's lament ("O eyes, no eyes but fountains filled with tears") was burlesqued as we might parody "To be or not to be." It is, however, safe to say that the success of *The Spanish Tragedy* with the popular audience did not stem from its poetry or its convenient tags but from the complexity and excitement of its action. Kyd has brought order out of the chaos of the native tradition while retaining the aspects of that tradition most appealing to the audience.

Native tragedy had heretofore concerned itself with the success and failure of some great figure, characteristically with the Falls of Princes; classical tragedy, as typified in Seneca's *Thyestes*, with the swift accomplishment of a long-plotted scheme of vengeance. The combination of the two traditions effected by Kyd established the revenge play or tragedy of blood as the most popular and most enduring form of Elizabethan tragedy. It is, therefore, entitled to extended consideration in spite of its artistic shortcomings.

The Spanish Tragedy

Kyd chooses to tell the story of a father's revenge for the murder of his son. In the hands of Seneca, the action of the play would have begun at the end of the fourth act, where Hieronimo decides on a method of working justice upon the villains; the precedent action would be digested into long speeches of expository narrative. In Kyd's play the exposition is dramatized, over three acts being given to the double motivation of Lorenzo's murder of Horatio, the deed itself, Hieronimo's discovery of the criminals, and his arrival at a determination to seek revenge. In Seneca, too, the action of the dramatized portion of the story would be further reduced by suppressing Hieronimo's performance of *Soliman and Perseda* in favor of a report of the event. While Kyd showed no reluctance to insert lengthy passages of description, he never misjudged his audience: blood they wanted, and blood they got, produced liberally and on the stage itself.

It is true that the death of Don Andrea is only narrated, and at Senecan length, in the opening scene. Later, however, the audience is to *see* the murder of Horatio, the murder of Serberine, the hanging of Pedringano, the suicide of Isabella, the murder of Balthazar, the murder of Lorenzo, the suicide of Bel-Imperia, the murder of the Duke of Castile and the suicide of Hieronimo. The action also displays the several scenes in which Isabella and Hieronimo run mad, as well as the dreadful moment when Hieronimo bites out his tongue rather than reveal what the Duke required. We have supped full of horrors; yet Kyd provides more. He deliberately adds at the beginning of the play a series of scenes involving the grief of the Viceroy of Portugal over the false report of the death of his son Balthazar. There is bustling action enough here to gratify the most insatiable among the groundlings; but it is all *significant* action—relating to the central problem of the play and working out the basic conflict in a series of increasingly tense situations—not a restless succession of incidents.

The major action of the play, Hieronimo's revenge, is introduced by the ghost of Don Andrea returned from the infernal regions to see justice done upon his murderer and to "serve for Chorus in this tragedy"; the theme of vengeance is thus announced long before it appears in the action, and on a level removed from reality, from natural events. The supernatural figures do not intrude upon the action, for Kyd is concerned with the working out of justice in this world, but they lend a grandeur, a magnitude, to the theme wholly lacking in earlier popular tragedy. The action proper may be divided into three "movements"; in the first, Horatio is killed, in the second, Hieronimo comes to a decision, and in the third, the revenge is completed. These three movements are introduced by passages of dialogue between the Ghost and the allegorical figure of Revenge, and correspond to the five-act divisions of classical tragedy. The audience, because of the nature of the staging, would be conscious of the divisions in the action only from the interruptions of the supernatural pair. They remained in cheerful ignorance of an "act" in the classical sense, or in the sense of the play's later editors.

The parallel between the intentions of the Ghost and those of Hieronimo suggests the motive behind other apparently unrelated incidents in the play. Even the kindest of critics has had some reservations about the Villuppo situation, since the "transition to the Portuguese palace is a far and sudden flight." We must bear in mind, however, that the nature of the staging required no far and sudden flight, that the emphasis is always on the action and never on its location. Thus Kyd has provided a doubling of the emotions, a kind of foreshadowing of his main plot in the Portuguese parallel. In I,2, the Viceroy mourns over the death of his son, as Hieronimo is to do in II,4. The first scene of the third act in which the Viceroy recovers his son immediately precedes Hieronimo's most famous lament, intensifying it by contrast and suggesting the eventual working out of the Spaniard's dilemma. So too the major villain is paralleled by Villuppo, equally ruthless and ambitious, whose exposure and death are a further foreshadowing of the end of the play. The entertainment which Hieronimo presents before the king in the first act is preparation for the play-within-a-play in the last. There are other parallels and foreshadowings to demonstrate the author's skill in construction, and not the least of these is the highly dramatic foreshadowing of the eventual defeat of Lorenzo in the detection and execution of his tool, Pedringano.

This is not to suggest that *The Spanish Tragedy* is a perfectly constructed Elizabethan tragedy. There is still plenty of undigested narrative and the messengers are kept nearly as busy as their classical models. The Ghost who quotes Seneca and paraphrases Virgil has a parallel rather than a personal interest in the action and actually watches without emotion while his widow woos his best friend. The plot progresses by means of a good deal of overhearing and eavesdropping and the characters are great letter writers, but Kyd does try, however artificially, to prepare in each instance for the event. The influence of Senecan tragedy is apparent in the least successful portions of the dialogue, the set descriptions of the battle in the first act, and the stichomythia of the scene in which Balthazar becomes prisoner to Bel-Imperia's beauty is in the most artificial tradition of Renaissance wit. Kyd at his worst is perhaps to be pointed out in Balthazar's analysis of his position:

> LORENZO. How likes Prince Balthazar this stratagem?
> BALTHAZAR. Both well and ill; it makes me glad and sad:
>   Glad that I know the hinderer of my love,
>   Sad that I fear she hates me whom I love;
>   Glad that I know on whom to be reveng'd,

Sad that she'll fly me if I take revenge.
Yet I must take revenge, or die myself,
For love resisted grows impatient.
I think Horatio be my destin'd plague!
First, in his hand he brandishèd a sword,
And with that sword he fiercely wagèd war,
And in that war he gave me dang'rous wounds,
And by those wounds he forcèd me to yield,
And by my yielding I became his slave. . . .

This is, as Mercutio might say, to make poetry by the book of
arithmetic, and Kyd's "bombasting" of a blank verse line was not
unjustly parodied by later playwrights.

Two characters in the play require especial notice, Old
Hieronimo and Lorenzo. Hieronimo is an ironic type, a good
man whose position is such that he must take justice into his own
hands and become a murderer to avenge a murder. His hesitancy,
his determination to "by circumstances try what I can gather to
confirm" such early evidence as he has, even his madness, real or
assumed, are as inseparable from the Revenger as rant from
Herod. His soliloquies, revealing his inner misgivings, his grief
and passion, tend to increase the sympathy of the audience and
to humanize his position. The Duke's son, Lorenzo, is also destined to establish a type, the complete villain, soulless, heartless
and ruthless. No stratagem is too devious, no means too monstrous for the accomplishment of his ambition: his sister, his
friend, his servant, and his servant's servant all are tools to be
manipulated with impersonal calculation. For he can smile, and
murder whilst he smiles, and meet his end without compunction.
Craft, stratagem, policy are his watchwords and self-interest his
guiding principle: "I trust myself," he declares, "myself shall be
my friend." Lorenzo, the first wholly wicked character, was the
founder of a family of distinguished villains.

It is necessary to reiterate that, however successful in its own
right, *The Spanish Tragedy* is of greatest importance as prototype
of the tragedy of revenge. Typical is the panoramic action—telling the *whole* of the story rather than just its climax—falling into
three movements paralleling the three parts of *de casibus* tragedy;
typical is the focus on a single hero and his struggle to obtain
"grounds more relative" before confronting the typical villain;
typical are such lesser matters as the appearance of a ghost and
the intermittent madness of the hero. Most typical of all, perhaps,

is the final catastrophe, better described as a holocaust, after which scarcely enough members of the cast remain alive to bear off the dead; this is the over-all irony which is at the heart of the revenge play—the villains are exposed and killed by their own schemes in the play-within-a-play which reproduces their villainy, but the revenger himself is engulfed in the general slaughter. The possibilities for great spiritual tragedy are implicit within the form, but the possibilities for debasement and melodrama are obvious. The popular theater did not hesitate to make the most of them.

Almost immediately, Christopher Marlowe demonstrated what possibilities lay in the Lorenzo-type. In his melodrama *The Jew of Malta* (c. 1588) he continues in his own tradition of the one-man play, save that the major character is neither a heroic tyrant nor an aspiring scholar, but a Machiavellian villain. The Elizabethan popular misconception of Machiavelli pictured him as a crafty politician (a noun of evil implication to an Elizabethan) who placed statecraft above morality, and whose name was associated with atheists and mockers of all religion and virtue. Barabas, the Jew of Malta, is such a schemer:

> A reaching thought will search his deepest wits,
> And cast with cunning for the time to come. . . .
>
> Hast thou no trade? Then listen to my words,
> And I will teach thee that shall stick by thee:
> First be thou void of these affections,
> Compassion, love, vain hope, and heartless fear,
> Be moved at nothing, see thou pity none,
> But to thyself smile when the Christians moan.

In the brief autobiography which he recounts to his apprentice-villain, Ithamore, he describes his activity as a poisoner, an "engineer," usurer, indeed any activity which offers the possibility of slaughtering or torturing Christians or driving them to despair.

The play is obviously anti-Semitic, the reflection of the popular prejudice. But Barabas very quickly ceases to be a Jew (as Shylock does not) and becomes simply a villain. Further, in at least the earlier scenes wealth is conceived in terms not unlike the aspirations of Tamburlaine and Faustus.

> What more may Heaven do for earthly man
> Than thus to pour out plenty in their laps,
> Ripping the bowels of the earth for them,
> Making the seas their servants, and the winds
> To drive their substance with successful blasts?

There is even some attempt to humanize the character at the beginning by providing him with a daughter, Abigail,

> whom I hold as dear
> As Agamemnon did his Iphigen,

a declaration at once pathetic and prophetic. When she has shut herself into a nunnery to help him recover the money hidden there he cries,

> O my girl,
> My gold, my fortune, my felicity!
> Strength to my soul, death to mine enemy!
> Welcome the first beginner of my bliss!
> O Abigail, Abigail, that I had thee here too!
> Then my desires were fully satisfied:
> But I will practice thy enlargement thence.
> O girl! O gold! O beauty! O my bliss!

There are moments in the first two acts of the play when it is possible either to sympathize with Barabas or to laugh at him. Marlowe, if he intended him as a sop for an anti-Semitic audience, more than matched him with the Christian members of the cast who are, laymen and clerics, scarcely models of Christian virtue.

The Jew of Malta quite obviously was conceived as a revenge play, with Barabas scheming to recover the property taken from him by the Maltese officials. From Barabas' words, quoted above, it is apparent that the loss of his gold is, for him, the equivalent of the loss of Hieronimo's son. And the plotting of his revenge to involve the deaths of Matthias and Don Lodowick is the equivalent of Hieronimo's action. However, his victory is not the play's catastrophe but occurs at the beginning of the third act and he must spend the remaining acts avoiding the consequences of his revenge. At this point he becomes a double-dipped Lorenzo, not only plotting to overthrow his enemies but to rid himself of his accomplices (Abigail and Ithamore) in the process. As Pedringano betrayed Lorenzo, so Ithamore betrays Barabas, but he is saved for still further villainy by the timely arrival of the Saracen army.

The final scene presents a properly horrendous ending for the monster's career. He appears on the upper stage busily preparing a trap door through which his new-found Turkish allies are to be plunged into a boiling caldron. The passionate aspiration of a Marlovian hero, of which there were some hints in the earlier part of the play, is almost burlesqued as Barabas asks the audience

> Why, is not this
> A kingly trade to purchase towns
> By treachery and sell 'em by deceit?
> Now tell me, worldlings, underneath the sun
> If greater falsehood ever has been done?

The boast is barely out of his mouth when one of his intended victims springs the trap and Barabas tumbles into the kettle—a sensational effect for which the Elizabethan theater was well adapted. True to his villain-type he dies unrepentant and cursing the fate which prevented him from completing his course of evil. It is plain that Marlowe had exhausted the possibilities of the aspiring hero, but the Machiavell's career was just begun.

The native English form of chronicle history was, as we have seen, a dramatization of a series of events in the reign of whatever king happened to be the chosen hero. Its structure was chronological or epic with little attempt at climax or compression; the result was formless and undramatic, of no interest save to the audience of the moment, closer to journalism than art. The successful shaping of chronicle history into chronicle *play* is further evidence of the original genius of Christopher Marlowe.

Edward II (1591-92) is, at first reading, a disappointing finish to Marlowe's brief career. The dramatic sweep and tragic power of aspiring Tamburlaine and Faustus, and even Barabas, are replaced by the weak and rather negative portrait of a defeated king. The high astounding terms of the mighty line have been replaced by a more utilitarian verse. A closer reading, or better still a theatrical production, reveals a considerable advance in dramatic technique over its predecessors, an advance that was of great service to Marlowe's successors in general and to Shakespeare in particular. In view of the dramatic advance, the mod-

ern reader must grant, however reluctantly, that the mighty
line may be well lost.

Which is not to say that Marlowe has ceased to be a poet in
becoming a better dramatist. The melody, the unforgettable
phrase, is still ready, but it has been adjusted to the character of
the hero, imprisoned by his wife and her lover:

> For such outrageous passions cloy my soul,
> As with the wings of rancour and disdain
> Full often am I soaring up to heaven,
> To plain me to the gods against them both.
> But when I call to mind I am a king,
> Methinks I should revenge me of my wrongs,
> That Mortimer and Isabel have done.
> But what are kings when regiment is gone
> But perfect shadows in a sunshine day.

The brave words, the rant, are reserved for Mortimer, the
Machiavell, who goes to execution to the older tune:

> Base fortune, now I see that in thy wheel
> There is a point to which when men aspire
> They tumble headlong down; that point I touched,
> And, seeing there was no place to mount up higher,
> Why should I grieve at my declining fall?—
> Farewell, fair queen; weep not for Mortimer,
> That scorns the world, and, as a traveller,
> Goes to discover countries yet unknown.

Like the earlier writers of histories, Marlowe derived his
material from Holinshed's *Chronicles;* unlike them he treated his
source with great freedom. Where they were interested in providing gratification for the illiterate jingoist, Marlowe is concerned
with the nature of man, even though that man be a king. The
portrait of Edward provided by his source is a strange one for
him to choose for his gallery. One of the poorest of England's
kings, he was a weak and willful executive, blind to the faults of
his favorites, and unjust and capricious in his treatment of those
outside his own circle; yet in an era which respected only strength
in a ruler, the dramatic Edward becomes a tragic figure. The
events covered by the play begin with the return of Piers Gaveston in 1307 and end with the execution of Mortimer in 1330; at
one point (after III,1) there is a gap in the historical action of
nearly ten years though the dramatic action is continuous. In
other words, Marlowe is using the materials of history for the

purposes of drama, not accepting them as dramatic in themselves.

He does not spare Edward in the early part of the play. The king is portrayed as wholly in the power of the corrupt Gaveston, insulting the good barons who are concerned only with the welfare of the kingdom, tyrannizing upon the Church, neglecting his devoted queen. Nor can the audience rejoice at Edward's momentary triumph over his rebellious subjects in the third act. Almost at once, however, and with great skill, Marlowe begins to woo sympathy for the despicable king. Young Mortimer, escaping from his captors, makes his way to France to head a second rebellion and takes the queen as his mistress. Mortimer is now revealed as a Machiavell, and the queen as a weak and vicious woman. The king is captured and treated with the grossest indignities—and it should be remembered that to the English of this period a god was not more glorious than a king. The poet makes much of this contemporary attitude, larding Edward's speeches with images of the sun, the lion, the royal vine; his very mood is controlled in the abdication scene by the fact that he is wearing the crown. The loyalty of Kent, a plainly good man, who switches from the rebels to the king, and the firmness of the king's young son are used dramatically to arouse the sympathy of the audience for Edward.

Most effectively, Marlowe invented the character of Lightborn, a hired assassin, to doubly emphasize the cruel and shameful nature of the king's murder. The death scene is extended and detailed, completely in the tradition of Machiavellian villainy and only the swift capture and punishment of Mortimer makes it bearable. At the end of the play the words of Edward III can be spoken without irony:

> Sweet father, here unto thy murder'd ghost
> I offer up this wicked traitor's head;
> And let these tears, distilling from mine eyes,
> Be witness of my grief and innocency.

With *Edward II* the chronicle is established as a dramatic unit. Marlowe demonstrated how the facts of history may be compressed, altered, or revised to suit the purpose of the playwright. He added to history the technical advances of the revenge play in plotting and of the *de casibus* drama in characterization and in elevation of the dialogue to tragic heights. *Edward II* thus es-

tablished the pattern not only for future chronicle plays, but for
a large number of the greatest English tragedies which, while appearing to be True Histories, are really descriptions, great in
depth and breadth, of Man.

At about the same time that Marlowe and Kyd were stabilizing
the form and dignifying the treatment of tragedy, two others of
the University Wits were creating, out of a combination of native materials and classical and native techniques, a form of
comedy usually called romantic. As in the case of tragedy, it is
impossible to determine with any assurance which of the romantic comedies is entitled to priority. Because of its profusion
of folk elements, however, George Peele's *The Old Wives' Tale*
(c. 1590) may be considered first. It is, admittedly, a desperately
difficult play to read, a potpourri of fairy tales and romantic adventures, rustic entertainments, literary satire, and realism. Yet,
once the reason for its structure is understood, the play becomes
a fitting precursor of the most popular and enchanting of the
English comedies. The key, of course, is in the title and in the
realistic induction. This is to be a story told by an old wife, and
a very particular old wife as her prefatory remarks indicate:

Once upon a time [she begins] there was a king, or a lord, or a duke,
that had a fair daughter, the fairest that ever was; as white as snow and
as red as blood: and once upon a time his daughter was stolen away:
and he sent all his men to seek out his daughter; and he sent so long
that he sent all his men out of his land. . . . O Lord, I quite forgot!
There was a conjurer, and this conjurer could do anything, and he
turned himself into a great dragon, and carried the king's daughter
away in his mouth to a castle that he made of stone; and there he kept
her for I know not how long, till at last all the king's men went out so
long that her two brothers went to seek her. O, I forget! She (he, I
would say) turned a proper young man to a bear at night and a man
in the day, and keeps by a cross that parts three several ways; and he
made his lady run mad—Ods me bones, who comes here?

And enter the Two Brothers to tell Gammer's tale for her, with
action, and in just such rambling fashion as she has begun. The
play is intended to be a jumble of clichés and incidents begun
(and some finished) without regard for order, as in the narration
of an inexperienced story teller. To keep this point clear to the
audience, to maintain perspective, the prologue characters remain on the stage throughout, and Madge occasionally interrupts
with a comment to remind us that this is her story.

It is the familiar story of the romantic quest. The king's daughter, Delia, has been enchanted by Sacrapant. In search of her come four men, Huanebango a foolish pedant, Eumenides, her lover, and her two brothers. The brothers fall into the magician's power, Huanebango is magically blinded and married to a shrew, and Eumenides discovers the magic formula by which Sacrapant may be overcome. Although the formula, traditionally ambiguous, seems impossible of realization, Eumenides by his own natural goodness enlists certain magic forces—including a ghost—and is able to conquer the magician with ease. The ending is most appropriate to the spirit of romance; Jack hath his Jill, the oppressed are liberated, and evil is destroyed.

The play, for all its apparent shapelessness, proceeds in three movements, marked by the interruptions of the prologue characters and a nondramatic chorus of harvesters. The first movement, introduced by the most charming of songs of impatient love, "When as the rye reach to the chin," establishes the situation, the quest and the magic formula; the second, announced by the song of the farmers "sowing sweet fruits of love," ends as Eumenides has unknowingly acquired the instruments whereby his sweetheart will be freed; and the third, after the farmers "with women in their hands" sing of reaping their "harvest-fruit" (of love), brings the quest and the love-affair to a happy conclusion. *The Old Wives' Tale* is an inconsequential play but its lyric optimism, and its spirit of freshness and good humor are the very essence of romantic comedy. For later playwrights, it was a lesson in giving a spiritual and tonal unity to a patchwork of materials.

Robert Greene's *Friar Bacon and Friar Bungay* on the record of its contemporary popularity established romantic comedy as a type to be attempted by all aspiring playwrights. First produced about 1590, it remained in the regular repertory for half a dozen years, was revived in 1603, and was still being shown as late as 1630. It is, like *The Old Wives' Tale*, a mixture of elements which had proved their success with audiences. *Dr. Faustus* is the obvious inspiration for the choice of Friar Bacon; from pastoral romance comes the love story of Lacy and Margaret; from chronicle history, Prince Edward and Elinor, and from the Moral play, Miles, the vice. These elements, however, are treated in the most popular manner: the history is utterly falsified and the supernatural is "harmless" white magic in contrast with the tragic black art of Faustus.

But the play has been planned with great care, and the various elements are united in more than tone and spirit. We have already seen parallelism in situation and incident as far back in the native tradition as the *Second Shepherd's Play,* and in the humanistic tradition in *Fulgens and Lucres.* In the later popular drama the same parallelism was observed in *Faustus* and *The Spanish Tragedy.* But in *Friar Bacon and Friar Bungay* two fully developed plots with apparently no unity beyond the mechanical use of characters common to each merge into a single whole with a *unity of theme.* The structure is, therefore, of greatest importance to the development of panoramic drama and repays close analysis.

The titular plot concerns the feats of Roger Bacon, who had been commemorated by an anonymous pamphleteer as a famous magician. At first his hocus pocus is merely theatrical; he is toying with magic in transporting the Hostess of the Inn as a practical joke on Burden. The initial manifestation of his magic glass, wherein Edward beholds Lincoln's all too successful wooing of Margaret, is done merely to oblige the Prince and has no serious outcome; indeed he invites the Prince to "Sit still, my Lord, and mark the *comedy.*" Still comic and theatrical is his defeat of the German Vandermast, an event which Greene does not fail to make the most of as gratifying to a patriotic English audience. But the final demonstration of the powers of the magic glass, though undertaken with good intentions, is directly responsible for the deaths of two young scholars; Bacon himself has a premonition as he declares to Bungay, "I smell there will be a tragedy." And when this magic power, even though used with the best will in the world, proves itself to be fundamentally evil, the friar foreswears it.

The second plot centers in Margaret, the Fair Maid of merry Fressingfield, whose beauty attracts the roving eye of Edward, Prince of Wales. Toying with her love, he sends Lacy, Earl of Lincoln, to woo her in disguise, but, in what has become the established pattern, true love develops between the messenger and the maiden. She chooses to become Lacy's wife rather than Edward's mistress, and Edward is rewarded for his generosity in giving her up by winning the Princess Elinor as his own wife.

The seriousness of Margaret's love is now demonstrated as two local squires fight over her, and Lacy subjects her to the accepted medieval test, pretending to forsake her for another. Her love for him proves to be so strong that, rather than choose another man, she will become a nun; and then, when he returns to her, she rejects Heaven for him:

> The flesh is frail; my Lord doth know it well,
> That when he comes with his enchanting face,
> Whatsoe'er betide, I cannot say him nay.
> Off goes the habit of a maiden's heart,
> And, seeing fortune will, fair Framlingham
> And all the show of holy nuns, farewell!
> Lacy for me, if he will be my lord.
> LACY. Peggy, thy lord, thy love, thy husband.

The two plots are mechanically joined according to the old custom by allowing characters to move from one to the other. Edward consults Bacon to see how Lacy is faring on his errand; Bacon entertains the King of Castile and his daughter, Elinor. The joining, however, is far more than mechanical. It is facilitated by the nature of the Elizabethan theater: while Bacon and Edward are watching the magic glass in the inner stage, the scene which they observe is enacted on the outer stage. While the two squires kill one another on the outer stage for the love of Margaret, their sons observe the event in the inner stage and instantly fall to fighting. The relationship of the Margaret plot and the Bacon plot is made apparent to the spectator in action and by the staging. Margaret's power to awaken love is fatal to Lambert and Serlsby as Bacon's power to control supernatural forces is fatal to their sons. As William Empson has observed, the power of love is here paralleled in the action with the power of magic, and the theme of the play might be expressed in a simile: the power of love is like the power of magic. Further, this simile is fundamental to the structure of the play. The incidents are so arranged that the play might almost be described as a dramatized simile or, since the comparison is never expressly uttered, as a *dramatized metaphor*. For a century or more, the native drama had been experimenting with the double plot and parallel situations. In *Friar Bacon* the experiment is successfully concluded and the perfected form is ready for the use of future playwrights.

It is perhaps the most purely English aspect of the panoramic drama.

Other aspects of Greene's comedy are worth comment. Miles, Bacon's scholar-servant is, like Faustus' Wagner, clearly descended from the Vice of the Moral play, and, like his progenitors, is borne off on the Devil's back in the last scene. A parallel character in the Edward-Margaret-Lacy plot is Ralph Simnell, the King's jester. He, like the Vice, takes an active part in the story, suggesting means for the conquest of the lady. His advice, however, is purely comic and his suggestions are meant to display his wit, not his malice. Ralph, as contrasted with Miles, shows the derivation and development of the court jester, a stock character of such romantic comedy as *Twelfth Night* and *As You Like It*, and even of tragedy, as the Fool in *King Lear*.

Margaret herself is generally described as the first romantic heroine in English drama. This is true insofar as her position and behavior are more nearly in the later tradition than were those of Lucres or Zenocrate or the heroines of Lyly. In Edward's description she becomes the type of all men's dreams:

> Whenas she swept like Venus through the house,
> And in her shape fast folded up my thoughts.
> Into the milkhouse went I with the maid,
> And there amidst the cream bowls she did shine
> As Pallas 'mongst her princely huswifery.
> She turn'd her smock over her lily arms,
> And dived them into milk to run her cheese;
> But, whiter than the milk, her crystal skin,
> Check'd with lines of azure, made her blush
> That art or nature durst bring for compare.
> Ermsby, if thou hadst seen, as I did note it well,
> How Beauty plays huswife, how this girl,
> Like Lucrece, laid her fingers to the work,
> Thou wouldst with Tarquin hazard Rome and all
> To win the lovely maid of Fressingfield.

The Goddess of Beauty, yet a good housewife. And if her conversation is somewhat overfraught with classical imagery, she is, after all, out of the Renaissance pastoral tradition, and she can, when the occasion warrants, speak plainly enough:

> Why, thinks King Henry's son that Margaret's love
> Hangs in the uncertain balance of proud time?
> That death shall make a discord of our thoughts?

> No, stab the Earl, and 'fore the morning sun
> Shall vaunt him thrice over the lofty east,
> Margaret will meet her Lacy in the Heavens.

There is no doubt that Margaret is a man's woman, created by a male author for a predominantly male audience, as Edward is a man's prince. Furious though he is at Lacy's interference in his passion, a passion that has led him to address Margaret as no woman save Zenocrate had been saluted and almost in Tamburlaine's words:

> In frigates bottom'd with rich Sethin planks,
> Topp'd with the lofty firs of Lebanon,
> Stemm'd and incas'd with burnished ivory,
> And overlaid with plates of Persian wealth,
> Like Thetis thou shalt wanton on the waves,
> And draw the dolphins to thy lovely eyes,
> To dance lavoltas in the purple streams;
> Sirens, with harps and silver psalteries,
> Shall wait with music at thy frigate's stem,
> And entertain fair Margaret with their lays.—

furious though he is, he yet places male friendship above romantic love, forgives the Earl of Lincoln, and graciously consents to a double wedding ceremony at the end. This man's-eye view of woman, love, and friendship is characteristic of romantic comedy so long as it remains the concern of the popular audience. The more sophisticated spectators of the court and private theaters were to effect a shift of focus in the early years of the next century.

One final structural note will emphasize the importance of *Friar Bacon* in crystallizing the panoramic form. It has been suggested before that the native drama tends to be constructed in three movements rather than in five acts. This is not true in all cases, of course, especially when the dramatist has deliberately copied the classical pattern (*Gorboduc, Ralph Roister Doister*). But it was plain in the craft cycle as a whole, and within the individual miracle play, it was true of popular tragedy, of the Marlovian heroic play, of *The Old Wives' Tale. Friar Bacon,* where the double plot is first perfected, can also be divided into three distinct movements. The first begins the action: Edward loves Margaret, Lacy woos and wins her, and Edward vows revenge; Friar Bacon's first demonstration of magical powers suggests an ambiguous value. The second develops the action: Edward, torn between love of a friend and love of a woman, gives up the woman; Lacy determines to test his betrothed, and Lambert and Serlsby quarrel over her; the second demonstration of Bacon's magic enables him to triumph over the German, but the project of the Brazen Head comes to nothing. In the third the action is concluded: Lambert and Serlsby die, their sons die, Bacon foreswears magic, and his servant is carried off by a devil; Edward and Elinor are betrothed, Lacy sends for Margaret and she turns from the nunnery to be his wife.

5. SUMMARY

Before turning to a consideration of the major Elizabethan dramatists, it will be useful to recapitulate the characteristics of the form which they inherited. Since it had its roots in English soil and had grown with the nation, it was ideally suited to the English climate of opinion. To the Elizabethan—whose habit of mind was allegorical, and whose way of life was violent—the world was a place of sharp contrasts, good and bad, black and white. This accounts for, among other things, the rigidity of dramatic characterization; a man is very good or he is very bad, and normally his character does not alter in the course of the action. If it does, the change is extreme, the villain reforming completely, the good man plunging to the depths. As one critic has observed, this complete reversal is very like exchanging one mask for another, like the queen in *Edward II,* or Cambises. So too, the characters in general are either young or old: Faustus does not age in the twenty-four years spanned by his play; Edward II, on the other hand, is emphatically a youth in the first act and just as emphatically an old man, for the sake of the pathos, in the last—although he was, historically, only forty-three —and no sense of passing years is conveyed by the action. The idea of a social order of sharp contrasts is further expressed in the familiar convention whereby the upper classes and members of the nobility commonly speak in verse, while the lower orders employ prose, a convention especially resorted to in tragedy.

The survival of the allegorical tradition contributes to the rigidity of character. The frequent use of a presenter (as in *Faustus*) or an induction (as in *The Old Wives' Tale*) is retained from the devices of the Morality Play and inevitably would suggest to the audience the morality tradition that the characters which followed were personifications of abstract qualities. The Elizabethan drama is thus largely populated by types: the Machiavell (Lorenzo), the villain whose defect or peculiarity sets him apart from the world (Barabas), the cheated tool (Pedringano), the revenger (Hieronimo), the bluff soldier (Kent), the *miles gloriosus* (Roister Doister), the pathetic child (Praxaspe's son), the vice-jester (Ambidexter, Wagner, Ralph Simnell), the superhuman hero (Tamburlaine, Hieronimo). This last type governs particularly the characterization of kings who are entitled, even when they are "bad" kings, to unswerving obedience and who frequently serve the plot as *deus ex machina* (*Friar Bacon*).

The heritage of the Morality Play is also evident in the frequent dumb shows with their allegorical figures and symbolic actions. This is true even for such a plot as *Gorboduc* which has sworn allegiance to Seneca and pretends to have adapted its dumb shows from the Italian theater. The symbolic property (a throne, a bed) is used when locality must be indicated, and the symbolic costume is much in evidence. (See particularly the last scenes of *Tamburlaine*.)

The plotting of the plays can be either extremely simple or extremely complex. *De casibus* tragedy, recounting the fall of a hero, is normally cumulative in structure, one incident following directly upon another in the manner of the epic, from the beginning of his rise to the end of his fall. Behind this structure, of course, lies the medieval concept of the turning wheel of Fortune, the panoramic form in its most elementary manifestation. The double-plot play, still panoramic, is complicated by the English love of parallelisms and echoes. It is to this that we owe the common device of a play-within-a-play in the final scene of *The Spanish Tragedy,* the incident repeated on a lower level in *Faustus,* and the whole action reiterated in *Fulgens and Lucres.* The achievement of *Friar Bacon* in establishing a more than mechanical relationship between two plots has been considered at some length; it was of first importance as a guide to the major dramatists, though it was, of course, too complex for the lesser hack-writers.

The classical unities were generally ignored, since neither the theater nor the nature of panoramic drama required them. TIME was forgotten: a quarter of a century might pass in an hour's action, the action of an hour be compressed into five minutes. When time could serve a dramatic purpose, adding to suspense as in *Faustus,* the playwright made much of it. But he did not hesitate to show two actions at once, or to move backward to pick up the beginning of a second action; the "double time" which has so confused the critics of *Othello* has its origin in this convention which could be illustrated in many early plays, most clearly in *Friar Bacon*. PLACE, too, was ignored unless localization was demanded by the action. Scene after scene transpires in space, unlocated, without any member of the audience recognizing that the actors were now in "Another Part of the Forest." The action and the actors were the thing, not the place or the time of the action, and the structure of the theater was ideal for such emphasis. ACTION was consecutive if the necessity of the story demanded, but the playwright had no hesitation in allowing the action to move in any direction, or to break completely if greater dramatic effectiveness could be achieved.

A Stage Beggar

Much of the action was as conventional as the characterization. The Elizabethan audience was prepared to accept love at first sight, last minute conversions, the impenetrability of disguise, the magic powers of sleeping potions, and battle scenes performed by token armies in token maneuvers. They welcomed the folk situations of the tested wife (Margaret in *Friar Bacon* is given the Griselda treatment), the participation of the devil, the comic cuckold. Special rôles for favorite clowns, or for actors successful in particular types, were written into the scripts at the expense of congruity; the text was larded with long passages of moralizing, and brief sententious remarks to suit the taste of the audience rather than the demands of the play. Songs and dances were provided for the child actors, plenty of opportunities to display acrobatic prowess for the professional men's companies. The unrealistic soliloquy and aside were as much a part of the convention as the painstaking realism of atrocities—murders, hangings, beheadings.

The panoramic form, as left by the University Wits, was full of paradox and contrast. It was as exuberant and expansive as its age. There was room in it for every aspect of life, the whole world was its stage and any man or woman high or low, good or bad, ancient or modern, native or foreign, might sooner or later find himself an actor upon it.

$\sim 3 \sim$

Panoramic Drama: The Second Movement

If classification of individual titles by appropriate types was a difficult task in Tudor drama, in the Elizabethan-Jacobean-Caroline periods it becomes a quixotic one. For a clearer notion of the richness and variety of the Elizabethan dramatic repertoire, we must turn once again to our own popular theater—the movies. There are the familiar types: the western, the mystery, the love story, the society drama, and so forth. But there are also combinations—the mystery-western, for instance—where it is difficult to decide which element is dominant, or which has the greater appeal for the audience. Such combinations result from a deliberate attempt on the part of the producers to collect as many disparate elements as they can into a single picture to attract the greatest possible number of customers.

To the Elizabethan playgoer this was a familiar trick. His grandfather might have told him of the "conceits of clownage," the rough-and-tumble interludes distributed through the serious moralities and tragedies of the professional troupes. His father would certainly remember the buffoonery of Jockey in the historical pageantry of *The Famous Victories of Henry the Fifth*. He himself was more than glad to drop his penny into the door-keeper's box to see such things as *If It Be Not Good, The Devil is in It,* in which Pluto and his assistants Shacklesoul, Lurchall, and Ruffman participate in a plot involving a romantic love story, a vitriolic attack on usury, a burlesque of monastic life, Guy Fawkes, and a magical Golden Head. All this is by way of cautioning the reader about the grouping of plays in the following chapter. They have been here "classified" purely for the sake of convenience; there is nothing absolute about such, or any, classification. For other purposes, the plays might be considered chronologically, alphabetically by title, author or subject. For the study of the English drama as an art form, a grouping by type and combination of types, however imperfect, seems to be necessary. This, further, will avoid the misleading distinction between Shakespeare and the "Minor Dramatists" (the term *minor* jumbling together such men as Jonson, Webster, and Shirley) and will perhaps give a more accurate notion of the richness of the repertory. Shakespeare is, of course, head and shoulders above his fellows, but he is also head and shoulders above all the playwrights of the post-classical world. To apply the epithet *minor* to Jonson and Webster is to do them a gross injustice, and such obviously lesser men as Middleton, Beaumont and Fletcher, and Ford can on occasion rise far above mediocrity. Not all the Elizabethan playwrights were men of genius—there is a strictly limited amount of that article available to any literary generation —but as one looks back from the twentieth century, it would seem that the Elizabethans had more than their share.

1. ROMANTIC COMEDY

Until the turn of the seventeenth century, England was an expanding social group. Fortune rode with the banners of her army and upon the prows of her ships. Her merchants grew prosperous and powerful, the New World offered limitless promise. The intellectual aspirations of the Renaissance were being matched by the material aspirations of an economic and political awakening. This happy breed of men, governed by the almost deified Gloriana, were confidently prepared to shock the three corners of the world though armed against them. And their confidence, their happy optimism was reflected in their drama. 1590-1600 is the great decade of romantic comedy and chronicle history. Realistic comedy and the greatest tragedy must wait upon a change in the climate of opinion.

The exuberant optimism and vitality of Elizabethan society is precisely mirrored in Thomas Dekker's *The Shoemaker's Holiday* (1599), a romantic comedy in the school of Greene. The conventional romantic pattern has been readjusted to the requirements of an increasingly commercial temper—the noble does not woo a country maiden but the daughter of a merchant who frowns upon the match, ostensibly because "citizens must not with courtiers wed," actually because the suitor does not respect the proper value of money. The substitution of Simon Eyre, shoemaker rampant, for Friar Bacon is a determined gesture in the direction of realism. Put money and cobbling aside, love is our theme, that magically-enduring love-at-first-sight which is the basic convention of romantic comedy.

Dekker tells two love stories at once: how Rowland Lacy, nephew of the Earl of Lincoln, deserted his command in the King's army and disguised himself as a Dutch shoemaker to woo and win Rose Oteley, the Lord Mayor's daughter; and how Jane, the cobbler's wife, tricked by Master Hammon into believing that her husband was a casualty of the war, was rescued only by the united efforts of the cobblers of London. For added measure, Dekker recounts the historical tale of the rise of Simon Eyre from shoemaker to Lord Mayor of London and introduces at the end, as a kind of *deus ex machina* to straighten out the lovers' difficulties, the King of England.

Here is certainly the gallery-gods' plenty, yet Dekker controls his materials with a firm hand. The structure is highly regular and both love stories maintain their parallel developments with great precision. In both plots there are the three movements typical of the structure of the panoramic form: (1) The lovers are parted by the call to arms; (2) The men seek their ladies in disguise (Lacy actually disguised as a Dutchman, Ralph deformed by a battle-injury); (3) True love is made to triumph by the intercession of superior beings (the King unites Lacy and Rose, the shoemakers of London, Ralph and Jane). It is this final element—the achievement of dignity and social power by the artisans as symbolized by Eyre's mayoralty—that makes the play so remarkable a mirror of its day; for all his light-heartedness Dekker was dramatizing one of the most significant and revolutionary aspects of his society: the growing independence of the common man.

The two plots are unified to a degree by the presence in each of Master Hammon who woos first one lady then the other, permitting each to demonstrate faithfulness after her fashion. When he, as a hunter, attempts to conquer Rose he gets for his pains a series of witty insults:

HAMMON. My heart is lost.
ROSE. Alack good gentleman!
HAMMON. This poor lost heart would I wish you might find.

ROSE. You, by such luck might prove your heart a hind.
HAMMON. Why, Luck had horns, so I have heard some say.
ROSE. Now, God, an't be his will, send Luck into your way.

Simple Jane has not the wit or the position to fend off his attacks in such a manner. When Hammon approaches her, as a tradeswoman she must be civil, but as a wife she is honest:

> I have but one heart, and that heart's his due.
> How can I then bestow the same on you?
> Whilst he lives, his I live, be it ne'er so poor,
> And rather be his wife than a king's whore.

The social distinctions between the characters are maintained, as usually in romantic comedy, by the dialogue styles. The more elevated characters speak in blank verse, the less elevated mainly in prose. In addition the love scenes are mostly in rhyme, imparting a certain lyrical color and a distinguishing mood and tone. For it is not Dekker's intention that his audience shall forget that love is his subject. In direct contrast with the Lord Mayor's snobbish remarks in the opening scene:

> Too mean is my poor girl for his high birth,
> Poor citizens must not with courtiers wed,
> Who will in silks and gay apparel spend
> More in one year than I am worth by far . . . ,

the King in the closing scene declares:

> Dost thou not know that love respects no blood,
> Cares not for difference of birth or state?

Love is a great leveler, a statement which could have come with no greater grace than from the mouth of this particular king, Henry the Fifth, whose merry boyhood as Prince Hal had been spent among the citizens and artisans of London.

Success is also a great leveler, as the story of Simon Eyre demonstrates. Simon and his craftsmen are the most attractive part of the comedy and his rise to dignity—which does not by any means involve a loss of his native high spirits—is the complete dramatic realization of Elizabethan optimism. Like his play, Simon has everything: he is patriotic, public-spirited, good-humored. His laughter is infectious, his burlesquing of pomp irresistible. He is never at a loss for words, for wisdom, or for a stratagem. "Prince am I none," he declares over and over, "yet am I princely born," perhaps quoting the tag from a bombastic play, and his speech as he sends Ralph off to war is the *reductio ad absurdum* of the romantic notion of chivalry. Yet there is honor and chivalry in Simon, too:

> Sim Eyre knows how to speak to a Pope, to Sultan Soliman, to Tamburlaine, an he were here, and shall I melt, shall I droop before my sovereign? No, come, my lady Madgy! Follow me, Hans! About your business, my frolic free-booters! Firk, frisk about, and about, for the honor of mad Simon Eyre, lord mayor of London.

This promise to his wife he makes good when the king comes to dine with the shoemakers:

> My liege, I am six and fifty year old, yet I can cry humph! with a sound heart for the honor of St. Hugh. Mark this old wench, my King: I danced the shaking of the sheets with her six and thirty years ago, yet I hope to get two or three young lord mayors, ere I die. I am lusty still, Sim Eyre still. Care and cold lodgings bring white hairs. My sweet Majesty, let care vanish, cast it upon thy nobles, it will make thee look always young like Apollo, and cry humph! Prince am I none, yet I am princely born.

It was possible to laugh with pleasure, in the London of 1600, at a man who could cry with such pride, "I am Simon Eyre, still." Only a few years would bring about a sharp change in the climate of opinion: the woman who is to cry, "I am Duchess of Malfi, still," will be standing on the verge of a tremendous tragic experience. For the moment, however, a Londoner may rise in his society to greater and greater security with no feeling that he dwells in "the suburbs of hell"; he may glory in his individuality, in his skill as a craftsman, in his nationality as an Englishman. Through the world of Simon Eyre, and the London of Thomas Dekker, Pippa might pass with confidence.

For most twentieth century readers the romantic comedy of the 1590's is dominated by Shakespeare. After tentative experiments in various comic styles—the classical *Comedy of Errors,* the romantic *Two Gentlemen of Verona,* and the courtly *Love's Labour's Lost*—Shakespeare settled upon the romantic and produced *A Midsummer Night's Dream* and *The Merchant of Venice.*

The Dream, hypothetically intended as a part of the entertainment for a noble wedding, though as insubstantial as its title would suggest, is a notable achievement in the union of diverse elements: characters from fairyland, from mythic history, and the English countryside mingle in complete harmony. The subject, like the treatment, is entirely appropriate to the occasion. Very nearly everybody in the play is in love, and, as at a wedding, the lovers are gently ridiculed. Love is still the mysterious spell of Greene's comedy, but the playwright chooses to emphasize the farcical rather than the tragic possibilities in its power. In *The Dream* love is less magical than irrational.

The action is set in the framework of the preparations for a royal wedding—duplicating on the stage the situation in the audience. Theseus has won the love of Hippolyta by the completely illogical device of defeating her in battle. Egeus would, by paternal command, force his daughter to love a man whom she despises. The rude mechanicals of the town rehearse a play based on the star-crossed loves of Pyramus and Thisbe which, because of their grotesque incompetence, becomes a burlesque of both Egeus' attitude and Shakespeare's own early *Romeo and Juliet*. Once the characters of the play move into the enchanted forest the whole subject of the irrationality of love is made overt by the actions of Oberon as he despatches his servant Puck to drop love-potion into the eyes of The Lovers (they are kept deliberately puppet-like to emphasize the situation) and Titania and Bottom. The ultimate of love's absurdity is reached in the very center of the play when the gossamer fairy, Titania, falls in love with Bottom, whose mortal grossness is intensified as Puck "translates" him into an ass. She awakens as he brays a vulgar song:

> TITANIA. I pray thee, gentle mortal, sing again.
> Mine ear is much enamoured of thy note;
> So is mine eye enthralled to thy shape;
> And thy fair virtues force (perforce) doth move me,
> On the first view, to say, to swear, I love thee.

BOTTOM. Methinks, mistress, you should have little reason for that. And yet, to say the truth, reason and love keep little company together now-a-days.

The tangled skein of love is unwoven with the aplomb of an accomplished prestidigitator in the final act, Titania awakened, the four lovers properly paired, Theseus and Hippolyta wed, and Bottom restored to his comrades for their hilarious "tragical

mirth" of *Pyramus and Thisbe*. This final comic moment coming
on the heels of Theseus' famous statement,

> The lunatic, the lover, and the poet
> Are of imagination all compact,

again restores the play to the audience, for like the actors they
too were watching (though let us hope somewhat more politely)
the acting of a play about love. *The Dream* is light and fanciful
but it betrays a skill in execution far beyond that of many of its
more thoughtful competitors.

A more startling example of the ability of the form of romantic
comedy to create an artistic unit of inharmonious materials is
offered by *The Merchant of Venice* (1596-1597). Where *The
Dream* story had combined romantic and supernatural elements
with a slight injection of realistic farce, *The Merchant* boldly
joins the fairytale-like story of the Three Caskets to the grim
near-tragedy of Antonio's bond. If the ending is pure romance,
the beginning is very nearly pure business: the scene, The Rialto,
the Wall Street of Venice; the characters, merchants and factors;
their talk of ships and trade and money made slightly unreal by
the rich argosy of their diction but firmly based on matters commercial. Shylock, the dominating figure of this aspect of the
whole plot, is in no sense a fairytale villain, but a man, a Jew,
and an avenger. In one of his most famous speeches, he cries,

> I am a Jew. Hath not a Jew eyes? Hath not a Jew hands, organs,
> dimensions, senses, affections, passions? . . . If you prick us do we not
> bleed? If you tickle us, do we not laugh? If you poison us, do we not
> die? And if you wrong us, shall we not revenge?

A good many of the scenes and incidents of *The Merchant* are
intended to illustrate these "dimensional" qualities of Shylock,
and Shakespeare's success with him, the first great character in his
gallery, very nearly turns the play into a tragedy for the modern
theater.

But not quite. For Shakespeare is at some pains to create a
balance and a relationship between the two plots. It is no longer
the simple relationship of *The Dream,* where each plot was in
some way concerned with irrationality in love. *The Merchant* is
a play of strong contrasts, of love and hatred, of mercy and
justice, of the Leaden Casket and the Pound of Flesh. It achieves
its unity not by parallel actions or by characters common to both

plots, but by a theme, a single idea which both plots are designed to dramatize. Like most themes, it is not a new idea but a general truth which requires reiteration from time to time:

> And earthly power doth then show likest God's
> When mercy seasons justice.

Shylock stands for strict justice, for the execution of his bond. In a sense, also, he represents the values of a mercantile society in which human life (a pound of flesh) is a mere commodity on the Rialto. But Bassanio, a young gentleman of that same mercantile society, leaves the Rialto and goes to Belmont to woo an heiress. Belmont is another world, characterized by its presiding genius, Portia, all wit and love; it is, in fact, to be equated with the enchanted forest of *The Dream*. In Belmont, under the spell of his love for Portia, Bassanio suddenly acquires a new set of values, chooses the Leaden Casket, and wins the lady's hand. This, however, brings Portia and the world which she represents, the world of love in its larger sense of charity and mercy, into opposition with Shylock, and her defeat of Shylock is thus only in part a triumph of legal quibbling.

For a modern audience it is difficult to see the major issue of the play because of the reality of Shylock. Modern actors, too, have been accomplices in obscuring the work as a whole: it is hard to resist the temptation to make this "tragedy of Shylock" into a kind of pro-Semitic document. But more to the purpose is an examination of the handling of Shylock's story. For so dominant a character he appears very seldom on the stage. Some of the "big scenes" in his plot are only narrated; Solanio, for instance, a veritable puppet, relates Shylock's discovery of his daughter's elopement and diminishes the tragic effect of the situation into mere gossip. The climax of his plot in the trial scene is not the ending of the play, but, in the interchanging of rings, furnishes substance for the final act. While Shakespeare may have taken advantage of contemporary anti-Semitic feelings, the focus of his play is always upon love and its power to conquer hate, law, and curiously-minded fathers. Portia's love for Bassanio defeats Shylock and finds a loophole in the law; Bassanio's love for Portia enables him to see through the cranky fancies of her father's will; and Lorenzo's love for Jessica enables him to take from Shylock "the flesh of his flesh." In the last situation, of course, there is an ironic reference to the pound of flesh required of Antonio by the undying hatred of Jessica's father.

The Merchant, then, demonstrates the organization of divers elements into a unified pattern through the use of a dominant theme. Where *The Dream* had employed parallel situations and incidents, *The Merchant* is constructed on the principle of contrasts: love against hate, paralleled by mercy against justice. With such an organizing principle the playwright can take full advantage of the possibilities of the Elizabethan theater; the vulgar wit of Gobbo seizes the audience's attention when the Prince of Morocco has scarce finished his dignified formalities, the curses of Shylock are still in their ears as Portia conducts her lover to his test. The dramatic structure likewise shows the playwright's license: the world is as he creates it; natural time and natural space cease to exist. The maturing of the bond requires, by Shylock's own statement, three months, the winning of Portia something like two days—yet both occur simultaneously in the play and with no sense of incongruity, so skilfully have the scenes been interrupted and the developing plots juxtaposed. And, the usurer's plot completed, this freedom from realistic time and place is used to the full as Shakespeare takes nearly one-third of his last act to create the final mood of the play, by poetry, moonlight, and music to suggest the beauty of the world in which love is the harmonizing influence. The view of the world is simple and uncritical, perhaps, but most persuasively presented.

Two years later, Shakespeare once again turned to romantic comedy in *Much Ado About Nothing* (1599), followed in the next year by *As You Like It,* and in 1601 by *Twelfth Night.* In these three plays the diversity of plot materials, the panoramic structure, and the emphasis on romantic love carry on the patterns established by *The Dream* and *The Merchant.* But, while their tone is still optimistic, there is a kind of seriousness in their central themes, for here paradoxically enough, the playwright is using the form and subject matter of romance and pastoral to sing the praises of simple humanity. A discussion of *Twelfth Night* will indicate something of the general tenor of all three plays.

The scene is a remote and fanciful world, the Duchy of Illyria. Unlike Belmont, however, it is a romantic place without being held up as ideal. True, it offers refuge to Viola and Sebastian, twin victims of a shipwreck while voyaging in the "real" world. But the governor of the country is a sentimentalist in love with the idea of being in love; Olivia, his heart's desire, has permanently withdrawn from society to mourn the death of her brother; and Malvolio, her steward, is an inhuman and self-righteous precisionist. Shakespeare does not pretend that such unnatural behavior is wholly appropriate in the romantic world he has created. He adds to the cast an "all-licensed fool," Feste, whose official function is to deflate pomp and, by ridiculing eccentricity, to persuade his employers to "be themselves."

This is the theme, the organizing principle, of the comedy and all the absurdities are designed to illustrate it. The romantic conventions are still to be observed: love-at-first-sight functions in a most miraculous way; Viola, disguised as a boy, can fool even a member of her own sex; the Fool is the paradoxical symbol of good sense. The two plots—the wooing of Olivia and the exposure of Malvolio—are still united by the superficial means of characters common to each. And the surface atmosphere is always gay and light of heart. Journeys end in lovers' meetings as surely as the rain raineth every day. The puritanical steward is revealed as only too human in his final anguished cry for vengeance; Olivia readily relinquishes her unnatural love for the memory of her brother when the right "man" presents himself; even the love-sick Duke finds a cure in genuine as opposed to sentimental love.

There are moments in the other romantic comedies of this period when the dramatic world is somewhat less cheerful. *Much Ado* contains a subplot as grim as Shylock's and as unpleasant as the major plots of the later realistic comedies. In *As You Like It*, the action is intended to demonstrate that the world of nature—the Forest of Arden—is the world of true values as opposed to the artificial values of courtly society. But Arden is no conventional enchanted wood. The shepherds are hard-handed and, however foolishly they may behave when in love, their daily life is careworn. There is just a hint, in other words, of the shift to realism which was to occupy English comic writers for most of the first decade of the seventeenth century. Romance, when it once again appeared, was to find itself in very different circles and turned to very different purposes. After 1600 it no longer represented the comic vision of the human situation.

2. CHRONICLE HISTORY: SHAKESPEARE

The ten years which preceded the opening of the seventeenth century witnessed the greatest prosperity and popularity of the chronicle history and, again in the hands of Shakespeare, its reshaping into a unique vehicle for tragedy. In origin a loosely-articulated series of scenes dramatizing the events of the historical past in the manner of the medieval craft cycles, the chronicle history had been given form and made into a dramatic unit by Marlowe in *Edward II*. By such fundamental devices as centering the whole interest in the king, eliminating the extraneous distractions of farce and buffoonery, and distorting the facts of history when necessary, Marlowe turned a pageant into a portrait and effectively demonstrated that figures from the past could be given significance far greater than their place in history warranted.

There has been some dispute about how much of the three parts of *Henry VI* and *Richard III* are Shakespeare's unaided work, and how much may be credited to Marlowe and Peele. However there is no question that *Richard II* is his work alone and it demonstrates immediately that his interest in chronicle was incidentally in its patriotic appeal and primarily in its opportunities to exhibit characters of a certain magnitude in actions of a certain importance. *Richard II* both adheres to the conventions of the form and departs from them. Like Marlowe's Edward, the hero is a weak king, and like Edward, the story of his reign is derived from Raphael Holinshed's *Chronicles of England, Scotland and Ireland,* the great source book for the historical playwrights. Shakespeare makes some alterations of the accepted facts as Marlowe had done. Richard's queen was actually ten years old at the time of the king's abdication. In the play she is approximately Richard's own age, increasing the pathos of the hero's situation as he is separated from her. Pathos and dramatic effectiveness are gained also by setting Richard's abdication before the full parliament of England, instead of before a few lords in the Tower. It was not necessary, however, for Shakespeare to telescope historical time as drastically as Marlowe had done. *Richard II* covers scarcely two years of the king's life and makes no attempt to include both the whole of his "troublesome reign *and* lamentable death."

It was part of the older convention to invent non-historical incidents—usually involving characters from low life—to enliven and add to the amusement of the chronicle. Marlowe is careful that his inventions, like Lightborn, shall have a direct relationship to his central figure, shall increase the dramatic effect of Edward's downfall. Shakespeare's major invention is likewise closely related to the downfall of Richard, but not, as in Marlowe, merely to the *action* of the play. For it is evident that Shakespeare is not only relating history and examining a puzzling figure, but is concerned with a larger and more general theme: the nature and functions of the ideal governor. It is a theme that was very much on his mind, not only in his series of histories but throughout his great tragedies also. In *Richard II* it is presented dramatically in the persons of two gardeners who discuss (III,4) the political state of England as they go about their work. These two figures from common life have almost nothing to do with the high action of the play, yet they have everything to do with its theme. Through their discussion of statecraft in terms of husbandry they make immediate to the least educated listener what might seem a rather remote problem. In comparing the state to a garden they speak metaphorically, and the metaphor is a poetical device for clarification. But this metaphor is not merely in the poetry. The gardeners are real and since they bring their very real garden with them, the metaphor becomes dramatic, becomes realized upon the stage. This dramatic use of metaphor is one of Shakespeare's major contributions to the art of the Elizabethan stage, and a careful reading of *Richard II* will disclose other important instances of its use to clarify the theme, or some particular situation of the play.

Richard II ends as Bolingbroke is about to ascend the throne of England. In *Henry IV* (two parts, 1597-1598) Shakespeare resumes the story and the theme. The first part of this play is both the high-point of chronicle history and a nearly perfect panoramic drama; on both counts it repays careful study. Shakespeare here uses the material of history to dramatize an idea of universal concern and importance. For the Elizabethan audience the major interest of the play must have been in the character of Prince

Hal, the young ne'er-do-well who was to become England's ideal
king. An earlier success, *The Famous Victories of Henry the Fifth*
testifies to their constant delight in the reformation of the
prodigal son of Bolingbroke. Shakespeare did not disappoint
them. He created the monster attraction, Sir John Falstaff, and

Sir John Falstaff

a fine farcical subplot, to show Hal
playing at profligacy while remaining
the good young man at heart. But in
the careful relationship established between this invented action and the
historical main action and in the juxtaposing of Hal, Falstaff, and Hotspur,
the larger theme emerges—not simply
the education of an Elizabethan prince,
but the general education of youth.

The parallelism of the plots is clear.
Falstaff and his rascally crew of the
Boar's Head plot to rob the king's
treasury at Gadshill and are defeated
by Hal's counterplot. Hotspur and his
rebels plot to rob the king of his do-
main and powers and are thwarted by Hal's superior ability on
the battlefield. The relationship of the three major figures goes
deeper than this parallelism of action. Hotspur and Falstaff each
represent a way of life, dramatized in their conduct and ver-
balized in their contrasting attitudes towards honor. Hotspur is
the complete romantic, totally blind to the necessity for compromise and coöperation in the social group; Falstaff is the complete realist, indeed the complete egoist, concerned only with his
own comfortable survival at whatever cost to others. Between
these symbols of extremely different ways of life stands Prince
Hal—stands, in the larger sense, any young man—and his decision
as to his own future is the major business of the play.

Yet *I Henry IV* is no dramatized Youth Club Lecture; it is not,
openly, a morality play. Falstaff, whatever his ancestry in the
great catalogue of medieval Vices, is a fully-rounded character
in his own right, witty in himself and the cause of wit in others.
It is a theatrical proverb that all the audience loves a rogue, and
when the rogue is such a hill of flesh and such a leviathan of
humor and invention, it is not surprising that he comes close to

swallowing the play. He was tremendously popular from his first appearance. Shakespeare was obliged almost at once to provide a sequel to the play in which Falstaff occupies a more prominent part and, in *Henry V*, seems to have killed him to obviate his certain diminishing of the luster of his hero-king. But by the royal command of Elizabeth herself, so the legend goes, Falstaff was resurrected and made the central figure of a comic love story in *The Merry Wives of Windsor*. Small wonder that so vigorous a character should assume almost a life of his own, independent of Shakespeare or his works, for the romantic critics of the late eighteenth and early nineteenth centuries.

But the point must be emphasized that, apart from his play, Falstaff has no life of his own; and within the play Shakespeare has been at some pains to equate him with Hotspur. That hot valiant Scot, whatever his affinities with Tamburlaine, is also presented to the life. He idles with his wife, cavils with Glendower, rages with his uncle, and makes noble and foolish vows in the field. If he is a symbol of a way of life, he is as far from *Everyman*'s Cousin as Falstaff is from *Everyman*'s Good Fellowship. By such fully realized characters and by the parallelism of action, *I Henry IV* becomes the perfect dramatic presentation of a theme, and its theme provides the perfect unifying device for its panoramic action.

In 1599 Shakespeare produced the final play in his Prince Hal trilogy, and in a sense *Henry V* is the sum of the two parts of *Henry IV*. Its central character, "the mirror of all Christian Kings," is the product of the princely education set forth in the earlier plays. To the modern audience he is perhaps a less-appealing figure though there are reminiscences of the democratic Hal in his attractive scenes around the campfires the night before the battle of Agincourt and his good-humored wooing of the Princess Katharine. Falstaff is only a memory, his death being reported in the first act, but Hotspur is somewhat in evidence in Henry's reply to the news that his depleted forces are far weaker than the French:

> If we are mark'd to die, we are enow
> To do our country loss; and if we live,
> The fewer men, the greater share of honor.

Like Hotspur, too, he scoffs at poetry. There is, finally, something of the Marlovian Tamburlaine in his words and actions as he moves from victory to victory against his enemies; but the "high astounding term" is a typical aspect of the hero-king, and the Marlovian excesses are tempered by the honesty of the final love scene.

It has been frequently said that *Henry V* is more an epic than a drama and it is certainly obvious that the carefully devised structure of *I Henry IV* has been abandoned for the older chronicle history form. The play follows the course of history with few changes of fact and time sequence. The comic action, involving some familiar faces from the Boar's Head Tavern and a group of army officers, is only casually connected with the historical action, and there is a plethora of long speeches in the manner of an earlier theatrical day. On the other hand, Shakespeare works up the character of the French Dauphin as a worthy opponent for Henry at Agincourt, departing from history for the sake of a strong dramatic conflict.

But the emphasis is always upon Henry, the ideal king, and the symbol of England's glory. The effect is that of a kind of patriotic hymn to the power of a victoriously united country. If the Dauphin taunts Henry with his gift of tennis-balls, Henry's equally taunting reply is followed by the more effective gift of cannon-balls. If the French can outnumber the English on the field, the English can outfight them; nor does Shakespeare hesitate to appeal to nationalistic sentiments by quoting at length comparative casualty lists. And in the speeches of the Chorus, the playwright suggests that all the available resources of the theater, all the dramatic devices at his command, are insufficient to convey the splendor of his subject:

> with rough and all-unable pen
> Our bending author hath pursu'd the story
> In little room confining mighty men,
> Mangling by starts the full course of their glory.

The Chorus begs that the audience will use its imagination, that it will piece out the imperfections of Elizabethan production with their thoughts that the "mockeries" of acting and staging may become images of truth. This is perhaps a more accurate statement of the function of the acted drama than Hamlet's more famous declaration that the purpose of playing is "to hold, as t'were, the mirror up to nature." At any rate, it is a more precise

definition of the practice of the Elizabethan dramatists in their
non-realistic theater; their imaginative audiences, by willing sus-
pension of disbelief, accepted the symbol for the reality.

Henry V thus emerges as a gigantic symbol of the exuberant
patriotism that had dominated England since the victory over
the Spanish Armada. But the year of its production, 1599, is significant. In that year Essex returned defeated from Ireland and
his resultant fall from favor brought to public attention the
palace intrigues which darkened the last years of Elizabeth's
reign. Society was becoming increasingly urban as the gentry were
drawn from the simple pleasures of country life to the glittering
sophistication of the court. The Puritans grew in power among
the lower classes, and the social harmony which had dominated
a decade of security began to be broken. The thoughts of Englishmen turned more and more to internal economic, social, and
political questions. The drama, too, turned inward to examine
the nature of man in his relations with society in tragedy and
realistic comedy.

3. TRAGEDY: THE REVENGE THEME

This shift in interest is strikingly illustrated by the early writing of John Marston. His first independent play for the public
theater, *Antonio and Mellida (c.* 1599), is a combination of
romantic elements, the hero disguised as an Amazon to rescue the
heroine from the clutches of a usurper, corpses suddenly returned
to life, a reforming villain, and a promise of more to come in a
sequel. As acted by the Children of Paul's, its prologue wishes the
audience "the wreath of pleasure, and delicious sweets." However, the prologue to the sequel, *Antonio's Revenge (c.* 1599)
begins in a different mood:

> The rawish dank of clumsy winter ramps
> The fluent summer's vein: and drizzling sleet
> Chilleth the wan bleak cheek of the numb'd earth. . . .
> O now, methinks, a sullen tragic Scene
> Would suit the Time with pleasing consequence.

The materials of the first part of *Antonio and Mellida* were
drawn from romance, the materials of the second part, *Antonio's
Revenge,* from Thomas Kyd; the elements which had proved
so popular in *The Spanish Tragedy* were revived and intensified.

Piero, the usurping governor of the first part, reappears as a
Machiavellian of the most livid complexion. To secure his position he would "Poison the father, butcher the son, and marry the
mother," to say nothing of defaming his own daughter and
slaughtering numerous minor obstacles to his goal. In his statement of principles, he gives the cue to a line of distinguished
successors:

> Now, now, now, now, now, my plot begins to work.
> Why, thus should statesmen do,
> That cleave through knots of craggy policies,
> Use men like wedges, one strike out another;
> Till by degrees the tough and knurly trunk
> Be rived in sunder.

And when he has "poisoned the father," there is nothing for the
father's ghost to do but return and demand that his son, Antonio,
avenge him. This Antonio is conventionally willing to do, dis-
guising himself as a Fool that he may remain close to his intended victim, since the "plump cheeked fool"

> hath a patent of immunities
> Confirm'd by custom, sealed by policy,
> As large as spacious thought.

Piero's plot is conventionally complex, and Antonio's revenge
must be equally involved. Piero must be made "to feed on life/
Till he shall loath it." His young son, Julio, the "pathetic child,"
is horribly butchered by Antonio as a kind of sacramental blessing
of his purpose, and Piero's own murder is accompanied by
masquing and torture as the ghost of Antonio's father complacently remarks: "Sons that revenge their father's blood are
blest."

Antonio's Revenge is a play of great violence and vicious passion well described in the concluding speech: "Never more woe
in lesser plot was found." With simple-minded brutality, Marston
creates a villain and hounds him to death. There is no judgment
on the revengers; at the end of the play they are alive and triumphant, confident that a little water will clear them of their
deeds. As a result the play is more melodrama than tragedy
although Marston, in his prologue, claims to possess a "common
sense of what men were and are," and "what men must be."

Marston's later and most popular play, *The Malcontent* (1604), is another kind of illustration of the simple and non-tragic view of the revenge situation. The moral issue is ignored or blunted when the initial villain, another usurping Duke, is replaced half-way through by a scheming Machiavellian. But his plots are foredoomed since his accomplices prove to be his intended victims in disguise. The deaths in the play are all feigned, the faithless wife repents and is forgiven, and even the villain receives no more serious punishment than Mak, in *The Shepherd's Play*. The conventional elements of the revenge play: horror, disguise, death, even the concluding masque or play-within-a-play, are here turned to the purposes of comedy. The use of such elements in place of more romantic ones for comic purposes is, of course, symptomatic of the changing Elizabethan world, but the final emphasis is on the happy outcome of the revenge pattern.

From the popular acclaim which greeted such comedies and melodramas there can be no doubt that Thomas Kyd's legacy to his successors was, financially at any rate, a golden one. Dealing with horrors and excitement for their own sakes, the revenge play invites both melodrama and a happy ending; in itself it is remote from tragedy, from the attitude which grows out of the thoughtful observation of man, not in the artificial world of romance or the theater, but of man in society. The revenge play was non-Christian in accepting, as did the ghost of Andrugio in *Antonio's Revenge,* the principle of vengeance as a proper motivation for its hero. In employing death as a mere dramatic device, a convenience for advancing or concluding the plot, it ignored the depth of emotion with which the typical man of the Renaissance regarded his inevitable end. "O eloquent, just, and mighty Death," wrote Sir Walter Raleigh, "thou hast drawn together all the far-fetched greatness, all the pride, cruelty, and ambition of man, and covered it all over with these two narrow words, *hic jacet.*" When the conventions of the popular revenge play were infused with the tragic contemplation of life, the result was a body of dramatic literature thoroughly typical of its period and yet universal in its power to move the hearts and mold the minds of future audiences.

The fusion is evident in Shakespeare's *Hamlet* (1600). A reworking of an older play, which may have been written by Kyd himself, *Hamlet* preserves all the conventions of the type: vengeance is imposed on the hero as a duty; the vengeance must be worked on a villain so highly placed that the ordinary processes of the law cannot reach him; the hero feigns madness for self-protection and to stay close to the villain. Other devices of the revenge play are retained in somewhat altered form. The ghost, who is only a spectator of *The Spanish Tragedy,* is the inciting force in *Hamlet.* Hieronimo's play-within-a-play is the actual vehicle of his vengeance; Hamlet's "mousetrap" is a scheme to gather evidence against the king. And the wholesale slaughter which concludes the earlier play, though not totally abandoned, is somewhat mitigated as a few deaths are distributed in the middle action.

The major difference lies in the choice of a revenger. In place of Hieronimo or Antonio, who subscribed without question to the bloody code of an eye for an eye, the central figure becomes Hamlet, the philosophical, Christian scholar, whose thoughts throughout the play are haunted by the Renaissance view of death. In moments of understandable emotional elation, as he interviews his father's ghost, as his play succeeds in trapping the king, he throws off the bondage of thought and abandons himself to the base desire to drink hot blood and achieve his revenge. But his scholarly habit of mind soon regains control of him and he is lost in the contemplation of the everlasting dreams which may come with death.

In contrast to Hamlet, the play exhibits another revenger who unquestioningly accepts the code. Laertes is put into a situation exactly like Hamlet's—he must avenge his father's murder—but his behavior is strikingly different. Unable or unwilling to think precisely on the event, he arms himself and sets out to achieve his vengeance without regard for the evil he may do to the innocent on the way. A good, if thoughtless, young man, he is persuaded by Claudius to become not a judicial murderer but an assassin by craft. Claudius is a Machiavellian villain, and Laertes, by yielding to his persuasions, becomes a Machiavellian also. Thus, without comment, without overt statement, and wholly in terms of dramatic action, Shakespeare turns the conventions of the melodramatic revenge play to the uses of tragedy.

The freedom with which Shakespeare employs the traditional devices of the revenge play clarifies his tragic purpose. Hamlet's play-within-a-play is not a means to achieve his goal, but a delaying device; characteristically the scholar is unwilling to commit himself, he must have further proof. The deaths of Ophelia and Polonius, distributed through the earlier acts of the play instead of reserved for the catastrophe, point up the completely unjudicial nature of revenge: there is no justification for their deaths; they are unfortunate victims of an inhumane code. It might almost be said that *Hamlet* as a revenge tragedy is an anti-revenge play.

But revenge is only the vehicle for the tragedy of Hamlet. It is the concrete symbol of a larger human problem: the continuing conflict between the individual and the code of his society. It is also the vehicle for the expression of disgust with that society which became the literary fashion with the development of satire in the early seventeenth century. Some of Hamlet's cynical remarks clearly anticipate the misanthropy of the malcontented hero of Marston's revenge comedy, and of Bosola in *The Duchess of Malfi*. This union of the malcontent and the revenge theme is a major feature of Cyril Tourneur's *Revenger's Tragedy* (1606-7).

The union is announced symbolically in the striking opening scene as the ruling family of a corrupt Italian duchy passes across the upper stage by torchlight while Vendice on the main platform stands clutching the skull of his murdered mistress and rails at them:

> Duke! royal lecher! go, grey-haired adultery!
> And thou, his son, as impious steeped as he:
> And thou, his bastard, true begot in evil:
> And thou, his duchess that will do with devil:
> Four excellent characters!

Four *typical* characters, at any rate, from a court so dissolute and vicious that a poor scholar like Vendice can only retire to his study to pray for the deaths of those who live "i' the world."

> Vengeance, thou murderer's quit-rent, and whereby
> Thou show'st thyself tenant to tragedy;
> O keep thy day, hour, minute, I beseech,
> For those thou hast determined. Hum! whoe'er knew
> Murder unpaid? faith, give revenge her due,
> She has kept touch hitherto.

Under the persuasion of his brother, the easy-going Hippolito, Vendice consents to disguise himself and enter the court. The ensuing play employs a kind of double plot as Vendice's mistress and the wife of the courtier Antonio are both revenged upon the Duke, with the addition of a series of interlocking minor revenges: Spurio against his legitimate brothers, the legitimate brothers against first Lussurioso and then Spurio, and Ambitioso against Spurio. There is even a grim burlesque of the subject as Vendice, to maintain his disguise, is forced to pretend to seek vengeance on himself.

The Revenger's Tragedy has been described as the archetype of Elizabethan dramaturgy because of the complexity of its action and because it seems to proceed by a series of situations established, developed, and resolved, rather than by a single conflict leading to a climax and denouement. Actually, its structure emphasizes its singleness of purpose, to portray the world as totally corrupted by lust and gold and dominated by the imminence of death. Vendice's initial attitude, that he despises the world and holds himself aloof from it, is indicated both by his opening speech and by the physical separation provided by the balcony and platform stages of the Elizabethan theater. When he enters the world of evil, he at first retains his spiritual independence by assuming a disguise, but his very disguise soon leads him to dishonorable actions. As the villain's misanthropic servant he is given the duty of persuading his own mother to prostitute his sister to his master. At first he is furious and would defend his family's honor with his sword. Then,

> now angry froth is down in me,
> It would not prove the meanest policy,
> In this disguise, to try the faith of both.
> Another might have had the self-same office;
> Some slave that would have wrought effectually,
> Ay, and perhaps o'erwrought 'em; therefore I,
> Being thought travelled, will apply myself
> Unto the self-same form, forget my nature,
> As if no part about me were kin to 'em,
> So touch 'em—

though he adds as an afterthought that he would venture his salvation upon their virtue. From this point, he is drawn deeper and deeper into the plots and counterplots of the court until at the end of the play he kills the chief villain and three of his nobles in a masque.

Then, by an unexpected twist of the plot, the crown passes to
honest Antonio:

> HIPPOLITO. Now the hope
> Of Italy lies in your reverend years.
> VENDICE. Your hair will make the silver age again,
> When there were fewer, but more honest men.
> ANTONIO. The burden's weighty, and will press age down.
> May I so rule, that Heaven may keep the crown!

Vendice is now moved to confess his part in bringing about this
happy ending:

> We may be bold to speak it now,
> 'Twas somewhat wittily carried, though we say it—
> 'Twas we two murdered him.
> ANTONIO. You two?
> VENDICE. None else, i'faith, my lord. Nay, 'twas well-managed.
> ANTONIO. Lay hands upon those villains! . . .
> You that would murder him would murder me.

The very suddenness of this turn of events emphasizes that the
moral order has been restored, that Vendice has been blinded to
the distinction between murder and justice. The latter he acknowledges in his final speech,

> 'Tis time to die, when we're ourselves our foes.

Unlike Hamlet, Vendice has allowed his revenge to pervert his
own sense of values, and the play is well named *The Revenger's
Tragedy.*

In the major plays of John Webster, *The White Devil* and
The Duchess of Malfi, the elements of the revenge convention
become pegs on which to hang a picture of a decadent world
whose moral order must be restored. Perhaps because of a growing consciousness that, as Shakespeare indicates in *Hamlet,* the
code of revenge was in opposition to the code of Christian justice and mercy, the chief interest of these plays lies in the complexity rather than in the single-mindedness of the central
characters, and the structure of the plays is designed to emphasize
this complexity while de-emphasizing the conventional revenge
pattern.

The first movement of *The White Devil* (1611) presents Vittoria Corombona persuading her lover Brachiano to murder her
husband. Brachiano accomplishes this through the good offices

of his tool, Flamineo, Vittoria's brother; Brachiano also disposes of his wife by means of a poisoned picture. The audience at once sympathizes with the moral indignation and passionate grief of Francisco de Medecis, Duke of Florence and brother to Brachiano's wife. In the second movement, however, it is difficult not to feel some admiration for Vittoria as she boldly defends herself in a trial which is a travesty of justice, declaring, "I scorn to hold my life/At yours or any man's entreaty, sir." Even Brachiano gains in stature by refusing to be bullied by a corrupt churchman. Francisco, determined to prove a revenger, becomes somewhat less noble as he leafs through a list of available criminals and selects a tool for his purposes. The third movement comprises his revenge, first on Brachiano who dies declaring his love for Vittoria, and then on the White Devil herself who dies defiant. But Francisco is completely blackened. After Brachiano has been murdered the tool villain declares, "our action's justified." To this the Duke cries,

> Tush for justice!
> What harms it justice? We now, like the partridge,
> Purge the disease with laurel; for the fame
> Shall crown the enterprise, and quit the shame.

Like Vendice, Francisco has been so caught up in his monstrous plot that his moral values have been destroyed. "Tush for justice!" At the end of the play, young Giovanni, heir to the state, orders the murderers punished and prays for the restoration of justice under law.

The Duchess of Malfi (1613-1614) develops further Webster's variations on the revenge theme. Where Vittoria had been a completely evil character at the start of her play, Giovanna, the Duchess of Malfi, is introduced as little worse than willful and proud. Her sins involve a breach of family honor and a questionable concupiscence, but they do not involve murder and adultery. If she deserved punishment, as by Elizabethan standards she apparently did, she did not deserve the brutal "justice" of her tyrannical and depraved brothers. Typically the play is composed of three movements, in the first of which Giovanna disobeys her brothers (who represent the Church and the State), in the second she is tortured and killed, and in the third her judges and executioners pay with their lives for her murder.

Webster is careful that both the arrangement of incidents and
the images of the poetry shall clarify his point. In the opening
movement Duke Ferdinand and his brother, the Cardinal, are
allowed a clear stage and a long scene to declare plainly their
purpose that the Duchess shall not remarry—so plainly that she
observes,

> I think this speech between you both was studied,
> It came so roundly off.

Her own willfulness, her scorn of the laws of Church and State,
are next depicted as she woos and weds Antonio, her steward,
in secret. Her maid, Cariola, concludes this scene with an editorial comment,

> Whether the spirit of greatness or of woman
> Reign most in her, I know not; but it shows
> A fearful madness: I owe her much of pity.

In the central movement much time is devoted to Ferdinand's
mad desire to avenge both his family honor and his slighted commands, and to a detailed presentation of the torture and death
of the Duchess, which the imagery of the verse constantly com-
pares to the purification of a condemned soul in purgatory. Ferdinand, looking upon her dead body, makes this explicit with
one of Webster's mighty lines:

> Cover her face; mine eyes dazzle. She died young.

All the taints of the world have been removed by the torments he
has caused her to undergo and he, at last, comes to a realization
of his own evil nature. In the final movement, he is totally insane
and is murdered, along with his wicked brother, by Bosola, who
had been their tool throughout the play.

It is not sufficient to point out that *The Duchess*, like *The
White Devil* and *The Revenger's Tragedy*, is compounded of
peripeteias, sudden reversals of the situation which may be either
melodramatic or ironic. The bearing of such incidents upon the
world-view of the play must be determined. Vendice, for instance,
is corrupted by the evil world into which he entered in hopes of
doing the work of justice. In Webster's plays two characters stand
in positions equally ironic and tragic.

Flamineo, in *The White Devil,* is the brother of Vittoria. At
various times in the play, he is the tool villain of Francisco and

malcontent for his own protection. His misanthropy is conventional enough, but his excuse for his villainy is only too reasonably a part of the social code in which he has been raised. Bearing in mind Vendice's horror at being ordered to solicit his sister's favor for his employer, observe Flamineo seizing every opportunity to profit by his sister's lustful behavior. And when his mother remonstrates, he excuses himself:

> Pray what means have you
> To keep me from the galleys or the gallows?
> My father proved himself a gentleman,
> Sold all's land, and, like a fortunate fellow,
> Died ere the money was spent. You brought me up
> At Padua, I confess, where I protest,
> For want of means (the university judge me)
> I have been fain to heel my tutor's stockings,
> At least seven years: conspiring with a beard
> Made me a graduate; then to this duke's service.
> I visited the court, whence I returned
> More courteous, more lecherous by far,
> But not a suit the richer: and shall I,
> Having a path so open and so free
> To my preferment, still retain your milk
> In my pale forehead? No, this face of mine
> I'll arm, and fortify with lusty wine
> 'Gainst shame and blushing.

The corruption of Vendice by the evil world has occupied a play; the corruption of Flamineo is disposed of in a speech. He becomes but one more symbol, and not the least ugly, of a damned society. He cannot redeem himself, as his society cannot redeem itself. The moral order is re-imposed, from the outside, by Giovanni who is too young to have been corrupted.

Bosola, the tool villain of *The Duchess,* is one of the most complex characters in the Elizabethan repertory and for that reason one of the most satisfying. Like Vendice and Hamlet a philosophical man, he has like Flamineo sought preferment at court. His major service has been to take the blame and the punishment for a crime committed by the Cardinal. As the play begins he is claiming his reward for two years of imprisonment in the galleys. That the Cardinal ignores both his merits and his claims intensifies his natural cynicism and his willingness to place self-interest above all other considerations. Yet his natural habit of mind cannot be wholly denied; on the least occasion he will

produce a malcontent's soliloquy in the Hamlet manner, which
is only in part an affectation. To Ferdinand and the Cardinal he
can be a pliant if sharp-tongued tool. But to the Duchess, whom
he must torture, he brings "comfort," first reminding her that the
greatest sin is pride:

> What's this flesh? a little crudded milk, fantastical puff-paste. Our
> bodies are weaker than those paper prisons boys use to keep flies in;
> more contemptible, since ours is to preserve earthworms. Did'st thou
> ever see a lark in a cage? Such is the soul in the body: this world is
> like her little turf of grass; and the Heaven o'er our heads, like her
> looking glass, only gives us a miserable knowledge of the small compass
> of our prison;

and that death is an escape from a world of corruption and
decay. He sings a song of purification:

> . . . A long war disturbed your mind;
> Here [in death] your perfect peace is signed.
> Of what is't fools make such vain keeping?
> Sin their conception, their birth weeping,
> Their life a general mist of error,
> Their death a hideous storm of terror—
> Strew your hair with powders sweet,
> Don clean linen, bathe your feet. . . .

When he has finished, the Duchess is at peace, and it is the
sight of this peace that drives her wicked brother mad. However,
it also reëstablishes in Bosola the sense of values which his preoccupation with worldly success had kept dormant.

> I stand like one
> That long hath ta'en a sweet and golden dream:
> I am angry with myself, now that I wake.

Over the Duchess' body he sheds tears and as he bears her off
he determines that his final actions shall be those of a righteous
man. It is, he declares, "the fool's pilgrimage . . . to sue to Fortune any longer." But seeking to aid Antonio he kills him, and
must himself kill Ferdinand and the Cardinal, in

> Revenge for the Duchess of Malfi murdered
> By the Arragonian brethren; for Antonio
> Slain by this hand; for lustful Julia
> Poison'd by this man; and lastly for myself,
> That was an actor in the main of all
> Much 'gainst my own good nature. . . .

The Duchess of Malfi in its moral position advances beyond the code of revenge, beyond even the corruption of a good man by a society for which revenge is an acceptable code. The structure of *The Duchess* is designed to show that an essentially moral man, however corrupted, may be given the courage to declare for the right:

> Let worthy minds ne'er stagger in distrust
> To suffer death or shame for what is just.

From the standpoint of Bosola, at least, the play is very close to a *de casibus* tragedy, as the central figure is brought to a clearer vision of man's fate.

In *The Atheist's Tragedy* by Cyril Tourneur (1611) the revenge play becomes almost a problem play in the modern sense. It has been often noted that the play is completely artificial; symbolic characters are moved through symbolic situations to make a point, somewhat in the fashion of the old secular moralities. The point is explicit in the subtitle, *The Honest Man's Revenge,* and in an overt statement of the hero at the conclusion:

> Only to Heaven I attribute the work
> Whose gracious motives made me still forbear
> To be mine own revenger. Now I see
> That patience is the honest man's revenge.

The "atheist" D'Amville symbolizes the materialistic spirit of the new century, of those who exalted Nature—as Edmund in *Lear*—above the supernatural, and who desired only immediate and measurable delights. He says,

> if Death casts up
> Our total sum of joy and happiness,
> Let me have all my senses feasted in
> The abundant fulness of delight at once,
> And, with a sweet insensible increase
> Of pleasing surfeit, melt into my dust.

To secure earthly position he murders his brother, to ensure the immortality of his name he marries his sickly son to Castabella and, when no issue seems likely, attempts incest with her. Material ambition and spiritual blindness drive him from one evil act to another until he is confounded by the deaths of his two sons, goes mad, and kills himself by accident.

The novelty of the play does not lie wholly in the new treatment of the Machiavell, as much as in the new treatment of the ghost. Montferrers has been murdered by D'Amville and in revenge-play fashion he reappears at intervals, but not to demand the villain's eye for his. The hero, Charlemont, is provoked to kill D'Amville's son, crying,

> Revenge, to thee I'll dedicate this work.
> *Enter the ghost of* MONTFERRERS
> MONTFERRERS. Hold, Charlemont.
> Let him revenge my murder and thy wrongs
> To whom the justice of revenge belongs.   [*Exit.*]

Vengeance is the Lord's and, according to *The Atheist's Tragedy,* is inevitable. The honest man, who trusts in divine justice, refuses to take matters into his own hands and is unstained at the end of the play.

In the dozen years between *Antonio's Revenge* and *The Duchess of Malfi* the code of the revenge play had been variously accepted, disputed, and rejected. In all these plays, however, the idea of revenge is treated with utmost seriousness, and in all save the first with larger tragic implications. The greater number are transformed almost into *de casibus* tragedy which, as part of the medieval heritage, expresses the most deeply-rooted Renaissance convictions about man's life.

4. TRAGEDY: THE *DE CASIBUS* THEME

The revenge play is of course only a small part of the Elizabethan tragic repertory. It is possible to distinguish other types, among them *de casibus* tragedy, dealing with the "Falls of Princes," and domestic tragedy, dealing with the fate of humbler men. Yet all these types may overlap and interlock until the modern audience concludes too easily that, to its ancestors, tragedy meant simply a multiplicity of violent deaths. To a certain extent this is true. "When the bad bleed, then is the tragedy good," wrote Tourneur. But the good bleed also. Whatever the change in the national temper with the advent of the seventeenth century, the ethics, morality, and symbolism of medieval Christianity continued to flourish in the public mind and in the minds of those who provided amusements for the public. One evidence of this is the persistent recurrence of the image of the goddess

Fortuna and her wheel as a symbol of the life of man. Man rises only to fall. At the moment of triumph, at the height of earthly glory, Death beckons. Princes fall, not because of any flaw in their character, not even because of *hubris* or pride, but simply because, as princes, they have reached the top of the wheel and "the wheel must come full circle."

Such a theme interpenetrates both the speech and structure of George Chapman's *Bussy D'Ambois,* performed by the Children of Paul's in 1604. As a play it was a great popular success, repeated constantly up to the closing of the theaters and revived early in the Restoration. To the modern reader it seems, perhaps, naïve, over-simple, and quite possibly non-tragic. The central figure is an adulterer and intriguer with a tendency to bullying and rant. His associates are colorless and petty, the nobility of an ignoble court. The play, that is, has much of Marlowe's extravagance without Marlowe's elevation; yet it is not, as such a statement might imply, melodrama. In structure as well as content it is the dramatic realization of the pervasive tragic symbol of Fortune's wheel.

The plot is based on the very nearly contemporary career of an historical figure, Louis de Clermont d'Amboise, Seigneur de Bussy, whose exploits as a swordsman and a soldier won him a place at the French court of Henri III. But Chapman does not bind himself to historical fact and his alterations illustrate the nature of *de casibus* tragedy.

The play may be divided into the conventional three movements: the rise of Bussy, his triumph, and his downfall. The hero first appears "poor"—that is, the physical details of costume and make-up are to emphasize the turning of the wheel, very much as we might speak metaphorically of going "from rags to riches." He soliloquizes almost as a Malcontent *de contemptu mundi,* and rails against Fortune:

> Fortune, not Reason, rules the state of things;
> Reward goes backwards. Honor on his head;
> Who is not poor is monstrous. . . .
> Man is a torch borne in the wind; a dream
> But of a shadow. . . .
> We must to Virtue for her guide resort,
> Or we shall shipwreck in our safest port.
> *He lies down.*

From this low estate both physical and spiritual he is raised immediately by "Monsieur," the king's brother, who has use for his skill as a swordsman. His rags are shifted for noble raiment, he freely insults the Duke of Guise, participates in a duelling match and wins a pardon from the king himself. These events show Bussy's progress and it will not do to complain that his behavior is something less than admirable to modern eyes. His actions result from the pursuit of that *virtù* to which he referred in his opening soliloquy, the sum of all the Renaissance excellences. Over and over we are told of his "greatness," that is, in the Aristotelian sense his *magnanimity*. Says Tamyra:

> though his great spirit something overflow,
> All faults are still-borne that from greatness flow.

In the second movement, Bussy, "Fortune's proud mushroom," reaches the summit of his career by winning the love of Tamyra whose chastity not even the king's brother could tempt. It is his triumph that leads to his fall, for at the very moment of his success, the scorned lover begins to plot against him. Monsieur, in a philosophical moment, expresses the *de casibus* theme:

> here will be one
> Young, learned, valiant, virtuous, and full mann'd;
> One on whom Nature spent so rich a hand
> That with an ominous eye she wept to see
> So much consum'd her virtuous treasury.
> Yet, as the winds sing through a hollow tree,
> And, since it lets them pass through, lets it stand;
> But a tree solid, since it gives no way
> To their wild rage, they rend up by the root;
> So this whole man,
> That will not wind with every crooked way,
> Trod by the servile world, shall reel and fall
> Before the frantic puffs of blind-born chance,
> That pipes through empty men, and makes them dance.
> Not so the sea raves on the Lybian sands,
> Tumbling her billows on each other's neck;
> Not so the singer of the Euxine sea
> Near to the frosty pole, where free Boötes
> From those dark deep waves turns his radiant team,
> Swell, being enrag'd even from their inmost drop,
> As Fortune swings about the restless state
> Of virtue, now thrown into all men's hate.

As in much of Chapman's verse the idea is crabbedly expressed, but the ensuing action is clear enough. Bussy is attacked by the husband he has cuckolded and is about to best him in swordplay —a part of his *virtù*—when he is shot by pistols fired offstage. Despite "greatness," *virtù*, rank and achievement, Bussy is defeated by the inevitable turning of Fortune's wheel. He ends as he began, on the ground, and describing his career as

> a falling star
> Silently glanc'd, that like a thunderbolt
> Look'd to have st[r]uck and shook the firmament.

Chapman's debt to Marlowe has been often noted: the focus on a single powerful individual, the long speeches in soaring verse. In the conjuring of devils, too, there is something of Marlowe and a stage device employed in Greene's *Friar Bacon*. Chapman's classical leanings are apparent in the formal narrations of the Nuntius, in the Ghost of the Friar, in the almost Homeric similes and in passages adapted from Seneca. But into *Bussy D'Ambois* has crept some of that tragic vision which dominates the serious playwrighting of its period. It is still relatively simple in its expression, and the hero goes to his death without any clear recognition of the relation between the workings of Fortuna and his own virtues and failings. *De casibus* tragedy was capable of greater, because more human and more universal, expression.

In its later development, *de casibus* tragedy is the vehicle not simply for the medieval theme of the vagaries of Fortune, but the universal theme of the human dilemma: to live is to make choices, decisions, but such choices and decisions must be made in ignorance of their outcome and are determined for every man by his own peculiarities, his temper, his shortcomings, his virtues and his faults. Only in the consequences of such choices can man come to full knowledge of himself, and in the drama such knowledge comes only through suffering the consequences of ignorance. As the Duchess of Malfi says, parting from her young son,

> Farewell, boy:
> Thou art happy that thou hast not understanding
> To know thy misery; for all our wit
> And reading brings us to a truer sense
> Of sorrow.

The progression from blindness to vision, from ignorance to knowledge has been the theme of the greatest tragedy of all races and eras, but it acquires special significance in the Christian culture. The Elizabethan is primarily a moral drama, and the audience expected from both the action and the overt statements of the play examples of the teachings which it had inherited from the past and could hear expounded regularly from the pulpit.

Shakespeare's *King Lear* (1605-1606) may be taken both for its familiarity and its appositeness as an illustration. To begin with, it is a double tragedy, relating parallel stories on different social and intellectual levels. On the lower level, the Duke of Gloucester, an easy-going, sensual, credulous man is duped by those qualities into an erroneous course of action, is physically blinded and then, through a series of tortures and trials led to a recognition of the true state of things and to a reconciliation with his son Edgar, the symbol of the accepted Christian values. On the higher level, Lear makes the same kind of error in blindness and ignorance and suffers spiritual and intellectual tortures which restore him to his senses. The action of the play is calculated to develop this moral idea: Lear is presented first as a wilful, proud man, blind to the natures of his own children—the flesh of his flesh—and acting in a completely irrational, illogical way. For two long acts he is subjected to abuse and violence from his daughters and from the elements until he is driven out of his mind. When he is restored to Cordelia and to his senses he recognizes himself for what he is, "a foolish, fond, old man."

Once his vision is restored, however, Lear does not live happily ever after. For it is one of the essences of tragedy to take the full view of life; Lear has, through his own error, given strength and opportunity to his wicked daughters as Gloucester has to Edmund. These forces are not to be tricked back into their bottles as easily as Oriental genii. Once freed they will work out their destiny, and their inevitable defeat will not lessen the price the tragic hero must pay for his education. The bad bleed, but the good bleed also. Edmund, Goneril, Regan are dead at the end of the play, but so too are Gloucester, Lear, and Cordelia. By no easy twist of circumstance does the tragic hero avoid the consequences of his blindness.

The tragic view of life is neither pessimistic nor despairing. If the Duchess of Malfi's increased understanding brought her a truer sense of sorrow, and Hamlet greeted death as the escape from this harsh world to a world of felicity, neither play stops with the final words of its central figure. It has long been recognized as a convention of the Elizabethan drama that the person of highest rank left alive at the end spoke the concluding speech. This is clearly intended, not merely to get the cast off the curtainless stage with dignity, but to announce to the audience the restoration of the moral order. After five acts of error, violence, and sin, the whole community, the dramatic world, has been purged along with the tragic hero. Kent and Edgar at the end of *Lear* are directed to "Rule in this realm, and the gor'd state sustain"; power has descended upon those who have demonstrated their fitness to rule. Delio's concluding remarks in *The Duchess of Malfi* are more than an Aesopian period:

> Let us make noble use
> Of this great ruin, and join all our force
> To establish this young hopeful gentleman
> In's mother's right. . . .

Jacobean *de casibus* tragedy is a rich and exciting form, reflecting as drama must the ideals and interests of its audiences. Any subject was grist for its playwrights. The Renaissance had awakened admiration for classical times; North's translation of Plutarch and other Roman stories were plundered for the plots and heroes of *Julius Caesar, Antony and Cleopatra, Sejanus, Catiline, Lucrece, Timon of Athens, Coriolanus.* Thomas Heywood ambitiously dramatized the whole body of Greek mythology in five plays: *The Golden Age, The Silver Age, The Brazen Age,* and the two parts of *The Iron Age* (1611+), a project so tremendous that it seems to have been produced as a joint effort of at least two of the acting companies. The interest in English history and legend, awakened by the patriotism of the last century, is turned to the uses of tragedy in *King Lear, Macbeth, Bonduca.* French history provided Chapman with the plots of *Bussy D'Ambois* and *The Conspiracy and Tragedy of Charles Duke of Byron* and *The Tragedy of Chabot Admiral of France.* The Englishman's conception of Italy as the home of intrigue and vice is reflected in *Othello* and in the plays of Webster and Tourneur. Whatever their source, the plays resemble one another in violence, as their characters are alike in passionate determination, in energy and single-mindedness. Whatever his subjects, the dramatist's approach is colored by a strong sympathy for the sweetness of life

and the finality of death expressed in verse which is the greatest
glory of a poetic age.

It must be noted, however, that in the midst of this body of
romantic drama treating by preference the careers of kings and
princes, noble warriors and classical heroes, there existed a small
group of plays which provide the tragic equivalent of the trend
toward realism in comedy. These domestic dramas, as they are
commonly called, are few in number and generally trade on the
popular interest in some current, widely-publicized crime. Theatrically they correspond to the Elizabethan popular ballad, or
to the yellow journalism of modern times, though on occasion
they could rise to a somewhat higher aesthetic level.

To the earliest survivor of this class, *Arden of Feversham* (1592),
Kyd may have made some contribution. The plot is taken from
Holinshed's account of a wife who, for love of another man,
hires two ruffians to do away with her husband, a classic tragic
subject here "writ small." The passions of Mistress Arden and
her lover Mosbie are treated in sordid detail and the two killers,
Black Bill and Shakbag, are recognizable in their modern counterparts, the gunmen of gangster films. The play, largely concerned with the failure of various attempts on Arden's life, is
totally lacking in the elevation or vision of tragedy and stands as
an isolated example of domestic drama at the beginning of the
great decade of romantic expansiveness.

With the trend towards tragedy at the end of the century, the
domestic drama reappears in *A Warning to Fair Women* (1599)
dealing with love and murder in a middle-class London setting.
There are several other examples, including *A Yorkshire Tragedy* (1608) falsely ascribed like many anonymous plays to "W.
Shakespeare," and they are not all inferior as works of art. The
one recognized masterpiece of the form is Thomas Heywood's
A Woman Killed with Kindness, but even *Othello,* set in England instead of Italy, might be grouped with these plays of domestic crime and punishment.

Although it is the archetype of domestic drama and the one
example generally read, *A Woman Killed with Kindness* (1603)
differs from its fellows most significantly in that it is not based
upon English matter at all but is adapted from two or three
Italian fictions. This fact only emphasizes the remarkable realism,
the remarkable Englishness, of Heywood's art. No play yields

so detailed a picture of provincial life in Elizabethan times, the squires, their servants, their domestic affairs, their amusements. The audience is present at a country wedding, a below-stairs dance, a falconry match, a card game. The hero enters "as it were brushing the crumbs from his clothes with a napkin, as newly risen from supper," a homely touch as is the booting and spurring of the hero to ride out on a matter of business which replaces the familiar arming for battle of more elevated tragedy.

The action first establishes the completely felicitous marriage of Master Frankford and Anne, each party being almost a symbol of masculine and feminine perfection. Master Wendoll, bosom friend of Frankford, is driven by lust to cuckold him and the guilty lovers are betrayed by a loyal servant. Wendoll escapes and Frankford, instead of murdering his wife in wrath, sends her to live at another of his estates, vowing that he shall never more look upon her. However, when she is at the point of death, he comes to her and forgives her. She dies embracing him, a woman "whom her husband's kindness killed."

It should be noted first that Frankford's "kindness" does not consist in sparing Anne's life. The accepted punishment for adultery was not death but public exposure, after which the wronged husband was freed of all responsibility for his wife's support. Dramatically, this custom is developed at length in the concluding scene of *Bussy D'Ambois* where Montsurrey banishes his erring wife forever. Frankford, on the other hand, plans to continue to support his wife, even though separated from her. This is his "kindness," increased, of course, by his willingness to forgive her in the final scene:

> My wife, the mother to my pretty babes!
> Both those lost names I do restore thee back,
> And with this kiss I wed thee once again.
> Though thou art wounded in thy honored name,
> And with that grief upon thy death-bed liest,
> Honest in heart, upon my soul, thou diest.

In the second place, Heywood is at no pains whatsoever to motivate Mistress Anne's fall from grace. Deeply in love with her husband, a woman chaste in body, mind, and soul, she yields to Wendoll after two impassioned speeches and regrets her submission even before the sin is consummated. Since this unmotivated reversal of character is one of the most difficult of Elizabethan dramatic devices to accept, it must be emphasized that Heywood does not motivate because he is not interested. The focus of the play is upon Master Frankford, his actions and reactions. His wife must behave in such-and-such a way to motivate *him,* and therefore she does. For the motivation of the essentially chaste wife who becomes unchaste, we must turn again to *Bussy D'Ambois* and Tamyra. There the progress of her decline into wantonness is of primary importance to the plot, in arousing the jealousy of the villain as well as of her husband; it is presented explicitly and at some length. But Heywood's subject is the behavior of an honest man towards an erring woman whom he has loved. It is therefore enough that she err, and the situation is handled as economically as possible—too economically, perhaps, for audiences and readers who have been turned by modern psychology into motive-hunters.

There has been some not altogether unreasonable criticism of Heywood's dramatic extravagance in including the subplot of the feud between Sir Francis Acton and Sir Charles Mountford. At first glance it appears to be the conventional double plot used to pad out the story, and indeed the integration of the two actions is not very close. There are, however, certain parallels: Sir Francis Acton's attempts on her chastity are indignantly repulsed by Susan in the scene following Mistress Anne's submission to Wendoll; Sir Francis' scheme to win Susan by her gratitude for his rescue of her brother is set in the midst of Master Frankford's plan to trap Wendoll and his wife through overconfidence; Sir Francis' evil designs are put to shame by the sight of brother and sister hand-in-hand and determined to sacrifice themselves for honor in the scene preceding Frankford's forgiveness of his repentant and heartbroken wife. The parallels are closer in mood and tone than in action and only by visualizing the play as produced on the Elizabethan stage can their effectiveness be appreciated.

It is probably inevitable that this "simple and home-born" play should be more pathetic than tragic. Both the characters and the situations are dangerously close to sentimentality. Mistress Anne sins and repents at once. Sir Charles, having murdered in a fit of temper, falls a-weeping like a milkmaid who has upset her pail. Master Wendoll wanders through the concluding scenes stricken with grief. Frankford himself would be an almost impossible monster of perfection did he not try to kill Wendoll in his first rage, though he promptly rejoices that a nameless maidservant catches his arm and holds him back. To intensify her shame and grief Anne's two little children are paraded before her and she is at last led to describe herself as "a woman made of tears."

Pathos and sentimentality seem to be inseparable from domestic tragedy wherever it appears in the later history of the drama. It must be granted that Heywood has handled his material with affecting simplicity. The verse seldom rises above the situation into rant and never descends beneath it into disordered prose. Frankford's outcry as he finds his wife and Wendoll asleep in each other's arms has the precise amounts of the commonplace and the universal to be characteristic as well as moving:

> Stay, let me pause awhile!—
> O, God! O, God! That it were possible
> To undo things done; to call back yesterday;
> That Time could turn up his swift sandy glass,
> To untell the days, and to redeem these hours!
> Or that the sun
> Could, rising from the west, draw his coach backward;
> Take from th'account of time so many minutes,
> Till he had all these seasons called again,
> Those minutes, and those actions done in them,
> Even from her first offence; that I might take her
> As spotless as an angel in my arms!
> But, O! I talk of things impossible,
> And cast beyond the moon. God give me patience;
> For I will in, and wake them.

In the whole repertory of panoramic tragedy, the domestic occupies a relatively small part. The public, when it paid for serious drama, apparently demanded the larger passions and a less restricted vision of man; had bourgeois subjects been desired, playwrights would have learned to provide them. Instead, in the first decade of the seventeenth century, realism and domestic situations replaced the romantic as materials for comedy, whence, cultivated by the tribe of Ben, they were never wholly to be uprooted.

5. REALISTIC COMEDY

Realism, to be sure, had frequently played a part in comedy before 1600. The story of Mak inserted into the Nativity play, the farcical events ensuing when Gammer Gurton lost her needle, are sufficient evidence of the comic writers' instinctive resort to humble matter. Even Dekker's *Shoemaker's Holiday*, basically romantic in its determination to show that love conquers all, depends for much of its effectiveness on the rough-and-tumble commonplaceness of its chorus of cobblers. The rustics in *Gammer Gurton's Needle* are pawns in the game instigated and played by Dikkon, the Vice. Dekker's cobblers constitute an earthy *deus ex machina* used to bring about a happy ending for an apparently impossible situation. The comic realism of the years after 1600, on the other hand, is more than a matter of incident or character; it is a change of emphasis, a change in the motivation of the plots; it is an underlying realism of attitude and an all-pervading realism of tone.

As far as the story is concerned, the various actions and counter-actions of such a completely romantic comedy as *Twelfth Night* are intended to bring about a happy marriage founded on an ideal love; the emphasis is always upon the beauty, faithfulness, and poetic instincts of its men and women. In the realistic comedies with which we are now concerned, the purpose of the plot is generally the acquisition of material wealth as the acknowledged basis for a happy marriage; the emphasis most often lies on the stupidities, vanities, and weaknesses of its men and women. Seventeenth century realistic comedy thus becomes a parallel expression of that spirit of the age which led to the development of tragedy and satire.

About 1598, in the very middle of the period when Shakespeare was inventing his moon-struck Athenian woods and Belmont gardens, and his fairylands of Illyria and Arden, William Haughton set the scene of his patriotically-named comedy, *Englishmen for My Money*, in London's financial district. His plot is romantic enough: three English merchants triumph over three foreigners in wooing the daughters of Pisaro, a Portuguese usurer. Pisaro bears something of a professional resemblance to Shylock; his business dealings are close, not to say crooked, and in preferring French, Italian, and Dutch to English sons-in-law he is reproducing Shylock's antipathy to Christians. Like the earlier play, *Englishmen for My Money* is in blank verse, and great use is made of disguise for complicating and advancing the plot. The tone is good-humored, however, the various disguisings produce highly comic situations, and Pisaro gracefully accepts his inevitable defeat.

The play also differs from *The Merchant* in its insistence upon the "London-ness" of its setting and characters. Much of the dialogue deals with mercantile affairs and the customs of the Exchange. The menace to a happy ending is not the conspiracy of Neptune and the unfriendly gods of the weather but Spanish pirates. Some of the humor arises from the attempts of the foreigners to speak English and of the Englishmen to imitate them. One whole scene depends for fun and effectiveness upon an intimate acquaintance with the street- and place-names of London, and a Bellman plays a small but important part in the intrigue. However, the lovers are still dominated by idealistic motives and the acquisition of material possessions is of lesser importance to them than the winning of their sweethearts.

About this time also, Henry Porter returned to the realistic materials of country life in his *Two Angry Women of Abingdon* (1598). The very title suggests that it belongs in the native tradition of *Gammer Gurton,* although the motive and the cue for passionate anger between Mistress Barnes and Mistress Gourcey is marital jealousy and not simple neighborly bad temper. This is a considerable advance, dramatically, over the older play, since the action, instead of being instigated externally by a Vice, arises out of the characters. But the play is old-fashioned, for all of that, concluding with a long scene of farcical mix-ups in the dark, the two wives—completely in the tradition—kicking and clawing one another, peace being restored only when the daughter of one marries the son of the other. The dialogue, too, smacks of an older day. Father Barnes is attempting to persuade daughter Mall to hearken to her lover's pleas:

> BARNES. Well, this is it, I say 'tis good to marry.
> MALL. And this say I, 'tis not good to marry.
> BARNES. Were it not good, then all men would not marry.
>   But now they do.
> MALL. Marry, not at all. But it is good to marry.
> BARNES. Is it both good and bad? How can this be?

MALL. Why it is good to them that marry well,
   To them that marry ill, no greater hell.

In the light of future developments, note that at no time are
these country people satirized as rustics. Country customs are sympathetically presented. The country women are honest in themselves, if suspicious of each other; even the country knight with
a bad reputation comes to the aid of distressed virtue. Rural life
is neither romanticized nor sneered at; it is simply accepted as
proper setting and materials for a realistic comedy.

This new departure was fully acceptable to the audience, for
Porter's play was sufficiently successful to warrant a sequel, *The
Two Merry Women of Abingdon*. At least such a sequel was con-
templated and advance payments made by the theater manager.
There is no record that it was ever completed or produced, but
almost coincidentally there appeared in 1600 William Shakespeare's *The Merry Wives of Windsor*, which was both a sequel
(though to *2 Henry IV*) and a realistic comedy of country life.

It is only in its latter capacity that *The Merry Wives* is tolerable. As "The Further Adventures of Falstaff" it is a disappointment; indeed, its central figure is not the Falstaff of the *Henry*
plays but a witless clown. He is tumbled from a basket of foul
linen into the Thames; ignobly disguised as a woman, he is
soundly beaten by a jealous husband; wearing antlers, he is
pinched and burned by fairies in the woods—all to prove that
"Wives may be merry and yet honest too." That Sir John Falstaff
should be brought to this!

Fortunately there are other interests in the play. Shakespeare
has recalled his Stratford youth with affection, and *The Merry
Wives* is full of country life and pastimes. Page and Slender
discuss greyhound racing and Slender boasts of his daring in
handling trained bears. The gentlemen hunt deer and the ladies
are busy about their servant problems. Master William Page
demonstrates his aptness as a Latin scholar and rejoices in a
"playing day," when school does not keep.

There is a love story, too; a simple but important one. Mistress
Anne Page has three wooers: Slender, her father's choice; Dr.
Caius, her mother's; and Master Fenton, her own. Since Shakespeare makes it plain from the start that the play is a comedy,
there is no question as to which lover will win. Of importance

is Page's reason for opposing Fenton. Mine Host of the Garter Inn presents the young man's qualifications:

> He capers, he dances, he has eyes of youth; he writes verses, he speaks holiday, he smells April and May. He will carry 't, he will carry 't! 'Tis in his buttons, he will carry 't.
>
> PAGE. Not by my consent, I promise you. The gentleman is of no having. He kept company with the wild Prince and Poins. He is of too high a region; he knows too much. No, he shall not knit a knot in his fortunes with the finger of my substance. If he takes her, let him take her simply. The wealth I have waits on my consent, and my consent goes not that way.

Mrs. Quickly

To Page, the small business man, Fenton is a bad investment, an attitude towards marriage which later realistic comedies were to develop almost to the exclusion of the older idealistic notions.

In other ways, also, *The Merry Wives* is a part of the developing tradition of realistic comedy. Falstaff's assaults on the virtue of Mistress Page and Mistress Ford are doomed to fail before they are undertaken, since the ladies declare their honesty at once. Nonetheless, a large portion of the action is concerned with the making and interrupting of assignations, and a large part of the dialogue with various aspects of cuckoldry. Elaborate disguises are employed, and some humor is wrung out of the attempts of a Welsh parson and a French doctor to speak English. These are to become the staples of bourgeois comedy: burlesqued foreigners, loose-moraled city wives, wild young gentlemen, and a completely materialistic interpretation of the basis for marriage and a happy life. For the future, the scene shifts almost exclusively to London. Shakespeare's picture of Windsor is very nearly the last appearance of country joys and rural virtues to be set before a community and (inevitably) a theater that was becoming increasingly self-conscious and provincial.

Westward Ho, Eastward Ho, and *Northward Ho,* a curious trio of plays growing out of a theatrical rivalry in 1604-1605, illustrate the conventions of bourgeois realistic comedy. The first, by Dekker and Webster was performed with such sensational

success by the Children of Paul's that Chapman, Jonson, and
Marston were set to work to provide the second for the Children
of Blackfriars, a company that had hitherto devoted most of its
talents to romantic comedy. The good-natured contest (the prologue to *Eastward Ho* frankly confesses that its model "was good,
and better cannot be") was concluded by Dekker and Webster
with the third play, in which they took only indirect note of their
competitors by a gentle spoof of Chapman in the character of the
poet Bellamont.

In all three plays, the reader is at once informed *"scaene,* London." The action of the first transpires at such typical city meeting places as a brothel and an ordinary, or tavern. *Northward
Ho* includes a visit to Bedlam, the hospital for the insane, to see
what "merry Greeks" are there, and in *Eastward Ho,* the action
moves up and down the Thames from London to Cuckold's
Haven as one group of characters prepares to set out on a voyage
to the Virginia plantations.

In all three plays the major characters are citizen merchants,
their flighty wives, and the young rakes who prey upon the wives
and are preyed upon by the husbands. Justiniano in *Westward
Ho* first equates the merchants and their consorts as he upbraids
his own wife unjustly for receiving a lover.

MISTRESS JUSTINIANO. The gentleman you spake of hath oft solicited
   my love, and hath received from me most chaste denials.
JUSTINIANO. Aye, aye, provoking resistance: 'tis as if you come to buy
   wares in the City. Bid money for't, your merchant or goldsmith says,
   "Truly I cannot take it"; lets his customer pass his stall, next, nay
   perhaps two or three; but if he find he is not prone to return himself,
   he calls him back, and back, and takes his money. So you, my dear
   wife.—O, the policy of women, and tradesmen: they'll bite at anything!

The woman's point of view on the subject is set forth by Mrs.
Birdlime, a bawd who would persuade Mistress Justiniano to
make the most of her opportunities:

Strike while the iron is hot. A woman when there be roses in her
cheeks, cherries on her lips, civet in her breath, ivory in her teeth,
lilies in her hand, and licorice in her heart, why, she's like a play.
If new, very good company, very good company, but if stale, like old
Jeronimo [*The Spanish Tragedy*]: go by, go by.

Quicksilver, the idle apprentice of *Eastward Ho,* in rehearsing to become a young gentleman of fashion, reveals the characteristics of his type; he gambles and goes a-whoring, borrows recklessly and cheats inveterately, lards his conversation with playhouse scraps (notably from such plays as *Tamburlaine* and *The Spanish Tragedy* which had become laughing-stocks with the more sophisticated audiences of the private theaters), and prides himself on rising every morning with a hangover. For confirmation of the reality of the portrait, the reader may turn to Dekker's pamphlet, *The Gull's Hornbook,* but for dramatic purposes no confirmation is required. The would-be gallant is well adapted to the setting and to his place in the cast of characters.

In the matter of theatrical amusement or sociological information there is little to choose among the three plays. Each involves a complicated intrigue carried on with elaborate disguises. In *Westward Ho,* Justiniano, a naturalized Italian, suspects his English wife of infidelity and disguises himself as a tutor-pander in the hope of obtaining evidence against her. Since she is a completely chaste woman his stratagems expose his own jealous folly; but they also expose Mabel Tenterhook, Judith Honeysuckle and Clare Wafer, citizens' wives. These ladies are determined to "strike while the iron is hot," justifying their determination—*after* it has been taken—by the discovery that their husbands have been most devoted in attendance upon a notorious Mistress Luce. Nothing comes of the ladies' resolution; their virtue asserts itself, and they punish their husbands and their would-be lovers in a scene of good farce and high spirits. The theme, if the play may be said to have one, is that of their virtuous sisters of Windsor:

> We'll leave a proof by that which we will do,
> Wives may be merry, and yet honest too.
> We do not act that often jest and laugh;
> 'Tis old but true: Still swine eats all the draff.

Eastward Ho, taking the opposite compass-point from its predecessor, also takes a somewhat firmer ethical stand. The work of three eminent students of the classics who could also turn their hands to satire and morality, it nevertheless is willingly, if lightly, fettered to the conventions of the type. The moral issue is raised at once by the main plot, a standard situation of Roman comedy adapted to the business world of London. In place of the classical father with two sons of differing temperaments are substituted Touchstone, the goldsmith, and Quicksilver and Golding, his idle and honest apprentices. For good Jacobean measure, Touchstone is provided with two daughters; Mildred who is contented with her lot, and Gertrude who aspires to become a lady and escape from her bourgeois surroundings. The action of the play then presents a norm, or standard of bourgeois behavior, in the modest aspiration and happy wedding of Mildred and Golding, as opposed to the deviations from that norm, as Quicksilver and Gertrude come to absurd and total grief.

The comedy was a deserved success, both in its original version and in later revisions by Massinger (*The City Madam*, 1632), Nahum Tate (*Cuckold's Haven*, 1685), and Charlotte Lennox (*Old City Manners*, 1775). The complexities of the plot are skilfully handled and the catastrophes visited upon each of the foolish aspirants are suitably comic and symbolically effective, as, for example, when the braggart explorer, would-be abductor and penniless projector, Sir Petronel Flash is swamped in a rowboat off the Isle of Dogs, while his would-be mistress is washed ashore at St. Katherine's, a woman's reformatory. There is plenty of secondary humor in the play also. Gertrude's footman, through no coincidence at all, is named Hamlet, and is described as fit only to run behind her coach on the highway. Much is made of the current interest in the Virginia colony and Seagull, skipper of Sir Petronel's ship, describes it at length in the manner of a local booster, with details which some of the audience were expected to recognize as coming not from the Virginia countryside, but from Sir Thomas More's *Utopia*. Finally, as in these plays generally, great sport is made of the mangling of the King's English by foreigners, and here particularly by Scotsmen. The recent accession to the English throne of James VI of Scotland and his indiscriminate creation of knights (Sir Petronel was a "thirty-pound knight") were inexhaustible sources of humor.

Northward Ho was clearly designed by Dekker and Webster to cash in on the popularity of the title and subject matter of their first collaboration and the equally successful contribution by Jonson, Chapman, and Marston. Once again the plot concerns a merchant who fears cuckoldom, and a brace of gallants who would make free with the city wives. One of these wives, Mistress Mayberry, rejects the advances of Luke Greenshield who, in

revenge, boasts to her husband that he has enjoyed her. Mayberry's public pose is to understand that Greenshield is talking
about some other citizen's wife; in private he rages and storms
at his wife and will not listen to her protestations of innocence.
Wise woman that she is, Mistress Mayberry bides her time and
by the end of the play tricks her husband into an apparently
compromising position. And there the play ends with the wife's
comment: "Virtue glories not in the spoil, but in the victory."

The ending is typical of all three plays. No great harm has
been done to established morality in any of them; wives that
seemed loose were but sportive, husbands who feared horns were
by that fear made attentive to their wives, and the young gallants
thinking to make fools of the husbands were by the wives given
impressive lessons in being fooled. Only in *Eastward Ho* does
the action of the play overtly present a moral standard. In the
others morality is present by implication, as perhaps it was in
the daily life of the London merchant, whose code was that of
William Touchstone, goldsmith:

I will not be gallanted out of my moneys. And as for my rising by
other men's fall, God shield me! Did I gain my wealth by ordinaries
[gambling]? by exchanging of gold? no! by keeping of gallants' company? no! I hired me a little shop, fought low, took small gain, kept
no debt book, garnished my shop, for want of plate, with good wholesome thrifty sentences: as "Touchstone, keep thy shop and thy shop
will keep thee"; "Light gains makes heavy purses"; " 'Tis good to be
merry wise." And when I was wiv'd, having something to stick to, I
had the horn of suretyship [responsibility] ever before my eyes. . . .
And I grew up, and, I praise Providence, I bear my brows now as high
as the best of my neighbors.

There was, however, another sort of merchant with another
sort of code. He is a prominent figure in the world of Thomas
Middleton, the generally acknowledged master of Jacobean realistic comedy, a world whose colors are somewhat sharper and in
which deviations from the code of mercantile shrewdness are
punished with finality. In Middleton's plays the intrigue is no
less complex, the situations no less ingenious, and the humor no
less lusty than in the works just considered. But in their tone
and attitude lies a difference. The material values of an urban
society take complete possession of the stage.

The Middletonian merchant appears in a full-length portrait

in *Michaelmas Term* (1605-1607). Quomodo, a woolen draper, cozens Master Easy out of his country estate. The details of the cheat are given precisely and with much relish, as are the details of the cheat whereby the merchant in turn is done out of his ill-won profits. The play, that is, is but another variant of the ancient theme of the biter bit, but we are not expected to be prejudiced in favor of either the merchant or his victims. We are, rather, expected to accept the situation as a necessary part of an established way of life which Middleton presents to us almost as a case history, without indignation or approval.

So with Quomodo himself and his motivation the audience is to take it as a matter of course that the citizen should aspire to the status of a country gentleman—nothing is to be placed above the possession of "property" in the scale of moral, social or cultural values. Says the merchant:

> There are ways and means enow to hook in gentry,
> Besides our deadly enmity, which thus stands,
> They're busy 'bout our wives, we 'bout their lands.

And his factotum Shortyard replies:

> Your revenge is more glorious.
> To be a cuckold is but for one life;
> When land remains to you, your heir, or wife.

When the cheat works, and Quomodo takes possession of Master Easy's estate, he shouts with joy and anticipates future blessedness:

Now come my golden days in. Whither is the worshipful master Quomodo and his fair bedfellow rid forth? To his land in Essex. Whence come those goodly loads of logs? From his land in Essex. Where grows this pleasant fruit, says our citizen's wife in the Row? At master Quomodo's orchard in Essex. . . .

A fine journey in the Whitsun holy days, i'faith, to ride down with a number of citizens and their wives, some upon pillows, some upon side-saddles, I and little Thomasine i' th' middle, our son and heir, Sim Quomodo, in a peach-color taffeta jacket, some horse-length, or a long yard before us;—there will be a fine show on's, I can tell you. . . . To see how the very thought of green fields puts a man into sweet inventions!

Quomodo is gulled in his turn, but not as a punishment for avarice or unfair trade practices. In his eagerness merely to see what will eventually become of the land he has acquired he pre-

tends to die, thus hoping to learn what his wife and son will do.
He is thoroughly disconcerted when his "widow" marries the
very man he has cozened and returns the property to him.

Similar cozenings and similar characters occur in all of Middleton's bourgeois comedies. They appear also, as we shall see, in
the humour comedies of Ben Jonson, but there the vicious person
is exposed and the vice satirized. Middleton's interests lie in
intrigue and complex action placed in familiar London settings
and populated with familiar types. Morality enters only by implication and the sole virtue to be rewarded is cleverness; the hero
of *The Roaring Girl* declares that success in this world can be
achieved only

> By opposite policies, courses indirect,
> Plain dealing in this world takes no effect.

A Mad World, My Masters! deals with the attempts of young
Follywit to acquire before his grandfather's death that part of
his estate which is to be his by inheritance; if he achieves his end,
it is because he is clever, not because he is virtuous. And clever
he is. First, he gulls his grandfather, Sir Bounteous Progress, by
visiting him disguised as Lord Owemuch. During the night, he
and his comrades further disguise themselves as robbers, plunder
the house, then, reassuming their former disguises as guests, bind
themselves and pretend to have been robbed also. Next, Follywit
disguises himself as Frank Gullman, Sir Bounteous' mistress,
visits his home and robs him for the second time. Finally, with
his comrades disguised as travelling players, he undertakes to
present a drama entitled *The Ship,* first borrowing from his
grandfather certain necessary properties—a watch, a chain, a
jewel—which promptly disappear along with the strolling company.

Disguise is of course a basic device in a comedy of intrigue, but
few playwrights are as lavish in its use as Middleton. In *Your
Five Gallants,* all five title characters are disguised at one time or
another in the play, and Goldstone and Frippery appear in two
different disguises. In the case of Frippery, his second disguise is
that usually worn by Fitsgrave, and is so convincing that he is
taken for Fitsgrave by Pursnet, in disguise, who sets upon him
and trounces him soundly. In the masque of the final act, all the
gallants and courtesans assume disguises as actors, while the

gentlemen as spectators also disguise themselves. "To heap full
confusion!" In less skillful hands, the result would have been a
mad succession of unintelligible incidents with strange and unknown characters appearing on the stage with every new scene.
But Middleton's interest in intrigue comedy was equalled by his
technical skill in handling complex plots. Though masks run
riot, confusion is not there.

The most famous of Middleton's comedies, *A Trick to Catch
the Old One* (1605) simply reverses the plot situation of *Michaelmas Term*. Instead of a city sharper gulling a countryman, we are
introduced to Witgood, a country gentleman who has wasted his
substance and is plotting with his ex-mistress to gull his city
uncle, Lucre, out of his money. He is so triumphantly ingenious
that he not only bilks the old man of his money and marries a
virtuous London maiden, but manages to marry the "honest drab"
to Citizen Hoard, his uncle's bitterest enemy and business rival.
There is no moral justification for Witgood's success, unless it be
that Uncle Lucre deserved punishment for keeping from Witgood the wherewithal for continuing his dissolute course. But the
moral issue is not raised, in part because Lucre is as vicious an
old man as Witgood a young one, and in part because this is a
picture of reality and not a comment or satirical attack on it.

Some questions have been recently raised as to the accuracy of
Middleton's "realism." While it is true that many of his plots
bear a resemblance to the standard plots of Roman comedy, they
are not simply adaptations from Plautus and Terence. However
impossible they seem in bare synopsis, to anyone familiar with
the literature of the Elizabethan underworld (the *Cony-Catching*
pamphlets and *The Seven Deadly Sins of London,* among others)
they assume an almost documentary character. As in the *Ho*
plays, the streets, the taverns, brothels, and prisons, the shops and
merchants' homes furnish the background for the action, clearly
a declaration of realistic intention. Always there is the intangible
and unexpressed realism of the citizen-audience's attitude towards
material goods. Lovers are regularly separated by parental covetousness; in *The Roaring Girl* a ne'er do well son is to be cured
by being sent to debtors' prison: "No way to tame him like it.
There he shall learn what money is indeed, and how to spend it."
Profit and possessions was all the law, and terms that had formerly been reserved for an object of spiritual or romantic devo-

6. THE COMEDY OF HUMOURS

Side by side with the dispassionate, virtually objective, realistic comedy there developed about the turn of the seventeenth century the satirical, frequently bitter comedy of humours associated, for good reason, with the work of Ben Jonson. Actually Jonson was neither its inventor nor its sole practitioner, but under humour comedy his masterpieces may be classified, and nearly all the masterpieces of humour comedy are by him. As a type it is actually a blend of the conventions of classical Roman comedy and medieval Morality, and only in its satirical intention is it to be carefully distinguished from the realistic comedy of Middleton and Dekker.

The word *humour* has caused more than its proper amount of distress to modern readers. According to the medieval *materia medica* every man's temperament and disposition was determined by one of the four elemental fluids in his body. If blood were predominant the man was of a sanguine disposition; if choler, choleric; if black bile, melancholic; if phlegm, phlegmatic. By Jonson's day, the term was used more loosely, very much as modern psychological terms have lost their strict definition through popular use. In the Induction to *Every Man out of His Humour,* Asper [Jonson himself], in a burlesque of pedantry, clarifies his usage:

> Why, humour (as 'tis *ens*) we thus define it
> To be a property of air, or water
> And in itself holds these two properties
> Moisture and fluxure. . . .
> 　　　　　and hence we do conclude
> That whatsoe'er hath fluxure and humidity,
> As wanting power to contain itself,
> Is humour. So in every human body
> The choler, melancholy, phlegm, and blood,
> By reason that they flow continually
> In some one part and are not continent,
> Receive the name of humours. Now thus far
> It may by metaphor apply itself
> Unto the general disposition:
> As when some one peculiar quality
> Doth so possess a man that it doth draw
> All his effects, his spirits, and his powers
> In their constructions all to run one way,
> This may be truly said to be a humour.

For Jonson *humour* was some deep-seated characteristic—obsession might be a modern equivalent—which controlled the actions and reactions, the behavior and feelings, of any given man. Thus Kitely, in *Every Man in His Humour,* is completely dominated from the start of the play by a "humour" of jealousy which drives him from one act of folly to another. In *Othello,* on the other hand, the jealousy is implanted in the hero by the stratagems of the villain who, rather than Othello's humour, determines the direction of the future action. A similar comparison might be made between Ralph Roister Doister and Bobadill, the braggart warrior of *Every Man in His Humour.* Both characters typify cowardice and the desire for self-glorification, but Bobadill works himself into situations where he cannot fail to be exposed, while Roister Doister is directed by Matthew Merrygreek.

Each character in Jonsonian humour comedy is motivated by a single human folly, emotion, or desire, such as avarice, jealousy, vainglory, and from that humour derives his name: Cash, Sir Epicure Mammon, Littlewit, Fitz-dotterel, Sir Diaphanous Silkworm. After the second act of *The Staple of News,* several members of the "audience" discuss the play. They are old-fashioned, and object to the piece as lacking the elements of sixteenth century popular drama. Yet in their criticism they indicate how closely the comedy of humours is related to the medieval tradition.

CENSURE. Why, this is duller and duller! intolerable! scurvy! neither devil or fool in this play! . . .

MIRTH. How like you the Vice i' the play?

EXPECTATION. Which is he?

MIRTH. Three or four: old Covetousness, the sordid Penny-boy, the Money-bawd, who is a flesh-bawd, too, they say.

TATTLE. But here is never a fiend to carry him away. Besides, he has never a wooden dagger! I'd not give a rush for a Vice that has not a wooden dagger to snap at everybody he meets.

MIRTH. That was the old way, gossip, when Iniquity came in like Hokus-Pokus in a juggler's jerkin, with false skirts like the Knave of Clubs! But now they are attir'd like men and women o' the time, the vices male and female! Prodigality like a young heir, and his mistress Money (whose favors he scatters like counters) prank't up like a prime lady . . .

"But now they are attir'd like men and women o' the time, the vices male and female." The plot of the older morality was made up of the conflict of abstractions representing moral vices and virtues and the intent was didactic; the plot of the later comedy of humours develops from the conflict of men and women "of the time," each dominated by his characteristic human vice, folly, or virtue, and the purpose is satire.

The earliest writers of humour comedy were not students of the medieval tradition but classical scholars of some standing. Jonson prided himself on the observance of classical rules of construction and style and his two tragedies, *Catiline* and *Sejanus*, are full of long passages translated from Roman historians and orators. Chapman is perhaps more famous as the translator of Homer than as a playwright. John Marston wrote satires in imitation of Juvenal. It is not surprising to discover therefore that humour comedy copies many of the conventions of the Roman comic writers, Plautus and Terence, both in structure and characterization.

In characterization, particularly, there was little difference between the Roman and the medieval tradition. Both tended to create types—the ancient Jolly Companion can be equated with the medieval Fellowship, the ancient Adulescens with the Tudor Lusty Juventus. As the morality figure behaved according to the vice or virtue which he personified, and the humour character according to his dominant whim, so the character of classical comedy according to the type to which he was assigned.

The comedy of humours has also a third affinity—with realistic comedy. Although the settings of Chapman's *An Humourous Day's Mirth* and *All Fools,* and Jonson's first version of *Every Man in His Humour* seem to be declaring for the romantic tradition, which was of course popular when these particular plays were first produced, it is evident that for Italy or France we are intended to read London; Jonson admitted as much when he revised his play and gave the characters their corresponding English names. Indeed the declared purpose of this play, to ignore romantic nonsense and unrealistic language and situations, and to deal only with

> deeds and language such as men do use
> And persons such as comedy would choose
> When she would show an image of the times,
> And sport with human follies, not with crimes,

might almost be the epigraph for the plays of Middleton.

The major distinction between the comedy of humours, and
Roman comedy, realistic comedy, and the Morality, lies in its
satiric purpose. By exposing to laughter the follies of mankind,
it earnestly hopes to reform those follies and persuade mankind
to abandon affectation, exaggeration, whim; to follow the dictates
of reason and nature. Here, of course, it is at one with all great
comedy, whether it be the burlesque extravaganza of Aristophanes, the romantic fantasy of *Twelfth Night,* or the dialectic
wit-combats of Bernard Shaw. The words of George Chapman
establish the satiric direction of the comedy of humours: "we will
with rhyme and reason *trim the times."*

Chapman's first attempt, *An Humourous Day's Mirth* (1597),
seems originally to have been called simply *A Comedy of
Humours.* That title is indicative not only of the new dramatic
type which it introduces, but of the very structure of the work,
for the slight plot is a series of practical jokes intended to expose
the peculiarities of the *dramatis personae.* The play is given a
unity in that the exposings are arranged and carried out by
Lemot (who has himself a kind of humour to set people where
their humours will run wild) and in that three of the situations
in which he interferes are parallel: old Labervele is jealous of
his puritanical young wife Florilla, the old Countess of Moren is
jealous of her young husband, and the Queen is jealous of the
King. Further, the exposings are so arranged as to culminate
simultaneously in the fifth act scene at Verone's tavern. This is
a primitive kind of structure, to be sure, but it is the basic pattern
of the comedy of humours and it serves its purpose where a more
complex plot might fail. The interest of the spectator is constantly focussed on the *character* before him. He cannot fail to
be more concerned over the true nature of Florilla, who speaks
Puritan but behaves otherwise, than over the outcome of the
romance of Martia and Lord Dowsecer, the melancholy student.

The same kind of simple plot, practical jokes to expose folly,
makes up the action of Ben Jonson's *Every Man in His Humour.*
The types, or humours, presented can be ticked off without difficulty: Elder Knowell, the worrying father; Young Knowell, the
poetical student; Kitely, the jealous man, and so on. Out of the
contrast and paralleling of humours the structure of the play is
built—Kitely and Dame Kitely set against Cob and Tib, Young
Knowell against Matthew, Downright against Bobadill. Egged on

by the witty young gentlemen, Brainworm, whose humour is pride in his ingenuity and who is descended on one side from the medieval vice and on the other from the clever servant or parasite of Roman comedy, disguises himself, invents messages and rumors, and variously exploits the weaknesses of the other characters until all are assembled at Justice Clements' chambers for the final untangling. Since the Justice is himself a man of humour (both in the Jonsonian and more general sense of the word) no serious punishment is meted out and the characters depart satisfied or, at least, resigned; an appropriate ending for a slight play.

In *Every Man in His Humour* and the sequent *Every Man out of His Humour* Jonson was merely experimenting with a theory of comedy and characterization. The second play has almost no discernible plot, but is rather a succession of scenes in which humourous figures are satirically lashed and exposed by Macilente and Carlo Buffone. *Every Man out of His Humour* was not a success in the theater, and, although Jonson tried to justify himself by rushing it into print, the reason must have been clear to him. More than humours, more than satire, and more than deeds and language such as men do use must go into the making of a successful play. When he finally returned to the comedy of humours after various attempts at satire and tragedy, Chapman's second humour play and his own experience with such a comedy as *Eastward Ho* made plain to him the importance of the missing ingredient: a plot.

It might indeed be confessed that George Chapman's *All Fools* (1605) was somewhat too elaborate a lesson in plotting. Determined apparently to improve upon the simplicity of *An Humourous Day's Mirth,* Chapman selected from his classical models not one but two plots and added for good measure a subplot dealing with the familiar humour of a jealous husband. The main plot is also familiar, handling the favorite Terentian theme of the education of youth as exemplified by contrasted parents, one stern and one liberal. But the disguisings and sudden reversals of situation, while amusing and skillfully managed, require closer attention than the average audience of comedy is willing to bring. The intriguing slave of ancient Rome has been neatly "Englished" into a younger son, a student whose humour like Lemot's is to manipulate the lives of other people. In the fifth act, before the general unravelling, he explains himself to the spectators:

Fortune, the great commandress of the world,
Hath divers ways to advance her followers. . . .
My fortune is to win renown by gulling.
Gostanzo, Darioto and Cornelio,—
All which suppose in all their several kinds
Their wits entire, and in themselves no piece—
All at one blow, my helmet yet unbruisèd,
I have unhorsed, laid flat on earth for gulls.

Over-complicated as it is, *All Fools* was a guide to the intricacies of comic plotting, to the adaptation of classical stories to the Jacobean theater, and particularly to the fitting of the parasite or clever servant into contemporary situations. The scene is Italy, but no commentator was required to suggest that the audience need not stretch its imagination too far from the Blackfriars Theatre, London. Since Ben Jonson had been working side by side with Chapman, had even collaborated with him, it is not surprising that he should profit from his experience.

The fruit of this early experimentation was *Volpone* (1606), one of the greatest of English comedies though so bitter in its satirical exposure of mankind that it often verges on tragedy. The marks of the humourous play are at once evident. Although the scene is Venice, the Italian names of the characters are transparent: Volpone the Fox, Mosca the Fly, Voltore the Vulture, Corbaccio the Raven, Corvino the Crow. Scholars have pointed out the sources of these character names in the Beast Epic of the Middle Ages; for the average spectator, it is enough that they are all types of viciousness and evil. Set against them are the somewhat colorless, completely good hero and heroine, Bonario and Celia, and the burlesqued Englishmen, Sir Politick and Lady Would-Be. As a further mark of humour comedy, the humour of each of the major characters drives him at length to expose himself for the vicious fool that he is, and justice is dispensed to each according to his deserts in a final courtroom scene.

Volpone, however, goes far beyond the pattern of humour comedy. The beast-men of the cast are dominated not by whim or extravagance or such all-too-human emotions as jealousy or vainglory. Volpone, Corvino, Corbaccio and Voltore are slaves of avarice, one of the Seven Deadly Sins, and Jonson does not spare the rod in exposing their warped minds and souls. Corvino, for example, is incidentally afflicted with the humour of jealousy, but so great is his greed for gold that he will even prostitute his chaste wife to Volpone. Corbaccio will disinherit his son for the same passion. In the trial scene, one of the judges remarks in an aside that the corrupt and wealthy Mosca would be a suitable match for his daughter. And that no one may escape, Jonson throws the play into the laps of the audience in the mountebank scene.

This situation and its effect is one for which the Elizabethan public theater was uniquely adapted. Volpone, as a peddler of patent medicines, mounts his little cart in the "Venetian Square," actually the center of the outer stage. Around him stand the straggling supernumeraries who made up the theatrical mob, and around them the audience in the pit. As Volpone addresses the stage-crowd, he at the same time addresses the audience—and "sells" them his painless cure for all human ills for the smallest coin of the realm. All fools, indeed; not only the avaricious Volpone and his gulls, but greedy Everyman who believes in the illusion of something for nothing.

The play begins with a most innocent prologue, disclaiming any intentions of satire or railing, and pretending to introduce a "quick comedy" along strictest classical lines:

> The laws of time, place, persons he [Jonson] observeth,
>   From no needful rule he swerveth.
> All gall and copperas [vitriol] from his ink he draineth;
>   Only, a little salt remaineth;
> Wherewith he'll rub your cheeks, till red with laughter,
>   They shall look fresh a week after.

Such a prologue is better suited to Jonson's next three comedies; for *Volpone* it is, to say the least, deceiving.

These comedies, *Epicoene, The Alchemist, Bartholomew Fair,* are a little like Banquo in the witches' prophecy: "Lesser than *Volpone,* and greater." They are lesser in passion, in satiric intensity, and greater in comic spirit. *Volpone* ends with the administration of strict justice to all the characters, these plays end with the more general comic convention of forgiveness. They are laughing comedies, truer to Jonson's original avowal to "*sport with human follies.*"

The technique of the developed comedy of humours is very plain in *Epicoene, or the Silent Woman* (1609). The plot is simple and direct, the juxtaposition of contrasted humour characters. Morose, the old miser who can bear no noise, is brought together with La Foole and the Collegiate Ladies who do nothing but talk. The conjunction is managed artificially but effectively by Truewit, who thus exposes both extremes of folly. By this exposure Morose is punished, not *for* his humour but by means of it, for cheating his kinsman, Dauphine.

The structure and dramatic technique of *The Silent Woman* repay examination. In true panoramic fashion, the showing up of Morose is accomplished in three movements: in the first the approaching marriage is revealed to the audience as a trick of Dauphine's; in the second, Morose discovers after the wedding that his wife is only too able to talk; in the third, after he has been led to the final indignity of pretending impotence to rid himself of this plague, "she" is unmasqued as a boy. Unlike *Volpone* and *The Alchemist* part of the scheme whereby Morose is gulled is kept back until the final scene of the play. The audience, like Morose, does not know that the Silent Woman is only masquerading—again a skillful use of the Elizabethan stage convention for dramatic effect, since all "women" in the plays were actually boy-actors. The anticipated climax gains in comic effectiveness as the audience suddenly realizes that, while supposing itself completely on the inside of the whole gulling, it too has been fooled.

Typically Jonsonian, also, is the method of introducing characters before their entrance. They do not simply appear and behave in the manner of their humour; instead their appearance is anticipated and the audience carefully prepared by character sketches woven into the preceding dialogue. Thus, as Truewit describes Tom Otter at the end of the second act, Dauphine interrupts with, "No more of him. Let's go see him, I petition you." The device is intended to arouse in the audience the same expectation. It puts a considerable burden on the playwright, for the characters' behavior must thereafter surpass the sketch and the expectation, but in miniature it is typical of the larger Jonsonian structure.

In *The Alchemist* (1610), for example, the entire plot of the play is presented in the opening scene. As in *Volpone* (and indeed in such non-satirical realistic comedies as *A Trick to Catch the Old One*) the audience is immediately introduced to the "villains" and informed in detail of their scheme to gull the other characters. Then, one by one, the other characters are brought on and gulled. *The Alchemist* makes a further interesting contrast with *Volpone* in that the principal vice exposed is avarice and the schemers are themselves defeated by their own stratagems.

Constructed around the discredited and forgotten "science" of alchemy the play might be expected to have little attraction for subsequent generations, but few comedies have stood the test of time so well. There are sharpers in every age, and pseudo-scientists (even today) by promising miraculous results can acquire a wide following of credulous devotees, Subtle, Face, and Dol Common, were seeking the Philosopher's Stone which would turn base metal into gold. Their believers came to them in ignorance, but not in innocence, for their own selfish purposes. Few scenes in comedy are more hilarious than the efforts of Sir Epicure Mammon (his name fully characterizes him) to maintain the appearance of devout humility before Subtle while almost overcome with greedy anticipation. So varied are the victims of Subtle's art—merchants, puritans, roaring boys, law clerks—that the Philosopher's Stone itself expands from a particular stage-property into a general symbol.

*A Stage
Simpleton*

The structure of the play has been greatly admired, and with reason. Although the first scene would seem to anticipate merely a series of gullings, the seeds of the denouement are present. Face, Subtle, and Dol are obviously moved by the same greed which moves their victims, and only the slenderest thread of common interest keeps them working together; and it is evident from the start that although Master Lovewit has abandoned his house during the plague epidemic, he will one day return. Lovewit's arrival in the last act is the substitute for the law courts of *Every Man in His Humour* and *Volpone*. As a kind of *deus ex machina*, he is above the particular follies here satirized and hence dispenses comic justice and forgiveness with an unbiased hand. According to moral law, Subtle and Face are as deserving of punishment as Volpone and Mosca; but according to the law of comedy they have taken advantage only of those who were eager to be taken advantage of.

But when the wholesome remedies are sweet,
    And, in their working gain and profit meet,
He hopes to find no spirit so much diseas'd,
    But will with such fair correctives be pleas'd.

Bartholomew Fair (1614) is less tidy in its plotting, but as lively
and rowdy a public entertainment as its subject. The Fair itself
is the excellent unifying device for a series of plots and counterplots, becoming like the Philosopher's Stone a generalized symbol
of that which provokes men to folly. The play's two major plots
involve parallel romantic situations, the wooing of Dame Pure-
craft by Zeal-of-the-Land-Busy and the rescue of Grace from
Cokes.

This equating of the sanctimonious puritan with the addlepated
Cokes was only the beginning of Jonson's attack on the brethren.
Developing the sketches of Tribulation and Ananias in *The
Alchemist,* he draws a full length satirical portrait worthy of a
place beside Sir Epicure Mammon and, perhaps, the great Volpone. Busy is observed from every angle and in every conceivable
situation: he preaches, he prays, he woos. If it is wonderful to
watch him hypocritically bend dogma to permit himself to eat
pig at the Fair, how much more wonderful—and to an audience
which was growing resentful of Puritan efforts to censor the
amusements of the people—to see him completely outargued on
the justification for stage plays by a wooden-headed puppet in a
booth.

The typical denizens of the Fair are presented with great
relish: ballad singers, horse coursers, pickpurses, gingerbread
women, toy sellers, and, best of all, Ursula, the proprietress of the
barbecue stand, a comic mountain of flesh fit to stand beside
Falstaff for more reasons than avoirdupois. In Justice Adam
Overdo, Jonson satirizes his own favorite device for unravelling
a plot. In his zeal, his humour, to execute the laws, he goes in
disguise to the Fair to anticipate disorders and capture offenders.
But, Jonson seems to say, only a fool would insist upon order
in a Fair. There is a time and place for everything, even law and
order. Overdo should have practiced his wholly admirable ambition to be like Junius Brutus where it was desired and needed.
Like the ending of *The Alchemist,* the situation could hardly be
approved in a solemn court of law, but in a good-natured comedy nothing could be more appropriate.

No other play of Jonson's is so full of gusto or takes such true and lively pleasure in the everyday world in which it is set. In a sense it may be said to conclude the Jonsonian repertory, for none of his later comedies approaches it in technical skill or sheer good spirits. The shadow of Zeal-of-the-Land-Busy bulks larger and larger over the playhouse and the year of his ultimate triumph is not far off. Before that year arrives, however, some great plays are to be written and some curious developments to take place in the theater. The form which Ben Jonson developed out of the comedy of humours, temporarily eclipsed, was to rise with renewed vigor in final and enduring victory over its self-righteous opponent, "as fresh a hypocrite as was ever broached, rampant." Jonson's legacy, ably transmitted by his immediate heirs, the tribe of Ben, was the structural basis of Restoration comedy of manners, of eighteenth century sentimental comedy, of Victorian neo-classical comedy—indeed its vital force has not been entirely expended in the modern theater.

~~~ 4 ~~~

Panoramic Drama: The Third Movement

1. TRAGICOMEDY

Under the impetus provided by Marlowe and the other University Wits, the English theater developed its unique panoramic form in about a decade. In a dozen or fifteen years this form produced the magnificent repertory generally called Elizabethan (or Renaissance) drama. The decline of the form was slow, extending over a quarter-century, and interrupted with occasional flashes of familiar brilliance. Although it is easy enough to mark the terminal point of the decline by the closing of the theaters in 1642, it is more difficult to mark precisely its beginning. First evidences can be detected as early as 1608 or 1609, though several of Jonson's comedies and both of Webster's tragedies fall after those years. Perhaps no exact date is needed, since the decline, the decadence, is a matter of tone and taste, not years. When playwright and spectator had, in general, tired of satirical and realistic comedy and took little pleasure in *de casibus* tragedy, they turned their attention to sensation drama. In the theater, that is the beginning of decay.

Dominant in the final period of panoramic drama were two types: tragicomedy and the comedy of manners. They had appeared sporadically in the earlier periods; now they become characteristic. There is, traditionally, no accounting for tastes, but the shift in dramatic popularity may be credited in part to the increasing control which the court and the upper classes exercised over the theater. One of the first acts of King James had been to issue his personal license to the Globe company to perform officially as "The King's Men." Similar licenses were issued other companies, giving royal patronage to the "rogues and vagabonds" and in turn making them conscious of the tastes of the court. In 1608-1609, Burbage and the Globe company reclaimed their lease of Blackfriars from the Children of the Revels and commenced using that private, indoor theater for winter seasons. In the course of time they discovered that their receipts at Blackfriars were something over double their receipts at the Globe. In the theater this could mean but one thing: the Blackfriars audience would be catered to. Because of the theater's location and higher admission prices, it recruited its audience mainly from the upper classes, and their tastes were increasingly reflected in the repertory of the company. Other private theaters, like the Cockpit or Phoenix in Drury Lane, from their proximity to Whitehall, were even more strongly under the influence of the Court. As the Puritans made increasing headway in the middle classes, the players became more and more dependent upon the aristocracy and the various degrees of gentry, professional and academic. The striking effect of this reorientation on the theatrical repertory may be gathered from a list of plays performed at court during the winter of 1630-1631 by the King's Men. Of twenty plays, ten are by Beaumont and Fletcher, the court's darlings, one (*A Midsummer Night's Dream*) is by Shakespeare, two (*Volpone* and *Every Man in His Humour*) by Jonson, and one (*The Duchess of Malfi*) by Webster. During the years from 1615 to 1642, the court commanded three performances of *A Winter's Tale* to one of *Hamlet*. An examination of the new plays of the final period of panoramic drama will suggest that this is more than a mere statistic.

Sensation drama was not, of course, originated by the demands of the court; suggestions of it may be found in Shakespeare and the other writers for the popular theater in what may be called, with some stretching of the term, *problem plays*. In *Measure for Measure* (1604), for instance, Shakespeare provides a comic, or at least a fortunate, outcome for an essentially tragic situation. The play is now generally read as a parable of the Christian principle of mercy; one wonders if its appeal to its contemporary audience was not that of an insoluble problem solved by the circumstantial presence of a *deus ex machina*.

The two parts of Dekker's *The Honest Whore* (1604, 1605) seem even more clearly to be problem plays. In the first part, Bellafont, reformed by Hippolito, manages to persuade Matheo, her original seducer, to confer honesty on her by marriage. In the second part, Hippolito, the reformer and defender of the principle of chastity, is overcome by lust for Bellafont and attempts to seduce her. The latter situation is closely parallel to the situation of the corrupted Angelo of *Measure for Measure:*

> Oh cunning enemy that, to catch a saint,
> With saints dost bait thy hook.

Both plays are in the tradition of realistic comedy; Shakespeare's Vienna, like Dekker's Milan, is but a thin veil for Jacobean London. The intrigue is complex and the subplots deal with characters from low life, objectively observed. Some of the Shakespearean action transpires in a brothel, some in a court of justice, some in a prison; the action of the first part of *The Honest Whore* is unravelled in a madhouse, the second part in a prison for errant females. Although Shakespeare takes a firm grip on Christian morality and ethics, Dekker betrays a more popular attitude in combining the sentimentality of Hippolito's long preachment against prostitution with passages of *double-entendre* of the grossest sort.

The sensational had always been a part of the popular dramatic tradition from the day of *Cambises;* in *The Honest Whore,* however, it is a sensationalism not so much of action as of idea. Although the play is thoroughly moral in its conclusion, it toys dangerously with morality. Just such a morbid or prurient toying with moral standards was eagerly seized upon by the court playwrights.

A second ingredient was romance. Gentlemen and courtiers affected to scorn the romantic popular drama. This scorn was dramatized by Francis Beaumont in his satire, *The Knight of the Burning Pestle,* which failed when produced by a children's company at Blackfriars in 1607, but was completely successful in later revivals when the upper classes dominated the audience. Both Beaumont's youthful high spirits and contempt for the popular old fashion of playwrighting are equally evident in *The Knight* which, if we except Peele's *Old Wives' Tale,* is the first of a distinguished series of dramas burlesquing dramatic taste.

As the play begins the company is about to present a realistic comedy entitled "The London Merchant," an obvious reference to the *Westward Ho* type. Before the actors have fairly got their wind, they are interrupted by a Citizen who mounts the stage with his wife and demands that these "girds at citizens" cease, and that his own apprentice, Ralph, be put into the play to "do rare things." The ensuing play is a mélange of elements from the popular drama and from *Don Quixote*. In the "London Merchant," as the actors strive valiantly to present it, a virtuous 'prentice outwits a grasping mother for the hand of the merchant's daughter. The professionals must reckon with Ralph, the grocer's apprentice, who intrudes with his own plot, defeating a monster [a barber], wooing the daughter of the King of Moldavia, and otherwise comporting himself as a "grocer-errant." In his scenes, Ralph shows more than a passing acquaintance with the more extravagant moments of the popular drama as, with Hotspur, he hauls up drownéd honor by the locks and departs his theatrical life with a palpable paraphrase of *The Spanish Tragedy*. In 1607, the fantastic adventures of the romantic hero and the unrealistic attitudes of such as Hotspur were fit for burlesque by Francis Beaumont. In 1609, he collaborated with John Fletcher in the writing of *Philaster, or Love Lies a-Bleeding*.

Like Beaumont, Fletcher had written a failure, though in attitude *The Faithful Shepherdess* (1608) is the very obverse of *The Knight of the Burning Pestle*. Like *The Knight,* the *Shepherdess* was destined for approval some years later when the court dominated theatrical taste. It is a pastoral in the neo-classical tradition, involving a satyr and a river god, highly idealized country characters, and thrilling events. It rejects the realism with which commoners had been handled in comedy, finds miraculous solutions for apparently tragic situations, makes free use of song and rhyming speech, and pays frequent respects to sentimental notions of love and honor.

Disappointed at his failure, Fletcher blamed it on the unfamiliarity of the audience with the new type of drama with which he was experimenting. To justify himself he added a preface to the printed text defining *The Faithful Shepherdess* as a "pastoral tragi-comedy" and explaining: "A tragi-comedy is not so called in respect of mirth and killing, but in respect it wants deaths, which is enough to make it no tragedy, yet brings some near it, which is enough to make it no comedy." That is to say, tragi-comedy is not a juxtaposition of the grave and the gay but a mixture; grave events threaten grave conclusions which are averted in a skillful denouement at the last moment. The action

of tragedy and comedy is frequently the result of the nature of
the characters; the action of tragicomedy is wholly dependent
upon the ingenuity of the playwright. Modern critics condemn it
as "escapist" since it removes the audience to a fictitious world
where cause and effect are totally unrelated and where the laws
of nature and morality do not hold. Its popularity with a court
which was increasingly burdened with political and social troubles in its real world is easily predicted.

In 1609, the year after the failure of *The Faithful Shepherdess*,
Fletcher joined forces with Beaumont to write *Philaster*. The
locale of the action is Sicily, but it might as well be ancient
Greece or cloud-cuckoo-land; it is related neither to historical
events nor contemporary life. The plot is a tissue of familiar
situations: the rightful heir to the throne is pushed aside by a
usurper whose daughter he loves. The lady is slandered by a
jealous woman, the hero attempts to kill her in a fit of rage, is
arrested but saved from execution by a sudden uprising of the
commoners. The princess, who was only wounded not killed, is
restored to her hero (to whom she had been secretly married) and
the play seems about to end happily when the slander against
the heroine is repeated with apparently circumstantial evidence.
However, the "man" with whom she is suspected of having relations is unmasked as a woman. The King remarks as the play
ends,

> Let princes learn
> By this to rule the passions of their blood;
> For what Heaven wills can never be withstood.

The "lesson" is obviously to be taken no more seriously than the
dutiful reference to "Heaven." The will of the playwright dominates the world of tragicomedy.

Philaster invites comparison with *Hamlet* because of its inciting situation. Though such a comparison inevitably results in an
evaluation unfavorable to Beaumont and Fletcher, it is instructive in revealing the precise nature of tragicomedy and the level
of seriousness at which it aims. In Shakespeare's tragedy the emphasis is continually upon right reason and morality. His hero is
a scholar with a philosophical cast of mind; Hamlet is tormented
by the past, not only his own injuries but his father's. His opponent, Claudius, though evil, is hedged with divinity, an intelligent
man with both passion and conscience, a sturdy opponent for the

revenger. Hamlet is very nearly alone; his sweetheart is excluded from the main action; only Horatio and the grizzled spectre of his father are on his side.

The emphasis on *Philaster* is always on love and the various emotions, such as jealousy, that spring from it. The morality is questionable, as Philaster himself is outraged by the conduct of Pharamond and Megra, though his own relations with Arethusa are open to question, since their wedding has been kept a secret. Philaster himself is a paler Hotspur, a noisy defender of honor, surrounded by friends who take arms against his sea of troubles and end them for him. Unlike Hamlet, for whom the past has reality, Philaster promptly forgets his injuries as the play comes to an end. The King, his opponent, is a cardboard ruler without the attribute of divinity and is treated with notable indignity by the other characters. The leading lady's rôle is developed until it is nearly as important as the hero's, further emphasizing the love motif. And the ending of the play is the unveiling of surprises—the secret wedding, the identity of Bellario—which might have come at any other time in the play and put an end to the misfortunes of Philaster.

The verse of *Philaster* also invites comparison with Shakespeare. Purely as verse it is on a level with the finest Elizabethan achievements. Philaster's speech as he enters the woods (IV,2) is the essence of the pastoral attitude; Bellario's address to Arethusa as the messenger of Philaster stands not far behind its model in *Twelfth Night:*

> ARETHUSA. Does he speak of me
>   As if he wished me well?
> BELLARIO. If it be love
>   To forget all respect of his own friends
>   With thinking of your face; if it be love
>   To sit cross-armed and sigh away the day,
>   Mingled with starts, crying your name as loud
>   And hastily as men i' the streets do fire;
>   If it be love to weep himself away
>   When he but hears of any lady dead
>   Or killed, because it might have been your chance;
>   If when he goes to rest (which will not be),
>   'Twixt every prayer he says, to name you once,
>   As others drop a bead, be to be in love,
>   Then, madam, I dare swear he loves you.

This is good verse, but as dramatic verse it is mere hokus-pokus. It colors the situation and gives it a false importance; it does not grow out of the situation as in Viola's wooing of Olivia. Arethusa has made no secret of her love for Philaster. Bellario's speech is more decorative than organic. The same charge can be brought against the characters and the action of tragicomedy generally.

This is not to say that tragicomedy fails to fulfill its purpose, or that its purpose is worthy of condemnation. It is, however, important to recognize the *differences* between its methods and intentions and the methods and intentions of tragedy. The reader should also recognize the differences between these courtly romantic plays and such romances as *Friar Bacon* and *Twelfth Night*. Although the common theme is love, in the older plays it is treated from a masculine point of view. The woman's rôle was largely passive, the object of affection. If it became necessary for her to act, she was likely to resort to male disguise. In tragicomedy the heroine's rôle is equal in importance with the hero's; frequently it is superior. This again is a response to audience demand. In the social life of the upper classes women were a major factor; in a few years a new queen will introduce the modern French equivalent of the medieval court of love, and the masculine ascendancy in the subject matter of drama will diminish further.

Whatever the complexion and tastes of the Blackfriars audience, to the modern reader *Philaster* can have little but historical interest; it simply and obviously illustrates the characteristics of tragicomedy, a type which furnishes the largest part of the serious repertory of the latter-day panoramic drama. Other products of the Beaumont-Fletcher collaboration together with some of Shakespeare's experiments have more universal appeal.

In *A King and No King* (1611) Beaumont and Fletcher, not too boldly, take up the subject of incest. Arbaces falls in love with his newly discovered sister, Panthea; she loves him in return and he, deciding that love is stronger as a passion than morality as deterrent, prepares to indulge his sinful affection. Before the tragic event can occur, of course, evidence hitherto withheld is brought forward to prove that Arbaces is only by adoption the child of the late king and therefore neither king nor brother to Panthea. By marrying her, he thus legalizes his position and justifies his love. Two subplots are ingeniously interwoven, one paralleling the idea of a love-affair with insuperable obstacles to its consummation, the other paralleling in comic vein the pride of Arbaces which must be humbled. Mechanically, *A King and No King* is a perfect example of its type; the question arises, what is the function of this perfect machine?

The answer to the question is perhaps plain in the choice of incestuous love as a motive. No situation in a romantic drama could be more shocking, create greater tension in an audience. When handled as skillfully as in this play, no revelation than that incestuous love was honest love after all could produce greater relief and satisfaction. The purpose of tragicomedy was to arouse emotion by a series of shocking incidents and to relieve emotion by fortuitous and unexpected turns in the plot. The structure of tragicomedy is a series of scenes designed, in the words of Arthur Mizener, "to generate in the audience a patterned sequence of responses." That is, although *A King and No King* may be read as a play about the humbling of the pride of Arbaces, this theme is not kept constantly before the audience as, say, the humbling of Angelo in *Measure for Measure*. More than in the developing of a theme, Beaumont and Fletcher are interested in exploiting any given feeling to its limits without running the risks of melodrama, with which tragicomedy is closely to be identified. In a sense, this is the purpose of all drama of escape: to move the audience without insisting upon the reference of events in the drama to the actual estate of mankind.

Even *The Maid's Tragedy* (1611), whose title suggests a serious and morally oriented work, demonstrates how completely this emotional structure controlled the writing of Beaumont and Fletcher. The situations are made up of a series of highly theatrical ironies. Evadne, the King's mistress, requires a husband to cloak her dishonorable position. She selects the honorable, brave and intelligent young soldier, Amintor, already betrothed to Aspatia, one of her attendants. By the King's command, the honorable Amintor is forced to break his vow to Aspatia. Evadne's pride would not allow her to choose a fool, who might have been happily complaisant, and the King would not trust a less honorable man. All of Amintor's good qualities, then, lead to his unhappiness.

When he discovers his plight, he is at first enraged. However, as long as Evadne is firm in her resolve to remain true to the

King, Amintor takes no action. Only upon her repentance is he moved to attempt the King's life. He is restrained, however, by Melantius, Evadne's brother, who appeals to his sense of honor:

> Amintor,
> Think what thou dost; I dare as much as valour,
> But 'tis the King, the King, Amintor,
> With whom thou fightest!

The hero is immediately repentant:

> What a wild beast is uncollected man!
> The thing, that we call honor, bears us all
> Headlong to sin, and yet itself is nothing.

The irony here is doubled; not only was the honorable Amintor on the verge of the almost sacrilegious crime of regicide, but Melantius, whose fortunate interposition reminds him of his nature, is himself involved in a plot against the King's life.

Irony is, of course, a standard tool of the tragic playwright, but the ironies presented in *The Maid's Tragedy* have not the organic relationship to a theme or nucleus of idea characteristic of the greatest tragedy. They are related rather to the successive situations and intensify the constantly shifting emotions which the play is designed to arouse or gratify. Compare, for instance, the masque of the first act with the masque or play-within-a-play of *The Spanish Tragedy*, or *Hamlet*. In those plays the masque was a functioning part of the plot, advancing the action, bringing about the denouement. In *The Maid's Tragedy* it is simply added entertainment for the audience, a development of a traditional lover's plea. This conventional subject matter prepares the audience for a conventionally happy marriage and thus intensifies the shock of Evadne's revelation, but the elaboration is primarily to gratify the audience's taste for spectacular entertainment.

The skill with which this emotional structure is handled by Beaumont and Fletcher can be demonstrated from a number of scenes in the play. In the opening of the second act, Evadne is being prepared for her wedding night by her ladies. The first dialogue, between the bride and Dula, is the inevitable bawdy jesting. Into this gay, if smutty, atmosphere, Aspatia is introduced, the slighted maiden, to sing her beautiful dirge, "Lay a garland on my hearse." The mood shifts back immediately as

Dula contributes her little song of the inconstant lover. Evadne departs and Amintor arrives. There is a moment of sweet pathos as Aspatia forgives him and bids him adieu. The ladies exeunt, leaving Amintor to soliloquize his misgivings. But the entrance of Evadne drives away all idle fears:

> Yonder she is, the lustre of whose eye
> Can blot away the sad remembrance
> Of all these things.—Oh, Evadne, spare
> That tender body; let it not take cold.
> The vapors of the night will not fall here:
> To bed, my love. Hymen will punish us
> For being slack performers of his rites.
> Cam'st thou to call me?
> EVADNE. No.

Similarly effective are the scenes in which Melantius drives Evadne to repentance, and the conclusion in which Evadne, Aspatia and Amintor commit suicide. These scenes are only theatrically effective. The reader is constantly aware of the manipulation which has brought them about. Aside from Melantius the characters are not endowed with much vitality; Amintor and Aspatia are more sentimental than tragic, and the sudden conversion of Evadne, though perfectly conventional in the Elizabethan dramatic tradition, is melodramatic and unconvincing. *The Maid's Tragedy,* in fact, might be taken as the equivalent for an aristocratic audience of such a play as *A Woman Killed with Kindness.* Both are good theater while falling short of great drama, although *The Maid's Tragedy* is perhaps more sensational and is certainly superior poetically. A Restoration critic decided *The Maid's Tragedy* to be a "moral" lesson on the dangers attending incontinence, with the King as the central figure; in the eighteenth century, a critic felt the "moral" rather to be the dangers attending perfidy to a betrothed mistress, with Amintor as the central figure. However, the title of the play places the emphasis on Aspatia, whose rôle in the action is small. The modern reader may conclude that this confusion arises from the fact that there is no "moral" in the play, at least no fixed moral attitude, and to that the failure of the play to reach the tragic level may be charged. Although it concludes with the deaths of the major characters, *The Maid's Tragedy* belongs to the tradition of the tragicomedy.

Shakespeare, as a professional writer, was immediately aware of the revived demand for romantic drama and the corresponding development of tragicomedy. In the very year of *The Faithful Shepherdess* he may have written *Pericles, Prince of Tyre,* a sensation drama which rambles over most of a fancifully-conceived ancient world. Granted *Pericles* as a kind of trial error, in *Cymbeline, The Winter's Tale* and *The Tempest,* and in *The Two Noble Kinsmen* written in collaboration with Fletcher, Shakespeare demonstrated the same ability to transmute effective theater into lasting drama as, at the beginning of his career, he had done with chronicle history. In each of these plays, apparently insoluble tangles are unravelled by the romantic expedients of disguise and surprise; *The Tempest* even makes free use of white magic.

The Winter's Tale (1610-1611) takes up the theme of *Othello,* unwarranted marital jealousy, and finds a happy rather than a tragic solution. There are, to be sure, pathetic, if not tragic, events: little Prince Mamillus dies and the faithful retainer, Antigonus, is fatally clawed by a bear. However, both deaths occur offstage: on stage the sorrows of the first three acts are effaced by the chorus, Father Time, who "unmakes error"; the unhappy court of Leontes is replaced by the golden lads and lasses of the Bohemian countryside, and a statue comes to life to make the point that if sorrow and evil exist in the world, so do joy and goodness, and Time is a great healer. The theme is no more commonplace than the themes of the greatest tragedies; the point is that *The Winter's Tale* has a theme, a nucleus of idea. It presents a view of life and takes a moral stand as lesser tragicomedies do not.

The Tempest (1611) has been generally considered Shakespeare's last independent work, his farewell to the theater. Without stressing the fact that he is known to have had a hand in two later plays, it is the better part of criticism to examine it as a play rather than as autobiography or last will and testament. *The Tempest* is a tragicomedy according to our definition though it employs some of the technical devices of the masque. It illustrates the favorite Shakespearean theme of forgiveness and is, actually, a kind of final treatment of the revenge play.

Prospero, by the aid of his learning in occult arts, manages to bring all his enemies together on his enchanted island. He has been grievously wronged, deprived of his rightful office in the state, exiled, set adrift at sea with his infant daughter. His revenge should be terrible and complete since his enemies are completely at his mercy. Also under his spell are his two island servants, Ariel, the personification of various spiritual qualities, and Caliban, the very image of bestiality. Caliban, like Prospero, is seeking vengeance against the master who has, he believes, treated him unjustly. But in the final act, Prospero, like Ariel, changes his purpose from vengeance to forgiveness, releases his chastened enemies, foreswears his magic art, and returns to the world.

None of Shakespeare's plays except perhaps *A Midsummer Night's Dream* realizes so completely the fairy world of romance; none of the comedies is more economically organized as the vehicle for an idea. Early in *The Tempest,* Ariel sets out to find Prince Ferdinand and comfort him over the supposed drowning of his father. He sings a famous song, "Full fathom five thy father lies," pointing out that the tragic event has had a marvelous outcome:

> Nothing of him that doth fade
> But doth suffer a sea-change
> Into something rich and strange.

This is true of all the characters in the play. Prospero by coming overseas to the island has long since changed from an idle bookworm to a magician-philosopher, a man who puts his special talents to practical use. The evil men, shipwrecked, are changed through new experiences into good men; Ferdinand wins the love of Miranda. The heroine's joyous discovery may be taken in a double sense: "O brave new world, that hath such creatures in it."

The Tempest and *The Winter's Tale* show the possibilities of tragicomedy. Without ceasing to be fanciful or entertaining, it may still develop a theme and thus achieve universality. Such a universal theme will then give vitality to the work, enabling it to survive the changes of theatrical taste which accept and reject generation by generation those plays aimed solely at contemporary appeal. It is the universality of the themes that makes it possible for the most skeptical modern to accept the statue-scene in *The Winter's Tale,* or the magic and supernatural beings of *The Tempest,* while refusing to take seriously the concepts of love and honor which bring about the fortunes and misfortunes of Philaster, Arbaces, and Amintor.

The affection of the Jacobean-Caroline audiences for such concepts was endless, and playwrights who could manipulate them with ingenuity were assured of success. The extremes to which this ingenuity might go are well illustrated in William Davenant's *Love and Honour* (1624). The plot is so complex as to defy summary, but some acquaintance with it will illuminate not only the tastes of the Caroline audience but the later aristocratic audience of the Restoration. The brother of the Duke of Savoy has been taken and killed in battle by the Duke of Milan; in revenge Savoy has sworn to kill without mercy any members of Milan's family he can capture. The play begins at the conclusion of a battle in which Savoy's troops are victorious and the young Count Prospero has captured Evandra, Milan's daughter—and promptly fallen in love. Savoy's son, Alvaro, discovers Prospero's prize, straightway loves Evandra also, and, fearing that his father will carry out his vow, forces Prospero to secrete the lady until she can make her escape to safety. Evandra has a third suitor, a captive Milanese named Leonell. The vital problems are set forth at once and argued at length: should Alvaro obey his father (honor) or protect his lady (love); should Prospero serve his prince (honor) or announce his feelings to Evandra (love)?

But Evandra, too, has a sense of honor, and rather than let either of her Savoyard suitors suffer a breach of their sworn duty to their superiors, she tricks them into entering her hiding place, locks them up, sets Leonell to protect them (!) and prepares to give herself up to the Duke. Evandra's lady-in-waiting disguises as her mistress and persuades a courtier to take her to the Duke in Evandra's place, but Evandra overhears, dresses as the lady-in-waiting, and finally reaches the Duke. Both women are condemned to death and the execution is made ready. The three lovers of Evandra exchange confidences and discover their common love; Alvaro's reaction is completely in the tradition:

> O what a prompt and warm delight I feel
> When others' reasons are inclined unto
> My choice! 'Tis strange the senseless world should so
> Mistake the privilege of love, the best
> Of objects!

They then join hands and swear to effect a rescue.

As the execution is about to take place, Leonell steps forward
and surprises the Duke with the revelation that it was *his* father
and not Evandra's who killed the Duke's brother. He is promptly
substituted for the ladies at the block. At this moment a mysterious ambassador removes his false beard and announces that
he is Milan, Evandra's father, and the real assassin. He changes
places with Leonell, but before the sword can fall, a second
stranger removes *his* beard and proclaims himself the brother
mistakenly supposed dead. So much for the working out of
Savoy's vow. The love plot is disposed of with equal facility. It
is revealed that Alvaro had visited Milan in disguise some years
before and betrothed himself to Evandra's lady-in-waiting. The
lady reminds him of his vow, he resigns Evandra to Prospero,
and the Duke concludes the exercises:

> Come, to the temple, and let's join those hearts
> That with such pious courage have endur'd
> The trial of a noble constant faith,
> Whom tortures nor the frowns of death could move,
> This happy day we'll consecrate to love.

Love and Honour, coming after the vigorous dramas of the
Elizabethan and Jacobean theater, seems still-born. But it was
this play, with its thoroughly unrealistic motivations, its seesaw-
ing between one artificial extreme of conduct and the other, that
was revived almost at once when the theaters were opened after
the Restoration and gave the cue for the whole genre of heroic
tragedy.

2. TRAGEDY

While tragicomedy dominates the "serious drama" of this final
period, tragedy makes an occasional appearance among the new
plays and is constantly present, of course, in the revivals. Such
performance records as survive, however, indicate a decline in
its appeal partly due to the change in the audience, and partly,
no doubt, to the exhaustion of strong tragic situations. At any
rate, the tragedy of the third and fourth decades of the seventeenth century leans heavily upon sensationalism and shock in
idea and situation—the sensational and shocking *action* had been
inseparable from the greatest tragedy, whether it be Faustus conveyed to hell by devils, Lear buffeted on the heath, or Bosola
strangling the Duchess of Malfi.

Beaumont and Fletcher, singly, together, and in collaboration with a variety of playwrights were most nearly successful in *The Maid's Tragedy;* but their special genius was for tragicomedy and comedy. Philip Massinger assumed the tragic mask for *The Fatal Dowry* (1619), *The Virgin Martyr* (1620), and *The Roman Actor* (1626), earnest, dignified, and dead plays. Quite unexpectedly,

A Changeling

the greatest tragedy of the period is the work of the comic writer, Thomas Middleton, in collaboration with a playhouse hack, William Rowley.

The Changeling (1622) would be a remarkable play in any repertory. In a theater dominated by the easy optimism, the escapism of tragicomedy, it is almost unbearably passionate. The authors return to the earlier practice of tragic structure in setting up a double plot to dramatize their theme. The main action concerns De Flores, an ugly man governed by his desire for the heroine, and Beatrice-Joanna, who loathes him but will use him or any other person with cold calculation to attain her ends. In the course of the play Beatrice-Joanna employs the infatuated De Flores to murder her bridegroom, uses her maid-servant to cover up the shame of the price De Flores demands for his crime, assents to the murder of the girl and, in the end, betrays her tool without compunction. From an egocentric virgin, the action of the play and her own character have made her the most dishonest of whores.

The subplot, thoroughly unpleasant to modern tastes, is nonetheless closely related to the main action and serves the normal function of clarifying the tragic point. Antonio pretends to be a half-wit to win the love of Isabella, wife of the keeper of a madhouse. The connection with the theme of the play is stated overtly in the final scene:

ALSEMERO. What an opacous body hath that moon
  That last chang'd on us! here is beauty changed
  To ugly whoredom; here servant-obedience
  To a master sin, imperious murder;
  I, a suppos'd husband, changed embraces

With wantonness,—but that was paid before,—
Your change is come too, from an ignorant wrath
To knowing friendship,—Are there any more on's?
ANTONIO. Yes, sir, I was changed from a little ass as I was to a great fool
as I am; and had like to ha' been changed to the gallows, but that you
know my innocence always excuses me.
FRANCISCUS. I was changed from a little wit to be stark mad,
Almost for the same purpose.
ISABELLA [to her husband]. Your change is still behind, but deserve best
your transformation. . . .
ALIBUS. I see all apparent, wife, and will change now
Into a better husband. . . .

The most powerful scene of *The Changeling,* in which Beatrice-
Joanna is forced to yield to De Flores, distinguishes the play from
all but the greatest of its contemporaries. Here is no unexplained
yielding, as in *A Woman Killed with Kindness,* no sudden conversion, as in *The Maid's Tragedy.* Beatrice has effectively
trapped herself; however she may struggle, she has no alternative
except death. And death is the alternative to which her will to
live cannot permit her to turn. When De Flores demands his
payment as the murderer of her intended husband, she protests:

> Why, 'tis impossible thou canst be so wicked,
> Or shelter such a cunning cruelty,
> To make his death the murderer of my honor!
> Thy language is so bold and vicious
> I cannot see what way I can forgive it
> With any modesty.

With this sentimentality, De Flores will have nothing to do. He
recalls her to reality, and reminds her of her complicity:

> Push! and you forget yourself.
> A woman dipped in blood, and talk of modesty!

The point is made allegorically and dramatically, to be sure.
The beautiful Beatrice employs the ugly De Flores for evil purposes and, finding herself totally in his power, is changed into
a complete demon. But the point is made in human terms, also,
as Beatrice, completely degraded, protests that she could not
have acted otherwise, that Fate controlled her actions. For Fate
read Fortune, and the relation of *The Changeling* to the Elizabethan tradition is established. For Fate read Character, particular human motivation, and the relation of *The Changeling* to

the timeless and universal matter of tragedy is established. Passion has driven the guilty to destruction, and the moral order is restored, as Alsemero, the only character in the play not overpowered by willfulness, declares:

> justice hath so right
> The guilty hit, that innocence is quit
> By proclamation, and may joy again.
> Sir, you are sensible of what truth hath done;
> 'Tis the best comfort that your grief can find.

The moral issue is clear, and it is not necessary, as in tragicomedy, to invent a conventional tag to the effect that kings must be good if they are not to be bad. At the same time, however, the playwrights manage to convey a sense of pity for their unhappy characters. One by one they are trapped, not by a desire to do evil, but by a desire for that which in any other situation might be good. The epilogue of *The Changeling* is neither sentimental, nor coldly puritanical:

> All we can do to comfort one another,
> To stay a brother's sorrow for a brother,
> To dry a child from the kind father's eyes,
> Is to no purpose, it rather multiplies:
> Your only smiles have power to cause re-live
> The dead again, or in their rooms to give
> Brother a new brother, father a child;
> If these appear, all griefs are reconciled.

This is not the conventional appeal for applause, it is the convention turned to a larger human purpose, akin to the purpose of all great tragedy, to increase the spectator's comprehension of his own lot in life and his sympathetic understanding of those who are passion's slaves.

The strangely muted tragedies of John Ford were designed to illuminate the tragic theme in terms especially comprehensible to a court strongly influenced by the reading of Burton's *Anatomy of Melancholy* and by Queen Henrietta's cult of Platonic love. The melancholic had long been a popular dramatic type; Burton's treatise, a semi-scientific and exhaustive study of the humours, gave a certain authority to what formerly had been a theatrical device. As Jonson was able to construct a comedy by the juxtaposition and opposition of humours, Ford can apply the same method to tragedy. Melancholy is "the mind's disease," and the actor list for *The Broken Heart* specifies the "quality" of each character, very much as Jonson explicitly lists the "humours" of each of the characters of *Every Man out of His Humour*.

The Queen's revival of the medieval Court of Love may have been responsible in part for Ford's favorite theme: love as a dynamic force, which neither law nor custom can deny. Incest, adultery, erotic frustration are his subjects, and for those of his characters whom love has driven to sin he has sympathy, not revulsion. Incestuous love is treated with timid relish by Beaumont and Fletcher; but for his unfortunate Annabella, Ford has only "Pity."

> Love is the tyrant of the heart; it darkens
> Reason, confounds discretion; deaf to counsel
> It runs a headlong course to desperate madness.
> [Ford, *The Lover's Melancholy*]

The reader who approaches Ford's major tragedies with some knowledge of his background and intention will not be led astray by the sensationalism of his subject matter. In *'Tis Pity She's a Whore* (1633) it is not incest but love with which the playwright is concerned: the power of love demonstrated in the most tragic of romantic situations. There is a curious and significant echo of Marlowe's Faustus in the opening speeches of the young scholar Giovanni as he resolves to put away his learning and yield to his passion for his sister. The power of black magic led to the damnation of Faustus, the power of love to the damnation of Giovanni. Here is a reminiscence of *Romeo and Juliet* also, with the lovers divided by moral law rather than a family feud, and with an honest friar to guide and warn them. As Giovanni confesses his love and by specious logic justifies himself, the Friar replies:

> O ignorance in knowledge! long ago,
> How often have I warned thee this before!
> Indeed, if we were sure there were no Deity,
> Nor heaven nor hell; then to be led alone
> By nature's light—as were philosophers
> Of elder times—might instance some defence.
> But 'tis not so; then, madman, thou wilt find
> That nature is in Heaven's positions blind.
> GIOVANNI. Your age o'errules you; had you youth like mine,
> You'd make her love your heaven, and her divine.

Ford exercises considerable dramatic tact in selecting a vehicle to direct the audience's sympathy to lovers it would normally reproach. Annabella has three suitors: Soranzo, Grimaldi, and Bergetto. Soranzo has seduced the wife of Richardetto, Grimaldi is a dishonorable murderer, and Bergetto a fool. In their schemes and counterschemes to win Annabella, Giovanni's love is made to appear more honest—it is her beauty and her virtue that awaken his passion, not her social status or her dowry.

Although *'Tis Pity* begins as a love tragedy it soon turns into a revenge play. The conventions, however, have been transmuted almost beyond recognition. The moral issue raised and argued by Shakespeare, Tourneur and Webster, is never referred to— vengeance is simply a device for complicating and advancing the plot. It is an ingenious structure: three men love Annabella. Thwarted by her love for her brother, two turn to seeking revenge: Grimaldi on Soranzo, and Soranzo on Annabella; Bergetto, the fool, is content to wed the daughter of Richardetto and Hippolita. Three characters seek revenge on Soranzo: Richardetto for his wife's seduction, Hippolita for his desertion, and Grimaldi as his rival for Annabella. The outcome of each of the revenge schemes is very useful to the maintenance of the plot interest, but is in every case accidental. The action transpires in a world of moral anarchy like the world of tragicomedy. Giovanni's final entrance, with Annabella's heart upon his dagger is so violent a shock that the reader fairly sympathizes with those older critics who label the playwright decadent and his audience as jaded.

The Broken Heart (c. 1632) is perhaps a fairer test of the power of "psychological" tragedy to arouse pity, since it does not involve so abnormal an example of love-madness. Once again the theme is vengeance growing out of a frustrated love-affair. Orgilus and Penthea are in love, but the lady is forced by her brother Ithocles to wed a nobleman, Bassanes. Orgilus comes to her after the marriage and claims that by the laws of love (that is to say, Platonic Love) she is his wife. Penthea does not deny her love for him, but she is determined to prove chaste.

> ORGILUS. . . . . advise thee better:
> Penthea is the wife to Orgilus
> And ever shall be.
> PENTHEA. Never shall nor will.

Her chastity, her resistance to the fateful pressure of love drives her out of her wits. From her ravings it becomes apparent that she conceives of herself as an adulteress:

> There is no peace left for a ravish'd wife
> Widow'd by lawless marriage; to all memory
> Penthea's, poor Penthea's, name is strumpeted.

She dies, the victim of love though completely virtuous.

Ithocles, her brother, becomes smitten with love for the princess Calantha who is about to wed the prince of a neighboring country. Thus, ironically, Ithocles comes to appreciate the wrong which he has done his sister in forcing her to marry without love. Before his penitence can make itself felt, however, he is trapped by Orgilus and killed for vengeance. This scene is comparable in shock and violence to the final entrance of Giovanni in *'Tis Pity*.

It is followed, however, by two remarkable scenes in which the focus of the play shifts to Calantha, the princess. While dancing at the wedding of Prophilus, friend of Ithocles, and Euphranea, sister of Orgilus, she is informed successively of the deaths of her father, her friend Penthea, and her beloved Ithocles. With noble self-control she refuses to interrupt the ceremonies and only at the end of the dance proclaims herself Queen. In the final scene, effective use is made of spectacle and music as Calantha weds the corpse of Ithocles:

> Thus I new-marry him whose wife I am
> Death shall not separate us;

and dies of a broken heart.

It is possible, if not easy, to dismiss these plays as too unreal for tragedy. Yet in the world of his own creation, Ford's characters behave in appropriate fashion. Recall that it is a world created to embody the special attitudes towards passion and reason represented by Burton and the cult of Platonic love. For those who cannot tolerate impediments to the marriage of true minds, *The Broken Heart* and *'Tis Pity* are genuine tragedies.

It is common to praise Ford as a poet, but it is only just to point to his skill as a dramatist. His complex plots are handled with ease. The situations, save for an occasional unhappy effort at comedy, all derive from or are related to the central idea; and much of the action has the virtue of being dramatized metaphor, as in the two last scenes of *The Broken Heart*. Added to this rather mechanical virtue are Ford's talent for grave and musical verse and his human pity and understanding.

As much cannot be said for those of his fellows who essayed tragedy. Typical of their ingenious but unsuccessful efforts to arouse pity and terror is James Shirley's *The Cardinal* (1641) with its mechanically perfect plot of three successive and interlocking revenges: Colombo on Alvarez, the Duchess on Colombo, and the Cardinal on the Duchess. The play is, quite simply, a thriller, a swiftly-moving series of unexpected reversals which the author was pleased to think the best of his not inconsiderable "flock." The prologue carefully conceals from the spectator the nature of the play; we are kept in the dark as to whether it will be comic or tragic, and many of the devices Shirley employs are the devices of tragicomedy. There is no question, however, that it is meant for tragedy since the bad bleed profusely. Though the play cannot fail to arouse and hold interest, it does not awaken sympathy. Here, at the very end of the career of panoramic drama is a play that is completely in the tradition and yet falls short of genuine tragedy. One is conscious always of the author's hand as in tragicomedy; the world of the action is not sufficiently convincing for unquestioning acceptance of the events that transpire within it; the characters of the play are stock types propelled about the stage without much attempt on Shirley's part to understand them. The speech is dutifully elevated to poetry, but like a once-celebrated brand of toothpaste, it comes out like a ribbon and lies flat.

It is probably fruitless to search for the ultimate cause of the utter collapse of panoramic tragedy. In part the audience and in part the playwright must bear the responsibility. The fact here is the important thing: the great tragic period had ended, and the ideal combination of a dramatic form, a group of dramatic poets, and a widely-accepted tragic view was never to recur. When, in the year after the production of *The Cardinal*, the Puritans found a means of closing the playhouses the action was unconsciously symbolic. Panoramic tragedy was dead.

3. COMEDY OF MANNERS

The comedy of manners made its first appearance in the English theater about 1620. Like most dramatic classifications, comedy of manners may be defined in various ways, but in its origins it was intended to be a joyous and witty reflection of the fashionable life of its time. Accepting without question the social code of the upper classes, it is a development of the realistic comedy of Middleton and the humour comedy of Jonson.

The comedy of humours was not, of course, completely superseded by the new type. In the works of "The Sons of Ben," followers of Jonson like William Cartwright and Richard Brome, it continued with only slight modifications to attract audiences to the public theaters. These modifications are best illustrated by Philip Massinger's *A New Way to Pay Old Debts* (*c.* 1625) which combines the Jonsonian humours with the intrigue of realistic city comedy. A villainous extortioner, Sir Giles Overreach, is cheated out of his ill-gotten gains by a clever deceit practised by Frank Wellborn, his nephew. Wellborn, one of his uncle's victims, pretends to be the prospective husband of a wealthy widow, Lady Allworth, and Sir Giles, blinded with joy at the prospect of robbing the same victim twice, returns his nephew's property and is bilked of his own. It is not an original plot; if Sir Giles had spent more time in the theater and less in his counting-room, he would have realized that he was being cheated as Pecunius Lucre was cheated by *his* nephew in *A Trick to Catch the Old One*. That Massinger was aware of the source of his intrigue is evident from his awkward attempts to disguise it. Middleton in his opening scene presents Witgood and his mistress discussing their whole plan; Massinger begins his intrigue with a whispered confidence between Wellborn and Lady Allworth, and keeps the audience in the dark as long as possible. A similar device of a secret confidence is employed in the secondary plot as Lord Lovell pretends to woo Margaret while actually assuring her of his assistance in thwarting Overreach. The sudden introduction of a document written in disappearing ink does not add to the verisimilitude of the events. The most conventional situation of the revenge play is employed for denouement as the tool villain turns upon his employer and publicly exposes him.

If an example of decadence in the panoramic drama is required,

it is surely in such inability to conceive new and vital situations
and in the failure to clothe the old in anything more than
reminiscent, if serviceable, blank verse. Even Sir Giles, drawn
from the notorious contemporary figure of Sir Giles Mompesson,
is a kind of Volpone. Says one of his servants:

> Such a spirit to dare and power to do were never
> Lodg'd so unluckily.

As his nephew tries to worm his purposes out of him, Sir Giles declares his
"atheism": "My thoughts are mine and
free." Like Volpone, he is the biter bit,
caught in the trap erected by his own avarice.

The difference, the originality of Massinger, lies in the changed tone of the play.
Watching the machinations of Volpone or
Subtle, the audience can take a certain
pleasure in the way their (admittedly evil)
devices get the best of a series of fools
before leading to their own downfall. For

*William Rowley as
The Fat Bishop in
A Game at Chess*

Sir Giles there is only loathing; he is not a
fox, but a wolf, a vulture, a terrifying figure. Nor, as in *A Trick to Catch the Old
One,* is the audience beguiled by watching the triumphant career of a prostitute made honest through the intrigue. For Middleton's Jane, a courtesan, Massinger employs the respectable,
sentimental, and honest Lady Allworth. The whole atmosphere
of delight in immoral skullduggery is changed in Hazelton
Spenser's phrase, to one "sweating moral earnestness at every
pore." That this is not an isolated instance may be shown from
Massinger's *The City Madam* (1632) which similarly elevates the
plot of *Eastward Ho.*

Elevation, but not moral earnestness, is also characteristic of
the comedy of manners. Shoemakers and 'prentices and merchants
and their wives have little place in its cast of characters. The
court of Charles I, cut off from the bourgeois world of London,
desired to see itself and its interests dramatized. Playwrights, of
course, hastened to oblige, and witty young gentlemen and their
witty young mistresses take possession of most of the stage.

These plays and their characters were not to popular taste which continued to patronize revivals and imitations of old thrillers and romances in the public theaters. On one occasion in 1640, the Blackfriars company was forced to produce a court comedy at the old Globe and the author, James Shirley, equipped it with a none too complimentary, but revealing prologue:

> All that the Prologue comes for is to say
> Our author did not calculate this play
> For this meridian. . . .
> No shows, no dance, and what you most delight in,
> Grave understanders, here's no target fighting
> Upon the stage; all work for cutlers barr'd,
> No bawdery, nor no ballads—this goes hard—
> But language clean, and what effects you not;
> Without improbabilities the plot;
> No clown, no squibs, no devil in't; oh now
> You squirrels that want nuts, what will you do? . . .
> But you that can contract yourselves, and sit
> As you were now in Blackfriars pit,
> And will not deaf us with lewd noise and tongues,
> Because we have no heart to break our lungs,
> Will pardon our vast stage, and not disgrace
> This play, meant for your persons, not the place.

The isolation of the court and the courtly drama, so clearly expressed in Shirley's prologue, manifested itself also in the elaborate masques designed exclusively for aristocratic audiences, and in the plays written by wealthy amateurs, like Sir John Suckling. King Charles I himself, took great interest in the theater, suggesting to Shirley the plot of *The Gamester* (1633) and being complacently satisfied with the result. Queen Henrietta took part with her ladies in a pastoral drama. So closely did the comedy of manners mirror its audience that the censor required Shirley to make extensive alterations in his comedy *The Ball* (1632) after it had been acted by the Queen's men, because "there were divers [im]personated so naturally, both of lords and others of the court, that I took it ill."

On the surface, the comedy of manners seems closer to the older comedy of humours than is actually the case. The cast is frequently filled with Allworths and Littlewits and Scentloves and Kickshaws who are clearly indebted to the Subtles and Dol Commons of Jonson for their nomenclature. It will be noticed, however, that the so-called humour names of the comedy of manners do not inevitably designate temperaments or even dominant characteristics, but quite frequently professions or occupations; Master Haircut is a barber, Furnace, a cook, Madame Decoy, a bawd. Intrigue is the essence of the plot of the comedy of manners as of the comedy of humours, but it is often intrigue for its own sake, not for the sake of satire. The satire of the later form, in fact, is almost wholly directed at country characters, who are too dull to understand the courtly code, or at vulgar pretenders, who are too foolish to recognize their own inability to fit into the world of fashion. It is in this matter of worlds, in fact, that the major difference lies. The comedy of humours deals in universals, with the eccentrics of the world-at-large; the comedy of manners is concerned with its own small world, as artificial and as isolated as the special world of tragicomedy.

One of the earliest, and certainly one of the best, of the comedies of manners is *The Wild Goose Chase* (1621). It was so pleasing when first produced that even its naturally modest author, John Fletcher, found himself applauding the "rare issue of his brain" in the midst of the thronged theater. And well he might for the play is written in his sprightliest blank verse and makes merry with three love-affairs interwoven in a multiplicity of incidents and with remarkably little confusion. This is due, perhaps, to Fletcher's use of an adulterated comedy of humours pattern. Instead of juxtaposing intense passions and playing them off against each other, he creates three young gentlemen of varying "humours" or attitudes concerning the opposite sex: Mirabel the Wild Goose, "a great defier of all ladies in the way of marriage," Pinac, "of a lively spirit," and Belleur, "of a stout, blunt humour." Mirabel is opposed to Oriana who declares vigorously that "my thing is marriage," the sprightly Pinac to the apparently serious-minded Lillia-Bianca, and the bluff Belleur to the "airy" Rosalura.

In a series of four moves, the young men are mated. In the first the dashing Pinac puts on a serious mien and goes after his "frozen snowball" while Belleur is emboldened to attempt the apparently silent Rosalura. Oriana meanwhile announces her intentions regarding Mirabel, only to be laughed at when she mentions marriage. Mirabel's companions are completely thwarted when their ladies turn out to be in the first instance

giddy and pleasure seeking and in the second voluble to a fault.
In the second move, the pursuers fare better by a series of decep-
tions, Pinac pretending to be betrothed, Belleur inventing an
excuse to lose his temper and with it his stage-fright, and Oriana,
on the other side, pretending to have a wealthy suitor to arouse
Mirabel's interest. Oriana alone fails: Pinac and Belleur are
momentarily successful. In the third move the pursued once more
triumph as the two over-confident young men expose their devices and are thoroughly mocked by their young ladies. Oriana,
however, is almost successful. Mirabel is informed that she is near
death, and her performance is so convincing that he is very nearly
trapped:

> Is't possible my nature
> Should be so damnable, to let her suffer?
> Give me your hand.

He announces that he repents his cruelty "truly," but when he
sees that he has been deceived, he reneges. In the fourth move,
as anticipated, all the lovers are united, Pinac and Belleur made
into reasonable facsimiles of acceptable gentlemen and Mirabel
into a willing husband. Oriana's final trick is somewhat extreme,
not to say obvious, but perhaps the object of the chase had realized that final escape from so determined a pursuer was impossible. At any rate, he concludes, "We have won o' both sides."

Aside from the dexterity of the plotting, the character of
Mirabel is perhaps the most interesting aspect of *The Wild Goose
Chase*. Unlike the normal hero of romantic comedy, he is the
pursued not the pursuer. To him, also, are attributed a series of
affairs of the most unsavory sort, of which he boasts, and which '
do not in any way diminish his credit with the respectable ladies
of the cast. It is to be noted, however, that Mirabel *talks* a check-
ered past. After one of his boasts, Oriana's brother declares his
skepticism:

> I believe ye as ever I knew ye
> A glorious talker, and a legend-maker
> Of idle tales and trifles; a depraver
> Of your own truth; their honors fly about ye!

Mirabel is not unsentimental. When Oriana appears to be dying,
she stirs his heart. When she appears to have gone mad for love
of him, he is totally lost, even after he realizes the trick:

> I thank you! I am pleased you have deceived me,
> And willingly I swallow it, and joy in't.

Then he must add "And yet, perhaps, I knew you," not so boldly as Falstaff but for the same purpose.

The typical Caroline comedy of manners will follow the pattern of *The Wild Goose Chase*. Its action will be wooing and its goal matrimony; wild young gentlemen will reform "truly" in the final scene; there will be much talk of loose sexual behavior, but little evidence of it. The morality of these plays, while seldom referred to in the dialogue, is sound enough, and the chief delight which they yield to an audience is the universally enjoyed experience of a love-chase, with a priest in view.

The favorite playwright of the court of Charles I, and the major producer of its comedies of manners was James Shirley, author of the decadent revenge play, *The Cardinal*. If his comedies are no less imitative in plot, they are fresh in tone and accurate mirrors of the taste and temperament of their audiences. Like Fletcher he retains the nomenclature and blank verse of the Jonsonian humour comedy but employs them as vehicles for intrigue comedy rather than satire. Like the writers of realistic city comedy, he prefers his action to take place in scenes familiar to Londoners, but to Londoners of the upper classes. Thus, instead of assembling his characters at Bartholomew Fair for a general exposition of the vices and follies of mankind, he takes them to Hyde Park to unravel romantic complications.

The comedy of *Hyde Park* (1632) makes good use of public interest in the newly opened pleasure-garden to add novelty to a somewhat hackneyed plot. The subject is again a triple wooing, with humour complications. Fairfield is after the wilful Carol, who is resolved to surrender none of her liberties; Lacy pursues Mrs. Bonavent whose husband has been missing at sea for seven years; and Trier woos Julietta but insists on making an extreme test of her chastity at the same time. The play has more than its share of light talk, but Julietta holds a firm moral line and does not hesitate to put the lascivious Lord Bonvile in his place:

> I must
> Be bold to tell you, sir, unless you prove
> A friend to virtue, were your honor centupled,
> Could you pile titles till you reach the clouds,

Were every petty manor you possess
A kingdom, and the blood of many princes
United in your veins, with these had you
A person that had more attraction
Than poesy can furnish love withal,
Yet I, I in such infinite distance, am
As much above you in my innocence.

After more of such speeches, Lord Bonvile remarks aside, "I do
not like myself," and soon reforms. It is important to notice such
situations and their handling by the court's favorite poet in the
light of the multiplying attacks by Puritans on the immorality of
the drama.

Hyde Park, and Caroline manners comedy generally, does not
go very deeply into the relationship between the sexes. It was
more interested in clever intrigue and the lighter aspects of the
game of finding a husband or wife. Towards the end of the
seventeenth century, however, the same kind of comedy was to
become more completely occupied with the realistic problems of
marital life. As a foretaste of the most famous solution presented
by this later comedy, the "proviso scene" of Congreve's *The Way
of the World,* it is worth noticing the "proviso scene" in *Hyde
Park.*

It develops out of the scheme of Fairfield to win the hand of
Mistress Carol. After a series of futile attempts he bids her farewell and requests that she grant him one boon. She is, not un-
naturally, suspicious and he assures her she may make any exceptions before he names the "boon." Still suspicious, she exempts
herself from loving him, marrying him, giving him any of her
possessions, and is then about to promise to grant his unnamed
boon, when a fashionable thought strikes her:

stay,
You shall not ask me before company
How old I am, a question most untoothsome.
I know not what to say more; I'll not be
Bound from Spring-Garden, and the 'Sparagus.
I will not have my tongue tied up, when I've
A mind to jeer my suitors, among which
Your worship shall not doubt to be remember'd,
For I must have my humour, I am sick else;
I will not be compell'd to hear your sonnets,
A thing before I thought to advise you of. . . .

The boon that Fairfield requests is that she shall never desire his company again—which of course provokes the wilful lady into desiring his presence for the first time. The "provisos" are not very serious, being the efforts of a humourous lady to live up to her humours, and they are only a device to advance the plot, yet they do reveal something of the growing independence of women which was to provide one of the major themes of the great period of English comedy of manners after the Restoration.

Shirley's *The Lady of Pleasure* (1635) is a step further towards the studied immorality of Restoration comedy. The moral note is still sounded, but it is muted and it is sounded late. The double plot juxtaposes the reckless Lady Bornwell, coming to the city in the pursuit of pleasure, and restored to her senses by the near-ruin of her husband's fortune, with the honorable Celestina, testing the faithfulness of a widowed nobleman by first tempting him to fall and then tongue-lashing him back to virtue. The general reformations in the last act are, however, more perfunctory than convincing. The young men in *Hyde Park* talked of their lurid past and sought honorable marriage; Lady Bornwell commits adultery with Alexander Kickshaw, whose name indicates his nature as a trifler.

The widening gulf between town and country is noticed, with disapproval to be sure, as Lady Bornwell's steward reckons the changes that urban residence has brought:

> The case is alter'd since we liv'd i' th' country:
> We do not now invite the poor o' th' parish
> To dinner, keep a table for the tenants;
> Our kitchen does not smell of beef; the cellar
> Defies the price of malt and hops; the footmen
> And coach-drivers may be drunk like gentlemen,
> With wine; nor will three fiddlers upon holidays
> With aid of bagpipes that call'd in the country
> To dance and plough the hall up with their hob-nails,
> To make my Lady merry. We do feed
> Like princes and feed nothing else but princes.

Scorn likewise is heaped by the country Lord Bornwell upon his wife's citified extravagances: unnecessary furniture and plate, huge looking-glasses, £80 dinners, expensive clothing, rich perfumes, and so many servants that, accompanying her carriage, they clog the streets until pedestrians and tradesmen alike curse her. She gambles, buys priceless gems, covers her richest cloth

with heavy embroideries, and revels the night through at "The
Ball," an assembly which cloaks licentious behavior. To this
Aretina can only reply:

> though you veil your avaricious meaning
> With handsome names of modesty and thrift,
> I find you would entrench and wound the liberty
> I was born with.

It is now the woman's privilege to be her own master.

The gentlemen of the town lead equally footling lives. Aretina,
who has made a careful study of the world of fashion, gives their
character:

> You, gentlemen, are held
> Wits of the town, the consuls that do govern
> The senate here, whose jeers are all authentic.
> The taverns and the ordinaries are
> Made academies, where you come, and all
> Your sins and surfeits made the time's example.
> Your very nods can quell a theater;
> No speech or poem good without your seal;
> You can protect scurrility, and publish;
> By your authority believ'd, no rapture
> Ought to have honest meaning.

They work not, neither do they study—the common occupations
of earlier comic heroes. They live only for sexual indulgence and
other city sports.

Evidence of the growing independence of women is to be found
not only in the actions of the vicious Lady Bornwell but in
Celestina, who is intended to be a model of sophisticated virtue.
Her purpose is to keep men dancing attendance upon her, but
not to wed, and not for love. She says:

> We hold our life and fortunes upon no
> Man's charity. . . .
>   My stars
> Are yet kind to me; for, in a happy minute
> Be't spoke, I'm not in love, and men shall never
> Make lean my heart with sighing, nor with tears
> Draw on my eyes the infamy of spectacles.
> 'Tis the chief principle to keep your heart
> Under your own obedience; jest, but love not.

This is the very reverse of the heroine of romantic comedy; nor
does Celestina's consciousness that she lives in a dissolute society

and her announced desire to find a faithful man wholly excuse
her brazen seduction of the anonymous Lord only to display her
wit in calling him back to his "honor." The conclusion of her
lecture indicates the audience for whom it was actually intended:

> Had not you
> So valiantly recover'd in this conflict
> You had been my triumph, without hope of more
> Than my just scorn upon your wanton flame;
> Nor will I think these noble thoughts grew first
> From melancholy for some female loss,
> As the fantastic world believes, but from
> Truth, and your love of innocence, which shine
> So bright in the two royal luminaries
> At court, you cannot lose your way to chastity.

The King and Queen, patrons of the licentious comedy of manners, are at the same time patrons of virtue and chastity. It is not
to be wondered at that Shirley became the favorite of the court,
or of the censor who would have him "the pattern to other poets
. . . for the bettering of manners and language."

This courtly life, reflected so vividly and with such wit and
accuracy in the comedy of manners, this world of idle gallants
and wilful ladies of fashion, this world of love intrigue and the
pursuit of pleasures, was growing smaller and more isolated daily.
The reader of the tragicomedies and the comedies of manners of
the last years of James and the reign of Charles and Henrietta
would never guess the clouds which hung over the apparent
gaiety. The plagues which had closed the theaters at intervals
throughout the century grew more frequent; the Puritan outcries
against the players carried greater and greater authority. By 1642
Scotland, Ireland, and the English Parliament were in open rebellion against the king and the court had fled north. In April, the
Prologue to Shirley's *The Sisters* was complaining:

> a Play
> Though ne'er so new, will starve the second day:
> Upon these very hard conditions,
> Our Poet will not purchase many towns;
> And if you leave us too, we cannot thrive.
> I'll promise neither play nor poet live
> Till ye come back.

The drama, by devoting itself to a coterie, lost its audience and
its life. On September 2, 1642 was issued "An Order of the Lords

and Commons concerning Stage Plays" that "while these sad causes and set times of humiliation do continue, public stage plays shall cease and be foreborne." For the two ensuing decades the English theater in effect ceased to exist, but the spark that had given vitality to the great period of panoramic drama had long since been extinguished. It would be many decades more before the conjunction of dramatists of penetrating insight and wide powers of expression with a full and understanding auditory would take place. Until that time the triumphs of the Elizabethan theater would be both an inspiring shade and a lodestar, fittingly memorialized by two of its most famous players John Lowin and Joseph Taylor, who, poverty-stricken and deprived of their profession, wrote in the preface to *The Wild Goose Chase* (pr. 1652):

And now farewell our glory! Farewell your choice delight, most noble gentlemen! Farewell the grand wheel that set us smaller wheels in action! Farewell the pride and life o' th' stage!

5

Neo-Classic Drama: The Restoration

The Order of Parliament was intended to suppress the theater for the duration of the civil war; in effect, however, it drove the theater underground. Entertainments were presented surreptitiously throughout the Commonwealth period, 1642-1660, particularly in the private homes of country gentlemen or at fairs, but on occasion in the playhouses of London. The latter performances were hazardous affairs for the actors. In 1648, a company which had taken over the Cockpit was raided in the midst of *The Bloody Brother.* They were imprisoned and their costumes taken from them, a most effective punishment. The old popular house, The Red Bull, seems to have been occupied more or less regularly, in spite of frequent raids, occasionally presenting full length plays, but more often a series of *Drolls.*

Drolls were particularly ingenious expedients for outwitting the authorities. They do not seem to have been original works, but "cuttings" of familiar Elizabethan plays. One, *The Bouncing Knight,* selects and joins together in a playlet the Falstaff scenes from *I Henry IV;* another, *The Grave-Makers,* is, as its name suggests, the grave-diggers' scene from *Hamlet. Bottom the Weaver* made his appearance along with farces or playlets extracted from Beaumont and Fletcher, and other established masters. In 1672 a collection of drolls was published by Francis Kirkman as *The Wits, or Sport upon Sport* with an apologetic preface:

I have seen the Red Bull playhouse, which was a large one, so full, that as many went back for want of room as had entered; and as meanly as you may think now of these drolls, they were then acted by the best comedians then and now in being.

The advantage of the droll, of course, was that although brief, it was the most popular essence of the play from whence it was

190

taken, and because brief it could be presented with little advance preparation, could be transported easily from one fair, festival, or theater to another, and was over before a raid could be organized.

In spite of Kirkman's testimony, most of the familiar names of the last age left the profession, either to follow the king and fight in his battles, as did Michael Mohun, or, remaining behind, quietly to adopt some less conspicuous occupation like innkeeping. George Jolly, a minor player in England, organized a troupe and went barn-storming in Germany. Sir William Davenant went into exile in France, undertook a royal mission to America, was captured and spent four years languishing in the Tower of London. Thus, if the traditions of the panoramic drama were kept alive in spite of the Order of Parliament, the traditions of Elizabethan stage-production were effectively weakened. The great actors could no longer train apprentices; the boy actors who were so important a part of the older system grew up and no replacements were enlisted. When the king came home again in August 1660, the way was cleared for a new theory of production which was to have a lasting effect on the reshaping of English dramatic technique.

The king who came home was the son of the king who had been executed in 1649. The life of an exile in France had developed to a greater degree in Charles II those qualities which the Puritans had found most offensive in his father. He was by nature witty and pleasure-loving, and the rootless, homeless life of even a royal wanderer had destroyed his sense of moral values. Members of his court-in-exile reflected their King. His poets, for want of matter, had taken to writing illustrations of the code of the Court of Love, and of all the artifices connected with the "Science of Friendship." Prose writers had imitated the endless fantastic adventures and the long-winded pointless debates of the French romances, especially *The Grand Cyrus* of Mlle. de Scudéry, and troubled themselves for pages without number over exemplary gallants, flawless in their chivalric behavior. So quixotic are their attitudes towards love and duty that it becomes a matter of rejoicing if a "friend" falls in love with one's mistress since it gives occasion for so much greater display of generosity and magnanimity. Sexual jealousy was the emotion, above all others, to be stifled, and sexual love in the noblest relationships was rejected. This was the artificial code of behavior for a social group seeking a release from boredom.

When the court returned to England, it took with it this artificial and unnatural code and, inevitably, its boredom. Having been wrenched from its native soil and traditions it could think of nothing to do but attempt to amuse itself. To this end the re-established English theater became its especial property, its toy. The king, again, set the fashion. He loved the playhouse, the crowds, the spectacle, the wit; he loved the actors, and freely gave them his robes to adorn their favorite rôles; and most of all, he loved the actresses.

One of his first actions upon resuming his throne was to issue two patents, one to Sir William Davenant and one to Thomas Killigrew, allowing them the exclusive monopoly of public theatrical entertainments in the capital. Killigrew was the first to establish a company, using as a nucleus Mohun and Charles Hart and other survivors from the pre-Commonwealth days. By permission they were known as the King's Company and opened at a makeshift theater, Gibbon's Tennis-Court in Vere Street, on November 8, 1660. Later Killigrew moved to a new building in Covent Garden and established the first of a succession of theaters to bear that famous name. Davenant was somewhat slower in getting started. After some months of indecision he came to an agreement with a group of tyros headed by Thomas Betterton to work for him under the title of The Duke of York's Company. He opened at the old Salisbury Court Theatre, November 15, 1660. In the next year a new theater in Dorset Garden was completed and occupied by Davenant's troupe. It remained here until 1673 when it removed to Drury Lane. Thus within thirteen years after the Restoration were firmly established the theatrical monopoly and the two National Theaters (the Legitimate, or Licensed Theaters) which were to endure unshaken and unshakable until the middle of the nineteenth century, and to prove an insurmountable obstacle to the free development of the drama.

For the moment, however, two theaters were enough, and frequently more than enough. Catering exclusively to an aristocratic group their new plays rapidly exhausted their audience; a novelty at one theater would frequently leave the other with too few spectators to warrant performance of the announced bill, and even a novelty might attract a discouragingly small house. Dorset

Garden apparently accommodated about 1200; at the opening of Dryden's *All for Love* in 1677 there were 249 paid admissions. Admission prices were necessarily high, from four shillings in the best seats to twelvepence in the gallery, but by a kind of gentlemen's agreement it was possible to see one act of a play without payment; a gallant might be admitted, apparently, on the pretense of "looking for a friend." At the end of the act he was expected to leave, but would very likely take himself to the other theater and repeat the process.

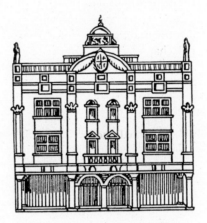

Dorset Garden

Performances began in mid-afternoon, at three-thirty or four, and, since there were no reserved seats in the pit, it was customary for a playgoer to dispatch a servant, or to hire a streetboy, to go to the theater about noon and hold his place for him. The audience in general came early and stayed late. The theater was a social gathering place and its habitués conducted themselves accordingly. The tavern and the playhouse were complementary; the gallant went to the former for food and liquor and to the latter for conversation. Shadwell, in *The Virtuoso* (1676), describes the spectators who "come drunk and screaming into the playhouse, and stand upon the benches, and toss their full periwigs and empty heads, and with their shrill, unbroken pipes cry, 'Damme, this is a damn'd play.'" Peace officers were stationed about the auditorium to keep order, but not much could be done with the loose-tongued and quick-witted aristocrats, since the audience obviously enjoyed their performances more than the efforts of the actors. The often-quoted experiences of Mr. Pepys as a theater-goer are typical: he was rather annoyed with the actors for carrying on their business while Sir Charles Sedley just in front of him was demonstrating his skill in repartee, and he quickly forgave a spectator who spit on him when he discovered her to be a charming female. The Restoration theater during a performance bore no resemblance to a shrine of the Muses, and only the supreme genius of an actor like Thomas Betterton could still the quarrelsome, exhibitionistic gentlemen and the raucous cries of Orange Moll and the girls who assisted her in hawking the fruit which had replaced nuts as playhouse refreshment.

The fourth act of Shadwell's *A True Widow* is an almost documentary picture of a Restoration performance. The principal characters assemble in a theater for the purpose of making assignations. The ladies are vizarded to protect their reputations.

> *Several young coxcombs fool with the Orange-woman.*
> ORANGE-WOMAN. Oranges! will you have any oranges?
> 1ST BULLY. What play do they play? Some confounded play or other.
> PRIG [*to Lady Cheatly*]. A pox on't, madam! What should we do at this damn'd playhouse? Let's send for some cards, and play at lang-trilloo in the box. Pox on 'em! I ne'er saw a play had anything in't; some of 'em had wit now and then, but what care I for wit?
> SELFISH. Does my cravat fit well? I take all the care I can it should; I love to appear well. What ladies are here in the boxes? Really, I never come to a play but on account of seeing the ladies. . . .
> 1ST BULLY. Damme! When will these fellows begin? Plague on't! here's a staying.
> 2ND MAN. Whose play is this?
> 3RD MAN. One Prickett—poet Prickett.
> 1ST MAN. Oh; hang him! Pox on him! he cannot write. Prithee let's to Whitehall. . . .
> *Enter several ladies and gentlemen.*
> DOOR-KEEPER. Pray, sir, pay me; my masters will make me pay it.
> 3RD MAN. Impudent rascal! Do you ask me for money? Take that, sirrah!
> 4TH MAN. No, I don't intend to stay.
> 2ND DOOR-KEEPER. So you say every day, and see two or three acts for nothing.
> 4TH MAN. I'll break your head, rascal!
> 1ST DOOR-KEEPER. Pray sir, pay me.
> 3RD MAN. Set it down; I have no silver about me. . . .
> THEODOSIA. What! do gentlemen run on tick for plays?
> CARLOS. As familiarly as with their tailors.

This was not idle satire on Shadwell's part. The author's payment for his labors depended upon the receipts of the third performance, commonly known as his "benefit," and he was consequently concerned not only that his play should be sufficiently pleasing to warrant a run of three days, but that the doorkeepers should be diligent in collecting admissions. Shadwell, himself, seems to have been the most lavishly rewarded of the playwrights, his share

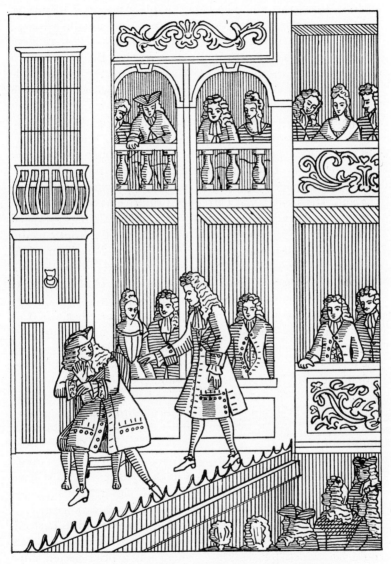

A Restoration Performance of The Plain Dealer

of the takings from *The Squire of Alsatia* amounting to £130. Such a success was not typical; a few plays managed to survive eight to twelve nights, but the longer runs were usually achieved by operas or other spectacular entertainments.

Spectacle, even more than wit or poetry, was the life blood of the Restoration theater. It was Davenant's interest in spectacle and his ingenuity in its employment that enabled the Duke's Company to outshine the more experienced players of the King's Company. As will presently appear, even during the Commonwealth he had produced public entertainments with the novel addition of painted scenery which, common enough in Italy and elsewhere on the continent, had hitherto been reserved for the masques and pageantry of private, aristocratic celebrations in England. His scenery was extremely primitive at first, consisting of a painted backdrop or shutter and a series of wings arranged in rows or grooves from the back of the stage to the front curtain. The curtain itself was an innovation; it seems to have been raised at the beginning of the performance and lowered only at the conclusion, scene changes being made in full view of the audience. The frequent stage direction, "the scene shuts," or "opens," refers to this method of changing by simply pushing together a pair of wings to make a new background for the action. Although the playhouse was roofed over and employed painted scenery set inside a proscenium frame, as in the modern theater, the old Elizabethan intimacy between actor and audience was maintained by the apron, or forestage, which projected in front of the proscenium as much as seventeen feet into the auditorium. The "front" curtain, in fact, seems to have divided the playing area into the equivalent of the older main stage and inner stage. On two sides of the apron were the stage boxes separated from the actors only by a narrow rail of wainscot. In a modern comedy it must have been difficult sometimes to distinguish the player from the playgoer. Here was the mirror held up to nature with a vengeance!

In addition to the innovation of painted scenery, the Restoration theater for the first time employed actresses. Until the ladies could be trained for their rôles there was a brief period after 1660 when the tradition of the boy-actress was retained. The coming of the female actress was inevitable, however, both because the courtly audience had been pleased with the French *comédiennes,* and because the long process of training boys had been interrupted by the Commonwealth. Only Edward Kynaston seems to have made anything like a success of impersonation in the old manner, and when he shifted over to heroes, Downes, the prompter, wrote in his notebook, "it has since been disputable among the judicious whether any woman that succeeded him so sensibly touched the audience as he."

The judicious forming only a small part of any given audience, there is no doubt that the new actresses were welcome arrivals.

Among the first was Mrs. Margaret Hughes who performed Desdemona with Killigrew's company in 1660, an event so notable that a special prologue was composed to call attention to it. It is, all too typically, a shabby affair with a deliberately provocative reference to the actress. For the women did not simply take over the rôles formerly filled by boys, they exploited themselves. In a revival of Shirley's *The Grateful Servant*, Mrs. Long was the first to take full advantage of the fa-

Nell Gwynn

miliar comic convention of the heroine who diguises herself as a man. Downes writes, "the first time she appeared in man's habit proved as beneficial to the company as several succeeding new plays." In these early actresses and their open treatment of their profession as an introduction to a more rewarding one ("more than one of them," says Colley Cibber, "had charms sufficient at their leisure hours to calm and mollify the Cares of Empire") is a symbol of the relationship of the drama and its audience during the Restoration.

1. RESTORATION COMEDY

From the lists of old plays revived immediately after the reopening of the theaters it is plain that the courtiers' taste declared itself without hesitation for Jonson, Beaumont and Fletcher in comedy. Shakespeare makes but a poor showing and one is not surprised when Mr. Pepys notes in his *Diary* that *A*

Midsummer Night's Dream is "the most insipid ridiculous play" he has ever seen. The comic world of romance was exchanged for the comic world of manners, a witty, cynical, intellectual, deliberately immoral world, an exact reflection of the tastes, interests, and code of behavior of its aristocratic audiences. If the term "manner" needs definition, we may rely upon that eminent lexicographer, Lady Froth of Congreve's *The Double-Dealer:* "Some distinguishing quality, as for example, the *bel air* or *brilliant* of Mr. Brisk; the solemnity, yet complaisance of my Lord, or something of his own that should look a little *je-ne-sais-quoish.*" In other words, a dominant characteristic which is not unconscious, like a Jonsonian humour, but an assumed grace, an artifice. It will be apparent that the principals of these plays may be ranked one above the other in the hierarchy of social acceptability in ratio to the success of their artifice.

Wit is the touchstone by which they are to be judged; it was perhaps the accomplishment on which the courtier most prided himself. "Wit was killed in the war," complains a speaker in *The Sociable Companions* (*pr.* 1668), only to be corrected, "you are mistaken; it was only banished with the Cavaliers, but now it is returned home." Taken in small doses the epigrammatic brilliance of this part of the English drama is its most attractive feature; the exquisitely turned phrase, the carefully balanced antithesis, the precise or surprising comparison is the perfect expression of a society for which style and not sincerity was a major concern. If tasted immoderately, however, it loses its flavor; the reader grows weary of the pun, of the reiterated reference to the cuckold's horns, the similitudes stacked cord upon cord in endless orderly dialogues. The central character of Cowley's *The Cutter of Coleman Street* (1661) is one Puny, whose "manner" is insatiable delight in fantastic similes, but it is sometimes difficult to distinguish his absurdities from the similitudes of the wits we are expected to admire. The question of the succeeding generation, whether Congreve's fools be fools indeed so brilliant was their dialogue, is one which still later generations have been tempted to reverse: Are the pretenders to wit greater fools than the wits themselves? Fortunately there are other criteria for judgment.

The admirable characters, the comic heroes and heroines of the Restoration, practice with grace and dexterity a code of behavior which is utterly beyond the comprehension, not to say abilities, of the fools. They are gallants, or fine ladies, and they are lovers, and each of these states has its special conditions. The Reverend Jeremy Collier (see p. 232), looking with a somewhat sour eye upon the gallant, sums him thus:

> A fine gentleman is a fine whoring, swearing, smutty, aethistical man. These qualifications, it seems, complete the idea of honor. They are the top-improvements of Fortune, and the distinguishing glories of Birth and Breeding. This is the stage-test for quality, and those that can't stand it, ought to be disclaimed. The restraints of conscience and the pedantry of virtue are unbecoming a Cavalier; future securities and reaching beyond life are vulgar provisions. If he falls a-thinking at this rate, he forfeits his honor, for his head was only made to run against a post.

The gallant requires a number of mistresses solely for "the sweet sake of variety" or as the hero of *She Would if She Could* declares, "A single intrigue in love is as dull as a single plot in a play." Living to this gallant is a "pleasant comedy," the pursuit of marriage its "main design," brightened and preserved from dullness by some "underplots."

The fine lady subscribes to much the same code. Profiting by the new importance which increasing freedom has given to women of the upper classes, her greatest pleasure is to keep as many lovers as possible in suspense for as long as possible. She will not marry without establishing elaborate precautions for the preservation of her "dear liberty," and she will never admit to any man's superiority in wit. Perhaps the most vivid picture of her is in Cibber's recollection of Mrs. Verbruggen as Melantha in *Marriage-à-la-Mode* at her first meeting with her intended husband, who has brought a letter of introduction:

> She reads the letter . . . with a careless, dropping lip and an erected brow, humming it hastily over, as if she were impatient to outgo her father's commands by making a complete conquest of him at once. And that the letter might not embarrass her attack, crack! she crumbles it at once into her palm, and pours upon him her whole artillery of airs, eyes, and motion; down goes her dainty, diving body to the ground, as if she were sinking under the conscious load of her own attractions; then launches into a flood of fine language and compliment, still playing her chest forward in fifty falls and risings, like a swan upon waving water; and, to complete her impertinence, she is so rapidly fond of her own wit, that she will not give her lover leave to praise it—silent assenting bows and vain endeavours to speak are all the share of the conversation he is admitted to, which, at last, he is relieved from by her

engagement to half a score visits, which she *swims* from him to make, with a promise to return in a twinkling.

"To think of a whirlwind, tho' 'twere in a whirlwind, were a case of more steady contemplation!" exclaims another hero treated to a similar performance. Mrs. Verbruggen's Melantha is a good image to bear in mind when reading of these Harriets, Gertrudes, Angelicas and Millamants. Though they are more the fine lady and less the pretender, they are compounded of the same airs, the same vitality, and the same enthusiasm for the dance of life.

It is when gallant and fine lady are brought together for a love scene that their true value may be tested. The intimacies exchanged by fashionable lovers partake of the quality of a verbal fencing match; they insult one another freely and profess the greatest reluctance to commit themselves to the permanence of the marriage contract. "A man would think," says a member of the audience during the play scene of *A True Widow*, "these lovers in plays did not care a farthing for one another when they find nothing to do but be florid, and talk impertinently when they are alone." The code of courtship was rigid, however, and if these scenes owe something to the behavior of Benedick and Beatrice in *Much Ado About Nothing* and Carol and Fairfield in *Hyde Park*, they are more deeply indebted to the traditions of courtly love exemplified in the French romances to which the Restoration reading public was devoted.

Treated seriously, the tradition of the French romance finds expression in Thomas Killigrew's *Thomaso* (*pr.* 1664) where the heroine excuses her sweetheart's loose living by an appeal to the principles of Platonic love: "I scorn to fear he can be such a fool as to give [his mistresses] his heart; and for his body, 'twas always the least of my thoughts." The double standard thus comfortably justified for men, it remained for the comic playwrights to establish it for the ladies also, and their success can be traced through a series of conventional "proviso" scenes in which each party lays down his conditions before consenting to marriage, again an echo of *Hyde Park*. One of the earliest of these occurs in Dryden's first comedy, *The Wild Gallant* (1663). Isabella states the provisos upon which she will enter into matrimony: to live in London, to be spared her husband's friends, to have control of the purse strings, and the choice of her own company, her own hours, and her own actions: "these trifles granted me, in all things

of moment I am your most obedient wife and servant, Isabella."
As the scenes multiplied, the conditions became more extreme.
In Dryden's *Secret Love* (1667) the consenting parties actually
swear an oath of inconstancy, as well as prohibiting jealousy, safe-
guarding the liberty of speech and action, and abolishing all
terms of endearment both of marital affection and platonic servi-
tude. The same conventional items are retained in the proviso
scene of Ravenscroft's *Careless Lovers* (1673), but all previous
lovers are outdone as the groom stipulates that his bride *must*
have a gallant and the bride that he *must* have a mistress. *The
Way of the World* (1700) turns upon the most famous of the
proviso scenes; the expected thing of earlier comedy becomes in-
tegrated, as will be pointed out below, with the plot and the
theme in a manner totally unexpected.

It is well to have these conventions in mind when approaching
the comedy of manners. Critics in the past who have read it solely
in the light of their own times have found it dull, smutty,
inhuman; or—equally aberrant—unrealistic, imaginative, and
charming. In both tone and incident it is a realistic portrait of
a transitional society. If its humor is cruel and its jokes practical,
so were the humor and the jokes of its audience; if its behavior
is licentious and totally opposed to any acceptable moral standards, the society for which it was intended was desperately searching for standards. The aristocrats established a code, imitated by
the dramatists, that inevitably clashed with human nature. Platonic, courtly love is a graceful game in literature; in life the
impulses of ordinary human behavior are in immediate conflict
with it. Out of this conflict between artificial code and human
nature grew the works of the Restoration comic playwrights.

Something has already been said of the continuity of English
dramatic conventions in spite of the interregnum; the effect of
this continuity and its manifestations in the comedy of manners
will presently be seen. But other influences were at work from
French comedy and, through the French, from Spanish comedy. It
is a curious fact that the golden age of the Spanish theater almost
precisely parallels the period of the Elizabethan drama, yet the
influence of that theater was not felt in England until the end
of the seventeenth century. On the serious level, the Spanish
theater had drawn its subject matter from the conflict between

love and duty which preoccupied the Caroline court dramatists; on the comic level it was a drama of intrigue, working out intricately interwoven love affairs in a way which was at once amusing and mathematically exact.

Typical of the plays inspired by the Spanish comedy of intrigue is John Dryden's *Marriage-à-la-Mode* (1673). The scene is Sicily, but might as well be Seville or London. Rhodophil is fashionably tired of his wife Doralice and woos Melantha to be his mistress. Palamede, his friend, returns home to marry an unknown bride—Melantha, of course—and falls in love with Doralice who is fashionably agreeable. Each man suspects the other, but cannot speak without revealing his own affair. In scene after scene the two pairs of lovers are presented, shifted, nearly discovered and rescued by the series of ingenious but mechanical reversals which is the essence of intrigue comedy.

The comic plot is not without some correspondence to the English social code, since Rhodophil is publicly tired of his wife only because a happy marriage is an inconceivable state for a gallant. He confesses to his friend: "I loved her a whole half year, double the natural term of any mistress; and I think, in my conscience, I could have held out another quarter, but then the world began to laugh at me, and a certain shame of being out of fashion seized me." In her first encounter with her future husband, Melantha is at once obeying dramatic convention and the social code when she lists the provisos by which their married life shall be lived: they shall never pay visits together, nor go to a play together, and each shall have his own friends and way of life. Melantha is being gently mocked, but her intentions were those of the most approved heroines.

Somewhat incongruously this farcical intrigue plot in prose is interwoven, not very skillfully, with a "serious" love and honor conflict in a kind of workaday blank verse. This plot is reminiscent of the tragicomedy of Beaumont and Fletcher as the usurper Polydamus orders his newly-recovered son, Leonidas, to marry Amalthea, a court lady, although he loves Palmyra, a shepherd's daughter also beloved of Argaleon, Amalthea's brother. The young man, that is, must choose between obeying his father (duty), or his heart (love). After much impassioned declamation on both subjects, it develops that Palmyra is really the child of Polydamus, and that Leonidas was put forth for reasons best

known to the playwright. Palmyra is immediately ordered to wed
Argaleon, and the same conflict between love and duty is repeated in her case. The entire debate is resolved by a disclosure
in the final scene that Leonidas is neither the child of the
usurper, nor an impostor, but the long-lost king. Love triumphs,
and even Polydamus is forgiven because he is the father of the
beloved.

Leonidas is the projection of the Restoration gallant into an
unrealistic world. For wit, substitute rant, for the comic, the serious treatment of the code of friendship and courtly love. Discovering for the first time that he is a prince instead of a simple
swain and taken to his "father's" court, he discloses his essential
nobility.

> POLYDAMUS. Come near, and be not dazzled with the splendor
> And greatness of a court.
> LEONIDAS. I need not this encouragement;
> I can fear nothing but the gods.

Later, discovering that he is not a prince and that Palmyra
is a princess, he thus replies to her offer of foster-brothership and
Polydamus' offer of a large pension:

> You are all great and royal in your gifts;
> But at the donor's feet I lay them down:
> Should I take riches from you, it would seem
> As I did want a soul to bear that poverty
> To which the gods designed my humble birth:
> And should I take your honors without merit,
> It would appear I wanted manly courage
> To hope them, in your service, from my sword.
> POLYDAMUS. Still brave, and like yourself.

Leonidas, as we shall see, is not as much of an individual as the
usurper's comment would suggest; he is but one of a large-souled
and large-mouthed company, the serious heroes of the Restoration stage.

Nor is he altogether out of place in this comedy. From his title,
Dryden would seem to suggest that he is examining marriage
according to the fashionable code, and, by implication, according
to the ideal also. Rhodophil and Palamede and their intrigue
represent love à la mode; Leonidas and Palmyra, true love. The
articulation of the two parts is crude, for Dryden was writing in
haste. If the hack writers of the Elizabethan theater produced

tightly-unified works out of diverse materials even though writing in haste, it was because they were also writing in good faith. Dryden was on both levels employing artificial, not deeply felt, standards. At the end of the play, Leonidas, happily married to Palmyra, delivers the author's explanation of his performance:

> Thus have my spouse and I informed the nation
> And led you all the way to reformation;
> Not with dull morals, gravely writ . . .
> But by examples drawn, I dare say,
> From most of you who hear and see the play. . . .
> Some stabbing wits, to bloody satire bent,
> Would treat both sexes with less compliment;
> Would lay the scene at home; of husbands tell,
> For wenches, taking up their wives: the Mall;
> And a brisk bout, which each of them did want,
> Made by mistake of mistress and gallant.
> Our modest author thought it was enough
> To cut you off a sample of the stuff:
> He spared my shame, which you, I'm sure would not,
> For you were all for driving on the plot:
> You sighed when I came in to break the sport,
> And set your teeth when each design fell short.

The lack of integrity in the play's writing is apparent when the leading character is permitted to define his function as being no more than "to break the sport."

Dryden, in such a play as *Marriage-à-la-Mode*, effected a combination of Spanish intrigue and Fletcherian tragicomedy. Of even greater importance was the fusion of older English elements with the comic method of Molière to be observed in the works of Sir George Etheredge. His first play, *The Comical Revenge, or Love in a Tub* (1664) brings together a gulling plot reminiscent of Middleton, with an impudent French servant, and a serious plot of love and friendship. *She Would if She Could* (1668) relates the ignominious exposure of Lady Cockwood, the ambitious pretender to the social graces, and the complex love-intrigues of Freeman and Courtall. The Lady is only the Restoration view of Lady Bornwell in Shirley's *Lady of Pleasure,* the outsider who seeks admission to the gay inner circle. In Shirley, she is a character to be rescued at all costs and restored to the sanity of country living; in Etheredge she is merely to be kept at a distance. In the end Lady Cockwood admits the defeat of her endeavors but not the death of her desire; she still would, if she could, be a fine lady.

The Man of Mode, or Sir Fopling Flutter (1676) is Etheredge's most famous and most complete realization of a society in which he played a leading part. St. Evremond is the authority for the statement that the hero is actually a portrait of the Earl of Rochester, the wittiest as well as the most dissolute member of Charles's court. Whether or not the rumor be true, the accuracy of the total picture is not to be questioned. The gullings of the plot, the cruel jests at the expense of the outsiders, are only the stage equivalents of the unpleasant practical jokes with which the courtiers amused themselves, as a reading of the *Memoirs of the Count de Grammont* will testify. Etheredge defends in the most complaisant terms the abuse of the "gay, giddy, brisk-insipid noisy fools" who are striving to make themselves a place in the only available urban society. "You must allow," says Mrs. Loveit, "'tis pleasanter to laugh at others than to be laughed at ourselves though never so wittily."

The scorn of the country is one of the recurrent motifs of the Restoration, and one of its strongest points of difference with that love of the pastoral so characteristic of the panoramic romance. In *Marriage-à-la-Mode,* the gay ladies shudder at the thought of being removed from the city to a place where they must be content with last year's songs and last year's gossip. "When I am out of town but a fortnight," Artemis says, "I am so humble that I would receive a letter from my tailor or mercer for a favor." Etheredge, more the courtier than Dryden, is more explicit in the horror image he draws in *The Man of Mode.* At the end of the play, Harriet is condemned to return to her country home:

HARRIET. To a great rambling lone house that looks as if it were not inhabited, the family's so small. There you'll find my mother, an old lame aunt, and myself, sir, perched up on chairs in a large parlor; sitting moping like three or four melancholy birds in a spacious vollary [aviary]—Does not this stagger your resolution?
DORIMANT. Not at all, madam! The first time I saw you, you left me with the pangs of love upon me, and this day my soul has quite given up her liberty.
HARRIET. This is more dismal than the country! Emilia, pity me who am going to that sad place. Methinks I hear the hateful noise of rooks already—kaw, kaw, kaw—There's music in the worst cry in London: "My dill and cucumbers to pickle!"

The structure of the play is based on the conflicts in the society which Etheredge reflects: the old, pre-war conventions against the new, the country against the city, the pretender against the successful wit. These oppositions are woven together by the multiple love-affairs of Dorimant. Tired of Mrs. Loveit, but too polite to tell her so, he contrives to match her with the pretender, Sir Fopling Flutter; currently engaged in an affair with Bellinda, he is strongly attracted to the country lass, Harriet. According to his code, he must appear complaisant to all three women and the lies which are forced upon him lead to most of the complications of the action and give him a series of occasions to demonstrate the polish of his social graces and the quickness of his wit. According to his code, he is a complete gentleman, as even Bellinda confesses when, although she discovers that his heart is intent on another woman, he refuses to get himself out of a scrape by revealing his affair with her: "He's tender of my honor, though he's cruel to my love."

More than by the honorable gallant, the spectator or reader is attracted by the title character, Sir Fopling, ancestor of a long line of Cock-fools. His major concerns are indicated when Dorimant describes him as "a senseless caper, a tawdry French ribband, and a formal cravat." Newly arrived from Paris he has set himself up as the "pattern of Modern Gallantry" and the vivid sketches of his manners and actions establish the type for subsequent dramatists and players alike.

MEDLEY. He was yesterday at the play with a pair of gloves up to his elbows, and a periwig more exactly curled than a lady's head newly dressed for a ball.

BELLAIR. What a pretty lisp he has!

DORIMANT. Ho! that he effects in imitation of the people of quality in France.

MEDLEY. His head stands for the most part on one side, and his looks are more languishing than a lady's when she lolls at stretch in her coach or leans her head against the side of a box i' the playhouse. . . .

BELLAIR. . . . a complete gentleman . . . according to Sir Fopling, ought to dress well, dance well, fence well, have a genius for love letters, an agreeable voice for a chamber, be very amorous, something discreet, but not overconstant.

From the action of the play it is apparent that Sir Fopling's code of conduct differs from Dorimant's chiefly in the significant item of success. Sir Fopling's behavior is satirized, Dorimant's treated as the comic predicament of a young man whose virtues constantly betray him into compromising situations.

Modern critics have noticed a more general satirical attack on the whole of Restoration society in the plays of William Wycherley. There is, certainly, in both *The Country Wife* and *The Plain Dealer* a sense that the ugliest realities of upper-class life are being displayed, but it is not always clear whether the author relished them or was disgusted by them. His treatment of his sources, for example, is puzzling.

The Country Wife (1675) is partially derived from Molière's *L'École des Femmes,* the story of an innocent ingenue whose guardian is foiled in his plan to wed her by her quickness in translating into action all the stratagems he unjustly accuses her of—after he has described them to her. Wycherley's ingenue, Margery Pinchwife, is chaste only because she has never been asked the question. Her jealous husband, a former gallant, is well aware of all the stratagems and wiles of gallantry and in his overzealous endeavors to protect his honor, he fairly throws her into the arms of Horner, thereby making her an adulteress. Both Pinchwife and Margery are treated with the same disrespect; after her experience with the gallants, she and her husband return to the country, she with no consciousness of what she is, and he an unrevenged, self-made cuckold. In Molière the theme is evident if trivial: property-mad suitors will inevitably be defeated by the strength and wisdom which true love affords their intended victims. Wycherley's theme, if he has one, seems to be the power of marriage to destroy a man's wit and his wife's moral sense.

Horner, the central figure, is of course engaged in other love-affairs and these make somewhat better satirical sense. In the true vein of Ben Jonson, but with the inevitable Restoration coloring, he is presented as a man whose schemes to gain his own purposes are based upon the humours or weaknesses of his victims, and whose actions result in the exposing of his victims for the fools they are. By announcing publicly, with the complicity of his physician, that he has been made impotent by sexual indulgence, he gulls the justifiably over-anxious husbands of his acquaintance into allowing him intimacies with their wives. The general cuckolding reaches its climax in a famous scene of *double-entendre* in which Horner exhibits his collection of "china" to the ladies of the cast one after another. But since, by the code, the husband was always wrong and the gallant always right, the play does not end as it began in the Jonsonian manner. Horner's own "humour" never leads to his discomfiture. Indeed, his triumph is emphasized by being set parallel to that of his friend, Harcourt, who manages to win the hand of Pinchwife's sister, Alithea, by proving that her suitor, Sparkish, is capable of the unfashionable (but human) emotion of jealousy. Neither wisdom nor folly, neither wisdom nor the pretense of it, is allowed to hinder the rake's progress in the comedy of manners.

In *The Plain Dealer* (1676), Wycherley draws on both Molière and Shakespeare without attempting to disguise his debt. He is so frank in calling attention to his source, using not only the Viola-Olivia situation from *Twelfth Night,* but the actual character-name Olivia, that he seems to be making a point of the difference between the romantic events in Illyria and his own besmutted versions of them. Situation after situation, also, is taken from *Le Misanthrope* of Molière; but the French Alceste is an honest man. His humour is an inability to compromise with his personal creed in order to live according to the social code. At the end of the play he resigns from society altogether. The English Manly, on the other hand, rails at society and its customs and at the human race in general while entrusting his heart, his friendship, and his fortunes to Olivia and Vernish, the most unscrupulous rascals of the lot. At the end of his play he is rewarded with the hand and fortune of the faithful and innocent Fidelia. Molière makes the point that Alceste's refusal to compromise with the world is as unnatural as the behavior of the complete worldlings, since man must live in society; to emphasize this point, he creates a pair of lovers, Philinte and Éliante, to act as norms or standards of reasonable behavior. In Wycherley, Philinte becomes Freeman, the Restoration ideal, engaged among other activities in a completely unscrupulous cozening of the Widow Blackacre to get her hand and fortune. To the audience he openly declares:

. . . out of love to her jointure and hatred to business, I would marry her and make an end of her thousand [law] suits and my thousand engagements, to the comfort of two unfortunate sorts of people: my plaintiffs and her defendants, my creditors and her adversaries.

The Widow Blackacre is a true Jonsonian humour; she is so governed by her passion for litigation that she would proclaim her son a bastard when he refuses to become a lawyer, although Freeman points out that such a position is dangerous to her own reputation. Voltaire acclaimed the Widow as the most amusing character ever brought on the English stage, and she is involved in several witty, if conventional, scenes of satire on lawyers and one, more original, with Major Oldfox, the poetaster. On the whole, however, she is more vicious than amusing, her humour more grim than laughable.

Grimness, in fact, is characteristic of the play. The double plot manages to include a cross-section of society from Plausible, the foppish lord, down to a bookseller's apprentice, and to suggest by its parallel action that the moral code is as corrupt as the legal code. Manly and Wycherley are fluent in their description and denunciation of this corruption, but Manly's violent verbal attacks on his fellows in Westminster Hall in Act III are less effective than the actions of the characters—the lawyer, for instance, will listen to his attacks as long as he seems to be wealthy; when he proposes a plea *in forma pauperis,* the lawyer finds an instant excuse to exit. The effective satire is in the action, not in the violent denunciations with which the playwright is liberal. Manly puts his finger on his own deficiency when he demands of Novel, a pretentious wit, "But is railing satire?"

The Plain Dealer was much admired in its own day, and is usually held to be Wycherley's masterpiece. The various actions are, it is true, skillfully interwoven, though there is typical carelessness in the handling of the exposition at the beginning and the explanations at the end. The tone of the whole is consistent; Manly's brutal "frankness" in the dialogue is matched by such incidents as the near-rape of Fidelia in the action. Manly himself, however intended by his adapter, is a vigorous expression of the Restoration dilemma, in terms of character. He loves where he should hate, just as the Restoration gallant was continually falling in love in spite of a code which forbade sincerity in romantic affairs. The callous vulgarization of the Shakespearean romantic plot, though deplorable, is symptomatic. Mr. Pepys would call the original insipid and would find the adaptation very much to his completely typical taste.

There are traces of Ben Jonson in all these plays, "manner" after all being but the Restoration substitute for "humour," and the Novels and Plausibles and Manlys are not too distantly descended from the Littlewits, Canters, and Subtles of the past age. If they differ, it is in intensity. Their peculiarities are a matter of behavior, manners, not instinct, humours. It is thus the age and the fashion that is satirized rather than the universal vices and follies of mankind. Thomas Shadwell, a true "Son of Ben" recognized this in the preface to his first play, *The Sullen Lovers* (1668) declaring:

> Most other authors, that I ever read, either have wild, romantic tales, wherein they strain love and honor to that ridiculous height that it becomes burlesque; or in their lower comedies content themselves with one or two humours at most, and those not near such perfect characters as the admirable Jonson always made, who never wrote a comedy without seven or eight excellent humours. I never saw one, except Falstaff, that was in my judgement comparable to any of Jonson's considerable humours. You will pardon this digression, when I tell you he is the man, of all the world, I most passionately admire for his excellency in his dramatic poetry.

Having thus announced his affiliation, Shadwell attacks the common practice of writers of manners comedy for employing "no such thing as a perfect character," but using as a hero "A swearing, drinking, whoring ruffian" and as a heroine "an impudent ill-bred Tomrig," and as their subjects "bawdry and profaneness." These, Shadwell set himself to reform, creating a play after the prescription of his master by assembling a collection of contrasting humours and propelling them through a regulation love-intrigue designed to expose their folly. In view of such a declaration, and such criticism of his fellows, it is somewhat surprising to discover that Shadwell could on occasion match vulgarity and obscene suggestion with the most accomplished, but even the great Dryden (Shadwell's confirmed enemy) was capable of reversing in the writing of a later play the solemnly reasoned principles announced in the preface to an earlier. Expedience, it might be remarked, is the virtue of those who must "please to live."

The very title of *Bury Fair* (1689) suggests its inspiration, and Oldfox, Trim, and Noddy are introduced in the opening scene in the time-honored manner. In a sense the scene is a union of two conventions of comedy, since Wildish is being dressed by his valet as was Dorimant in *The Man of Mode*, or any of a dozen other Restoration heroes, and, in Jonsonian fashion, is discussing the characters of the humour-ridden fools shortly to be presented. Oldfox is a "paltry, old-fashioned wit and punner of the last age that pretends to have been one of Ben Jonson's sons," Noddy, "a blunt, noisy, laughing, roaring, drinking fellow," and Trim, "a most complete and finished fop . . . , full of forms and empty of substance, all ceremony and no sense." Like Jonson, also, Shadwell sends his characters to the fair, but he uses the fair only as a novel and interesting background for his intrigue; it is not integral to the theme of the play as in *Bartholomew Fair*.

The social attitudes of the London audience are here, and not always satirized. Wildish, the model *beau*, despises the country for the fashionable reasons; Gertrude expounds the conventional attitude towards marriage, "this same whoresome marriage kills all love and makes best friends fall out"; Lady Fantast is gulled by her affectation of good breeding into making a match with La Roche, a French barber. But there are less familiar characters and attitudes in the play also. Bellamy, friend of Wildish, speaks praise of the country as free from "fools, knaves, whores, and hypocrites." He refuses liquor since it has always led him to do "some mad thing or other which made me ashamed to show my face." And he daringly, considering the audience, denounces the gallant's major occupation: "He that debauches private women is a knave and injures others; and he that uses public ones is a fool and hurts himself." In the major action of the play, Gertrude is shown to be a sensible young woman determined to tame her lover before she marries him, and Wildish, the rake, gracefully submits to the dominion of the heart and earnestly promises reformation. If the resolution seems somewhat hastily taken, Shadwell does not intend to suggest that it will be impermanent. The curtain falls on general rejoicing over a double wedding and the anticipation of a happy future. Some of his later plays are openly sentimental; in *Bury Fair* there is a strongly implied criticism of the code of manners, but it is the pretender to the code, Lady Fantast, rather than the complete gallant who is exposed as a fool. The comedy of manners was not yet ready to yield to the demands of morality.

In the history of the neo-classic drama in English, the comedy of manners was a rake that must be reformed. Before the inevitable denouement, however, there came the inevitable climax in which the rakish hero was displayed at the height of his bril-

liance as wit and intriguer. William Congreve's *The Old Bachelor*
(1693) was doctored by Dryden himself and greeted with enthusiasm by the audience. *The Double-Dealer* (1693) was somewhat slower in gaining approval. *Love for Love* (1695) was an
immediate and enduring triumph and *The Way of the World*
(1700), only moderately received at its original showings, is now
generally recognized not only as Congreve's masterpiece, but as
the masterpiece of the comedy of manners. After Congreve there
was time enough for reformation.

Congreve has one basic plot, the story of an honest love affair
brought to near catastrophe by the hero-gallant's relations with
some other woman in the play, relations which proceed not so
much from congenital looseness as from an unwillingness to act
contrary to the prescribed code of social behavior. In a way, this
is the basic plot of all comedies of manners, a hero cannot be a
plain-dealer and a gallant, but only in Congreve's final work does
it achieve the kind of statement which has universal validity.

Love for Love echoes several of the complications of Fletcher's
The Elder Brother and bears a close resemblance to the favorite
situation of Roman comedy—the son must outwit his father to
marry the woman of his choice. Congreve has also consulted the
theories of Ben Jonson for his minor characters: old Foresight,
the victim of superstition, Sir Sampson Legend who makes a
virtue of bluntness, and Tattle, the gossip-monger. Wycherley's
unpleasant account of the seduction of Mrs. Pinchwife is aped in
the scenes between Tattle and Miss Prue, the stupid country
wench, and there are the usual wit-combats between the fashionable lovers.

In the character of Angelica, the fine lady, there is at least
promise of great things to come. Like all Restoration heroines she
is unwilling to resign her heart to any man; love and life are
both games to be played for the sake of amusement according to
her own rules. In *The Mulberry Garden*, Sir Charles Sedley, king
of the wits and master of the chase, had written: "the great
pleasure of gaming were lost if we ever saw one another's hands;
and of love, if we knew one another's hearts: there would be no
room for good play in the one, nor for address in the other;
which are the refined parts of both." To this, Angelica subscribes,
but Valentine, the lover, has made all too plain an exposure of
the condition of his heart. Remembering, perhaps, *The Wild*

Goose Chase, he pretends to be mad for a double purpose; to avoid signing away his estate to his brother Ben, and to win Angelica's sympathy. She is not so easily trapped, mocks him, and refuses to give him any hope.

VALENTINE. You are not leaving me in this uncertainty?
ANGELICA. Would anything but a Madman complain of uncertainty? Uncertainty and expectation are the joys of life. Security is an insipid thing, and the overtaking and possessing of a wish discovers the folly of the chase. Never let us know one another better, for the pleasure of a masquerade is done when we come to show our faces. But I'll tell you two things before I leave you: I am not the fool you take me for, and you are mad and don't know it.   [*Exit*
VALENTINE. From a riddle, you can expect nothing but a riddle.

The riddle is explained, however, when Angelica rescues Valentine's estate for him under pretense of wedding old Sir Sampson, gaining possession of the necessary legal paper and declaring herself at the same time: "I'll use it as I would everything that is an enemy to Valentine." [*Tears the paper.*] It develops that she had been testing his constancy and virtue and finding that he would "persevere even to martyrdom" for her, had no longer hesitation about yielding. In the comedy of manners Patient Valentine has replaced Patient Griselda.

The Way of the World is the apotheosis of Restoration manners comedy. Commonly criticized as badly constructed, it is actually a remarkable demonstration of Congreve's technical skill as a playwright. A single reading of the play will, it is true, result only in bewilderment, for the relationships of the characters are complexly interwoven. On the stage, however, or on re-reading, the relationships straighten themselves out, and in their very complexity they are a symbol of the restricted society with which the play deals. Symbolic too are the three settings in which the action takes place: a chocolate house, St. James's Park, and the home of a lady of quality. These establish visually the limits of the world of the title; and, once the world is established, the action of the play never strays from Lady Wishfort's.

Usually production in the theater can reveal a mastery of dramatic technique which is not observable on the printed page, but even the most casual reader cannot fail to admire the construction of the fourth act of *The Way of the World*. Here is a succession of comic scenes which for variety, point, and juxtaposition for climax can scarcely be matched elsewhere in the drama. Beginning with a satirical portrait of Lady Wishfort determining how best to greet her new "lover" (already known to us as the servant, Waitwell, disguised), it moves to the witty "provisos" on which Millamant and Mirabell expect to found a happy marriage, then to a procession of drunkards climaxed by the whole-hearted farce of Sir Wilfull, and reaches its peak with the long-anticipated meeting of Lady Wishfort and "Sir Rowland."

The act is more than a demonstration of skill in the raising of laughter. The juxtaposition of Lady Wishfort's preparations for deceiving her suitor and the frankly outspoken provisos of the main characters is a statement in terms of the theater of the theme of the play. The way of the world, the world of chocolate houses, St. James's Park, and Lady Wishfort, is the way of deceit, of falseness and pretense, but it represents the only code established for the guidance of the inhabitants of that world. The play has exemplified, in Fainall and his wife, the behavior of a typical married couple who live according to the code in a relationship which is both undignified and unhappy. The proviso scene thus becomes more than mere comic convention as point by point the lovers provide a reasonable basis for their marriage.

Few critics of this play, whatever their attitude towards Restoration comedy as a whole, have been able to resist the spell of Millamant. She is a tease, a wit, a woman of the world; but she is chaste and determined to remain so. She is not perfect since she delights in the affectations and airs that grace a fine lady, but she knows her own value as an individual and she does not yield lightly to the persuasions of Mirabell. But having engaged herself to marry, she does not stipulate for his guarantee of reform; rather she relies upon her own demonstrated powers of entirely capturing his devotion and his imagination. Mirabell, at her first entrance, unwittingly describes her in a parody of the terms Milton applies to Dalila in *Samson Agonistes:* "Here she comes, i' faith, full sail, with her fan spread and her streamers out and a shoal of fools for tenders." And Dalila she is, for she completely subdues the strongest of gallants into a "tractable and complying husband." Though it may be open to question whether she will, in her wisdom, ever permit herself to "dwindle into a wife."

Congreve has not discarded the conventions of Restoration

comedy, but has adjusted them to his theme. The old and the foolish are burlesqued as expected, the country is despised, the usual humours are exhibited, and the dialogue is full of simili-tudes true and false. The norms of conduct are not secondary but central figures in the plot, and the girds at marriage are directly related to the theme. Every incident, farcical, satirical, or simply humorous, has bearing on the main design, to establish a rational marriage contract. Marriage itself only represents the larger social contract which the Restoration had struggled without success to establish for a society without traditions. Millamant and Mirabell were intended by Congreve as symbols of a new order. But reason and wit are impossible models for the world in general, and the comedy of manners, like the more conventional rakish-heroes, was to be reformed by sentiment and not provisos.

2. THE HEROIC PLAY

The serious counterpart of Restoration comedy is so utterly different that it is difficult to believe they were intended for the same theater and audiences. Instead of the amiable man-about-town with an epigram upon his lips and several hundred more up his sleeve, with little money, no heart, and a large troupe of creditors, with a wandering eye and a horror of permanent entanglements, the hero becomes a super man-of-the-world, richly robed in fantastic colors and materials, with a mass of ostrich plumes sprouting from his helm, and endless tirades of moral tags, vaunts, taunts, and epithets spouting from his lungs. The same actor, the same audience, each apparently accepting and believing in a totally different concept of virtue, a totally dif-ferent set of ethical values.

Like the comedy, the heroic play has a complicated ancestry, but to a large extent it derives from English traditions and the English theater. Officially, it may be credited to William Dave-nant whose plays before the closing of the theaters had dealt with the ideal conflicts of love and honor, the almost exclusive concern of the heroic play. During the Commonwealth period, Davenant had remained loyal to the King and had gone with the court to France where he published in 1650 a long heroic poem *Gondi-bert,* in the preface to which he pointed out the political value of the theater as a sop to keep the working man contented with his hard lot. Returning to England, he slipped a second piece of theatrical propaganda into the epilogue to his *First Day's Entertainment at Rutland House* (1656). This was a curious bastard form of drama disguised as declamation set to music and performed under the noses of the authorities. In the declamations, Diogenes and Aristophanes "debate" the question of public entertainments, and a Parisian and a Londoner "declaim concerning the pre-eminence of Paris and London." The lengthy harangues are separated by passages of choral music and the whole concludes with a veiled hint that it is time for the spectators to demand the reopening of the theaters:

> Where you by art learn joy, and when to mourn;
> To watch the plot's swift change and counterturn;
> When Time moves swifter than by nature taught;
> And by a chorus miracles are wrought;
> Making an infant instantly a man—
> These were your plays, but get them if you can.

Disguised as a musical debate against a painted setting in the tradition of the masques or other private entertainments, *The Entertainment* was performed without molestation and Davenant was emboldened to press his luck.

In the same year, also at Rutland House, he wrote and produced *The Siege of Rhodes; Made a Representation by the Art of Perspective in Scenes, and the Story sung in Recitative Music.* The inference of "the story sung in recitative music" is, of course, that *The Siege of Rhodes* was a narrative poem and not a play, and that it was somehow "represented" in painting rather than acted. Such legalistic quibbling was intended either to confuse the issue or save the faces of authorities no longer fanatically interested in preventing the revival of the theater. For *The Siege of Rhodes* is a musical *play*, acted and sung in character on a framed stage against representational scenery; it was an instant success, was revived in 1658, and, after the Restoration, opened in Lincoln's-Inn-Fields in 1661 where it remained long in the repertory.

Davenant undoubtedly deserves more credit as a patron of the drama than as a dramatist. *The Siege of Rhodes* was produced under the most adverse conditions: the stage was but fifteen feet deep and had to contain "the fleet of Soliman . . . , his army, the Island of Rhodes, and the varieties attending the Siege of the city"; the size of the playing area limited his cast to seven, with an apparently static chorus. But the innovations are of greater importance than the limitations. The stage not only represented the scene of the action with flats painted by John Webb, pupil of Inigo Jones, but these scenes were changed freely to indicate change of place. Among the seven actors was a woman, Mrs.

John Webb: Sketch for **The Siege of Rhodes**

Edward Coleman. The story of the play initiated the Restoration heroic theme: the presentation of the true hero and the picture of his constant struggle between the call of love and the call of duty or honor. "The story," wrote Davenant, "is heroical, and notwithstanding the continual hurry and busy agitations of a hot siege is, I hope, intelligibly conveyed to advance the characters of virtue in the shapes of valor and conjugal love."

The plot grows out of a geometrical arrangement of passions. Rhodes, besieged by the Turk, Soliman, is being defended by warriors from all Christian nations, among them Alphonso, a Sicilian duke. His wife, Ianthe, coming to join him, is intercepted by Soliman who is so impressed with her virtue that he gives her safe passage to the city and promises a passport home for her husband and herself. Alphonso's raptures at greeting his wife are immediately dampened as he suspects the motives behind Soliman's act, and is consumed by jealousy, the unforgivable passion in a lover. Roxolana, Soliman's wife, is consumed by the same passion, for the same reason. Soliman and Ianthe are, of course, both innocent.

The qualities of the heroic hero are at once apparent. Soliman rails upon one of his followers:

> hence, from my anger fly:
> Which is too worthy for thee, being mine.

Alphonso defines the supreme impulse that will drive the troops to their most strenuous exertions:

> Ianthe cannot be
> In safer company:
> For what will not the valiant English do
> When beauty is distressed, and virtue too?

The hero's passions are as large as his lungs and his pride is the deadliest of the virtues. In the general run of heroic plays he moves through a plot as mechanically as if he were solving a well-worn theorem.

In several ways, then, *The Siege of Rhodes* is the original of the heroic play. It differs from its successors mainly in the style of its dialogue and the grandeur of its execution. Since it was intended as the libretto of an opera, the metrical patterns of its "speeches" are varied, with heroic couplets used mainly to cement more extended passages in lyric measures. As to the quality of its execution, Dryden remarked that it lacked design and variety of characters, continuing:

An Heroic Play ought to be an imitation in little of an Heroic Poem: and, consequently . . . love and valour ought to be the subject of it. Both of these Sir William Davenant had begun to shadow: but it was so, as first discoverers draw their maps with headlands and promontories and some few outlines of somewhat taken at a distance, and which the designer saw not clearly. The common drama obliged him to a plot well-formed and pleasant, or, as the ancients called it, one entire and great action: but this he afforded not himself in a story, which he neither filled with persons, nor beautified with characters, nor varied with accidents. The laws of an Heroic Poem did not dispense with those of the other ["the common drama"], but raised them to a greater height: and indulged him a farther liberty of fancy, and of drawing all things as far above the ordinary proportion of the stage, as that is beyond the common words and actions of human life: and therefore in the scanting of his images and design, he complied not enough with the greatness and majesty of an Heroic Poem.

The heroic play is not, however, merely an imitation of an heroic poem. It is a mixture of elements from the classical, the contemporary French, and the Jacobean English stage. The dramatic romances of Beaumont and Fletcher (as well as the artificial prose-romances of France) yield the characters, exalted in rank, the settings, remote and unreal, and the typical plot, a series of sensational reversals with a happy ending. These popular elements were modified both by the "rules" of neo-classic criticism and by the practice of the French tragic writers. A serious play should, according to these rules, extol nobility and restraint, and the playwright should have a greater regard for propriety and decorum than for historical truth, aiming at heroic wonder rather than tragic awe. "Fletcher," said Dryden, "neither understood correct plotting, nor that which they call the decorum of the stage"; and the attempts of Restoration improvers to make orderly and decorous drama out of the chaotic masterpieces of the dramatists of the last age resulted in grotesque versions of Shakespeare, like Nahum Tate's *King Lear*.

Neither neo-classical rules nor French models could eliminate completely the true-born English nature of Restoration heroic drama. In spite of critical authority, dramatists were careful to supply plenty of violent action on stage, and comic or musical entr'actes which soon re-introduced the forbidden subplot, more or less fully developed. Comedy creeps into the most serious situations and the happy ending is very nearly inevitable. The heroic play is further demonstration of the power of the audience in determining the nature of its entertainments. In 1665, Sir Robert Howard provided both comic and tragic endings for *The Vestal Virgin,* and in 1672 Dryden was quick to alter his *Marriage-à-la-Mode* from heroic drama to comedy. "I confess," Dryden wrote, "my chief endeavours are to delight the age in which I live," and declared his willingness "to break a rule for the pleasure of variety."

In 1664 Dryden, in collaboration with Sir Robert Howard,

undertook to supply the heroic play with the elements of greatness and majesty which he found lacking in Davenant's work. Their joint work, *The Indian Queen,* and its sequel, *The Indian Emperor* written by Dryden alone in 1665, established the type and insured its popularity. The scene of the first play is laid in Peru, a considerable distance in time and space from the realistic settings of comedy. The intent behind such a choice of locale, as Dryden was later to explain, was that "the representation of such things, as depending not on sense, and therefore not to be comprehended by knowledge, may give the dramatist a freer scope for imagination." To be sure, Dryden's immediate reference is to the use of magic and supernatural beings, but it is equally applicable to the fantastic world of his action.

So too with the hero, Montezuma. At the beginning of the play he is about to slay the Inca for refusing him what he considers just reward for his services, the hand of the Princess Orazia in marriage. Prince Acacis restrains him.

> ACACIS. Hold, sir.
> MONTEZUMA. Unhand me.
> ACACIS. No, I must your rage prevent
> From doing what your reason would repent;
> Like the vast seas, your mind no limits knows,
> Like them, lies open to each wind that blows.
> MONTEZUMA. Can a revenge, that is so just, be ill?
> ACACIS. It is Orazia's father you would kill.
> MONTEZUMA. Orazia! how that name has charmed my sword!

Since his love for the daughter prevents him from killing the father, he resolves to seek revenge by fighting with the Mexicans, whom he has just defeated, against the Peruvians, whom he has just led to victory. This immediately raises the question of honor. Acacis is a Mexican and a prisoner, but he refuses to allow Montezuma to liberate him:

> I, as a prisoner, am by honor tied.
> MONTEZUMA. You are my prisoner, and I set you free.
> ACACIS. 'Twere baseness to accept such liberty.
> MONTEZUMA. From him that conquered you, it should be sought.
> ACACIS. No, but from him for whom my conqueror fought.
> MONTEZUMA. Still you are mine, his gift has made you so.
> ACACIS. He gave me to his general, not his foe.

As a result of this splitting of hairs, Montezuma, captor of Acacis, finds himself fighting for Acacis' country, and Acacis, the captive, finds himself preparing to defend Montezuma's beloved and her father against his attack. Yet even this is but preliminary to the real complications of the plot, in which Dryden and Howard more than compensate for the deficiency in "design" of *The Siege of Rhodes.* For however tiresome the ringing of changes upon the love and honor theme may be to the modern reader, he cannot fail to recognize that these plays are filled with violent, not to say melodramatic, events. Duels, battles, ambushes, visions, aerial choruses, courtly pomp, and religious ritual lend variety and color to the action, as the epilogue says, "To help out wit with some variety." As much emphasis was placed upon the spectacular settings as upon the text of the play. Again the epilogue,

> 'Tis true, you have marks enough, the plot, the show,
> The poet's scenes, nay, more, the painter's too;

and in the next year Dryden wrote the sequel, *The Indian Emperor,* in part to give occasion for the re-display of the scenery.

These plays, like Davenant's, were written in rhyming verse, but unlike his operas, in heroic couplets of great regularity. While this in itself is perhaps to be credited to the influence of French drama with its strict pattern of Alexandrine couplets, Dryden justifies the re-introduction of rhyme into English verse drama on a number of grounds: as an aid to the memory, as giving a particular grace to repartee, but most particularly as bounding and circumscribing the fancy. "Imagination in a poet," he writes in the Dedication to *The Rival Ladies,* "is a faculty so wild and lawless, that, like an high-ranging spaniel, it must have clogs tied to it, lest it outrun the judgement."

One of the most successful, as well as typical, of the heroic plays was Dryden's *The Conquest of Granada* (two parts, 1670, 1671). Two years earlier Dryden had published his famous *Essay of Dramatic Poesy* containing his equally famous definition of a play: "A just and lively image of human nature, representing its humours and passions, and the changes of fortune to which it is subject, for the delight and instruction of mankind." As an illustration of that definition, *The Conquest of Granada* is something of a surprise. The life which it images is completely fantastic and the instruction which it yields ambiguous. There is, to be sure, a fine assortment of humours and passions, but of human nature only the barest suggestion.

The background of the story is the historical re-conquest of Spain from the Moors by the Christian King Ferdinand in the fifteenth century, but Dryden, following a famous precept of the French Academy, has greater regard for "propriety" than historical truth—propriety meaning in this instance the true character of a great-souled hero. Two women are at the center of the plot, a bad one, Lyndaraxa, ambitious to be a queen (played, without irony, by Nell Gwyn!), and a good one, Almahide. Each is provided with two important lovers who are, of course, rivals. Since the ladies themselves are also rivals, the possible situations involving combinations and confrontations of characters are infinite and geometrical. A summary of Part One will exemplify the structure and technique of the heroic drama at its best.

Granada, the last remaining Moorish stronghold, is besieged by the Spaniards. During the first part of the play, however, Dryden concerns himself almost exclusively with the intramural contests of various Moorish factions, and the stratagems by which Lyndaraxa hopes to attain the throne. Boabdelin, the weak but voluble king, is scarcely able to keep his subjects from each other's throats, and in the first act they are actually about to come to blows when a mysterious stranger, Almanzor, arrives on the scene, instantly takes the weaker side and, when the king ineffectually orders the fight to cease, forces both factions to unite for the sake of future victories over the Spaniards. In the second act, Lyndaraxa scorns her lover, Abdelmelech, for Abdalla, the king's brother, whom she promises to wed if he will kill the king and usurp the throne. Abdalla discovers that the king has denied a boon to Almanzor and that the stranger is wild for revenge. Together they defeat Boabdelin, and Abdalla, momentarily, is king of Granada.

However, in Act Three, Almahide is introduced, the betrothed of Boabdelin. Almanzor is immediately smitten with her as is Zulema, the brother of Lyndaraxa. Abdalla, the new king, naturally takes Zulema's side, which drives Almanzor at once to Boabdelin whom he once more places on the throne, in the fourth act. Abdalla, no longer king and dismissed by Lyndaraxa, escapes from the city and flees to the Spanish camp. In the final act, Boabdelin promises Almanzor any boon he may desire as a reward for his services. Almanzor asks for the hand of Almahide, is denied, and goes into exile. In the Second Part, the stratagems of Lyndaraxa lead to the deaths of herself and her foolish lovers, and the brave Almanzor, revealed as the long-lost son of a Christian Spaniard, is united to Almahide in the inevitable *quod erat demonstrandum*.

The plot, it will be seen, is a series of reversals or re-groupings of the principal figures, generally dependent upon the passion which happens to dominate Almanzor at any given moment. The whole play turns upon him and it is his character which gives it such interest as it may retain. To Dryden he was the heroic hero *par excellence* drawn after the most acceptable models: Achilles, the Rinaldo of Tasso, and the Artaban of Calprenède. In a conventionally-fawning dedication to the Duke of York, the author confesses that Almanzor is not "absolutely perfect, but of an excessive and overboiling courage. . . . I designed in him a roughness of character, impatient of injuries, and a confidence of himself almost approaching to an arrogance; but these errors are incident only to great spirits." The term, "great spirits," is constantly associated with the hero and must, doubtless, refer to the Aristotelian quality of magnanimity, "great-souledness." Perhaps fearing that Almanzor's overboiling courage and arrogance might be misunderstood, Dryden is careful to put into the mouth of Abenamar, the king's counsellor, an editorial reminder:

> What in another vanity would seem
> Appears but noble confidence in him.
> No haughty boasting, but a manly pride;
> A soul too fiery and too great to guide.
> He moves eccentric, like a wand'ring star
> Whose motion's just, though 'tis not regular.

Almanzor is, in fact, a relic of the chivalric code so burlesqued in *Don Quixote,* and the most apt term to describe his actions is not arrogant but quixotic. At his first entrance he chooses to fight for the outnumbered Abencerrages without inquiring the nature or justice of their quarrel:

> I cannot stay to ask what cause is best;
> But this is so to me because oppressed.

When the king threatens to execute him for disobeying an express order, he replies with disdain:

> No man has more contempt than I of breath,
> But whence hast thou the right to give me death?
> Obeyed as sovereign by thy subjects be,
> But know, that I alone am king of me;

and spurns the guards sent to kill him with the command, "Stand off; I have not leisure yet to die."

In the third act, Abdalla approaches him with the scheme for overthrowing Boabdelin and promises to bring evidence to support his claims to the throne. This Almanzor takes almost as an insult:

> It is sufficient that you make the claim;
> You wrong our friendship when your Right you name.
> When for myself I fight, I weigh the cause,
> But friendship will admit of no such laws
> That weighs by the lump, and when the cause is light,
> Puts kindness in to set the balance right.
> True, I could wish my friend the juster side,
> But in the unjust my kindness more is tried.

Yet this mighty hero, for whom no odds are too great, no enemy sufficiently powerful, and who begs to be sent to fight outside the city since all he has accomplished

> is too little to be done by me. . . .
> I cannot breathe within this narrow space,
> My heart's too big, and swells beyond the place,—

this mighty hero is brought to his knees by his love for the virtuous and beautiful Almahide:

> Born as I am still to command, not sue,
> Yet you shall see that I can beg for you.

At the end of the play he takes the loser's part in a triangular love scene, and leaves the stage "undone" by love.

It is in this picture of a superman completely ruled by a woman that the heroic play finds a kind of affinity with Restoration comedy. However tremendous the historical or political, the ultimate motive is always love and the prime mover a woman. Nor is this the wholly idealistic concept of Platonic love. The relations between the sexes were matter for intellectual wit-combats in comedy and, in addition, were a very real part of the action; so in the heroic play, Almanzor and Almahide debate at length the problem of love versus honor, and Almanzor refers very frankly to the nuptial bed as his goal. Love is ever the victor in the repeated conflict with honor or political duty, but underneath the cloak of inflated diction and rant, it is not infrequently the same physical love which is the major concern of the plots—if not the provisos—of the comic writers.

Yet the popularity of heroic drama need not depend on its exaggeration of virtue and vice or its exaltation of love. In the hands of Dryden, at least, it could rise to genuine poetic statement. Here, for instance, is Almahide's farewell to Almanzor:

> Heaven will reward your worth some better way;
> At least, for me, you have but lost one day.
> Nor is't a real loss which you deplore;
> You sought a heart that was engaged before.
> 'Twas a swift love which took you in his way,
> Flew only through your heart, but made no stay.
> 'Twas but a dream, where truth had not a place,
> A scene of fancy, moved so swift apace
> And shifted, that you can but think it was:
> Let, then, the short vexatious vision pass.

Even the rants, the passages so much ridiculed in after years, were written to please a theatrical taste which by no means died out with the vogue of the heroic play. When the usurping king grants Almanzor a pardon, he gets the following speech of gratitude:

> If from thy hands alone my death can be,
> I am immortal, and a God, to thee.
> If I would kill thee now, thy fate's so low
> That I must stoop ere I can give the blow,
> But mine is fixed so far above thy crown
> That all thy men
> Piled on my back can never pull it down;
> But at my ease thy destiny I send
> By ceasing from this hour to be thy friend.
> Like heaven I need but only to stand still
> And not concurring to thy life, I kill.

It is true that this is spoken in a passion by a passionate man, but it can hardly appear other than absurd on the printed page. Yet Colley Cibber is our witness that worse rants than Almanzor's gave pleasure to an audience that prided itself upon cynical wit and classical taste. "When these flowing numbers," he writes, "came from the mouth of a Betterton, the multitude no more desired sense to them than our musical connoisseurs think it essential in the celebrate airs of an Italian opera."

The heroic drama was not, however, a form to be accepted without criticism by the wits. In 1671, a collaboration involving the Duke of Buckingham, Martin Clifford, Thomas Sprat and perhaps Samuel Butler, produced *The Rehearsal,* another of the burlesques of the theater which mark the stages of the development of the English drama. *The Rehearsal* seems to have been many years in the writing and the chief butt of its jokes is, variously, Davenant, Sir Robert Howard, and Dryden, but its major purpose remains constant: to mock the absurdities of heroic playwriting and Restoration stagecraft. Because it is so closely packed with contemporary allusion and "local hits," much of the amusement—it was extremely popular—is inevitably lost. Yet there is enough of a general comic nature to give the piece some vitality.

The situation is the familiar play-within-a-play: Mr. Bayes, the dramatist, invites two friends to the rehearsal of his new work, and the satire develops partly from their comments. Principally, however, the satire grows out of Bayes' heroic drama itself, the plot of which is so complicated the very actors cannot follow it. One actor explains to a comrade who cannot understand his rôle: "The grand design upon the stage is to keep the auditors in suspense, for to guess presently at the plot and the sense tires them before the end of the first act." Bayes contradicts his actor somewhat later when one of the spectators complains that a passage of comedy has nothing to do with the action, that the plot stands still. "Plot stand still!" he cries, "why, what the devil is the plot good for, but to bring in fine things?" Spectacular scenes, costumes, and dances are the main concern of the playwright, who wastes little time on plot or character, furnishing such trivia from his "Drama Commonplace Book" where he has noted down all the effective situations and speeches of his fellow playwrights. Passions and bombasts are introduced without warning and without relation to the plot, the exposition is conducted entirely in whispers, the kingdom is provided with two kings, all for the sake of novelty. As Bayes explains, "I despise your Jonson and Beaumont that borrowed all they writ from nature; I am for fetching it purely out of my own fancy, I."

The final target is always Dryden, however, and at his favorite devices the most telling shafts are aimed. The love and honor conflict is ridiculed by an unshod actor sitting down to draw on his boots:

My legs the emblem of my various thought
Show to what sad distraction I am brought.
Sometimes with stubborn honor, like this boot,
My mind is guarded and resolved to do't.
Sometimes again, that very mind, by love
Disarmed, like this other leg does prove.
Shall I to honor or to love give way?
Go on, cries honor; tender love says, nay;
Honor aloud commands, pluck both boots on;
But softer love doth whisper, put on none.

Dryden's very poetic technique is satirized as Mr. Bayes stands by to comment enthusiastically on Volscius' debate with Prince Prettyman:

VOLSCIUS. I gladly would that story from you learn;
But thou to love dost, Prettyman, incline;
Yet love in thy breast is not love in mine.
BAYES. Antithesis! thine and mine.
PRETTYMAN. Since love itself's the same, why should it be
Diff'ring in you from what it is in me?
BAYES. Reasoning! egad, I love reasoning in verse.
VOLSCIUS. Love takes, cameleon-like, a various dye
From every plant on which itself doth lie.
BAYES. Simile!

But it is with Dryden's hero, Almanzor, that the wit of the authors of *The Rehearsal* is most severely tried. It is not an easy task to make more absurd that which is already perilously close to the farcical. One of the friends inquires of the playwright:

Pray, Mr. Bayes, who is that Drawcansir?
BAYES. Why, sir, a fierce hero that fights his mistress, snubs up kings, baffles armies, and does what he will, without regard to numbers, good manners, or justice.

In the first scene of Act V,

A battle is fought between foot and great hobby-horses. At last DRAWCANSIR comes in and kills them all on both sides. . . .

DRAWCANSIR. Others may boast a single man to kill;
But I the blood of thousands daily spill.
Let petty kings the names of parties know:
Where'er I come, I slay both friend and foe. . . .
If they had wings, and to the gods could fly,
I would pursue and beat 'em through the sky;
And make proud Jove, with all his thunder, see
This single arm more dreadful is than he.

"There's a brave fellow for you now, sirs," comments the proud
creator. "You may talk of your Hectors and Achilles, and I know
not who; but I defy all your histories, and your romances too,
to show me one such conqueror as this Drawcansir." The reference to Dryden's own explanation of his Almanzor is apparent,
and line after line of *The Conquest of Granada,* along with lesser
plays, is skillfully parodied. *The Rehearsal* is further evidence of
the intimacy and the smallness of the Restoration theater and its
public.

That public did not, apparently, echo very insistently the conclusion of *The Rehearsal*'s epilogue: "Pray let this prove a year
of prose and sense." The vogue of the heroic drama continued
unabated. Dryden must have been supplying a demand with his
Amboyna, or the Cruelties of the Dutch to the English Merchants
(1673), and *Aureng-Zebe* (1675), and such playwrights as Crowne,
Orrery, Lee, and Settle did not lack hearers.

In 1678, with *All for Love, or The World Well Lost,* Dryden
cast off his once-loved mistress, rhyme, and returned to blank
verse, signalling a change not only in the manner but in the
matter of neo-classical tragedy. Since it is based on the story of
Shakespeare's *Antony and Cleopatra,* comparisons are inevitable
and are generally uncomplimentary to the later play. Such comparisons are not altogether fair, since they ignore the intentions
of the playwrights and the intellectual climate in which they
wrote. In proper perspective, *All for Love* is at its worst respectable, at its best, profoundly moving. In a famous essay "The
Grounds of Criticism in Tragedy" prefixed to his *Troilus and
Cressida* (1679), Dryden declares his allegiance to neo-classical
principles. Tragedy, he declares, should have but a single great
action, involving great persons. The moral of the action must
be determined first and the fable built upon it. The hero should
be a man with a preponderance of virtues, though not barren of
vices, and the characterization must follow the precept of *decorum,* be suited to the person in age and dignity, and be made
apparent in both speech and action. Finally, the language must
be seemly, since no man is at leisure to make sentences and
similes when his soul is in agony. In this, he assures the reader,
he is not attacking "height of thought," "pathetic vehemence,"
or "nobleness of expression," but only the "false measure" of

them in the wrong place. Of these neo-classical principles, *All for Love* is an ideal illustration.

Dryden does not see the story of Antony and Cleopatra as a conflict between worlds or ways of life but as a conflict, within the mind and soul of the hero, between love of his mistress and duty to his state. The entire action of the play is arranged to present this psychological struggle, the first act ending with the triumph of duty as Ventidius persuades him to resume his martial career, the second with the triumph of love as Cleopatra works her spell on the hero, and so on, with honor and love alternating until the fifth act in which the world (the state, duty) is well lost for love.

No subplot interferes with the progress of this conflict, and even the number of characters required to relate it is cut down by combination (Dryden's Ventidius represents both the Ventidius and Enobarbus of Shakespeare). Many of the scenes which are dramatized in the first two acts of the older play are compressed into expository speeches in Dryden's second act, after he has established the atmosphere, the emotional envelope, of his tragedy in Act One. The effectiveness of the play depends very largely, then, on the characterization of Marc Antony, on Dryden's ability to make him at once probable and heroic. It is a considerable achievement, as the playwright recognized when he wrote, "To invent a probability and make it wonderful is the most difficult undertaking of the art of poetry," quite the reverse of the problem which faced him in creating Almanzor.

Antony, on his first appearance, is far from the "bully" of the heroic play. He is full of love's melancholy, and like that other notable sentimentalist, Orsino, Duke of Illyria, calls for music that, "surfeiting, the appetite may sicken and so die." Ventidius intrudes with the direct speech of a bluff soldier and, in a scene which Dryden considered his very best, persuades Antony to choose the path of honor. The dialogue is vigorous and life-like as Ventidius' manliness puts heart into his melancholic leader.

> VENTIDIUS. You sleep away your hours
>   In desperate sloth, miscalled philosophy.
>   Up, up, for honor's sake; twelve legions wait you . . .
> ANTONY. Where left you them?
> VENTIDIUS. I said in Lower Syria.

ANTONY. Bring them hither;
   There may be life in these.
VENTIDIUS. They will not come.
ANTONY. Why didst thou mock my hopes with promised aids
   To double my despair? They're mutinous.
VENTIDIUS. Most firm and loyal.
ANTONY. Yet they will not march
   To succor me. Oh, trifler!
VENTIDIUS. They petition
   You would make haste to head them.
ANTONY. I'm besieged.
VENTIDIUS. There's but one way shut up: How came I thither?
ANTONY. I will not stir.
VENTIDIUS. They would perhaps desire
   A better reason.
ANTONY. I have never used
   My soldiers to demand a reason of
   My actions. Why did they refuse to march?
VENTIDIUS. They said they would not fight for Cleopatra.
ANTONY. What was't they said?
VENTIDIUS. They said they would not fight for Cleopatra.

The directness and simplicity of the speech illustrates Dryden's new principle that the language must be "seemly," while the irregularity, the broken lines, and the swift tempo convey—and more dramatically than tirades or extended similes—the emotion which underlies the situation.

All for Love does not, of course, turn its back completely on the heroic play. In getting rid of the rhymed couplet, it is perhaps merely following the poetic fads, and the theme and subject matter continue unchanged. However, the return to Shakespeare seems to have been educational. There is a quality in the play almost totally lacking from his earlier work:

ANTONY. How I loved
   Witness ye Days and Nights, and all your Hours
   That danced away with down upon your feet,
   As all your business were to count my passion.
   One day passed by, and nothing saw but love;
   Another came, and still 'twas only love:
   The suns were wearied out with looking on,
   And I untired with loving.
   I saw you every day, and all the day;
   And every day was still but as the first:
   So eager was I still to see you more.

On the other hand, the experience of writing in heroic couplet and working out the geometric complexities of heroic plots was salutary in re-introducing a sense of form into a drama which had grown, at the end of the panoramic period, diffuse and slovenly. It is noteworthy, at any rate, that from about 1678 a type of serious drama more closely related to the native English form, while displaying a consciousness of the neo-classical rules, begins to take possession of the stage.

~ 6 ~

Neo-Classic Drama: Sense and Sensibility

In 1688 James II was deposed and William of Orange placed on the throne of England in a bloodless revolution which was not without its significance for the drama. The Stuart courts had been notorious for their licentiousness and the courtiers, as the almost exclusive patrons of the theater, expected, and got, licentious entertainment. King William and Queen Mary re-introduced the domestic virtues at the very moment when the Restoration social code had become so excessive that a reaction was almost automatic. The noble vagabonds who had returned with Charles II in 1660 had had, after all, almost thirty years to settle down.

Further, the backbone of English society, the middle class with its strong Puritanical elements, was beginning to reassert itself. Deprived of a popular audience the Restoration theater had made but a precarious livelihood; to appeal to the popular audience certain changes were mandatory. Nor were "friends of the court" lacking to indicate the points at which improvement was desired.

Foremost among the censors was the Reverend Jeremy Collier who published, in 1698, *A Short View of the Immorality and Profaneness of the English Stage*. The effectiveness of Collier's attack has been variously over- and under-estimated, depending upon the convictions of the estimators. He was not, certainly, an Almanzor turning the tide of theatrical taste with a loud-mouthed rant and an invincible right arm. But neither was he a Don Quixote, a bright, ineffectual battler against imaginary enemies. The evil was real and Collier's attack was energetic; he was the most successful mouthpiece of widespread sentiment.

In part his success and his enduring fame must be credited to his completeness, his fundamental common sense, and his readability. If his weaknesses were many, his strength is obvious: Restoration comedy was indecent in its language, excessive in its profanity, and immoral in the tendency of its plots. With a kind

of Germanic thoroughness Collier went through the repertory of
the theater culling illustrations without fear or favoritism from
Dryden, Wycherley, Congreve, Vanburgh (*The Relapse* is treated
at length as particularly vicious), and the minor writers. Nor is
Collier wholly without a kind of wit in his censures. Complaining of the frequent indecent puns and *double-entendres,* he continues, "They have sometimes not so much as the poor refuge
of a Double Meaning to fly to. So that you are under the necessity either of taking ribaldry or nonsense. And when the sentence
has two handles, the worst is generally turned to the audience."
Or again, speaking of the immorality of the plots, "The stage
seldom gives quarter to anything that's serviceable or significant,
but persecutes worth and goodness under every appearance. He
that would be safe from their satire must take care to disguise
himself in vice, and hang out the colors of debauchery. . . . As
if people were not apt enough of themselves to be lazy, lewd,
and extravagant, unless they were pricked forward and provoked
by glory and reputation."

Like all censors, of course, Collier bedevils his subject into
absurdities. He first attacks Vanbrugh's *The Relapse* on the
grounds that the title, which applies to only half the plot, is a
misnomer, and "when a poet can't rig out a title page, 'tis but
a bad sign of his holding out to the Epilogue." His next point
is the well-taken one that the moral is vicious: "It points the
wrong way, and puts the prize into the wrong hand." The characters then come in for scrutiny and there is a certain sober-sided
justice in Collier's comment that they are hardly logical in conception and execution: "In short, either Lord Foplington [*sic*] and
Sir Tunbelly are fools or they are not. If they are, where lies the
cunning in overreaching them? . . . If they are not fools, . . .
why is their conduct so gross, so parti-colored, and inconsistent?
Take them either way and the plot miscarries. The first supposi-
tion makes it dull, and the latter incredible. So much for the
plot." However, the censor also holds up his hands in horror
when Loveless asks Berinthia to swear secrecy:

> LOVELESS. By what?
> BERINTHIA. By woman.
> LOVELESS. That's swearing by my Deity; do it by your own
> or I shan't believe you.
> BERINTHIA. By man, then.

At lovers' perjuries Jove may laugh, but not the Reverend Jeremy Collier.

So niggling an objection as the last is as typical of Collier's commentary as his larger and more fundamental strictures, and the reader is perhaps prone to seize upon the crass and let the creditable go. But to the playwrights and critics of the turn of the eighteenth century, the attack was a serious matter; it stung them, and they replied. The replies are for the most part feeble. Even Congreve expended most of his wit on Collier's eccentricities, but could find very little to say in reply to the major charges of immoral plots and indecent speech. Vanbrugh admitted that the *Short View* was "now a thing no farther to be laughed at," and Dryden, in the preface to his *Fables* (1700), was careful to point out "that I have written nothing that savors of immorality or profaneness. . . . I wish I could affirm, with a safe conscience, that I had taken the same care in all my former writings." In the immediate controversy the prize went to the "religious Lawyer," and although the stage was not at once purified, the ultimate victory was his also.

1. FROM WIT TO MORALITY

One of the earliest manifestations of a revived interest in the older code of morality is Colley Cibber's *Love's Last Shift*, produced in 1696, two years before Collier's attack. At first glance this is a not very witty and not very original Restoration comedy, opening in the accepted fashion with the man-about-town discussing the desperate state of his purse with his servant. We are almost at once introduced to Young Worthy who is bent on hoodwinking Sir William Wisewoud out of his daughter and her fortune, and to Sir Novelty Fashion, a pretender to wit and the social graces. There is much loose talk, and the expected jeers at marriage, and it is made plain by reiteration that the whole duty of man is to get money in order that he may live a life of pleasure.

Through this conventionally cynical plot, however, moves the unconventional figure of Amanda, "A woman of strict virtue," dressed in mourning for her husband who had deserted her ten years before and whom she mistakenly believes to be dead. Young Worthy, also, is not quite the callous beau we anticipate. Coming

upon Amanda's husband newly returned to England, he addresses
him in a manner to which we are not accustomed. "Faith, Ned,"
he says, "I am as much in love with wickedness as thou canst be,
but I am for having it at a cheaper rate than my ruin! Don't it
grate you a little to see your friends blush for you?" Imagine, if
you please, a Restoration wit daring to blush for the elegant
Dorimant, or Valentine, or Horner. What is worse,, Young
Worthy "preaches" the hoydenish Hillaria into matrimony with
his solemn brother so seriously that the audience quite forgets
his financial interest in their union. And finally, it is this same
young man about town who contrives the "shift" by which
Amanda wins back her errant husband, Loveless.

The shift is not very novel, to be sure. Having not seen his
wife for a decade Loveless is presumed to have forgotten her appearance, and she presents herself to him as a mistress. A day
later, he is a reformed character, having discovered that the
"happy life" is to be found in the arms of a "virtuous wife."
Loveless announces with conviction at the end of the play:

> All my life to come shall show how I approve the moral. . . . By my
> example taught, let every man whose fate has bound him to a married
> life beware of letting loose his wild desires; for if experience may be
> allowed to judge, I must proclaim the folly of a wandering passion.
> The greatest happiness we can hope on earth,
> > *And sure the nearest to the joys above*
> > *Is the chaste rapture of a virtuous love.*

In his *Apology for his Life* Cibber is becomingly modest about
this, his first play, quoting with approval Congreve's criticism
that it had "only in it a great many things that were *like* wit,
that in reality were *not* wit"; and admitting that he had written
it to give himself a good part in Sir Novelty Fashion. That he
had some misgivings about the reception of a play ending with a
reformed rake going with raptures into the arms of a mere virtuous woman is apparent from the epilogue, spoken (according
to a frequent repulsive Restoration custom) by a little girl:

> He fears he has made a fault you'll ne'er forgive,
> A crime beyond the hopes of a reprieve:
> An honest rake forego the joys of life!
> His whores, and wine, to embrace a dull cast wife!
> Such out-of-fashion stuff! But then, again,
> He's lewd for above four acts, gentlemen!

Forty years later, however, he acknowledged that the imitation wit, the puerility of the sentiments and the "frothy stage language" had little to do with its continuing success, which was due rather to the "mere moral delight received from its fable." It must be recognized, however, that the moral delight is superficial, that there is, once more to quote Prince Hal, but a pennyworth of reformation to an intolerable deal of corruption.

Sir John Vanbrugh's *The Relapse* (1696), which caused so much anguish to Jeremy Collier, is a sequel and a reply to, and in a sense an acknowledgement of Cibber's "moral" position. According to tradition, Vanbrugh scoffed at the notion that so experienced a rake as Loveless could rest reformed, and wrote his play in six weeks to illustrate his point. Loveless becomes involved in an affair with Berinthia, Amanda's cousin, Amanda's own virtue is sorely tempted by Worthy, and Sir Novelty (now elevated to Lord Foppington) finds himself the rival of his younger brother for the hand of Miss Hoyden, daughter of a country squire, Sir Tunbelly Clumsey.

Cibber had relied more upon farce than wit to keep his audience in a good humor; Vanbrugh does likewise. Although Amanda maintains her virtue and Loveless once again reforms after having paid Berinthia the "last compliment," *The Relapse* is in effect less moral than *Love's Last Shift*. There is a warmth, a passion, in the scenes of seduction which is nearly absent from the earlier Comedy of Manners and is only hinted at in the seduction scene of Cibber's play—where it is muted, of course, by the audience's knowledge that Loveless is wooing his own wife. Vanbrugh acknowledges the immorality of his comedy in the Preface: once by denial—"I am even to this day insensible of those two shining graces in the play (which some part of the Town is pleased to compliment me with) Blasphemy and Bawdy"; and once by indirect admission of the lifelikeness of the attempted rape of Amanda. Collier's objections are well taken both as to the dramatic weaknesses and moral ambiguities of *The Relapse*.

Vanbrugh was not discouraged from playwriting by Collier's analysis of his work, nor, in spite of disclaimers, was he encouraged to rise above the vulgarity of action and smuttiness of speech which are the more prominent in *The Relapse* for being mingled with morality. His characters are the stock types of neo-classical comedy, the gallant, the clever servant, the fop, the oafish country cousin, and the rest. His plots are the usual neo-classical intrigue and counter-intrigue for love and/or money, with last minute victory for the forces of youth and gallantry, and forgiveness and reformation all around. According to Cibber, the actors all declared "The style of no author whatsoever gave their memory less trouble than that of Sir John Vanbrugh," which may be taken two ways: that the dialogue is written with consummate ease and grace, or that it contains no complexity of thought.

It is generally true that as comedy moves closer to the standards of middle-class morality, to sentimentality, it moves nearer the surface of life. The comparison of George Farquhar's *The Beaux' Stratagem* (1706) with any typical Restoration manners play will indicate the degree of change. To begin with, leaving the monotonous round of London taverns, parks, and boudoirs, the scene is Litchfield, and the majority of the characters country people. The usual jeers at rural life are voiced by Mrs. Sullen, but since her objections are little more than mere fashionable patter the author's point of view may be represented by the skillful counter-arguments proposed by Dorinda, her rural sister-in-law.

Mrs. Sullen, in fact, is a rather old-fashioned character. She longs for the graces of London society and discusses the marriage-state as if she were participating in a comedy of Wycherley's some thirty years before. " 'Tis a standing maxim in conjugal discipline," she explains to Dorinda, "that when a man would enslave his wife, he hurries her into the country; and when a lady would be arbitrary with her husband, she wheedles her booby up to Town.—A man may not play the tyrant in London, because there are so many examples to encourage the subject to rebel." In her old-fashioned way, in the last act Mrs. Sullen finds herself in her bedroom with the hero of the comedy prepared to coöperate in cuckolding her husband. At this moment, however, a gang of thieves breaks into the house, and Mrs. Sullen is saved from an old-fashioned fate.

This reversal of the expected event is typical of Farquhar's play. Archer and Aimwell are two young penniless gallants from London fortune-hunting in the country. Money is their sole concern, for it is their maxim "that there is no scandal like rags, nor any crime so shameful as poverty." They have devised a complicated program of imposture for trapping a rural beauty with a large dowry—an accepted pattern of behavior for the Restoration man-about-town. The author's attitude toward them, however, is governed by his audience, and this audience, increasingly of the mercantile middle-class, regarded the pursuit of money as a serious, not a flippant, matter. Money becomes the reward of virtue not viciousness; the crown of life is a beautiful wife with a fortune, and as Aimwell frankly declares, "no woman *can* be a beauty without a fortune." Perhaps, therefore, there is an intentional irony in the opening situation: the young men, disguised for purposes of deceit, take up lodgings in a country inn whose owner is a fence and setter for a gang of highwaymen. At any rate both Archer and Aimwell must prove their honor and valor (as well as their wit) before they are permitted to marry their wealthy beauties.

The Beaux' Stratagem reverses Restoration practice in other significant situations. The proviso scene, in which fine lady and witty gentleman laid down the conditions of their marriage bond, was a regular and delightful item. Farquhar's "proviso" comes after the fact:

MRS. SULLEN. Pray, Spouse, what did you marry for?

SULLEN. To get an heir to my estate.

SIR CHARLES. And have you succeeded?

SULLEN. No.

ARCHER. The condition fails of his side.—Pray, Madam, what did you marry for?

MRS. SULLEN. To support the weakness of my sex by the strength of his, and to enjoy the pleasures of an agreeable society.

SIR CHARLES. Are your expectations answered?

MRS. SULLEN. No. . . .

SIR CHARLES. What are the bars to your mutual contentment?

MRS. SULLEN. In the first place I can't drink ale with him.

SULLEN. Nor can I drink tea with her.

MRS. SULLEN. I can't hunt with you.

SULLEN. Nor can I dance with you.

MRS. SULLEN. I hate cocking and racing.

SULLEN. And I abhor ombre and piquet.

MRS. SULLEN. Your silence is intolerable.

SULLEN. Your prating is worse. . . .

MRS. SULLEN. Is there on earth a thing we could agree in?

SULLEN. Yes—to part.

MRS. SULLEN. With all my heart.

SULLEN. Your hand.

MRS. SULLEN. Here.

SULLEN. These hands joined us; these shall part us—
    Away—
MRS. SULLEN. North.
SULLEN. South.
MRS. SULLEN. East.
SULLEN. West—as far as poles asunder.
COUNT. Begar, the ceremony be vera pretty!

Another reversal of the convention is the character of Lady
Bountiful, who corresponds in age to Lady Wishfort and the
other eager, ugly old women of Restoration comedy, but is here
portrayed as charitable and kindly, and foolish only in her blindness to her son's character. Marriage, too, is a serious, sentimental
business, and any one of the higher characters is apt at any
moment to slip into a kind of prosy blank verse for the elevation
of a commonplace into the appearance of original truth.

This is not to say that *The Beaux' Stratagem* is a solemn or
unfunny stage-piece. It is, in general, light-hearted and full of
comic bustle. If Boniface, the innkeeper, with his perpetual
tag-line, becomes tiresome, his daughter Cherry is a fine romping
ingenue, descended from Margery Pinchwife and Harriet Wood-
vil and Miss Prue, but with a heartiness and frankness which
furnishes little of the perverted satisfaction of hearing double
meanings from innocent mouths. The plot is complicated, but
not so involved as to bewilder the spectator, and the action moves
swiftly to its connubial conclusion. *The Beaux' Stratagem* is, in
short, a good early example of the type of comedy which will
dominate the English stage for two centuries, an intrigue plot
acted out by a mixture of stock and eccentric characters, ending
with the chime of wedding bells and the happy clink of golden
coins tumbling into the money bags of the leading man.

2. SENTIMENTAL COMEDY

The plays of Cibber, Vanbrugh, and Farquhar are really closer
to the Restoration than to the eighteenth century comic tradition. With the exception of the first, they make no profession of
moral intent and only in Farquhar is the hero required to earn
his good fortune. To Sir Richard Steele must go the credit, or
the blame, for returning the drama to its original purpose of

edification and for using the theater to propagate the newly discovered virtues of humanitarianism and morality.

As proprietor, with Joseph Addison, of The *Tatler* and *Spectator* he resolved to "enliven morality with wit and temper wit with morality." In a series of comedies beginning with *The Funeral* in 1701 and concluding with *The Conscious Lovers* in 1722 he carried the same program into his playwrighting, and indeed the prologue to the last declares its intention "To chasten wit, and moralize the stage." A play, to Steele, was an educational experience for the spectator, and a dramatist one who taught "by precept and example." A major concern of *The Conscious Lovers* is to attack the practice of duelling and to suggest that a man may refuse a challenge without being a coward or a knave.

The Conscious Lovers, with its combination of sentiment and farce, is typical of Steele's comedy. Based in part on the *Andria* of Terence, it is neo-classical in its structure and pathetic in its motivation. Two young ladies are at the center of the plot: Lucinda, daughter of Mr. Sealand a prosperous merchant, and Indiana, an orphan. Lucinda's father intends that she shall wed young Bevil; her mother, that she shall wed Cimberton, a country coxcomb. She is actually in love with Myrtle, friend to young Bevil, and Bevil, inevitably, is in love with Indiana. In earlier comedy, the intrigue would consist solely in the outwitting of the old by the young. That is also the problem confronting Steele's lovers, but it is complicated by sentimentality: they are dutiful children.

Young Bevil, upon rising in the morning, does not discuss intrigue or gallantry with his servant, or quote Suckling or *Pills to Purge Melancholy*. He makes his entrance with a copy of *The Spectator,* explaining, "Such an author, consulted in a morning, sets the spirit for the vicissitudes of the day better than the glass does the man's person." A moment later, his father, who has been waiting to see him, is let in by a servant:

BEVIL JUNIOR. Sir, you are the most gallant, the most complaisant of all parents. Sure, 'tis not a compliment to say these lodgings are yours. Why would you not walk in, Sir?

SIR JOHN BEVIL. I was loath to interrupt you unseasonably on your wedding day.

BEVIL JUNIOR. One to whom I am beholden for my birthday might have used less ceremony.

In the good old days of Charles and James, the gallant would never have deigned to bestow so polished a phrase upon a mere parent. But Bevil has more than polite speech for Sir John. Although in love with Indiana, he is determined to go through with his wedding to Lucinda so long as it is his father's wish. This puts him in an awkward position towards his dear friend, Myrtle, who has his own excesses of consciousness.

MYRTLE. I am told that you are this very day (and your dress confirms me in it) to be married to Lucinda.

BEVIL JUNIOR. You are not misinformed.—Nay, put not on the terrors of a rival, till you hear me out. I shall disoblige the best of fathers if I don't seem ready to marry Lucinda; and you know I have ever told you, you might make use of my secret resolution never to marry her, for your own service, as you please. But I am now driven to the extremity of immediately refusing, or complying, unless you help me to escape the match.

MYRTLE. Escape? Sir, neither her merit nor her fortune are below your acceptance.—Escaping, do you call it?

BEVIL JUNIOR. Dear Sir, do you wish I should desire the match?

MYRTLE. No—but such is my humorous and sickly state of mind since it has been able to relish nothing but Lucinda, that though I must owe my happiness to your aversion to this marriage, I can't bear to hear her spoken of with levity or unconcern.

As a final element in his character, observe young Bevil at the lodgings of Indiana, his beloved. Her (unacknowledged) aunt, Isabella, being of an older generation is highly suspicious of Bevil's attentions, and even Indiana has some misgivings about the possible return he may expect for supporting her. In a spirited defense of his actions, he sets her right:

If pleasure be worth purchasing, how great a pleasure is it to him who has a true taste of life to ease an aching heart, to see the human countenance lighted up into smiles of joy on the receipt of a bit of ore which is superfluous, and otherwise useless, in a man's own pocket. What could a man do better with his cash? This is the effect of an humane disposition, where there is only a general tie of nature and common necessity. What then must it be when we serve an object of merit, of admiration!

The reader cannot but agree with Fielding's Parson Adams that in this *comedy* "There are some things almost solemn enough for a sermon."

The plot, nonetheless, is lively and surprising if the spectator is not overfamiliar with Roman drama. Further, on the shrewd advice of Colley Cibber, Steele worked in a farcical subplot involving Phillis and Tom, a pair of servants who ape their "conscious" betters much as the Restoration fop aped the Restoration wit. The audience was amused, and frequently moved to tears, and the moral could be approved by the soberest citizen: "Your happiness is owing to your constancy and merit." As for the tears, Steele was quick to point out that no man need be ashamed of them. Did not Mr. Wilks say of a great general who wept unashamedly over Indiana's plight, "I warrant he'll fight ne'er the worse for that." And as for sentimentality in general, "the tears which were shed on that occasion flowed from reason and good sense, and . . . men ought not to be laughed at for weeping, till we are come to a more clear notion of what is to be imputed to the hardness of the head and the softness of the heart."

With the success of Steele and such co-workers as Cibber and Mrs. Centlivre, eighteenth century comedy donned the mask of sentimentality, the Lugubrious Muse. It was not the first time that sentimentality had appeared on the English stage, but in no previous period of the drama had tears, idle tears, so consistently stained the cheeks of actors and spectators. To the original impetus in the first quarter of the century were added at later periods the triumphant successes of the sentimental novels of Samuel Richardson and the *comédie larmoyante* of the Parisian theater. By the 'seventies, sentimental comedy dominated the stage and, despite the attempts of critics and historians and satirists to prove that it was a contradiction in terms, unclassical, or simply foolish, it has never been driven from the popular theater and forms today a major part of the entertainment furnished by radio and motion pictures.

Sentimental comedy is perhaps more important to the social historian for what it reveals of its audience than to the student of literature. It falls easily into melodramatics, false rhetoric, and awkward moral posturing which give it but a low place in the whole view of the drama. Richard Cumberland's *The West Indian* (1771) may exemplify the hundreds of sentimental comedies growing out of the humanitarian belief in the natural goodness of man, rather than the older comic conception of man's natural weakness.

Although *The West Indian* follows the familiar neo-classic comic pattern of an intrigue leading to marriage and a fortune,

Cumberland prided himself on having chosen materials that were fresh, heroes that had not hitherto been considered heroic, "noble game and new" as the Prologue announces. One of his heroes, therefore, is the Irish Major O'Flaherty presented sympathetically, not as the caricatured stage-Irishman of *The Beaux' Stratagem* and a hundred farces. O'Flaherty, in fact, is the major instrument in bringing about the denouement as he providentially overhears the villains plotting to do the romantic young gentleman out of his inheritance. Belcour, newly arrived from the West Indies, is intended as a rake but his motive and cue for action is always sensibility, and his reformation is accomplished without much difficulty by the virtuous heroine, Louisa Dudley. Charles, her brother, is the complete sentimental hero, bursting into tears on meeting his sweetheart, and hesitating even to express his thanks for the kindness she has done him because "there is a selfishness even in gratitude, when it is too profuse; to be over-thankful for any one favor is in effect to lay out for another; the best return I could make my benefactress would be never to see her more." This is refinement of motives almost to the vanishing point.

It is instructive to compare Act V, Scene 5 of *The West Indian* with the famous proviso scene of *The Way of the World*. The latter is the ultimate dramatic statement of a realistic acceptance of the comic view of life as Millamant and Mirabell consider their own natures and provide for future contingencies. Belcour and his Louisa have a totally different approach.

BELCOUR. Miss Dudley, I have solicited this audience to repeat to you my penitence and confusion: How shall I atone? What reparation can I make to you and virtue?

LOUISA. To me there's nothing due, nor anything demanded of you but your more favourable opinion for the future, if you should chance to think of me: Upon the part of virtue I'm not empower'd to speak, but if hereafter, as you range thro' life, you shou'd surprise her in the person of some wretched female, poor as myself and not so well protected, enforce not your advantage, complete not your licentious triumph, but raise her, rescue her from shame and sorrow, and reconcile her to herself again.

BELCOUR. I will, I will; by bearing your idea ever present in my thoughts, virtue shall keep an advocate within me; but tell me, loveliest, when you pardon the offence, can you, all perfect as you are, approve of the offender? As I now cease to view you in that false light I lately did, can you, and in the fulness of your bounty will you, cease also to reflect upon the libertine addresses I have paid you, and look upon me as your reform'd, your rational admirer?

LOUISA. Are sudden reformations apt to last; and how can I be sure the first fair face you meet will not ensnare affections so unsteady, and that I shall not lose you lightly as I gain'd you?

BELCOUR. Because tho' you conquer'd me by surprise, I have no inclination to rebel; because since the first moment that I saw you, every instant has improv'd you in my eyes, because by principle as well as passion I am unalterably yours, in short there are ten thousand causes for my love to you, would to heaven I could plant one in your soft bosom that might move you to return it!

LOUISA. Nay, Mr. Belcour.—

BELCOUR. I know I'm not worthy your regard; I know I'm tainted with a thousand faults, sick of a thousand follies, but there's a healing virtue in your eyes that makes recovery certain; I cannot be a villain in your arms.

LOUISA. That you can never be; whomever you shall honor with your choice, my life upon't that woman will be happy; it is not from suspicion that I hesitate, it is from honour; tis the severity of my condition, it is the world that never will interpret fairly in our case.

BELCOUR. Oh, what am I, and who in this wide world concerns himself for such a nameless, such a friendless thing as I am? I see, Miss Dudley, I've not yet obtain'd your pardon.

LOUISA. Nay, that you are in full possession of.

BELCOUR. Oh, seal it with your hand then, loveliest of women, confirm it with your heart; make me honourably happy, and crown your penitent not with your pardon only, but your love.

LOUISA. My love!—

BELCOUR. By Heav'n my soul is conquer'd with your virtues more than my eyes are ravish'd with your beauty: Oh, may this soft, this sensitive alarm be happy, be auspicious! Doubt not, deliberate not, delay not: If happiness be the end of life, why do we slip a moment?

Such a scene is the essence of the sentimental view of life, love, and human relationships.

3. LAUGHING COMEDY

Sentimentality, fortunately, was not quite the only wear for the muse of comedy. In the general surrender to humanitarianism some few playwrights maintained their sense of humor and even dared to attack the popular trend. Although Goldsmith did not actually coin the term until the last quarter of the century, *laughing comedy* is a convenient omnibus designation for the farces, ballad operas, and full-dress comedies that kept alive the older tradition from the end of the Restoration to the period of the

American Revolution. Most of these pieces are so ephemeral in nature as to deserve a place only in the most extended account of the dramatic literature of the century; a few have retained their comic vitality through the years. A sampling of the repertory of laughing comedy will correct the distorted picture of the eighteenth century theater which inevitably follows a consideration of its sentimentality.

The liveliest and most original dramatic work of the century is not really a play at all but a musical comedy and thus outside the proper scope of this volume. It is impossible, however, to ignore *The Beggar's Opera* (1728) since it stands so boldly for satire, laughter, and wit at a time when those comic virtues were melting away in tears. The masterpiece of John Gay, it has demonstrated its vitality in a stage life which extends over two centuries, beginning with a record-breaking run of forty performances at its premiere and including an even greater record-breaking run of some four years at a revival in 1919.

Gay's intentions have been variously interpreted as satirizing politics, society, or Italian Opera, and may very well have included all three. The satire on the pomposities of grand opera involves a setting in the London underworld, with whores, highwaymen, and receivers of stolen goods as characters, and an ending of the utmost whimsicality, "For you must allow, that in this kind of drama, 'tis no matter how absurdly things are brought about." More particularly, as the highwaymen are about to go forth on their business they sing a rousing chorus to the tune employed by Rinaldo, in Handel's opera, as he reviews the Christian troops who are about to fight the Saracens. The satire on society is something like Steele's in *The Conscious Lovers*. There, two servants imitate the manners and customs of their masters, here the Ladies of the Town discuss the lowest things with the greatest elegance, and the proud parent (a receiver of stolen goods) searches out motives with the scrupulousness of a Young Bevil. As the "author" points out at the end of the play,

Through the whole piece you may observe such a similitude of manners in high and low life, that it is difficult to determine whether (in the fashionable vices) the fine gentlemen imitate the Gentlemen of the Road, or the Gentlemen of the Road the fine gentlemen.—Had the play remained as I at first intended, it would have carried a most excellent moral. 'Twould have shown that the lower sort of people have their vices in a degree as well as the rich: and that *they* are punished for them.

The political satire of *The Beggar's Opera* was the most telling in its own day. Macheath, the principal robber, was intended as Walpole, the Prime Minister, a fact which that worthy acknowledged by leading the applause on the opening night, and by banning the sequel, *Polly,* which Gay published in 1729.

The play might pass as a general satire were it not for the sixty-nine lyrics inserted at frequent intervals in the text. Like the work as a whole, these songs satirize society, politics, and opera, and are set, not to the elaborate melodies of professional composers, but to the simple tunes of popular street-and-folk songs. Gay's success brought to the stage a flood of similar, though for the most part inferior, works which go under the generic label of Ballad Opera until mid-century when, popular tunes exhausted, librettists turned to "art music" and renamed the form Comic Opera or Musical Comedy.

One of Gay's followers was Henry Fielding who, before censorship drove him to the novel, was proprietor of the Little Theater in the Haymarket (*cf.* p. 269) for which he supplied an endless run of light farces, ballad operas, adaptations from Molière, and a straight comedy or two. In the tradition of *The Rehearsal* he wrote burlesques of current theatrical fashions, the most memorable of which is *Tom Thumb, or The Tragedy of Tragedies* (two versions 1730, 1731) published with elaborate annotations of sources and mockery of aesthetic theories. But Fielding's daring was as great as his spirits were high; from literary he turned to political satire, attacked Walpole, and found himself like his master, under a ban. Some of the blame for the success of sentimental comedy may thus be laid to the government authorities ever quick to sense the tinge of sarcasm in public laughter.

Equally light-hearted, but politically safe, were the characteristic trifles of Samuel Foote, the celebrated farceur and mimic. His little pieces were written with his own talents in mind, for he did not hesitate to imitate with the cruellest precision any figure of sufficient notoriety, carefully avoiding recognizable politicians. Of several dozen short plays, *The Mayor of Garret* is the best and perfectly typical. It is based upon a contemporary custom, the burlesque election conducted at Garret in South London when

various wits stood for the fictitious Mayoralty under pompous
names and titles. Foote elaborates the ponderous joke with a
trivial but bustling plot involving a henpecked husband, patent
medicines, citizen armies, the cockneys, politicians (but only in
the most general way), and a proviso scene in which the henpecked husband is prodded by his fellows into asserting his rights.
Such pieces are completely dependent upon the company for
which they are written, the eccentric talents of the individual
players, and the inventive skill of the stage manager. They are
important in the over-all view only as an indication that the
comic muse could still laugh, albeit vulgarly.

Foote and Fielding were involved in the management of
theaters as well as playwrighting. The same duality of interests
was behind the writing of the more important laughing comedies
of *The Jealous Wife* (1761) and *The Clandestine Marriage* (1766).
These were the joint work of David Garrick, actor and manager
of Drury Lane, and George Colman the Elder, manager of both
Covent Garden and the Haymarket. Garrick was notoriously opposed to sentimental comedy and Colman had written a slight
afterpiece, *Polly Honeycombe* (1760), satirizing a young lady who
devoured too many sentimental novels. The combination of their
talents promised well for the restoration of true comedy "holding
both her sides." Garrick merely advanced hints and gave advice
for *The Jealous Wife* which is a spirited adaptation of *Tom
Jones*. *The Clandestine Marriage* is a more complete collaboration, a completely successful fusion of sentimentality and the old
comedy of the Restoration. Only the greater popularity of Sheridan and Goldsmith overshadowed the comic achievement of Colman and Garrick.

Suggested by Hogarth's series of pictures, "Marriage-à-la-
Mode," *The Clandestine Marriage* recounts an intrigue in the
old manner with a novel complication. Merchant Sterling is
anxious to marry his elder daughter to Sir John Melvil, and Sir
John while concluding the arrangement finds himself attracted
rather to the younger daughter Fanny. Sterling at first resents this
change of affections but is brought round by a financial consideration. Thus the plot arrives at the familiar situation of the
stern parent forcing an unwanted mate upon his child. The
novel complication in this case is that Fanny is already secretly
married to her father's clerk Lovewell, a fact which neither has

the courage to reveal. The possibilities for either comedy or sentimentality are evident, and both are realized.

Two sets of characters are employed to work the several veins. Merchant Sterling, Mrs. Heidelberg, Lord Ogilby, Sergeant Flower and the lawyers are figures of fun from the old school; Lovewell, Fanny, and Sir John from the new. Fortunately, the first group dominates the action. Ogilby is introduced in his dressing-room, after the manner of the Restoration gallant and his servants, but with a comic twist. Ogilby's servants are assembling him for his day's visits, supplying the necessary cosmetics and stimulants to enable him to assume his character of the lively old buck. Mrs. Heidelberg is a monument of vulgarity, very much impressed with Ogilby's antique gallantries, and a woman of determination. When Sir John proposes to marry Fanny, she forthrightly declares:

> The man is out of his senses.—Can't that wise head of yours foresee the consequences of all this, brother Sterling? Will Sir John take Fanny without a fortune? No.—After you have settled the largest part of your property on your youngest daughter, can there be an equal portion left over for the eldest? No.—Does not this overturn the whole system of the fammaly? Yes, yes, yes.

In the final act the two comic veins are united as Lovewell and Fanny are trapped in her bedroom by the rest of the cast who speculate on the identity of the "lover" and prepare to expose him. Fanny enters and faints, bringing on Lovewell and a flood of sentimentality. Even Ogilby is overcome and offers to take the young couple under his protection. To which Lovewell replies,

> Your kindness, my Lord—I can scarce believe my own senses—they are all in a tumult of fear, love, joy, expectation, and gratitude; I ever was and am now more bound in duty to your Lordship. For you, Mr. Sterling, if every moment of my life, spent gratefully in your service, will in some measure compensate the want of fortune, you will perhaps not repent your goodness to me. And you, ladies, I flatter myself, will not for the future suspect me of artifice and intrigue—I shall be happy to oblige and serve you. As for you, Sir John—

But Sir John is able to speak for himself and cuts the frenzy of apology and fence-mending in which Lovewell is engaged. It will be noted that for all his passionate gratitude and self-abasement Lovewell is wise enough to keep his eye on the main chance, his employer-father-in-law, his job, and his wife's inheritance.

Sentiment dominates the conclusion of the play when Lovewell declares his title to be in Fanny's chamber:

> By that right that makes me the happiest of men; and by a title which
> I would not forgo, for any the best of Kings could give me.
> BETTY [*The Chambermaid*]. I could cry my eyes out to hear his magnanimity.

But if the audience was inclined to join Betty in a sentimental debauch, Garrick thwarted them by supplying a farcical epilogue ridiculing the taste for card-playing and the pleasures of opera among the aristocrats as opposed to the true love of the drama among the citizens. So deliberate a contrivance, outside the play itself, to raise a laugh was but a part of a general attack on sentimental comedy soon to find able leaders in Goldsmith and Sheridan.

Early in his career as an essayist, Goldsmith had complained "Does the poet paint the absurdities of the vulgar, then he is *low;* does he exaggerate the features of folly to render it more ridiculous, he is then *very low.* In short they have proscribed the comic or satirical muse from every walk but high life, which, though abounding in fools as well as the humblest station, is by no means so fruitful in absurdity." Sentimental comedy he further defined as "a kind of *mulish* production, with all the defects of its opposite parents, and marked with sterility." In 1768 he followed these remarks with what was meant to be a dramatic demonstration of the possibilities of laughing comedy, *The Good-Natured Man,* which has all the faults of Goldsmith's own nature in its careless construction and hasty characterization, although the author's professed aim was "to delineate character."

Amends were made, however, in his second play, *She Stoops to Conquer* (1773) whose stage history is practically uninterrupted to the present day. Goldsmith had made some preparations for an unfriendly reception by publishing an *Essay on the Theatre; or, a Comparison Between Laughing and Sentimental Comedy* the year before, debating whether "the exhibition of human distress is likely to afford the mind more entertainment than that of human absurdity." He appeals to authority, Aristotle, Boileau, Terence, Voltaire, declaring that distress is proper to tragedy as ridicule to comedy and that the two ought not to encroach upon one another.

The theme is continued in the prologue to *She Stoops to Conquer,* written by Garrick and spoken by Woodward, a comedian dressed in mourning and dabbing his eyes with a handkerchief. He is grieving for the old comedy in which he was trained, and is distressed to find that as a comedian he is unable to squeeze out a tear and is hence likely to lose his employment.

> But why can't I be moral?—Let me try—
> My heart thus pressing—fixed my face and eye—
> With a sententious look, that nothing means,
> (Faces are blocks in sentimental scenes)
> Thus I begin—"All is not gold that glitters,
> Pleasure seems sweet, but proves a glass of bitters.
> When ign'rance enters, folly is at hand;
> Learning is better far than house and land.
> Let not your virtue trip, who trips may stumble,
> And virtue is not virtue, if she tumble."
> I give it up—morals won't do for me;
> To make you laugh I must play tragedy.

He then announces that the play to follow is a kind of prescription intended to revive the dying comic muse with a potion,

> A kind of magic charm—for be assured
> If you will swallow it, the maid is cured.

For a century and a half audiences have been swallowing Dr. Goldsmith's prescription without a grimace,—a credit to the doctor's skill, since there are some elements in it which might be expected to go down rather hard. The plot, to begin with, is filled with improbabilities. Young Marlow is not the most intelligent of English comic heroes, but his spending an entire night at a private house without discovering that it was not a tavern seems a straining of verisimilitude. That Tony Lumpkin can sing Latin one moment and prove himself illiterate the next, or that his mother should, after a circuitous ride in a coach, kneel before her own husband in her own garden under the impression that he was a highwayman are not the most credible of situations. Yet to list such items is merely to emphasize Goldsmith's skill, for who ever notices their absurdity in the theater?

The plot is hardly novel enough to be startling. Aside from

the similarities with Farquhar's *The Beaux' Stratagem,* there is the fundamental familiarity of the basic situation—a young man in search of his bride and his fortune coupled with the freeing of a ward from the tyranny of a stern guardian. With this familiar plot, Goldsmith has (in the phrase of Mr. Bayes) brought in some fine things. The business with Miss Neville's jewels is very clever; Kate's "stooping" allows for easy comic irony, though it would doubtless be funnier if the times would have permitted her to be more like Cherry Boniface and less like a lady at a masquerade.

Goldsmith takes every opportunity to thrust at the genteel and the sentimental. In a rousing scene at the local alehouse, Tony Lumpkin and his fellows carouse and sing in the roughest manner and the oafish trainer of a dancing bear announces that he is a gentleman for all his occupation. "May this be my poison," he vows, holding up his glass of ale, "if my bear ever dances but to the very genteelest of tunes, 'Water parted' or the Minuet in *Ariadne."* Miss Hardcastle bluntly defines sensibility as hypocrisy, "there are few who do not condemn in public what they practice in private, and think they pay every debt to virtue when they praise it."

Something of the old comic manner is to be seen both in the separation of town and country, though the focus here is always rural rather than urban, and in the stock types in the cast. Hardcastle is descended from Major Oldfox, and his wife from the widow Blackacre, and Tony Lumpkin from Jerry Blackacre. The very two-facedness of the hero, a devil with a certain class of women but a good fellow underneath it all, is a more modest version of the Restoration rake. The resultant character, the "real" Marlow is a compromise between the sentimental hero and the rake, but Goldsmith is careful to mock both extremes, while particularly emphasizing that his sentimentality is only a mask assumed for social purposes.

There is, however, a touch of unmocked sentimentality in Marlow's reaction as his "barmaid" falls to weeping. It begins with an aside to suggest that it is an expression of his genuine feelings.

[*Aside*] By heaven, she weeps. This is the first mark of tenderness I ever had from a modest woman, and it touches me; [*to her*] Excuse me, my lovely girl, you are the only part of the family I leave with reluctance.

But to be plain with you, the difference of our birth, fortune and education, make an honorable connection impossible; and I can never harbor a thought of seducing simplicity that trusted in my honor, or bringing ruin upon one, whose only fault was being too lovely.

Could Bevil junior, or Lovewell have spoken more feelingly?

Yet criticizing *She Stoops to Conquer* is thankless and fruitless. Horace Walpole in a typical moment of spleen wrote to one of his correspondents that it was "set up in opposition to sentimental comedy and is as bad as the worst of them" though truthfulness compelled him to add that he had to laugh at it. Analysis fails to add to its virtues and such weaknesses as are revealed vanish before the good-hearted laughter of its multitudes of spectators. If Goldsmith could not drive sentimentality from the stage at least he was able to demonstrate the continuing vigor of laughing comedy.

In 1775 the second of a trio of comedies in the older tradition made its appearance, at first to catcalls but later to triumphant applause. *The Rivals* was the first play of Richard Brinsley Sheridan and it declared boldly for anti-sentimentalism. True to the old-school, the author puts together two related love intrigues with Absolute wooing in disguise Lydia Languish the very girl designed for him by his irascible father, and the capricious engagement of Faulkland and his Julia which treads close to the edge of the chasm of sensibility. In this latter plot, the characters are sometimes betrayed into a kind of blank verse as when Julia declares, "if I now more than ever, prize the solemn engagement which so long has pledged us to each other, it is because it leaves no room for hard aspersions on my fame, and puts the seal of duty to an act of love." Such situations and such speeches are not the best means of avoiding "weeping comedy."

Fortunately Sheridan seems to have been aware of this and equipped himself with a lively gallery of comic portraits. Many of these types come in pairs—Lydia and Julia are false and true sentimentalists; Captain Absolute and Faulkland are comic and sentimental lovers; Absolute and Mrs. Malaprop are a pair of stern guardians, and O'Trigger and Acres contrasted low characters. Lydia Languish comes from the stock of Polly Honeycombe and like her yearns for an elopement according to the best precepts of the literature of the circulating library. Sir Anthony is a complete humour character—"hasty in everything, or it would not be Sir Anthony Absolute," declares his servant with no less truth than dramatic theory. It is Mrs. Malaprop, however, who engrosses attention, and she is not so much an original as the supreme development of the Dogberry-Mrs. Quickly stock type. They were innocent abusers of the King's English; Mrs. Malaprop takes particular pride in her vocabulary, and therein lies her superiority. "An attack upon my language!" she exclaims, "What do you think of that? An aspersion upon my parts of speech! Was ever such a brute! Sure, if I reprehend any thing in this world, it is the use of my oracular tongue, and a nice derangement of epitaphs!"

Sheridan's more famous triumph, *The School for Scandal* (1777), has no such wonderful monster to keep it alive. But it is closer perhaps to the intention of the comedy of manners than is *The Rivals* which, like *She Stoops to Conquer*, is more comic drama than comic satire. *The School* is intended to ridicule social behavior, particularly, of course, the gossip-mongering, perhaps deriving its inspiration from Pope's *Rape of the Lock* in whose salons "at every word a reputation dies." But here, also for the first time in many years, are extended passages of witty dialogue, witty with a glitter that lacks only the poetic instincts of Congreve for final perfection. And here, most pointedly, is the familiar plot of the two brothers of differing characters, a plot as old at least as Roman comedy but now made into an instrument for an attack on sentimentality.

Joseph Surface is a man of sensibility, a humanitarian, full of wise saws and modern instances. In the scandal scene cannot he remark, "to smile at the jest which plants a thorn in another's breast is to become a principal in the mischief." Charles Surface, his brother, is a wastrel, a ne'er-do-well, a rake, desperate for money to pay his gambling debts and without a sentimental thought in his head. Yet it is Charles who will not sell the portrait of his uncle at auction, and it is Charles who pulls over the screen (a highly, if unintentionally, symbolic action) in Joseph's library to disclose the presence of Lady Teazle. And it is Charles who twists the knife as he quizzes the principals, one after the other:

Egad, you seem all to have been diverting yourselves here at hide-and-seek, and I don't see who is out of the secret. Shall I beg your ladyship to inform me? Not a word!—Brother, will you be pleased to explain this matter? What! is Morality dumb too?—Sir Peter, though I found you in the dark, perhaps you are not so now! All mute!—Well— Though I can make nothing of the affair, I suppose you perfectly understand one another; so I'll leave you to yourselves.—Brother, I'm sorry to find you have given that worthy man grounds for so much uneasiness.—Sir Peter! there's nothing in the world so noble as a man of sentiment!   (*Exit*)

As an anti-sentimentalist, Sheridan no doubt was pleased to think that in the Screen Scene and in Charles's exit speech he had dealt a severe blow to weeping comedy. No doubt the audience was so convinced. But such conviction rarely lasts out the epilogue. *The School for Scandal* remained the last great comedy of manners in English until the end of the nineteenth century, but sentimentality is a tougher bird than it appears and the sharpest and most gilded arrows from Sheridan's quiver fell almost unnoted at its feet.

4. TRAGEDY

As the comedy which succeeded the Restoration comedy of manners, though altered in tone and attitude, still resembled it in form and technique, so the tragedy which followed the heroic play, while reforming some of its extravagances, clung still to its basic attractive features. These, it will be seen, are rant, pathos, and the heroic conflict between love and honor. The reformation was largely a neo-classical purification of the more "romantic" elements. The settings are infrequently the exotic areas of the Western Hemisphere, or the Orient, but more often Rome, Greece or Italy, locales attractive to a generation that was to father the Augustans.

For example, Nathaniel Lee, the master of rant, chooses for his ranters not Almanzor and Montezuma but Nero, Alexander the Great, and Lucius Junius Brutus. His plays, however, are anything but galleries of classical statuary and his characters are bursting with over-articulate passion. *The Rival Queens* (1677), his greatest and most lasting success, pits Roxana and Statira the first and second wives of Alexander the Great against one another in extended self-examination and jealous recrimination. The whole action is carried on at the top of the lungs, and the situations are grandiose to match. At one point Lysimachus wrestles with a lion, pulls out his tongue, and kills him, a feat which wins him the accolade of "active prince," and should make him eligible for a corresponding membership in the Society of Munchausen. Few mad scenes are as frenetic as Alexander's in the last act, and Colley Cibber, who was no mean critic whatever he may have been as a playwright or manager, speaks justly of "the false fire and extravagance" of the play.

It is difficult to be just to Lee, to see beyond the appeal of violence which made him attractive to his age. Love, honest or perverted, is his constant theme, and in the analysis of the emotions arising from it he achieved his popularity. It is constructive to compare his (and Dryden's) version of *Oedipus* (1678) with the Sophoclean original, much of which is directly translated. The singleness, the simple structure of the ancient tragedy, is complicated by a subplot involving the love of Creon for Eurydice, daughter of Laius. Eurydice is also loved by the captive Adrastus, whom Oedipus has recently defeated in battle. This subplot serves a double purpose, irony and realism. It is ironic for Oedipus is able to forbid the marriage of uncle and niece as incestuous. It adds realism since Eurydice and Adrastus are blamed for the death of Laius, and hence are used to divert attention from Oedipus as the object of the oracle's predictions. A tremendous climax is provided as Creon, a sort of Richard III, kills Eurydice, Adrastus kills Creon and is himself killed by Theban soldiers, Jocasta murders her children before committing suicide, and the blinded Oedipus leaps from the bedroom window to his death. All this, it should be noted, is performed before the bedazzled eyes of the spectators, who no doubt left the theater with the virtuous satisfaction of having undergone a "classical" tragic experience.

The emphasis throughout is not upon the meaning of the oracle or on the tragic theme, but upon love. Oedipus becomes not the proud, ignorant king, but the great lover, and Eurydice wishes that all the excellences of womankind were hers for the sake of her sweetheart, then glosses the term "excellences" by adding,

No, 'tis too little all for him
Were I made up of endless, endless joys.

Love is likewise the theme of Lee's more famous contemporary, Thomas Otway, but with a difference. Otway, a harbinger

of things to come, is less interested in rant and bombast than in
their quieter counterpart, pathos. *The Orphan* (1680) and
Venice Preserved (1682), however, do more than suggest that
English tragedy is to develop in the direction of domestic drama
and pathetic romance. These plays mark the partial return of
the English drama to the panoramic tradition. Throughout the
Restoration, it had been Jonson who was the bright, particular
Elizabethan, and Shakespeare, though acknowledged, was re-
gretted as one who had not subjected himself to classical disci-
plines. His works were adapted and improved to suit the taste
of a more refined age, sometimes with respect (as Dryden's *All
for Love*); sometimes impudently (as Tate's infamous *King Lear*).
Otway, on the other hand, frankly imitates Shakespeare in matter, in manner, and even in speech.

The domesticity of *Venice Preserved* may not be at once apparent, since the plot deals with the Senate and nobility of
Venice and a conspiracy against the state. The mainspring of
the action, however, is not revolt against tyranny, but romantic
and filial love: Jaffier joins the conspiracy to get revenge against
his father-in-law, pledging his wife, Belvidera, for his good faith.
Renault, a villainous conspirator, attacks her and she escapes to
her husband whom she then persuades to discover the plot to the
senators, making the condition that his fellows shall not be
executed. When they are arrested and condemned, Jaffier is overcome with remorse and threatens Belvidera with death unless
she can secure their pardon from her father. She is successful,
but too late. In a blazing catastrophe, Belvidera goes mad, Jaffier
stabs Pierre on the scaffold and commits suicide, and Belvidera
dies of a broken heart.

If the action seems of a "certain magnitude," the emotions are
domestic, and the emotions are Otway's major concern. As
Dobrée remarks, he is examining man's capacity for feeling, for
self-torture, and many of the strongest scenes of the play depend
upon this searching out of emotion and sentiment. After Jaffier
has betrayed Pierre to the Senate, he must visit him in his dun-
geon and indulge himself in the luxury of self-abuse. Pierre,
understandably, strikes him and Jaffier whines:

> Thou hast disgraced me, Pierre, by a vile blow:
> Had not a dagger done thee nobler justice?
> But use me as thou wilt, thou canst not wrong me,

> For I am fallen beneath the basest injuries.
> Yet look upon me with an eye of mercy,
> With pity and with charity behold me;
> Shut not thy heart against a friend's repentance,
> But as there dwells a God-like nature in thee
> Listen with mildness to my supplications.

Belvidera's mad scene, too, resulting more from the necessity of the theater than the life of the drama, played upon the nerves of the spectators with memorable effect:

> Curst be my days, and doubly curst my nights,
> Which I must now mourn out in widowed tears;
> Blasted be every herb and fruit and tree,
> Curst be the rain that falls upon the earth,
> And may the general curse reach man and beast. . . .
> Say not a word of this to my old father,
> Murmuring streams, soft shades, and springing flowers,
> Lutes, laurels, seas of milk, and ships of amber.

A quarter century later, in 1715, the heroine of John Gay's amusing *What D'Ye Call It* entered "with her hair loose" accompanied by a "Chorus of Sighs and Groans" and went mad in the Belvidera tradition:

> Hah!—I am turned a stream—look all below;
> It flows, and flows, and will forever flow,
> The meads are all afloat—the hay cocks swim.
> Hah! Who comes here? My Filbert!—drown not him.
> Bagpipes in butter, flocks in fleecy fountains,
> Churns, sheep-hooks, seas of milk, and honey-mountains.

Otway makes no effort to disguise his Shakespearean references. In 1680 in his *Caius Marius* he had frankly re-written *Romeo and Juliet* down to the last line, as it were, resulting in such unconscious humor as, "Oh, Marius, Marius, wherefore art thou Marius?" In *Venice Preserved* he reproduces the scene from *Julius Caesar* in which Portia tries to persuade her husband to share his troubles with her. He prefaces the scene with a direct allusion to the situation in Shakespeare and gives to Belvidera a somewhat prosy paraphrase of Portia's entreaty. No doubt the blunting of the original resulted from that neo-classical spirit which led Dryden to "regularize" the famous description of Cleopatra's descent of the Nile; a briefer comparison between Otway's regularity and Jacobean luxuriance may illustrate the point.

In *The White Devil*, Brachiano cries furiously to Vittoria,

> O, ten thousand curses on't!
> How long have I beheld the devil in crystal!
> Thou hast led me, like an heathen sacrifice,
> With music and with fatal yokes of flowers,
> To mine eternal ruin. Woman to man
> Is either god or wolf.

The image of the sacrificial lamb is but glimpsed in a kaleido-scope of images pouring from a distracted man. Here is Jaffier, in *Venice Preserved*:

> Come, lead me forth now like a tame lamb
> To sacrifice; thus in his fatal garlands,
> Decked fine and pleased the wanton skips and plays,
>   Trots by the enticing flattering priestess' side,
> And much transported with his little pride,
> Forgets his dear companions of the plain
> Till by her bound, he's on the altar lain;
> Yet then too hardly bleats, such pleasure's in the pain.

The image, like the emotion, is done to death by being made over-explicit and over-literal. The play stands still.

The typical heroic psychological conflict between love and honor or duty here becomes almost exclusively Jaffier's problem. His fraternal love for Pierre and his duty to the revolutionary cause are set against his love of Belvidera; his hatred of Renault, her attacker, can be appeased only by an appeal to his arch-enemy, Priuli, her father. And, to avenge his wife, he must betray his friends. Pierre, on the other hand, is given the opportunity to display only several kinds of love, without the conflicting tug of honor—he trusts Jaffier, and forgives him for his betrayal, with a noble magnanimity productive of sympathetic and ap-proving tears. "Poets in honor of the truth should write," declared Otway in epilogue, but the over-all effect of *Venice Preserved* is neither truth nor tragedy, but pathos. As such, it is an early indication of the way the serious drama would draw closer to the comic in the coming century until the mingling streams became almost indistinguishable.

Congreve's single tragedy *The Mourning Bride* (1697) carries on the heroic tradition of the conflict between love and honor and the conventional plot of geometrically related passions. But the action proceeds by fits and starts and it is apparent that he,

like Otway, is interested in suffering and emotion for their own
sakes. Scene after scene is set up to illustrate some conflicting
passion, as when Almeria must plead with her father for the
life of his enemy, her secret husband. And, as in the case of
Otway, the attempt to analyze the passion at length frequently
reduces it to an intellectual specimen, seen as it were under a
glass case, and wholly without heart or spirit.

Almeria's mourning, for instance, is academic:

> Alphonso! O Alphonso!
> Thou are too quiet—long hast been at peace—
> Both, both—Father and son are now no more.
> Then why am I? O when shall I have rest?
> Why do I live to say you are no more?
> Why are all these things thus—is it of force?
> Is there necessity I must be miserable?
> Is it of moment to the peace of heaven
> That I should be afflicted thus? If not,
> Why is it thus contrived?

These are indeed good questions, but they are the abstractions
of an immature philosopher, not the outcries of a grief-stricken
heroine.

Dr. Johnson, whose own tastes were, of course, neo-classical, is
rather severe upon *The Mourning Bride;* he found himself more
intrigued by the plot than by "any true delineation of natural
characters." He speaks highly, to be sure, of the poetry, praising
Almeria's description of the tomb in Act II as the most poetical
paragraph with which he was acquainted. Even today there are
passages quoted, albeit unconsciously, from this once-famous,
now-forgotten tragedy; cries the slighted woman,

> Heaven has no rage like love to hatred turned,
> Nor hell a fury, like a woman scorned;

and declares the heroine,

> Music hath charms to sooth a savage breast—

but, to paraphrase Dr. Johnson, one would rather quote *The
Mourning Bride* than read it. In its conflict between love and
duty, in its plot in which most of the major figures are killed off
to provide a happy ending for the spotless noble lovers, it is
heroic drama. But in the situations which Congreve most delights to linger over it is pathos, sentimentality.

The intrusion of sentimentality into the heroic play anticipates somewhat the intrusion of the same quality into comedy. The fully formed and acknowledged pathetic tragedy of Southerne and Rowe parallels in the first instance, Cibber's tentative dabblings in sensibility and, in the second, Steele's complete surrender to it. As plays, the works of these men are negligible, as symptoms they are of importance for they were not only successful in their own day but clung to favor throughout the eighteenth century, an adequate test of their ability to bring on the "Chorus of Sighs and Groans."

Oroonoko (1695) dramatized by Thomas Southerne from a novel by Aphra Behn is, in addition to the usual love-tragedy, an emotional appeal to end negro slavery. The hero is an African prince sold with Imoinda, his wife, into bondage on a Surinam plantation. His princely spirit is evident in his address to his owner:

> Tear off this pomp, and let me know myself:
> The slavish habit best becomes me now.
> Hard fares and whips and chains may overpower
> The frailer flesh, and bow my body down;
> But there's another, nobler part of me,
> Out of your reach, which you can never tame.

The plot is exciting, centering in an uprising of slaves, but the problems which confront the hero were obviously of greater interest. As the governor's slave he feels himself duty-bound to obey his master, but that same master has made advances to Oroonoko's pregnant wife. As a man and a prince the hero is eager for an heir, as a slave he cannot tolerate the idea of bringing a child into the conditions of slavery:

> Methinks I see the babe with infant hands
> Pleading for life, and begging to be born.
> Shall I forbid his birth? Deny him life?
> The heavenly comforts of all-cheering light?
> These are the calls of Nature, that call loud;
> They will be heard, and conquer in their cause.

As the governor carries off Imoinda, Oroonoko flies into a passion and wishes the villain were not surrounded by guards,

> Else, lion-like, with my devouring rage
> I would rush on him, fasten on his throat,
> Tear a wide passage to his treacherous heart,
> And that way lay him open to the world.

The heroic fire had not been entirely smothered by tears.

Nicholas Rowe's *Jane Shore* (1714), accurately denominated a "she-tragedy," moves a step closer to pure sentimentality. Rowe had thoroughly soaked himself in the works of Shakespeare, of whom he was an early editor (1709). Consequently his play is full of reminiscent phrases and speeches:

> This morn I mean
> To probe him to the quick; then if he flinch. . . .
>
> Behold my arm, thus blasted, dried, and withered.

The subject of the play is a repentant sinner, a woman who is now more sinned against than sinning. The appeal is certainly to the women in the audience, as Jane complains of the double standard by which their errors are judged

> man, the lawless libertine, may rove
> Free and unquestioned through the wilds of love;
> While woman, sense and nature's easy fool,
> If poor weak woman swerve from Virtue's rule . . .
> Ruin ensues, reproach and endless shame,
> And one false step entirely damns her fame.
> In vain with tears she may the loss deplore,
> In vain look back of what was before:
> She sets, like stars that fall, to rise no more.

The speeches and the situations are generally overwritten for pathetic effect. The characters speak of themselves in self-commiserating terms; Jane weeps for her "poor, forsaken royal little ones"; and the audience is constantly reminded of the weight of penitent misery which she willingly bears. In a conclusion meant to be thoroughly touching, she dies, forgiven, in her husband's arms, though what purpose, what meaning, there can be in her death is never explained. Dealing with historical characters from high life, *Jane Shore* is not much removed in elevation and purpose from the older domestic drama, *A Woman Killed with Kindness*.

The famous tragedy *Cato* (1713) by Joseph Addison appears to have put aside both the mask of sentiment and the mask of the heroic to return to classicism undisguised. The prologue, written by Pope, states first the purpose of tragedy:

> To wake the soul by tender strokes of art,
> To raise the genius and to mend the heart,

> To make mankind in conscious virtue bold,
> Live o'er each scene, and be what they behold;

then disposes of the heroic play:

> In pitying love we but our weakness show,
> And wild ambition well deserves its woe.
> Here, tears shall flow from a more generous cause;

patriotism is the playwright's theme, and all the noble Roman virtues,

> A brave man struggling in the storms of fate
> And greatly falling with a falling state!

Quin as Coriolanus

The structure of *Cato* is laid out with the formality and perfection of parts of an Eighteenth Century garden. It observes the unities—the action proceeds without break in an unchanged setting, and the time of performance roughly corresponds to the time of the dramatic events; and it observes the classical virtues—duty to the state, to the family, and to virtue itself.

If, however, the whole pattern of the action is considered, instead of simply the announced intention or certain key speeches, a foreign element appears in the classical mechanism. Almost at once, the ancient Roman scene is invaded by Juba, a Numidian prince, who loves Cato's daughter, and whose father is Cato's enemy. Further, Cato's two sons, Marcus and Portius, are both in love with Lucia, a senator's daughter, and Portius, after the noble Roman custom, is forced to woo the lady for his less articulate brother. The conflict is familiar.

> What should I do! If I disclose my passion,
> Our friendship's at an end; if I conceal it,
> The world will call me false to friend and brother.

Love and honor, that is, are still our theme, though both qualities are somewhat metaphysical in Addison.

Cato himself is a monument of pride, though not so intended, and not Almanzor himself could have returned a more full-blown answer to Caesar's offer of amnesty:

> His cares for me are insolent and vain:
> Presumptuous man! The Gods take care of Cato!

When the body of his son, killed in battle, is brought on, Cato greets it with

> Welcome, my son! Here lay him down, my friends,
> Full in my sight, that I may view at leisure
> The bloody corpse, and count those glorious wounds.
> How beautiful is death when earned by Virtue!
> Who would not be that youth? What pity is it
> That we can die but once to serve our country!

One wonders if there may not have been a few in the original audience who agreed with Juba's aside, "was ever man like this!"

The language of the play is cold, elegant, and florid. Each act ends with a passion and a simile. As the villain becomes excited at the prospect of possessing Cato's daughter, his speech becomes warm:

> How will my bosom swell with anxious joy
> When I behold her struggling in my arms,
> With glowing beauty, and disordered charms,
> While fear and anger, with alternate grace,
> Pant in her breast, and vary in her face.

But Addison will not permit him to stop there; the inevitable simile must follow, marbellizing the human glow:

> So Pluto, seized of Prosperine, conveyed
> To Hell's tremendous gloom the affrighted maid;
> There grimly smiled, pleased with the beauteous prize,
> Nor envied Jove his sunshine and his skies.

In his endeavor to appear poetic, Addison neglects Dryden's excellent precept that the dramatic language should be seemly, that no man is at leisure to make sentences or similes when his soul is passionate. In his effort to re-create classical tragedy Addison partially deflates the heroic hero and overlays the typical heroic conflict with a thin veneer of antiquity. But the spectators of this dramatic bas relief will have only half an eye on the lonely figure of Cato, the noble Roman; their attention from long habit will be directed to Portius, torn between love of his brother and his sweetheart, and Juba, torn between love of

Cato's daughter and duty to Cato's enemy. And when a single battle conveniently eliminates Marcus and Cato, what spectator would be so unromantic as to complain that the reward of the patriot—the announced theme of the play—is somewhat less than the reward of the true lover?

In the tragic realm of domesticity unashamed, George Lillo's *George Barnwell, or The London Merchant* (1731) is the most famous example. The heroic conflict of love and duty is here reduced to the middle class level: the hero is in love with a vicious prostitute, and owes duty to his master, a man of commerce. In a sense, the play is a business man's tragedy and it was annually revived on certain holidays as a warning to any idle young men who might be inclined to trifle with their responsibilities in the world of trade, or not to show the proper respect for money. Its values are thus the values of sentimental comedy, a further instance of the contamination of types in the eighteenth century theater.

The play is pseudo-history. That is, it is based upon an Elizabethan popular ballad and the setting and costumes are of that period, but the sentences, passions, and morals are of Lillo's own day. Young Barnwell, having fallen into the clutches of the wicked Millwood, laments his lost innocence in a scene with his friend Trueman. He begins in the most high-flown style of pseudo-poetics:

> Will yesterday return?—We have heard, the glorious sun that till then incessant rolled, once stopped his rapid course and once went back; the dead have risen; and parchèd rocks poured forth a liquid stream to quench a people's thirst; the sea divided and formed walls of water while a whole nation passed in safety through its sandy bosom; hungry lions have refused their prey; and men unhurt have walked amidst consuming flames—but never once did time once past, return.
>
> TRUEMAN. Though the continued chain of time has never once been broke, nor ever will, but uninterrupted must keep on its course till, lost in eternity, it ends there where it first began; yet as Heaven can repair whatever evils time can bring upon us, we ought never to despair——But business requires our attendance; business, the youth's best preservative from ill, as idleness his worst of snares. Will you go with me?

The progression in these speeches from poetry to morality to business is almost a symbol of the development of eighteenth century dramatic art.

Thoroughgood, Barnwell's employer, is a business man and he speaks for the dignity of commerce as self-righteously as any of the honest merchants of sentimental comedy. He begins the education of a clerk with a moral:

Methinks I would not have you only learn the method of merchandise, and practice it hereafter merely as a means of getting wealth; 'twill be well worth your pains to study it as a science, to see how it is founded in reason and the nature of things; how it promotes humanity as it has opened and yet keeps up an intercourse between nations far remote from one another in situation, customs and religion; promoting arts, industry, peace and plenty; by mutual benefits diffusing mutual love from pole to pole.

It is against this code, this creed of the sacred mission of commerce, that Barnwell sins in stealing, out of "compassion and generosity," for a bad woman. When later he murders his uncle, the greater crime is made to seem the lesser since a complex piece of stage business turns the intended assassination into killing in self-defense. Barnwell's offense is more against business than against morality and as he pleads with the audience not to follow his example, his choice of words is significant:

> By my example learn to shun my fate,
> (How wretched is a man who's wise too late)
> Ere innocence and fame and life be lost—
> Here *purchase* wisdom, *cheaply,* at my *cost.*

The moral is, of course, that crime does not pay, and the word "pay" is to be taken in its most literal sense.

Although later critics have followed Charles Lamb's attack on *Barnwell* as a "nauseous sermon that makes uncle murder trivial," its theatrical life was long and prosperous. For reasons to be examined below (p. 274), it had few immediate successors in England, Edward Moore's *The Gamester* (1753) being almost the only one of note. On the continent of Europe, however, the type was both popular and productive. Lessing in Germany and Diderot in France introduced imitations and developments of the English domestic tragedy which were important factors in establishing a new dramatic tradition in those countries. In a few decades this European tradition would return to England, *via* translation, as domestic melodrama; a century later, a second invasion led by the domestic tragedies of Henrik Ibsen, would lay the groundwork for the serious drama of the contemporary theater.

The London Merchant was connected in its author's mind with such Elizabethan plays as *Arden of Feversham* (of which he seems to have prepared an eighteenth century adaptation). In the more romantic Elizabethan tradition was John Home's *Douglas,* produced in Edinburgh in 1756 and in London, with great success, in 1757. Since the subject was derived from folk-ballad material, the play is the dramatic equivalent of the developing romanticism of the poetry of Gray, Collins, and Wharton. From the moment that Lady Randolph enters and addresses the forest

> Ye woods and wilds, whose melancholy gloom
> Accords with my soul's sadness,

or finds time for so precise an image as,

> Have you not sometimes seen an early flower
> Open its bud, and spread its silken leaves,
> To catch sweet airs, and odours to bestow;
> Then, by the keen blast nipped, pull in its leaves
> And, though still living, die to scent and beauty!

and even the Machiavellian villain, Glenalvon, can thus analogize his schemes,

> Darkly a project peers upon my mind,
> Like the red moon when rising in the east,
> Crossed and divided by strange-colored clouds,

it is obvious that the playwright has a Pisgah sight of the new poetic world. And when, after an almost Popean personification of Nature, the young stranger identifies himself in the one famous passage of the play,

> My name is Norval: on the Grampian hills
> My father feeds his flocks,

intimations of Wordsworth are not difficult to discover.

Douglas does not succeed, of course, in escaping completely from the dominant conventions of its age. The plot structure is closer to the neo-classic than the panoramic; the action is single and more unified in time and place than most of the Elizabethan plays on romantic subjects. Home was not particularly skillful as a technician; the exposition is crudely handled, the audience is lectured on the various moral issues raised by the action, poetry frequently intrudes to halt the action instead of growing out of it, and most of the important action (in neo-classic fashion) transpires off stage. It must be feared that it was patriotism, rather than critical perception, that caused a member of the opening night audience in Edinburgh to inquire loudly at the end, "Whaur's yer Wullie Shakespeare noo?" Yet *Douglas* does have at least historical importance as a faint recognition of the new spirit stirring behind the classical façade of midcentury.

Home's innovations, like Lillo's, bore strange fruit. Romanticism like domestic realism appears in the late eighteenth century and early nineteenth century theater almost exclusively in melodrama. The settings, characters and incidents which were adapted to romantic treatment were usually also adapted to the popular Gothic style. Such titles as Walpole's *Mysterious Mother* (1768) and Jephson's *Count of Narbonne* (1781), a dramatization of Walpole's *Castle of Otranto,* suggest their relationship with the Gothic novel, while Sheridan's *Pizarro* (1799) and Colman the Younger's pseudo-historical dramas, *The Battle of Hexham, or, Days of Old* (1789) and *Feudal Times, or, The Banquet Gallery* (1799) turn the romantic taste for spectacular natural scenery to the uses of theatrical spectacle. Not by the farthest stretch of the definition could these plays be called tragedies; but, as has been indicated, tragedy made but a poor showing in the years after 1700.

It was plain, even to its devotees, that though the business of the theater was thriving through most of the eighteenth century the art of the drama was declining. Since the "decline" continued and was commented on frequently throughout the first half of the next century, its causes were clearly not simply the climate of opinion, or the taste of an age which after all produced some of the major poets, essayists, and novelists of English literature. For the causes we must look to the theater itself, its traditions, its policies, and its performances.

⌒ 7 ⌒

The Decline of the Drama

1. THE THEATER: 1700-1800

Bernard Shaw has remarked that the drama is always declining; it is never quite what it was when you were a boy, or
father was a boy, or grandfather was a boy. In a subjective sense
this is true, for the spectator will normally consider those conditions under which his taste was formed superior to any which,
in the course of time, may replace them. But in a larger sense,
taking the full view of English dramatic literature, it is apparent
that from about 1700 to about 1850 the drama generally was
in a decline. In the only artistic meaning of the word it was
decadent: playwrights produced limp imitations of bygone successes without reference to the life and opinion of the audience.
The rare exceptions to this generalization only emphasize its
fundamental truth.

It is exceedingly difficult to establish the specific cause of such
a decline. The theater, except during periods of economic de-
pression, was thriving, the arts of acting and production flourished, and audience generally ignored the lack of originality and
freshness in the programs. Perhaps it is sufficient to note the fact
of the decline. Yet the complex of conditions which may have
contributed to it are of some importance to an understanding of
the drama as a whole, however partial an explanation they may
provide for the particular instance. Among these conditions are
the royal patents and the theatrical monopoly which they fostered, the censor, the development of the theater building and
production methods, "Bardolatry," and the illegitimate playhouses.

The patents, it will be recalled, had been issued by Charles II
to Davenant and Killigrew, permitting them to establish theatrical companies and to divide between them the standard

repertory inherited from the days before the Commonwealth. Under the two patents, which were subject to renewal every twenty-one years, the theaters later known as Drury Lane and Covent Garden were founded and their exclusive right to the production of dramatic entertainments in London secured. The later history of the patents is intricate and hardly of concern to the present volume; it is enough to observe that they were jeal-

Hamlet: *The "Play-Within-the-Play" as Produced about 1740*

ously guarded and passed from proprietor to proprietor throughout the eighteenth and the first half of the nineteenth century.

It is plain fact that the theater, alone of the arts, thrives on competition; it cannot develop in the vacuum created by a monopoly. The holders of patents expended far more energy in prosecuting would-be competitors in the law courts than in beating them fairly on the stage. For in spite of the patents various attempts were made to establish other theaters under special licenses. The Haymarket was opened in 1720 with a troupe of French actors, but it was not until 1766, and after many vicissitudes, that it was granted a special patent to operate during the summer hiatus at the major houses. The theater in Goodman's Fields, opened in 1725 in a converted workshop, had a precarious career of scarcely a dozen years until the patentees found a means of suppressing it. In 1787 the Royalty Theater was constructed for Palmer, the actor, who foolishly believed that his announced intention of presenting musical plays and entertainments would exempt him from the prohibitions of the law; he achieved one performance only, but his subterfuge was to prove useful in a very few years in breaking the monopoly.

In the early years of the eighteenth century the holders of the two patents might appeal to history to justify their monopoly. Their predecessors in the Restoration had learned from sad experience that London was barely able to support two companies. Also, competition inevitably brought with it the search for novelty and sensation. When John Rich opened the theater in Lincoln's-Inn-Fields in 1714 he soon discovered that the available acting and writing talent was firmly committed to Drury Lane. In his struggle to survive he introduced programs of pantomime in the Italian manner, the adventures of Harlequin filled with the low farce and sensational transformation scenes which remain staples of this "illegitimate" form. Colley Cibber, at the time one of the three managers of the highly-successful Drury organization, later commented,

Two sets of actors, tolerated in the same place, have constantly aided in the corruption of the theater; of which the auxiliary entertainments that have so barbarously suffered the defects of weak action have, for some years past, been a flagrant instance; things even worse than childish pantomimes, set off with the decorations of scenes, habits, voices, and dancers.

It is possible that Cibber was speaking not only from his experience as a manager, but as an actor. When he first went on the stage in the last years of the seventeenth century, he was generally neglected until Thomas Betterton led a revolt of the leading players against the patentee and established a rival company. Cibber remained behind and perforce was made a principal actor, creating his reputation and increasing his salary at the expense of the then manager. He would not, it is certain, as a manager look with favor upon the same competition for the services of his actors. Further, in a theater protected by monopoly, there was little desire to develop new talent and no impetus to experiment with plays outside the established tradition. By 1730 Cibber's own style of acting was old-fashioned, but he saw no reason to change it, or to encourage actors who were better adapted to a changing audience, and to the end of his days he attempted to educate young players to perform in the sing-song, formal conventions of the heroic stage. The really vigorous and original theatrical productions of the early eighteenth century were thus to be found in the fly-by-night managements attempting to establish themselves in opposition to Drury. When Cibber rejected *The Beggar's Opera*, Rich caught at it for Lincoln's-Inn-Fields. Henry Fielding provided a series of lively satires and farces for various managements before setting up for himself at the Haymarket in 1736. David Garrick made his first appearance, anonymously, at Goodman's Fields in 1741.

It was against Fielding that the patent-holders levelled their strongest weapon, in the development of which they had the willing assistance of the state. Censorship had existed in England since the days of the Elizabethan Master of the Revels, but his activities had been restricted more or less to eliminating blasphemy and references which seemed to have political connotations. Since Elizabethan playwrights had little interest in social drama, this censorship was of minor importance and had small effect on the inhibition of talent. However, Fielding's attacks on Walpole and other officeholders in *Pasquin* (1736) and *The Historical Register for 1736* (1737) were so unmerciful that Parliament was induced to pass The Licensing Act of 1737 preventing the performance of any entertainment on the stage without a license from the Lord Chamberlain. As a result Fielding terminated his management of the Haymarket, Goodman's Fields

David Garrick as Macbeth

was effectively put out of business, and the patentees had the field to themselves.

It was an infamous victory. Fielding's highly promising talent was turned to the novel, and the first two plays forbidden were Brooke's *Gustavus Vasa* and *Eleanora* by James Thomson. Literary men soon learned that they might write what they pleased for book sellers but could write only what pleased the Lord Chamberlain for the theater. For any literary man of originality and independence there was no choice. Grub Street gained what Drury Lane and Covent Garden lost.

It must be said frankly that the managers were not aware of their loss. Hack writers were good enough for a theater with other interests, and there was an ample supply of hacks to keep actors and stage carpenters busy. The emphasis was upon theater and not upon drama, upon the actor and not the playwright, upon the production and not the script. No new play was as attractive as a great star in a favorite rôle, and among the happiest weeks of the season were those when two stars performed the same rôle at the rival theaters.

To our eyes the staging would appear primitive. The Restoration system of wing-and-backdrop was still in use, but attention to propriety was casual:

The scene shifters often present us with dull clouds hanging in a lady's dressing room, trees intermingled with the disconnected portions of a portico. . . . Sometimes King Richard's troops appear in the uniforms of the soldiers in St. James' Park with short jackets and cocked-up hats. King Richard, indeed, wears the dress of his time, but not so Richmond. . . . Again it is equally ridiculous to behold the actors making their entrances through plastered walls and wainscots [the apertures between the wings] instead of through doors.

However, improvements were gradually being instituted. Where formerly the stage had been lighted by candelabra hanging in full view, Garrick introduced footlights in 1765 and encouraged his scene painter and machinist, De Loutherbourg, in the development of systems of colored lights, of projected scenic effects, and of devices for increasing the realism of the settings. Charles Macklin, in a revolutionary interpretation of Shylock, demonstrated the value of realism in costume and founded a new school of naturalistic acting with which Garrick was quick to associate himself. These reforms were theatrical, however, and not dramatic. With the exception of a few brilliant comedies, the industrious managers applied themselves to uncovering new stage talent and keeping the hack writers in their places.

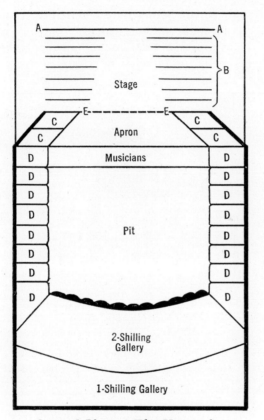

Ground Plan of The Haymarket
Theatre about 1825

A-A—Backdrop; B—Wings; C—Stage-Boxes;
D—Side-Boxes; E-E—Curtain

Perhaps the quietus to any attempt to revive the drama was given by the rebuilding of the patent theaters at the turn of the nineteenth century. In 1794, Sheridan opened the new Drury Lane in an edifice calculated to double the audience capacity of its predecessor. In 1808, Covent Garden burned to the ground to be replaced in the following year by a house built to contain nearly 3000 spectators. Both theaters burned again almost immediately but were replaced by equally imposing piles totally unsuited to the production of anything but the most grandiose and spectacular entertainments.

By 1810 both patent houses were about three times the size of the average modern theater, equalled only by our largest auditoriums and opera houses. As a consequence, in comedy, wit was replaced by the broadest farce, and in tragedy, pathos

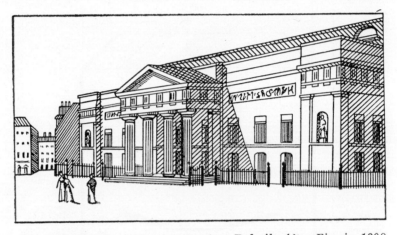

New Theatre Royal, Covent Garden, Rebuilt After Fire in 1808

and humanity by rant and violence. Shakespeare was butchered to make a leading actor's holiday and his plays filled with pageants and ballets to recompense the audience for what it was unable to hear. Such new tragedies as got produced, Shiel's *The Apostate* (1817) or Sheridan Knowles' *Virginius* (1820), depended on the long-windedness of performers rather than on the power of poetic dialogue. They are, in fact, only a "legitimate" form of melodrama, and their popularity stemmed from their resemblances to the hardly less crude drama produced at the "illegitimate" houses. On the other hand, it is not too much to say that Shakespeare became the leading playwright of the nineteenth century. The rising spirit of "Bardolatry" led to industrious but doomed attempts to imitate his works on the part of authors and a blind contempt for all other playwrights on the part of many critics. The players, of course, shared the responsibility since

they clung to their Shakespearean repertory as a badge of respectability, although to earn their bread even the greatest, John
Philip Kemble, Edmund Kean, William Charles Macready, were
forced to perform just as frequently in such tatterdemalion sensation pieces as Colman's *The Iron Chest* (1796), Sheridan's
Pizarro (1799), or Byron's *Werner* (acted, 1830). Even in the
standard repertory, melodrama held sway. Kean, possibly the
greatest actor of them all, fancied himself as Othello and Shylock, but his memorable triumphs were as Richard III and—
most revealing of all—Sir Giles Overreach.

Thus for complex and even contradictory reasons, the drama
declined, and the theater flourished. And with it flourished
melodrama, the dramatic weed.

2. MELODRAMA

The origins of melodrama have been traced to the French
boulevard theaters of the late eighteenth century, and to the
works of Pixérécourt, a specialist in Gothic romance. While it is
true that nearly one-half of all English melodramas, including
the first to be so labelled, are translations from the French, the
elements which we recognize as melodramatic are as English as
Yorkshire Pudding and the form itself is little more than the
panoramic drama debased. The panoramic dramatist, after all,
was constantly working on the audience's emotions, trying to
involve the spectator sympathetically in the struggles of the hero
in order that he might have an understanding of the final underlying meaning or theme of the play. In Elizabethan times it was
but a step from the passionate involvement with the sufferings
of Lear to arrive at a tragic vision of life, to the passionate
involvement in the fate of the Woman Killed with Kindness for
no other reason than the pleasure of a titillation of the emotions; hence the introduction of the little children in the final
scene of the latter to coax tears for a situation completely
unreal. So in the eighteenth century, the dramatist provided
sentimental comedy and bourgeois tragedy that the audience
might have "a good cry." In short, if the definition of melodrama
is the creation of thrills, excitement, horror, and emotional
twisting and wracking *for their own sakes,* it will be seen that

it was never wholly gone from the stage, and was not wholly a
creation of the late eighteenth and early nineteenth century.

As the almost exclusive offering of the minor or illegitimate
theaters, melodrama has also a special meaning for the English
stage. In the first decades after 1800 a series of small playhouses
had been erected in various parts of London with the intention
of profiting from a legal quibble over what constituted the theatrical "entertainments" described by the patents. The proprietors of the minors affected to believe, with Palmer of the ill-fated
Royalty, that the patents referred only to "legitimate" drama,
the standard repertory of five-act plays told wholly in dialogue
and action. The minors pretended to confine themselves to a
kind of opera: plays which made great use of lyrical interludes,
choruses, ballets, and other illegitimate delights. Since the patentees were indisposed to challenge them, the minor managers
were emboldened to insert songs into the standard works, even
of Shakespeare, and produce them as plays with music, or *melodramas*. In a few years what began as a scheme for evading the
law became a basic convention, the elaborate system of musical
cues which reinforce the passions, accompany the actions, and
serve as *leitmotifs* for the characters of this lively and popular
art.

Melodrama is an art with its own standards and conventions,
its own audiences and its own vision of man's fate. The world of
melodrama is a gaudy world, rendered in showcard colors; a
world of rose-covered cottages and wealthy homes filled with
gilt-and-ivory tables and chairs, with of course some mechanical
wonders to keep pace with nineteenth century inventiveness:
factories, telegraph, and railroad engines. The people of this
world are rarely kings and princes, but more commonly the types
who moved within the real world of the audience: policemen,
sailors, farmers and farmers' daughters, foundlings, revengers,
rent collectors, bailiffs, and bankers. The society of the world
of melodrama is divided into two classes, the rich and the poor;
two conditions, the happy and the unhappy; and two evalua-
tions, the good and the bad. That is to say, the world is made
up of the bad, unhappy rich, and the good, happy poor. As an
apologist for the minor theaters wrote:

[The stage] required something to excite the sympathies of the humbler
classes of society; something that . . . might teach them that poverty is

not always a sin, nor riches invariably the reward of merit.—That industry and good conduct will often overcome the inequalities of fortune, and where they do not absolutely produce wealth and distinction, they will inevitably command respect, and ensure a moderate competence.

In other words, the world of melodrama, while appearing to be realistic, was also and completely a world of fantasy as illusory as the Never-never-land of *Peter Pan,* a world of escape from reality.

It is perhaps difficult to realize how desperately the Victorian common man needed entertainment and escape from his grimy and hard-working life. He was a total stranger to the "comforts of home," unable or unwilling to read, and the theater was almost the only relief available. If he went to one of the great patent houses, he was thrust into a gallery a block from the stage, where he could not see or hear what was going on. Scorned by the pit and boxes and ignored by the actors, he was told stories he cared nothing for in a language he could not understand. So he turned to the minors, the illegitimate houses like the Surrey, the Lyceum, Sadler's Wells, or the Royal Victoria, where he could afford the best seats in the theater, and where the stories thrilled him to the core, and the sentiments of the characters could be understood and approved by every true-born Englishman, where the actors tore their lungs and three-sheeted their passions for his exclusive benefit.

Although melodramas are capable of classification by subject matter (romantic, domestic, nautical, and so on), there is little formal variation. Basically a group of stock characters is propelled through a series of conflicts until, after the requisite number of acts, scenes, hours, and thrills, the curtain falls on the triumph of the forces of good. Yet the platitudinous plots and the puppet-like characters can achieve a kind of dignity and charm enduring even in a theater which melodrama has abandoned in favor of the motion picture screen.

Douglas Jerrold's *Black-Ey'd Susan* (1829) is a good example. Its central figure, William, the honest tar, is as British as the flag and twice as colorful. Patriotic, simple, heroic, unabashedly sentimental and quaintly comic, there is something almost doll-like about his cocksureness, faithfulness, and jingoism. William has just returned from a long sea voyage to rejoin his beloved Susan whom he greets in appropriate style:

A Typical Scene from Melodrama

There's my Susan! Now pipe all hands for a royal salute; there she is, schooner-rigged. I'd swear to her canvas from a whole fleet. Now she makes more sail!—outs with her studding booms—mounts her royals, moon-rakers and skyscrapers; now she lies to it!

But life is not all nautical poetry for the lovers. As a preliminary, they must outwit Doggrass and Jacob Twig who would foreclose the mortgage on their cottage. Their main problem arises when William discovers his superior officer, Captain Crosstree, accosting his Susan, and "cuts him down like an old junk." He is promptly arrested and court-martialed and condemned to be hanged for striking a superior officer. The ceremony of the trial and the preparations for execution are reproduced in great detail, such matters being of surpassing interest to any popular audience as witness the courtroom scenes in a multitude of contemporary plays and movies. Surrounded by his praying messmates, William embraces the Union Jack, shakes hands with the Admiral, and is prepared to die when Crosstree rushes in with a paper. It develops (two minutes before the final curtain) that William had once saved Crosstree's life, and the Captain had written for his discharge:

> Villainy has kept back the document—'tis here, dated back. When William struck me he was not the King's sailor.—I was not his officer.
> ADMIRAL. He is free!

Cheers from the crew, a kiss from Susan, and tears of joy from the audience.

From such simple materials was shaped the only vital drama of the first half of the nineteenth century. Reading the endless repertory of melodramas one is often disgusted, more often stupefied. But there are times when the spirit suddenly becomes very powerful, when the innocence and naïveté of the *dramatis personae* find a responsive chord, when these Williams and Susans and their hundreds of counterparts assume an aspect not of life, but of faery, for they dwell in the suburbs of Arcady. The tolerant comment of a wise theatergoer might head any discussion of the literature of the minor theaters:

> The best in this kind are but shadows; and the worst are no worse, if imagination amend them.

3. THE FIRST REFORMS

It is pleasant to observe that the earliest reforms of the nineteenth century theater came from within the profession. They came in fact largely from the minor theaters, which were granted a degree of respectability by the Act for Regulating Theatres (1842), ending the monopoly held since 1660 by the patent houses. With their new dignity many of the proprietors of the minors acquired a new sense of responsibility towards their art, and undertook innovations in production, acting technique, and theater management. The earliest of these even preceded the Act by some months.

In 1841, Madame Vestris and her husband Charles Matthews, the actor-managers of the Olympic, a minor theater, produced *London Assurance* by Dion Boucicault. In this, his first successful work, Boucicault had written a five-act comedy in the accepted old-fashioned manner imitating the imitators of Sheridan. The production was a triumph, not for the conventionality of its writing but for the unconventionality of its staging. In it, Madame Vestris introduced for perhaps the first time in a London theater the modern box-setting, with three unbroken walls replacing the old wing-and-backdrop, with real doors and windows, with real carpets and potted plants, and with furniture and costumes appropriate to the locale and the characters. The innovation in a way simply did for legitimate drama what the producers of melodrama had done for their sensation scenes. About the same time during his incumbency as actor-manager at the patent houses, W. C. Macready introduced the same attention to realism and historical accuracy into his productions of Shakespeare and other classics, and developed many of the modern techniques of rehearsal, acting, and direction.

Realistic settings, however, cannot be shifted as readily as backdrops, and naturalistic acting is ill-suited to playwrighting in the grand manner, however decadent. The awakened consciousness of men and women of the theater to the relationship between art and the life of the times, their increasing attention to the most minute details of production, soon created a demand for a new type of play, one to replace the loosely constructed rambling plots of melodrama and the unreal and antiquated language of the traditional repertory. For inspiration, for mod-

els, and—all too often—for plays, they turned to the French theater and its thriving innovation, the *pièce-bien-faite*.

The well-made play is just what its name implies, a tidy,
logical, machine-made structure replacing the older jerry-built
structure of romantic melodrama. Its creator was Eugène Scribe,
an industrious hack, who devised a system of rules for playwrighting predicated upon clarity and "the logic of events."

Macready's Production of Virginius, *about 1840*

That is to say, every situation must be prepared for well in
advance, must grow logically out of what has gone before.
The novelty of this simple discovery can be realized by recalling
the completely fortuitous denouement of *Black Ey'd Susan* where
a piece of vital information was deliberately held back to make
a thrilling curtain. Subsidiary to the logical structure is, of
course, the careful handling of exposition which must now be
done "realistically" within the frame of the action and yet must
be always clear and precise. Scribe made a rule of giving every
important fact three times, once for the intelligent and attentive,

twice for the intelligent and inattentive, and thrice for the un-
intelligent and inattentive.

The characters of the well-made play were generally simple,
recognizable types and their goal was normally the effecting of
a marriage. A series of obstacles, sexual or financial, were placed
in the way of the achievement of the goal and increased or
removed by the ingenuity of the playwright. The plot was so
arranged that scene changes were held to a minimum, and suspense was kept at a maximum. The question always on the spectator's lips was, what will happen next? and the answer to that
question constituted the well-made play. In its origin, the well-
made play is simply the essence of what happened.

For a more serious-minded audience, however, a play must
have a kernel of truth to justify itself. The French successors
to Scribe, particularly Alexander Dumas *fils,* experimented with
the "thesis play" in which the well-made action was arranged
to illustrate a moral or ethical point. In *Le Demimonde,* for
instance, which has been described as a comedy of Scribe's "writ
tragic," the thesis confirms the conviction of the age that a bad
woman was unfit to marry into good society, but the thesis never
interferes with the *peripeteias,* the exciting reversals of situation,
which keep alive the suspense of the plot. A parallel might be
drawn with the modern detective story whose thesis is "crime
does not pay," but whose main interest lies in crime and not in
the moral.

The French well-made thesis play was ideally suited to the
well-made production methods which began to take over the
English stage shortly after mid-century. Some attempts had been
made earlier, in Bulwer-Lytton's *Money* (1841), in Tom Taylor's
The Ticket-of-Leave Man (1863), to treat contemporary conditions in a realistic, well-ordered manner, but the genuine reform of the drama is usually credited to the Wilton-Bancroft
production at the Prince-of-Wales' Theatre of T. W. Robertson's *Society* in 1865. Robertson had a long career as a theatrical
man-of-all-work behind him when he joined forces wth Marie
Wilton, an actress who shared his theatrical ideals and gave him
free reign. He found himself in a small theater, with a company
committed to the novel idea of the long run instead of repertory,
and to close attention to realism in production and acting.

The result is instantly apparent in a comparison of any of

this series of comedies, *Society, Caste, School, Ours, M.P.*, with
the comedies of his contemporaries and predecessors. The settings are painstakingly described:

A plain set chamber, paper soiled. A window, with practicable blind;
street backing and iron railings. Door practicable, when opened showing
street door (practicable). Fireplace; two-hinged gas burners on each side
of mantelpiece. Sideboard cupboard, cupboard in recess: tea-things,
tea-pot, tea-caddy, tea-tray, etc., on it. Long table before the fire; old
piece of carpet and rug down; plain chairs; bookshelf, back; . . . chim-
ney glass clock; a box of lucifers and ornaments on the mantel-shelf;
kettle on hob and fire laid; door mats on the outside of door. Bureau
in lower right-hand corner.   [*Caste*]

These "props," practicable doors and windows, and the rest
are not for mere stage decoration; they are a vital part of the
action. Robertson was one of the first to find dramatic uses for
the trivial things of everyday life. A box of matches, an um-
brella, an infant's coral necklace may form the nucleus of a
scene, or a character may be revealed as much by his smallest
action as by his longest speech. Such is the famous bit of business in the third act of *Caste* in which old Eccles fills his pipe,
or the bread-making at the opening of *Ours*.

Caste (1865) is his most famous play and it sufficiently illustrates the extent to which he escaped from the older traditions.
The three settings of the play contain its three acts; there are
but eight characters, none superfluous and each carrying his
full share of the whole action. The plot is simple, concentrating
on the marriage of the Hon. George D'Alroy and the dancing
girl, Esther Eccles, and the attempts of his mother, the Marquise
de St. Maur, to destroy it. And the theme, overtly and frequently
repeated, that "True hearts are more than coronets," is amply
proved. The dialogue at times catches the flavor of contemporary speech, and the characters, though recognizable types,
are sufficiently individualized to seem alive. When his sentimental heroine must describe the hardness of her lot as bread-
winner, she is cautioned in a stage direction not to speak "in
a tone implying hardship." Even Captain Hawtree, the sententious friend who must state the problem of the play, is permitted
to do so with a dash of slang:

My dear Dal, all these marriages of people with common people are
all very well in novels and plays on the stage, because the real people

don't exist, and have no relatives who exist, and no connections, and so no harm's done, and it's rather interesting to look at; but in real life with real relations, and real mothers and so forth, it's absolute bosh; it's worse, it's utter social and personal annihilation and damnation.

The shortcomings of the play for modern tastes are obvious. It is sentimental, both in its dialogue and in its theme; the Mar-

Caste

quise de St. Maur is, in the words of Oscar Wilde, a "monster without being a myth," a caricature; and old Eccles, for all his especially-designed character business, is a stock type from the older stage. Robertson's was a small talent but his experiments were instructive. His plays were successful with the Victorian audience, and after his day there was no excuse either for careless construction or slovenly stagecraft.

In a theater offering more attraction to men of letters Robertson's status would have been even smaller. The financial returns from playwrighting were so few, however, and the artistic satisfactions so far between that men of letters generally turned to the novel or poetry, where they might speak with some freedom, where they were not dominated by the vanities of a star-player, where they might expect a fair return for their labor. It was not until 1860 that Dion Boucicault tentatively suggested the modern system of royalty payments, and discovered that as a result *The Colleen Bawn* earned him £10,000 in contrast to the £100 or £200 he might have expected under the old system. Boucicault's suggestion that the playwright should share both the risk and the profit may be credited with a major part in bringing the literary man back into the theater.

Until after 1860, however, although the romantic poets, and Browning, Tennyson, and Dickens dabbled at playwrighting, only one literary figure devoted his talents exclusively to the theater. His works are among the most eccentric in the whole repertory—burlesques with a serious purpose, sentimental comedies with a cynical edge, and the most famous musical plays in the English theater. He is, of course, W. S. Gilbert, master of the world of Topsy-Turvy.

His originality has been many times called into question since such plays as *The Palace of Truth* (1870), *The Wicked World* (1873) and *Trial by Jury* (1875) have much in common with the mythological burlesques, fairy plays, and farcical operettas of the earlier illegitimate theaters. There is, however, a consistency about his works which is lacking in their predecessors. The Gilbertian world is unique, with laws and a logic all its own, very much as the world of Aesop or Gulliver or Lewis Carroll. His early Palace of Truth is a symbol of this world, for in that magical edifice every character must freely expose his innermost thoughts without realizing that he has abandoned the hypocrisies and defenses of his ordinary behavior. Throughout the celebrated Savoy Operas which are the crown of Gilbert's career (*H. M. S. Pinafore, The Mikado, Utopia, Ltd,* etc.), the most engaging moments are those in which the barrister, the aesthete, the major-domo, or the major general reveal their characters in the most naïve fashion.

Engaged (1877) shows Gilbert at his best as a legitimate playwright. Ostensibly the farce is realistic; that is, the characters are the everyday people of Robertsonian comedy. Their motives and manners, however, are Gilbertian. The sentimental heroine and her sentimental old father are driven by a greed for money so intense that it reminds the reader of the *Jew of Malta;* the simple pastoral swain, Angus MacAllister, describes his way of life:

> Yes, I'm a fairly prosperous man. What wi' farmin' a bit land, and gillieing odd times, and a bit o' poachin' now and again; and what wi' my illicit whuskey still—and throwin' trains off the line, that the poor distracted passengers may come to my cot, I've mair ways than one of making an honest living—and I'll work them a' nicht and day for my bonnie Meg!

One after another the sentimental clichés of the theater are exploited and turned topsy-turvy. When the romantic hero is revealed as a man who falls in love with and becomes engaged to every woman he meets, the most cherished convention not only of the theater but of the Victorian audience—the sacredness of romantic love—is grotesquely parodied.

Gilbert clearly stands alone among the playwrights of his age, both as a literary man and a critic of human foibles. Had he not devoted himself to his famous collaboration with the composer Sullivan in producing the Savoy Operas, he might well have become the founder of the modern English drama. As it is, he anticipates many of the techniques and attitudes of Bernard Shaw. But there are few theater-goers who would not declare his unwritten legitimate works well lost for the lyric adventures of Ko-Ko and Captain Corcoran and the Duke of Plaza-Toro.

Iolanthe

4. THE TRIUMPH OF THE WELL-MADE PLAY

The well-made play, transplanted from Paris, anglicized by Robertson, attempted with varying degrees of success by such of his successors as Henry J. Byron and W. S. Gilbert, and ignored by Henry Irving, the dominant actor-manager of the age, established itself in the last two decades of the nineteenth century as a staple of the English drama. For nearly three-quarters of a century, indeed, it has been the basic form of dramatic art for our theater as the panoramic was for the theater of the Elizabethans. It is difficult to realize that of the two men who brought it to perfection, one, Henry Arthur Jones, began as a writer of melodrama, the other, Pinero, as a writer of farce. The well-made play was so ideally adjusted to Victorian and post-Victorian society, and to their preferred theatrical subjects, that it effectively eliminated the older forms as models for contemporary playwrights and, in fact, very nearly put an end even to the revival of the classic plays which had long been the backbone of the theatrical repertory. Audiences quickly developed an insatiable taste for the "new realism," for seeing themselves and hearing their problems discussed upon the stage. That the problems were nearly always those growing out of love and marriage did not, of course, diminish the popularity of the form.

In general the well-made problem play of the eighties and nineties seldom descends below the upper middle classes for its characters, and lays considerable stress on the realism of its settings and costumes. The dialogue, in prose, makes an effort to ape popular speech, and is filled with contemporary local allusions and slang. The plot is single, carefully concentrated on a single problem or idea, to which all the characters and situations are adjusted. The "logic of events" still governs the structure (the selection and arrangement of incidents) of the play, and great care is expended on preparation, on foreshadowing of all future developments. Most of the dramatist's skill is thus employed in tying his characters into an apparently inextricable knot which his ingenuity will sever in an unexpected but "logical" and highly gratifying reversal or *peripeteia*.

The difference from Robertsonian comedy will hardly be apparent in a reading of Henry Arthur Jones's *Saints and Sinners* (1884), yet the latter is usually assigned the title of the first

English "modern serious drama." The claim is unimportant, but the difference is not. The difference, which becomes more apparent in Jones's later plays, lies in the attitudes of the authors to their work. For Robertson the theater had been a profession since childhood and his main interest was very likely in improving the attractiveness of the commodity which he sold for his daily bread. Sensible above all other things of the necessity of pleasing his audience, he was enough a man of his time to perceive that the audience was prepared for a change in the temper and tone of the drama. Yet Jones himself observes that most of Robertson's "pleasing characters and scenes" are "as essentially false as the falsities and theatricalities he supposed himself to be superseding." However real *Caste* may be in its stage management, it is false and theatrical in the foundation and conduct of its plot, employing a "social contrast that was effective on the stage, but well-nigh, if not quite, impossible in real life."

Jones, it will be seen, took the drama seriously as an art and earnestly desired to restore it to its mission as a criticism of life. A further quotation from his introduction to Augustin Filon's *The English Stage* will establish the aims of the "movement" in which he played a leading rôle:

> If I were asked what was the distinguishing mark of that movement, I should say that during the years when it was in progress there was a steadfast and growing attempt to treat the great realities of our modern life upon our stage, to bring our drama into relation with our literature, our religion, our art, and our science, and to make it reflect the main movements of our national thought and character. That anything great or permanent was accomplished I am last to claim; all was crude, confused, tentative, aspiring. But there was *life* in it.

Saints and Sinners makes use of a good many of those theatrically effective and socially false situations for which Robertson was condemned. Its conventional hero and villain, its last-minute sensation, its preoccupation with "stage justice" are the stuff of melodrama. But it also contained the first glimmerings of the attack on middle-class morality and respectability which was to be the preoccupation of the new domestic drama. Here Jones's theme was the complete separation of a man's religious professions and his action, dramatized by the stupid attempts of a local grocer to get his minister to preach against a coöperative store. The grocer's argument is at once logical and revealing: "If I support your chapel, I expect you to get the congregation to support my shop. That's only fair." The theme is emphasized as the heroine dares to express her discontent with the dreary life of a provincial town which values respectability above humanity.

A form of drama which was designed to expose the most cherished clichés of its audience could not fail to appeal to Oscar Wilde, who devoted much of his life to administering shocks to the middle class. *Lady Windermere's Fan* (1892) is remembered today largely for its epigrams and passages of wit, and its serious theme is ignored. But the action of the play supports the theme that absolute right and wrong are impossible standards and that to compromise with right and wrong is a human virtue. Lady Windermere, the "charming puritan" of the first act, recalls that her aunt taught her "what the world is forgetting, the difference that there is between what is right and what is wrong. *She* allowed of no compromise. *I* allow of none." By the end of the play, after she has placed herself in a compromising position and been saved by the self-sacrifice of the "bad" Mrs. Erlynne, she admits to herself, "There is a bitter irony in things, a bitter irony in the way we talk of good and bad women. . . . Oh, what a lesson!"

The obvious statement of the theme is fairly typical of the play as a whole, a curious mixture of polish and crudity in the dialogue and in the structure. Both crudities arise from the fact that Wilde's interest in his plot and his problem was only half-hearted; it is immediately apparent that his whole heart was given to mirroring the elegant *fin de siècle* society of which he was himself an ornament, and to displaying the glittering wit of which he was an unchallenged master. His interests thus lead him to such dramatically inefficient scenes as the epigrammatic debate among the fine gentlemen in Act III, or the botching of a climax with a totally unrealistic soliloquy, like Lady Windermere's as she rifles her husband's desk in the first act.

The structure of the play is equally artificial, juxtaposing three love-affairs designed to illustrate three fashionable attitudes towards marriage. The major plot, involving the triangle of Lord and Lady Windermere and Mrs. Erlynne, is artificial in the theatrical sense, hinging as it does on a highly melodramatic coincidence: that a mother who had deserted her daughter

in infancy should try to use her son-in-law as a means of regain-
ing her position in "good society." Equally melodramatic is the
son-in-law's resolution to keep secret the identity of Mrs. Erlynne in the face of his wife's suspicions and the certain threat
to their marriage. The second triangle, growing out of the first
in a way wholly natural—in the theater—, involves Lord Darlington's attempts to capture the affection of Lady Windermere in
her moment of revulsion. Running through the early part of the
play is a third love-affair, also completely artificial, but, unlike
the others, an accurate reproduction of a common situation in
the society of the time. The Duchess of Berwick arranges a marriage between her daughter and an eligible young man with as
much cold calculation as she would give to the getting up of a
dinner party. The juxtaposition is intended to emphasize the
romantic nature of the other love-affairs; perhaps, by depicting
the inhuman artificiality of the world of the play, it also justifies
to some extent the artificiality of the play's structure and technique.

Now it is obvious that no play can avoid artificiality, and a
study of the drama becomes in part a study of the *contrivances*
by which the dramatist arranges his material to make his point
or gain theatrical effectiveness. We applaud the allegorical techniques of the Middle Ages and Renaissance, the symbolism of
poetic drama, the double plots of the Shakespearean stage. But
the closer the drama moves towards realism, towards the pretense of an accurate reproduction of contemporary life, the more
conscious the audience becomes of contrivances which have not
been thoroughly camouflaged. During the last half of the nineteenth century, when the trend was all towards realism, playwrights expended great ingenuity in the art of preparation so
that no development might seem illogical or untrue to the life
portrayed. Wilde is content, however, with tricks, with the in-
expensive commodity of suspense, and the easiest of ironies.

The fan, for instance, though inanimate, is very nearly the
most important actor in the first two acts. It makes its entrance,
prominently, with two of the leading characters in the opening
moments of the play. Before the curtain falls, Lady Windermere
threatens to use the fan to strike Mrs. Erlynne should she dare
attend her ball, and directs her butler to speak the names of the
arriving guests with especial distinctness. At the ball, Lady Win-

dermere receives her guests with the fan prominently displayed, and as her husband asks for a word with her, she turns to her partner and says, "Will you hold my fan for me, Lord Darlington?" There is no reason for her not carrying the fan with her except the purely theatrical one, her action will focus the attention of the audience on the inanimate actor and increase the suspense.

Equally contrived are the entrances and exits. Just as his wife has renewed her vow to strike Mrs. Erlynne, and Windermere has decided (in an aside) that he must reveal the truth to avoid a scene—enter Mrs. Erlynne. In Act III, just as Mrs. Erlynne has persuaded her daughter to flee from Lord Darlington's rooms, enter Lord Darlington with, for added suspense, Lord Augustus with whom Mrs. Erlynne hopes to effect the marriage which will restore her to society.

Both situations, theatrically effective as they are, create the kind of ironies which the dullest in the audience can recognize. But the fundamental ironies of the plot are equally obvious. The action is so arranged that the virtuous Lady Windermere shall place herself in a compromising position from which she can be rescued only by the despised woman of easy virtue. Further, as the audience alone knows, the mother who once deserted her child now atones with a completely unselfish sacrifice. The whole action could be summed up in an epigram which would have cost Wilde much less effort.

But it must not be forgotten that Wilde's interests lay elsewhere. As a member of the society his play reflects, he is neither satirizing nor, very seriously, moralizing. There are fools at Lady Windermere's ball, to be sure, but there is also Lord Darlington, the epitome of Wildean virtue. To him fall most of the celebrated epigrams, and an examination of his wit reveals more than an ability to turn a cliché upside down or a pretense at insincerity in a desire to shock. Darlington is completely consistent: "I can resist everything but temptation; I think life too complex a thing to be settled by these hard-and-fast rules; we are all in the gutter, but some of us are looking at the stars." For the first time since the Restoration, the comic hero is both a member of his society and a commentator on it.

In a sense this is also true of the Duchess of Berwick. On the surface a babbling, inconsequential dowager, she reveals, not altogether ingenuously, a shrewd understanding of her society. Better than Mrs. Erlynne or Lady Windermere she has taken the measure of herself and of her world and set about to make the best of it. Whatever one may think of her views of marriage, they are certainly to be preferred to those of Lady Plymdale. She is wise and worldly and practical; and she has learned the same lessons about social relations as Mrs. Erlynne and Lady Windermere without for a moment compromising her own position or her family's. If *Lady Windermere's Fan* is still read and acted with delight, it is because of such as the Duchess and Darlington whom Wilde understood and respected and not because of its "problem" and its conventional lovers who are only the background for a comedy of manners *manqué*.

The most famous of the well-made problem plays is Sir Arthur Pinero's *The Second Mrs. Tanqueray* (1893). Indeed its immediate and enduring success has overshadowed Pinero's better plays *The Thunderbolt* (1908), and *Mid-Channel* (1909), but it is in so many ways the touchstone of its form that it must be treated at whatever cost to the author's reputation.

Unlike Wilde, Pinero was not writing a disguised comedy of manners. His intention was wholly serious, to describe a tragedy growing out of one of the "problems" of modern life. The question—one which has always been of intense moment in the theater—can a woman with a past ever acquire a position in polite society, is answered with a dogmatism highly satisfactory to the polite society that bought tickets to the play. In Pinero there is no uncertainty about the hardness and fastness of "rules," and no intention to shock his audience into a revision of moral attitudes. Instead we are called together to observe, in a world as real as the one we have just left to attend the theater, how right we are.

Pinero is insistent upon *reality*. No effort is spared to make the audience comfortable in a recognizable world full of recognizable people behaving in recognizable ways. It is instructive to observe the playwright's method. The curtain rises on a realistic-enough scene, Aubrey's richly and tastefully decorated chambers in The Albany, with plenty of real doors for exits and entrances, a table laid for dinner, and three middle-aged men over coffee and cigars (real coffee and real cigars, of course). Quite casually the play begins with a reminiscence by Misquith which leads to a comment on the absence of Cayley Drummle. Aubrey regrets Cayley's absence particularly since he had intended to make an announcement of great importance to his three oldest friends—he is going to be married, for a second time. The exposition is all very natural; he wishes to prevent the breaking up of bachelor friendships, although he is afraid that the second Mrs. Tanqueray will not be wholly acceptable to his social circle. A toast is drunk and Aubrey says, "As we're going to turn out by and by, let me scribble a couple of notes while I think of them," and most naturally withdraws to the other side of the room, leaving his guests to finish their coffee as best they may.

At this point, quite naturally, Cayley arrives with his story of Lady Orreyed's distress at her son's elopement. Aubrey steps in long enough to express his sympathy for the woman in the case—and returns to his letter writing. Naturally enough, the three men, left to their own devices, tell Cayley of Aubrey's impending marriage. This leads Cayley, the oldest of these close friends, to reveal to them *for the first time,* quite naturally, the story of Aubrey's first marriage, and the religious propensities of his young daughter. Now Aubrey, having quite naturally finished his letter writing, returns to his companions. Two of the friends take their leave, Cayley remaining behind rather pointedly to talk. After a few moments he breaks Aubrey down to the point of confessing the name of his intended bride and his determination to prove to the world that "it's possible to rear a life of happiness, of good repute, on a—miserable foundation."

The conversation is interrupted by the butler's announcement that Paula, the lady in question, has come calling. Cayley leaves and the butler brings in the mail, delivered at all hours in well-made plays, but before Aubrey can look it over, Paula enters. She has a letter of her own, too heavy to go for regular postage, a list of all her affairs and adventures which Aubrey is to read after her departure. This gesture of complete honesty on her part is rewarded when her future husband flings it unread into the fire, and she steps out with a gay laugh to fetch her cloak. Aubrey now has time to tend to his mail, which he quite naturally reads aloud. His daughter has resolved to leave the convent and come home to him. Paula returns in her bright cloak and Aubrey stares at her—a convent-bred maiden with an ex-prostitute step-mother. Curtain!

It is not to be denied that all this is handled with the greatest technical skill. When characters are needed they appear, when not they are got rid of; nor does Pinero balk at using coincidences if they will advance the action in a way that is dramatically effective. One might have a momentary misgiving that great plays are not written by pens stuck at one end of the long arm of coincidence, but life had served the convenience of the dramatist before *Mrs. Tanqueray*. There is, however, a difference

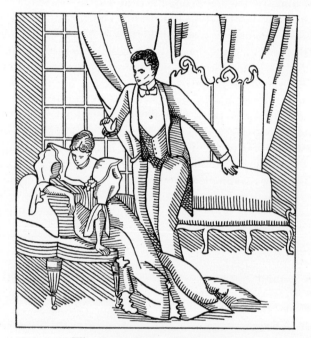

The Second Mrs. Tanqueray

between, say, the coincidence that Lear and Gloster misjudge their children in parallel ways at the convenient dramatic moment and that Paula Tanqueray's step-daughter should fall in love with one of her former lovers. The older playwright did not insist upon the contemporary naturalness of his action and he employed coincidence as a means to an end, not an end in itself.

Pinero might have thought that his coincidences also were means, and not ends. He wished to make the point that the marriage of an honorable man and a profligate woman could not succeed. But it is hardly a convincing proof to explain the inevitable failure on the grounds that the man's daughter may fall in love with one of his wife's kind keepers. It is a chance that any middle-aged widower has to take, perhaps, but the play is hardly a more convincing deterrent than *Ten Nights in a Barroom* which taught that a drinking man may very well murder his own father.

Coincidence does not spoil any play, it merely spoils a play that sets out to solve a problem and resorts to tricks to do it. There are as many tricks in Mrs. Tanqueray's play as in her former profession. Notice the handling of the opening scene in which Aubrey so "naturally" withdraws to write letters that the audience may overhear a passage of "natural" exposition. For that matter, count the number of letters written, received, intercepted: in these well-made plays the postman is the hardest-working member of the cast. Count those "practicable" doors and windows through which the actors can get in and out, and overhear, and be stowed away temporarily. All this is highly ingenious, and makes possible the telling of an entertaining story, but the result is neither a serious investigation of a social problem nor a tragedy of character. On the whole Jones-Pinero school of playwrighting Bernard Shaw comments:

I do not deny that an author may be driven by his own limitations to ingenuities which Shakespeare had no occasion to cultivate, just as a painter without hands or feet learns to surpass Michel Angelo in the art of drawing with the brush held in the mouth; but I regard such ingenuity as an extremity to be deplored, not as an art to be admired.

The well-made problem play is not a form to be despised or ignored. It still furnishes the major portion of the contemporary dramatic repertory, and in its emphasis on tidiness of structure it was and is the most useful model for beginning playwrights. Working with the form the novice learns the value of economy, preparation, and verisimilitude, and is instructed by precept and example that the play can and should support a theme of social or intellectual interest. Unfortunately, the well-made playwright seldom aspires beyond verisimilitude in the sense of realism, and is practically required to furnish a pat and comfortable solution for any issues he has raised.

After a very short course of study of the form, the reader soon learns to recognize the trains of action which the dramatist lays down in Act I for later explosion. When Pinero is careful to establish in the opening of *Mid-Channel* that at the back of the setting is a balcony five stories above the street, shortly before his heroine wonders àpropos of another matter, "Why is it that more people commit suicide in summer than in winter?—When I put an end to myself it will be the wintertime," the end of the play has been telegraphed to the wary.

Henry Arthur Jones was a master of the art of preparation. The setting of Act I of *The Masqueraders* (1894) is the bar of a country-inn. Against the bar, prominently displayed, are nailed charity lists. Within ten minutes after the rise of the curtain these lists have been referred to, explained and brought casually into the action, and the climax of the act is the auctioning of a kiss from Dulcie Larondie, the heroine, for the benefit of the unfortunate. With such apparent casualness does the everyday object become the cause of the first major conflict of the play that only the critical reader will observe the author loading the dice in his own favor. The heroines of these plays never have a chance to lead their own lives.

The situation in *The Masqueraders* is a good one, if completely theatrical. Sir Brice Skene, a habitual gambler, outbids David Remon for Dulcie's kiss and, with a strange chivalry, proposes marriage. The marriage is unhappy, Sir Brice gambling away his substance, but David, who has come into a small fortune, stands ready to assist Dulcie. She is too proud to touch his money, but Sir Brice becomes so abusive that David is finally driven to propose a gambling match, David's fortune against Sir Brice's wife and child. In an exciting scene, David wins, and rushes off with Dulcie to his mountain retreat, and it almost seems as if a blow were being struck at the institution of marriage as a kind of female slavery.

It is true that Jones was, unlike Pinero, critical of the middle-class morality which governed late Victorian ways of thinking, but he was also himself a late Victorian. In the final act of the play, Dulcie's sister points out that to win a wife in a game of chance is neither legal nor moral—though she says nothing about freeing her sister from her brutish husband. "She is not yours to take," she says very solemnly. "Save her to be a good mother to that little helpless creature she has brought into the world, so that when her girl grows up and she has to guide her, she'll not have to say to her child, 'You can give yourself to this man, and if you don't like him you can give yourself to another, and to another, and so on. It doesn't matter. It was what I did!' " Nor can the sister be swayed by rhetoric, sentiment, or reason. "The woman who gives herself to another man while her husband is alive betrays her sex, and is a bad woman."

The same rigid code operates in *Mrs. Dane's Defense* (1900) in which, once again, the woman with a past is ruthlessly shoved aside when she attempts to re-establish herself in a society which is not, as Jones pictures it, entirely spotless. The first act of this play should be studied as a model of economy in dramatic exposition and concentration in developing its theme. There are few scenes in the modern drama more thrilling than the masterly cross-examination in the third act in which the skillful lawyer traps the heroine into inadvertent confession. Yet the theme is, as before, a moral so often repeated that it begins to sound almost like a biological law: once fallen, no redemption.

Fortunately when outmoded moral issues begin to pall, there is always *The Importance of Being Earnest* (1895), "a trivial comedy for serious people." Here Oscar Wilde exploits all the devices of the well-made play and satirizes them while at the same time using them to support a theme of more universal significance than any of the serious plays for trivial audiences had succeeded in achieving. One recognizes the burlesque of the usual mis-sent letter in Ernest's misplaced cigarette case; indeed, he protests, "it's very impolite to read a private cigarette case." The plot, the individual situations, and the denouement all depend upon inanimate actors (the case, the handbag, the army records), yet they are all deliberately ridiculous objects to have so great an influence in the lives of the characters. But Wilde develops a theme of great seriousness out of the most farcical of his situations.

He makes huge sport of the fact that Gwendolyn has always vowed to love a man named "Ernest." It is not, look you, that he must be of an Earnest character, but simply that he must bear the label "Ernest." The situation is duplicated in the love of Cecily for Algernon Montcrieff, whom she knows also as "Ernest"—but it is the label in which she is interested, not the quality. The particular situation is capable of abstraction as a

~ 8 ~

The Revival of the Drama

The general revival of the arts of the theater at the end of the nineteenth century was the result of something more than the usual accidental conjunction of talent, intellectual climate, and social and economic factors. It was willed into existence by the determination of amateurs outside the Great Wall of Commercialism which surrounded the professional theater. They were men who had lived enough in the world beyond the stage door to realize that the drama alone of all the arts was unaware of the great changes in men and things the century had witnessed. Science, sociology, economics, politics, psychology, all revealed man in a new light; but the newly-employed carbon-arc spotlights and electric footlights and borders of the stage only cast a brighter glare on the painted imitations of reality in settings, on the conventional stock characters and mechanical evasions of the real problems of life in the plots.

Henrik Ibsen, a Norwegian poet and dramatist, is generally acknowledged as the founder of the modern drama. In his series of social problem plays beginning with *Pillars of Society* (1877), and including *A Doll's House, Ghosts, An Enemy of the People, Hedda Gabler,* and *Rosmersholm,* while making full use of the technical skills developed by the well-made playwrights, revolutionized the subject-matter of the drama. The conventional theatrical problems of the eternal triangle, or the fallen woman, were abandoned for attacks on the ignorance and corruption of a society willfully blind to its own best interests. In becoming the theatrical mouthpiece for the great liberal movements of the nineteenth century, however, Ibsen became something more. While adhering to the balanced and economic structural technique of the well-made play, he established a method of

299

characterization which owes almost nothing to the two-century-old traditions of the theater.

The method of the older dramatists had been to manipulate stock characters through a series of more or less novel situations. The audience recognized, and classified, the character upon his first appearance either through his cognomen or through the expository speech which introduced him. But the persons of Ibsen's plays are never fully understood until the final curtain has fallen. Following the scientific and sociological theories of the influence of heredity and environment on human character, his major interest is divided between the older dramatic convention of *what-happens-to-X,* and the newer naturalistic convention of *what-made-X-as-he-is.* Ibsen thus places great emphasis upon the uniqueness of his characters, their individuality. The tremendous theatrical climax of such a play as *Ghosts* depends not upon the catastrophe which befalls Mrs. Alving's son, nor upon her discovery of the flaw in her own character which had many years before made the catastrophe inevitable, but upon the skillful dramatic construction which brings about the catastrophe and the revelation at the same moment. Audiences familiar with the classic drama could recognize the return to Sophoclean structure, but those familiar only with the theater of their own day were both bewildered and revolted. Ibsen revealed things about human nature which were more comfortably forgotten. It was true that the same revelations could be found on the shelves of any public library, but mere print could be ignored. A play, with live actors and the illusion of reality, demands belief, at least while it is being enacted.

Ibsen's progress, his fairly rapid acceptance by the theaters of France, Germany, and Russia, is not a part of the present story. His acceptance in England was somewhat slower. As early as 1880 *Pillars of Society* had been staged at the Gaiety and in 1884 Henry Arthur Jones had made an adaptation of the German translation of *A Doll's House* as *Breaking a Butterfly,* a title which reveals all too clearly what happened to the original, for which Jones later begged forgiveness as a transgression of his "dramatic youth and ignorance."

Ibsen and the New Theater Movement in England received their first real impetus from the industry and devotion of J. T. Grein, a young critic who had been impressed by the success of various European "Free Theaters." Following their formulas, he organized the Independent Theater as a private club, with a subscription audience to escape the jurisdiction of the public censor, and a program of occasional Sunday performances of works which had already become classics of the New Drama in Europe. On March 13, 1891, he christened his series with the first English production of *Ghosts,* and the resultant tempest in the press—intended to kill—convinced him and his supporters that they were on their way at last to pulling the drama out of the backwater in which it had been stagnating. When press and public can be aroused to debate the merits of a work of art, the art is at least heading in the direction of adventure and discovery.

Grein's purpose, however, was not merely to introduce the London audiences to European masterpieces, but to give a hearing to new British playwrights. On looking about him, he discovered that the capable craftsmen were too busy turning out commercial vehicles to take time off for art, and the unproduced playwrights were for the most part striving only to imitate their successes. In a moment of inspiration he called on George Bernard Shaw, who for some years as novelist, critic, and socialist spell-binder, had been pointing out to the world the flimsiness of theatrical fare in the West End. Shaw was persuaded to complete an unfinished play begun some years before in collaboration with William Archer, and Grein produced it in 1892 as *Widowers' Houses.* In the author's own words, he "at once became infamous as a dramatist."

Widowers' Houses is a well-made play, but in the Ibsen tradition. That is to say, it follows the structure so popular in the period and employs the technique and dramatic devices of men like Pinero and Jones, but uses them to explore the evils of a contemporary problem: slum landlordism. It was the problem, not the form, that aroused the audience to protest. The socialists and regular subscribers to the Independent Theater applauded, the "ordinary" playgoers hissed, and the author bowed with equal delight to both camps. He had awakened his audience to the relation between the theater and life, and in so doing he had laid the cornerstone of the modern English drama.

A good many of the later stones in the edifice have been placed there by Mr. Shaw, for he anticipated most of the directions which the drama would take. If *Widowers' Houses* may be considered the origin of the "thesis play," in the sense of being concerned with the immediate problems of modern life, it also contains the seeds of the "discussion play" which finds its excitement in intellectual rather than physical conflicts. In the attempts to re-establish the poetic drama he has been perhaps the most successful, while *John Bull's Other Island* is in part a contribution to the great body of folk, or local color plays. It should be insisted, however, that his originality, like that of the dramatic tradition in which he was a pioneer, lies in his subject matter and themes, not in form. In the preface to *Three Plays for Puritans,* Shaw points out:

"John Bull's Other Playwright"

> Technically I do not find myself able to proceed otherwise than as former playwrights have done. True, my plays have the latest mechanical improvements; the action is not carried on by impossible soliloquys and asides; and my people get on and off the stage without requiring four doors to a room which in real life would have only one. But my stories are the old stories; my characters are the familiar harlequin and columbine, clown and pantaloon . . . , my stage tricks and suspenses and thrills and jests are the ones in vogue when I was a boy.

With so much by way of limiting the meaning of "new" in the "New Theater," let us examine some aspects of the movement, which, founded on the works of Shaw and the industry of Grein in the nineties, has not yet, fortunately, run its course.

1. G. B. S.

In the Preface to *Back to Methuselah,* Shaw surveys his early dramatic career: "I tried slum-landlordism, doctrinaire Free

Love (pseudo-Ibsenism), prostitution, militarism, marriage, history, current politics, natural Christianity, national and individual character, paradoxes of conventional society, husband hunting, questions of conscience, professional delusions and impostures." None of his fellows or followers can boast such a range of subjects but they have generally been faithful to his principle of devoting himself to the passions "which have produced the philosophy, the poetry, the art, and the statecraft of the world, and not merely those which have produced its weddings, coroner's inquests, and executions."

Shaw's earliest dramatic works, collected under the titles of *Plays Pleasant and Unpleasant* and *Three Plays for Puritans* may with certain (important) qualifications be classed as his contributions to the thesis drama. The importance of the qualifications becomes apparent in a discussion of nearly any of the nine plays. Each concerns itself with a kind of Gilbertian inversion of a standard theatrical situation: in *Widowers' Houses,* a romantic hero nobly declines to live on his fiancée's tainted dowry, only to discover that his own income is equally tainted; in *Candida,* an enlightened and poetic young man nearly destroys a happy marriage, only to be thwarted by the cold-blooded calculation of the wife; in *Arms and the Man*——

But *Arms and the Man,* because of its widespread popularity may serve as a more extended example of the basic Shavian technique. To begin with it is littered with the detritus of a thousand romantic operettas. The setting is that Middle Europe of gaudy costumes and quaint notions of honor and social behavior. The characters are a romantically moonstruck young heroine, a dashing cavalry officer, a mysterious stranger. As the result of the opening situation the heroine finds that her love has been transferred from her fellow countryman to her enemy, a romantic "problem" which had been the major concern of the authors of untold numbers of melodramas. It is perhaps significant that this introductory matter is conveyed to the audience at night, in the heroine's bed-chamber, in semi-darkness.

In the remaining two acts the full light of day is cast upon setting, characters, and action. Quaint and romantic Bulgaria proves to be a place of ignorance and filth; the heroic cavalry charge led by the Byronic Major Saranoff was the accidental result of his having been unable to dismount from a horse which was running away with him; the romantic fugitive is a professional soldier who carries chocolate creams instead of cartridges into battle. One by one the accepted conventions of the theatrical view of war are held up to the ridicule of common sense and, since these conventions represent the accepted views of the theatrical audiences, the spectator who laughed at *Arms and the Man* was actually laughing at his own unquestioning acceptance of outmoded and unrealistic assumptions. "I must," said Shaw, "warn my readers that my attacks are directed against themselves, not against my stage figures."

But if Shaw were simply attacking nineteenth century self-delusions, these first plays would be historical curiosities like the melodrama they satirized. Their continuing vitality is to be credited to their author's constant preoccupation with the larger meaning of the problems he raises and to his depth of human sympathy and understanding. The delusions dealt with in any one of the plays are but particular aspects of man's willingness to deceive himself, to accept blindly the symbols, images, and idols of his forefathers. As a consequence, *Arms and the Man* is equally valid as a commentary on an actual Balkan conflict, on the society that participated in the World War of 1914, or the World War of 1939, or on the social order between wars. That is, it dramatizes a general human truth and thus attains the universal meaning fundamental to enduring drama.

Shaw's method of characterization, derived from Ibsen, is very much his own. It was at first understandably bewildering to his actors who found it "artificial" in contrast to the style to which they were accustomed by (theatrical) nature. For example, an experienced professional would know in a moment how he was expected to growl and leer and bully if he were called upon to play the villainous exploiter of the poor. But the actor of Sartorius, in *Widowers' Houses,* was called upon to portray a slum landlord who extorts pennies from his tenants at the expense of their starving children, only to make a stronger case for his actions than the humanitarian hero can bring against them. Shaw abandoned the totally black villain and substituted a human being, shaped by heredity and environment, and able to justify his behavior in terms acceptable to the society in which he lived.

Equally radical is the Shavian hero. Like his creator, he is the completely articulate man, basing his actions on a "scientifically observed natural history." The first of the clan, Dr. Trench in *Widowers' Houses,* is thrust into the conventional position of despising the source of his father-in-law's income. Discovering that his own income is equally tainted, he accepts the reality of the fact and abandons a position which he recognizes as quixotic. The Caesar of *Caesar and Cleopatra* is as far as possible from the conventional stage conqueror or even from the popular conception of the Divine Julius. As one temptation after another, love, revenge, the heroic gesture, is placed before him, he remains true to his character and spurns them. For Shaw sees him as a man of sufficiently large mind to lead great armies to great conquests with great aims in view, a kind of superman who is not to be turned from his purposes by the petty passions to which ordinary men are subject. And there are many Caesars in the later plays, for the Shavian hero is not only the mouthpiece but frequently the image of his creator.

The Shavian heroine, the New Woman, is only partially indebted to the New Woman of Ibsen. Nora, in *A Doll's House,* ends her play by declaring her independence of her husband and by slamming the door on her exit. The Shavian heroine *begins* her play with the door slam. When Dr. Trench, in *Widowers' Houses,* pleads with his fiancée to accede to his scruples and abandon her dowry, to make a sacrifice in favor of sentimentality, she informs him quite realistically that two cannot live upon his income; a moment later she is observed flinging her maid about the set in a most unheroine-like manner. Candida is the most famous of the early heroines, and the most misunderstood. For several generations of theatergoers she has been a symbol of sentimental womanly attraction and wifely devotion. To Shaw she is completely realistic, true to her nature. She dismissed her husband's secretary for being young and attractive, she seduces her poet

just exactly as far as it is worth her while to seduce him. She is a woman without "character" in the conventional sense. Without brains and strength of mind she would be a wretched slattern or voluptuary. She is straight for natural reasons, not for conventional ethical ones. Nothing can be more cold-bloodedly reasonable than her farewell to Eugene: "All very well, my lad; but I don't quite see myself at fifty with a husband of thirty-five." It is just this freedom from emotional slop, this unerring wisdom on the domestic plane, that makes her so completely mistress of the situation.

The seeds of Shaw's structural innovation, the discussion play, may be observed in nearly all the early works. The method of the well-made playwrights may be simply described as exposition-complication-denouement; one event leads to another until the original force has spent itself. But in the Shavian play, events exist only for the discussion they may provoke. The intellectual rather than the physical complication is the dramatist's main concern, and it is Shaw's distinction that he has made the conflict of ideas as exciting as any of Boucicault's last-minute rescues. The secret may lie in the fact that Shaw is no abstract philosopher, but one who sees ideas always as a part of human problems. The essence of Bernard Shaw is his wit, the quintessence is his humanity.

In illustrating the discussion play, it is useful to take an extreme example, *Getting Married* (1908). Written in one act, it is intended to play a full evening without intermission, for, as the author explains with only the slightest trace of a smile, "I find in practice that the Greek form is inevitable when drama reaches a certain point in poetic and intellectual evolution. Its adoption was not, on my part, a deliberate display of virtuosity in form, but simply the spontaneous falling of a play of ideas into the form most suitable to it, which turned out to be the classical form."

At first glance *Getting Married* looks suspiciously like a debate; in the theater, however, it emerges as a lively play with an ample supply of strong conflicts and plenty of movement. The conflicts are all concerned with the single problem, not of marriage, but of *getting* married, and the various attitudes of the characters to that standard theatrical, and human, situation. For the sake of convenience, the play may be divided into four parts, the Prologue in which the characters are introduced, The Problem, The Attempts to Solve the Problem, and the Final Solutions.

The Prologue is a model of comic exposition. It is at once established that Cyril and Edith are about to be married and the various characters assemble to assist at the wedding. But each newcomer has his own marriage problem, or attitude towards the relationship. Mrs. Bridgenorth, mother of the bride, and

Collins, the caterer, take what must be called the everyday attitude towards an event which is a commonplace of their existence. General Bridgenorth has been for many years desperately in love with Lesbia, a "new woman" who, desiring children, is yet unwilling to surrender her independence to a husband. Reginald Bridgenorth has just been divorced by his wife, some years his junior, in order that she may wed St. John Hotchkiss, who is both younger and more entertaining. Bishop Bridgenorth, father

Getting Married

of Edith, is the recipient of love letters signed "Incognita Appassionata," declaring the writer's intentions of meeting him in heaven. The exposition is kept dramatic by a simple but effective (and typically Shavian) comic device. Each newcomer announces that there is one particular person to whom he has an invincible aversion, that person, of course, being the next to appear. General Bridgenorth, for example, despises his brother Rejjy for dragging the family name through the divorce court; Rejjy detests St. John for whom his wife abandoned him. Shaw assembles all these passions, aversions, and attitudes in the rectory kitchen, and allows us the pleasure of eavesdropping on the result.

The characters having been introduced at length (the "prologue" occupies the first third of the play), the major problem is presented: Edith and Cyril have been reading pamphlets about the barbarous nature of the English marriage laws and are refusing to go through with the ceremony. That there should be obstacles in the way of a marriage is, of course, a major tenet of any dramatist's creed; but these are not obstacles to be surmounted by outwitting a stern parent, paying off the mortgage, or proving the hero's valorousness. These obstacles can be removed only by reason and understanding, and the rest of the comedy is devoted to the attempts of the various characters to arrive at a reasonable compromise. Unfortunately, the personal marriage problems of the General and Rejjy and Lesbia and St. John continually interpenetrate the main discussion, resulting in a constant series of comic explosions, *peripeteias,* and ironies.

Since a partnership seems the best solution, three "outsiders" are brought in to assist in drawing up terms. The first of these is the caterer, a business man and local Alderman, who suggests that a lawyer is needed. The lawyer is provided in the character of Soames, the Bishop's curate, who had been trained for the Bar. But he proves to be a further comic complication, since he is not only a lawyer, but a confirmed advocate of celibacy. Finally the Lady Mayoress, Mrs. George, is sent for, a woman of affairs who can fall into trances and, in her mystic union with the forces of the universe, utter the precepts of wisdom. Mrs. George proves to be Incognita Appassionata as well as the wife of a coal merchant, and totally captures the heart of St. John, the complete snob. However, in her trance, she speaks as the Eternal Feminine, slave at once of the Life Force and of her husband:

> When you loved me I gave you the whole sun and stars to play with. I gave you eternity in a single moment, strength of the mountains in one clasp of your arms, and the volume of all the seas in one impulse of your souls. A moment only; but was it not enough? Were you not paid then for all the rest of your struggle on earth? Must I mend your clothes and sweep your floors as well? Was it not enough? I paid the price without bargaining: I bore the children without flinching: was that reason for heaping fresh burdens on me? I carried the child in my arms: must I carry the father too? When I opened the gates of Paradise, were you blind? was it nothing to you? When all the stars sang in your ears and all the winds swept you into the heart of heaven, were you deaf? were you dull? was I no more to you than a bone to a dog? Was it not enough? We spent eternity together; and you ask me for a little lifetime more. We possessed all the universe together; and you ask me to give you my scanty wages as well. I have given you the greatest of all things; and you ask me to give

you little things. I gave you your own soul: you ask me for my body as a plaything. Was it not enough? Was it not enough?

It is not idly that Shaw speaks of himself as a poet.

The final sixth of the play is devoted to the solutions of the problems. Edith and Cyril take out an insurance policy which will counteract the vicious marriage laws. Lesbia holds out for her dignity as an individual; Rejjy's divorced wife comes back to him as she convinces herself that the responsibilities of marital partnership are more satisfying than the luxury of being amused by a witty young man-about-town. But the last words belong to Soames and Mrs. George: both realize that the happiest marriage contract is based on Christian fellowship. And with that the evening's discussion ends, and the curtain falls on a comedy which is at once a biting satire on the artificial laws of human society and a hymn to the natural relationship of man and woman.

The doctrine of the Life Force has formed the basis of some of Shaw's finest comedies from *Man and Superman* (1903) to *Back to Methuselah* (1921). Quite simply, it is his phrase for Creative Evolution, the progressive development of the species from unicellular organisms to man. Shaw sees purpose in each step of the slow evolutionary process, and he sees great hope for the future development of the race, since we have already produced Supermen (like John Tanner) who have mastered the use of the highest product of evolution, the human brain. Tanner, in *Man and Superman,* like the Brothers Barnabas of *Back to Methuselah,* is an unyielding opponent of the social order, which can survive only by refusing to change. The opposition of the Superman, who realizes that the species must develop or die, and his society thus becomes a major comic theme and one which Shaw has exploited with all his own vitalism, optimism, and flair for the dramatic.

It is used, for example, with telling effect in *St. Joan* (1923) which is, to date, his masterpiece. Ostensibly writing in the form of a chronicle history, Shaw is at great pains to adhere to what appear to him to be the realities of the situations, and to counteract at every turn the dangerous misinterpretations of Joan's romantic biographers. Actually his subject is Superwoman against Men, the Saint against the World, the Radical against

Society. For Joan is portrayed as an individualist, responsible only to her own principles, unwittingly opposed to the religious and social forces which insist on the maintenance of the *status quo*. Her ability to work miracles, her ability to lead men to victory, is related to the mystical experiences of her youth. But these are for Shaw a symbol of her own development. By learning to use her own mind, she arrives at an understanding of life, and is thus able to determine what must be done, and to do it, until the forces of society become too strong for her.

The theme is clarified in the fourth scene, the debate on Feudalism and the Catholic Church between Warwick and Bishop Cauchon, an example of the discussion play at its most dramatic. The theme is made explicit at Joan's trial when she refuses to sign the recantation which would imprison her for life:

> You think that life is nothing but not being stone dead. It is not the bread and water I fear: I can live on bread: when have I asked for more? It is no hardship to drink water if the water be clean. Bread has no sorrow for me, and water no affliction. . . . I could do without my warhorse; I could drag about in a skirt; I could let the banners and the trumpets and the knights and soldiers pass me and leave me behind as they leave the other women, if only I could still hear the wind in the trees, the young lambs crying through the healthy frost, and the blessed, blessed church bells that send my angel voices floating to me on the wind. But without these things I cannot live; and by your wanting to take them away from me, or from any human creature, I know that your counsel is of the devil, and that mine is of God.

But *St. Joan* is a great play for more reasons than the greatness of its theme. Joan is the most human of the supermen, not the mouthpiece of a philosophical concept. And her fate is moving because she is herself unaware of her own position, unaware of the motives of the opposition. Even in the Epilogue which makes sport of the fantastic nature of social "realities," Joan is so much herself as to propose a return to earth now that she has been made a saint. At once the other characters of the play, who have been worshipping at her feet, recoil in horror and exeunt rapidly. Joan is left alone to lament, "O God that madest this beautiful earth, when will it be ready to receive Thy saints? How long, O Lord, how long?"

In a sense that speech is also the lamentation of Bernard Shaw, for it has been one of his convictions that the artist must be useful as well as entertaining, that he should enlighten and improve his audiences. Shaw has been for over half a century the most stimulating and optimistic of teachers for his fellow men. But he has also been the inspiration and guide of his fellow playwrights. One might classify with justice much of the modern repertory as the Shavian drama, as one classifies the Elizabethan repertory as Shakespearean.

2. THE COURT PLAYWRIGHTS

Grein's Independent Theatre which had borne the first plays of Shaw, survived until 1899 when it was re-organized as the Stage Society. Under its new title it continued to be small, occasional, and private, and although it gave London a glimpse of the wonders of the New Drama it made little impression on the commercial theaters of the West End. In 1904, J. E. Vedrenne, manager of the Court Theatre, invited Harley Granville-Barker, actor, director, and playwright for the Stage Society to produce a revival of *The Two Gentlemen of Verona*. Granville-Barker accepted with the understanding that six matinee performances of *Candida*, in which he had created the rôle of the poet, should also be given. The Shaw-Shakespeare experiment was so successful that the two men formed a regular partnership, leased the Court from its owners, and began a series of matinees. Within a year the matinees had become evening performances, and the Vedrenne-Granville-Barker management was an established success. In three years they gave nearly a thousand performances of thirty-two plays by seventeen authors, and although the critics were fond of referring to the Court as a Shavian temple (Granville-Barker produced eleven of Shaw's plays), plays of Euripides, Galsworthy, Yeats, Hankin, Ibsen, Hauptmann bore out Granville-Barker's declaration that it was rather a place "for the production of anything and everything that has genuine art about it."

One has, perhaps, only the justification of convenience in speaking of the "Court Theatre school" of playwrights. Subjects and styles as diverse as Gilbert Murray's translation of the *Hippolytus*, the Housman-Granville-Barker Pierrot play, *Prunella*, Shaw's "trifle," *The Man of Destiny*, and Galsworthy's realistic *The Silver Box* do not form a simple pattern. In the major playwrights first developed by the Court, however, Granville-Barker,

Galsworthy, and Hankin, there are significant resemblances: they are realists, critics of society, and they are very much a part of the modern movement which would remove the shackles of convention from the individual. In their subject-matter they are indebted to their immediate master, Shaw, as in construction they are indebted to the technical skills developed by the well-made playwrights. But if they lack Shaw's wit and gift for the fantastic, they are also free of excessive devotion to the "logic of events."

The Voysey Inheritance produced at the Court in 1905, was Granville-Barker's second play. His first, *The Marrying of Ann Leete,* produced by the Stage Society in 1899, is more in the tradition of Chekhov, an atmospheric play making a strong case for the irresistible force of progress, but that progress which is a part of the Life Force, not of society. The young lady of the title discovers that it is possible to break away from the prison in which society and convention have confined her and to realize her own possibilities. Thematically the play is Shavian, in the plainness of the dialogue and the quietness of the action it is characteristic only of its author.

Quietism and plainness are so much a part of Granville-Barker's technique that critics have sometimes found his plays "gray." They have nothing of the spectacular wit of Oscar Wilde or the comic invention of Shaw, for Granville-Barker was in his early writing a complete realist—as complete, that is to say, as a dramatist may be without ceasing to be an artist. The drama, to be sure, with its insistence on compression, on emphasis, on visual effect, places considerable limitations on the realist; he must employ "selective realism," to give the *illusion* of reality while avoiding the realism of the photograph.

The Voysey Inheritance is a good play to study in this connection. In the second act of this play, as in the first acts of *Waste* (1907) and *The Madras House* (1910), Granville-Barker sets himself the most difficult of dramatic tasks, the introduction of a large group of people to his audience without using any means which that audience can recognize as artificial. The Voysey family, assembled in its middle-class dining room, is presented without asides, without preparatory characterizing speeches. Through their conversation and actions alone they reveal themselves, and since they are commonplace people their talk is small. But a phrase here, or a sentence there, casually introduced, joins with other phrases, other sentences, to give a picture of the whole character in a manner so (apparently) artless that the spectator is completely won to belief in the truth of what he sees.

The problem, of course, is to sustain interest in the commonplace, to give a dramatic meaning to everyday reality. Granville-Barker's purpose is to comment, not favorably, on middle class morality, and he achieves it by means wholly theatrical, without once pointing a didactic finger. In the first act of the play, the father of the family has revealed to the son who will succeed him in business the fraudulent practices by which he has saved his firm and his family from bankruptcy and dishonor. After such a revelation, every line of dialogue in the second act acquires an overtone of irony. This is the art of the selective realist at its best, as it is described by Shaw in his preface to the translation of *Three Plays* by Eugène Brieux:

to pick out the significant incidents from the chaos of daily happenings and arrange them so that their relation to one another becomes significant, thus changing us from bewildered spectators of a monstrous confusion to men intelligently conscious of the world and its destinies.

Granville-Barker presents a picture of a society totally organized around money, peopled by those whose survival depends on a submission to its laws and values. Mr. Voysey maintains his reputation as an honest business man by being extra-skillful at fraud, hypocrisy, and sham. And this is the "inheritance" which he, and his society, pass on to his son, Edward. At this point, one might expect a dramatic renunciation of his inheritance by the idealistic Edward; as the conscience of his family, he might sacrifice himself, confess the state of affairs, and expiate the family sin in prison. But Granville-Barker is looking at life, not at the works of his predecessors. The heroic act is frequently irresponsible and selfish; the Voysey world cannot be so conveniently ignored.

In the manipulation of his customers' accounts, the elder Voysey had managed to keep his small investors solvent and his large investors contented; his family had the comforts and education proper to their position. A word from Edward and the small investors would be wiped out, the firm dishonored, and the family destitute. Edward must surrender his ideals or cause untold suffering and heartbreak. Not that the play is an attack on idealism, on just principles, or right reason. Its theme is the impossibility of such virtues, except as a self-indulgence, in the Voysey world. Responsibilities must be assumed, and Edward, like Prince Hal, must pay the debt he never promised.

In spite of the multitude of characters, each with his own life and problems, *The Voysey Inheritance* achieves unity by relating all events to the development of Edward's character. Scene by scene, we watch him change from a man of principle to a man of comprehension, and it is part of Granville-Barker's realistic attitude that Edward is neither priggish at the start (though his fiancée so describes him, half-seriously) nor debauched at the end. So complete is the concentration on Edward that the playwright chooses to ignore what would have been for Pinero or Jones the *scène-à-faire,* the indispensable scene, of his plot. The action of the play reaches its climax when George Booth, the father's oldest friend and heaviest investor, discovers the state of affairs and threatens first to go to law and then to withdraw his money with the understanding that all the firm's earnings will be paid to him until the deficiency is made up. Since this would ruin the smaller investors whom Edward is trying to protect, he laughs at the proposal and ushers the old miser to the door. A delicate irony is added to the situation as Edward's sister presents Mr. Booth with a basket of Christmas gifts to be distributed to his dependents. But the play stops before even a hint is given of what Mr. Booth will do to the firm. Granville-Barker is concerned only with Edward's progress; the audience is not permitted to indulge its appetite for sensational court-room scenes, or any other matter which is aside from the purposes of the dramatist.

This determination to be true to their own purposes is characteristic of the Court Theatre realists. In their plays there are few *peripeteias* to assist their heroes to easy solutions. In *Waste,* Granville-Barker permits his hero to be destroyed by a love-affair, but he refuses to conclude that the world is well lost for love. In *The Madras House* he depicts an ideal couple who have escaped "from the farmyard world of sex" to the greater realization of their possibilities as human beings. To emphasize his approval he presents them against the background of a middle-class husband-hunting family and a dress-shop where the baits for husband-hunters are provided. His position is radical, but his observation, as always, minute.

John Galsworthy, the second of the Court dramatists, was like Granville-Barker a realist. And like Granville-Barker's his realism was not that of the photographer but was, as he said "in every respect as dependent on imagination, construction, selection, and elimination—the main laws of artistry—as ever was the romantic or rhapsodic play." Like Granville-Barker, too, he was concerned with relating the particular problem with which he is dealing to the larger conflict of social order and human nature. Unlike Granville-Barker, he was at least by nature a reformer, concerned in part with mitigating the evils he undertook to depict.

As a reformer he had remarkable success. His *Justice* (1910) portrayed so graphically the conditions of the English prison system that the Home Secretary, Winston Churchill, was moved to an investigation which resulted in a general overhauling. Yet Galsworthy himself declared that his sights were on a higher object as well, that he intended "to elucidate the true proportions of the problem of Society face to face with the erring individual."

Justice, like Galsworthy's other social plays is scrupulously fair. The criminal, Falder, is not convicted on circumstantial evidence—his crime is real and acknowledged. But the punishment meted out to him takes into account neither his character as an individual nor his motives as a human being. It is not Galsworthy's intention that crime should go unpunished, but that the punishment should fit both the crime and the criminal. And since Falder's crime was the direct result of those marriage laws which other dramatists had been attacking for many years, it is Galsworthy's further suggestion that the justicers should look into their own hearts and minds before taking action.

The point is worth emphasizing that the play is neither a poster nor a one-sided piece of propaganda. The playwright is impartial in his reporting and bases his conclusions on that "natural history, scientifically observed" of which Shaw has been the advocate.

Because of the continuing immediacy of its subject-matter, *Strife* (1909) is perhaps the most vital illustration of his method and attitude. The struggle between capital and labor has not

grown less since *Strife* was first produced, nor was it the first
nor last play to find its central conflict in a strife. But few plays
before or since have failed to take sides, to support either the
working man or the boss. So skillfully are the materials of *Strife*
kept in balance that it would be difficult for the partisans of
either side to pick a quarrel with Galsworthy's treatment. His
play makes it clear that for him, at any rate, the struggle is not
between issues but between men, and thus he maintains his alli-
ance with the point of view which stresses the importance of the
individual over any system or convention, and the dramatic form
which concentrates on the revelation of character as its primary
function.

In the plotting, *Strife* is extremely simple. The strike at the
Trenartha Tin Plate Works is led by David Roberts on the part
of the workingmen, and opposed by John Anthony, on the part
of the company directors. John's children, Enid and Edgar (the
younger generation in plays of this school is generally enlightened), try to effect a compromise, but are unsuccessful in their
appeals both to their father and to Roberts. In the end, the
directors desert Anthony, fearing loss of dividends, and the work-
men desert Roberts, fearing loss of livelihood, or life itself. Before the final curtain the two opponents confront each other in
common defeat, and Tench, secretary to the board, and Harness,
an official of the trades union, are left to summarize the action:

HARNESS. A woman dead; and the two best men both broken!
TENCH. D'you know, sir—these terms, they're the *very same* we drew
up together, you and I, and put to both sides before the fight began?
All this—all this—and—and what for?

The whole interest of the audience in *Strife* is centered on the
two strong-minded men. They are men of principles and ideals,
not villains. Each sees and acts according to his lights, but each
is so blinded by his own light that he cannot see the other's
position. For this reason the play retains its validity when so
many "problem plays" have hopelessly dated. The condition
reflected in its plot is not merely the condition of labor conflicts
in particular, but human conflicts in general. If Galsworthy
is preaching, he is not preaching at capital and labor, but at
mankind. Anthony's battlecry is "Give way to the men once and
there'll be no end to it," and Roberts', "Mr. Anthony stands for

tyranny." Roberts is blind to the effect his determination is
having on his own wife, dying of starvation, to say nothing of
his fellow-workers; Anthony is equally blind to the necessities
of his partners. Galsworthy remarked that he might as well have
involved them in a political conflict as in class warfare or the
dispute of capital and labor. The individual, seen clearly and
completely, was his concern.

Galsworthy is fundamentally serious in his social attitude and
his artistic method. His ironies are grim, in contrast with the
sardonic ironies of Granville-Barker. But the Court was to introduce also St. John Hankin, a comic playwright, who, while
completely attuned to the new dramatic attitudes towards society, determined to reflect them in the style and with some of
the wit of Oscar Wilde. His first Court play, *The Return of the
Prodigal* (1905) resumes the ancient and familiar parable reflected in the title. But the "prodigal," Eustace Jackson, returns
without reformation and finds himself thoroughly unwelcome
in the bosom of his family. By trading on their false sense of
family honor, however, he gets the upper hand of them at once,
turns his hard-working, money-grubbing elder brother into an
accomplice, blackmails his father into giving him an annual
allowance, and departs for London with the promise (not to be
taken too seriously) not to woo his brother's fiancée.

Such a plot is of course a direct violation of all the laws of
theatrical propriety, but Hankin insisted upon its verisimilitude.
If a tragedy must come to a realistic conclusion, he reasoned, so
also may comedy. The Jackson family are middle-class, like the
Voyseys, with middle-class ideas and ideals, and are the slaves of
middle-class morality. An intelligent man who genuinely com-
prehends himself and his family and refuses to exaggerate the
importance of money or money-making will inevitably become
master of the situation. Eustace, therefore, is permitted to have
his own life as a character and is not forced into the stereotype
of the repentant prodigal gratefully chewing on that fatted calf
which is a symbol of his submission to familial convention.

Hankin's talents are more happily employed in *The Cassilis
Engagement* (1907). Here he takes up the problem which so
obsessed Galsworthy, the conflict between classes, but his method
is as unGalsworthian as possible. Geoffrey Cassilis, of a good
country family, becomes engaged to Ethel Borridge, daughter of

the proprietress of a London boarding house. At his mother's
invitation, he brings Ethel and her mother to stay at the Cassilis
mansion in Leicestershire "to get acquainted" before the wedding takes place. At the beginning of the play it is obvious to
Mrs. Cassilis and her country friends that the marriage is un-
desirable. After a week in the country it is also obvious to Ethel,
who breaks the engagement and returns to London. So much
of the plot is not remarkable for its originality, nor is the characterization of the vulgar harridan, Mrs. Borridge.

The originality lies in several novel and dramatically effective
juxtapositions. Mrs. Borridge represents the worst London has
to offer, to be sure, but she is set *vis-à-vis* Lady Remenham, the
worst the country has to offer. There is little to choose between
them, certainly, and there is an odor of cynicism in so balanced
a view of greed, vulgarity, and ignorance in *both* classes. More
shocking to the conventional-minded spectator is the portrait
of Geoffrey's mother. She is the epitome of the middle-aged
mother of high comedy: beautiful, gracious, and quietly witty.
She is also ruthless, hypocritical, and domineering.

Sight unseen she is determined that Ethel is no match for her
son and has carefully planned the strategy whereby she will,
under the guise of silken politeness and consideration for her
guests, contrive to expose them at every turn and bore them into
the bargain. She even goes to the length of introducing into
the party a notorious lady-killer, in the hope that he may be
tempted to seduce Ethel. Her sister is appalled at her unscrupu-
lousness, but she replies, "Of course it would be *pleasanter* to
be perfectly straightforward, and tell the girl I detest her. But
if I did she'd marry Geoff if only to spite me. So I must trap
her as she has trapped him. It's not a *nice* game, but it's the only
possible one."

Her son moves obediently through the play, picking up his
cues as if he had been rehearsed. For Mrs. Cassilis has taken the
measure of her Geoffrey as well as of Ethel. As a true member of
the landed gentry, if he sees a horse he will ride, or a hare he
will shoot. Though he has been called to the Bar, Lady Remenham's indignant question sums up the whole attitude of the
landed gentry: "What business has Geoffrey to be at the Bar!
Deynham has the best shooting in the Shires, and in the winter
there's the hunting. What more does he want? It's disgraceful."

In fact the only major character who emerges from the play in a sympathetic light is Ethel Borridge. She is very nearly a match for Mrs. Cassilis—it is the country itself that defeats her. She declares her independence by entertaining a dinner party with the rendition of a noisy music hall song, and regains her dignity by the decisive and kindly way she breaks her engagement with Geoffrey.

For all the wit of its dialogue *The Cassilis Engagement* is not a pleasant play, and Hankin had once again to defend his right to an unromantic ending in a comedy. The comic attitude may be just as realistic as the tragic in the modern theater and the refusal to provide the conventional happy ending is the comedian's declaration of his right to accurate observation and intellectual interpretation. Later writers of comedy have not been so scrupulous. Somerset Maugham in such plays as *Our Betters* (1917) and *The Circle* (1921) assumes a realistic attitude towards a social group for the purposes of satire but abandons it at his own convenience for the purposes of romantic sentimentality. Noel Coward (*Private Lives,* 1930) depends almost entirely upon situation and an affected sophistication in dialogue to provoke laughter, but the verbal glitter and farcical action are only the lacy decorations on what is basically a gaudy valentine. Sir James Barrie, on the other hand, is almost belligerently sentimental, and such plays as *What Every Woman Knows* (1908) and *Quality Street* (1901) depend for their effect upon his ability to create a world of his own and people it with characters of the most determined eccentricity. Yet Barrie has some right to be mentioned in a discussion of the new realism, since his subjects, regardless of his treatment of them, are often those which inspired Shaw, Barker, and Galsworthy. He pokes gentle fun at class conflict in *The Admirable Crichton* (1902), and portrays his own variety of the New Woman in *What Every Woman Knows.* But if Maggie, in the latter play, is descended from Nora and Ann Whitfield, she keeps it to herself; and it is the admirable butler who takes the step which destroys his classless Utopia.

In the repertory of the modern theater Barrie stands almost alone in both his attitude and his style. Realism, as it was developed out of Shaw's demand that playwrights be guided by natural history, is the fundamental attitude of the new theater.

It was not restricted to the Court, of course, although Barker and Galsworthy were courageous experimenters and good teachers. Perhaps their major contribution was to demonstrate that the realist, while reporting his observation with precision and faithfulness, could be sufficiently large-minded to relate his observation to the highest issues and greatest themes and thus to restore the drama as an art to be taken seriously by the most thoughtful members of its audience rather than (or perhaps, as well as) the most frivolous seekers of pastime.

3. THE ABBEY THEATRE DRAMATISTS

The seeds of the New Theater were scattered over the length and breadth of Britain, in London, in Glasgow, in Manchester, and most effectively in Dublin. Though Ireland had given to the English theater some of its most distinguished playwrights, the theater in Ireland had never been more than a poor relation of the theater in England. In 1898 under the leadership of W. B. Yeats, Lady Augusta Gregory, and Edward Martyn, an attempt was made to establish an Irish Literary Theater for presentation of "something better than the ordinary play of commerce." After several years of experimentation with methods of writing and production, developing both dramatists and an acting company, a series of appearances in London attracted the attention of Miss A. E. F. Horniman, an enthusiastic proponent of the new drama and the idea of a repertory theater. Miss Horniman was so impressed that she set about acquiring the Abbey Theatre, a small Dublin playhouse, which she rebuilt and presented to the company as a permanent home.

The Abbey was in many ways a unique establishment. Its actors were for the most part amateurs with no training in the professional theater and, in some cases, no contact with theater of any sort. Its playwrights were primarily literary figures, not dramatists whose experience had been totally confined to writing for the theater. It was a repertory theater. In a period when the dramatic fashion was for realism, the Abbey concerned itself with the creation of the folk-play.

It was not that the Abbey management was unaware of the heritage of Ibsen or was willfully blind to the problems confronting society. But the Irish National Theater was only one part of a general literary, cultural, political renaissance intended to awaken the nation to its responsibilities and potentialities. So, as Yeats declared, "A play should tell the people of their own life or the life of poetry where every man can see his own image. To ennoble the man of the roads, write of the roads, or of the people of romance or the great historical people."

Yeats's dramatizations of "the life of poetry where every man can see his own image" may be more properly considered later with other attempts to establish a modern poetic drama. The creation of folk drama was the especial province of his indefatigable coadjutor, Lady Gregory. She had spent much of her life among the peasants, collecting their legends, recording their speech, and gaining an understanding of their psychology. Consequently her little one-act comedies, *Spreading the News* (1904), *The Rising of the Moon* (1907), *The Workhouse Ward* (1907), are as precise in their observation as the most realistic of social playwrights. They are, however, informed with the imagination, the love of fantasy grounded on a sympathetic understanding of the ways of nature and man, so characteristic of the Irish. Mr. Shaw, in his "Irish National Drama," *John Bull's Other Island*, chooses to dispute the existence of this characteristic, but his play only demonstrates how much it is a part of his own makeup.

Structurally Lady Gregory's comedies are related to the convention of the well-made play. The plots are simple and the action direct. The development of the action often depends as much upon circumstance as upon character: the original impetus to the catastrophic rumor of *Spreading the News* comes from the deafness of an old woman. But in her characterization Lady Gregory is revolutionary; in common with her realist contemporaries she tried to see her characters as they actually were, and hence abandoned completely the red-wigged, thick-tongued, "begorraing" Stage Irishman of tradition. Her peasants are still quick-witted, still endlessly articulate, still superstitious and sentimental, but they are whole men and women, not convenient pasteboards.

Further, it was in her comedies that the style of dialogue so characteristic of the Abbey was fully established, a prose much like that of the Elizabethans, employing simple words, repetition, and a loose syntax which is an English approximation of

Gaelic. Here, for example, is Mike McInerny, roused to wrath in *The Workhouse Ward:*

Is it wishful for my death you are? Let it come and meet me now and welcome so long as it will part me from yourself! And I would say, and I would kiss the book on it, I to have one request only to be granted, and I leaving it in my will, it is what I would request, nine furrows of the field, nine ridges of the hills, nine waves of the ocean to be put between your grave and my own grave the time we will be laid in the ground!

Though such speech and such characters may often appear fantastic to foreign audiences, their reality to the Irish is attested by the numerous riots which have marked the history of the Abbey Theatre. Of these the most famous endured for the whole week of the first production of J. M. Synge's *The Playboy of the Western World* (1907) and ended in a public debate in the theater on the merits of the work. The riot was, apparently, inspired by the fears of local patriots that so accurate a reproduction of Irish character might damage the cause of home rule. The reader should, therefore, approach Synge's play with some assurance that it is as true in the particular as it is in the general.

The general theme is simple and familiar: the molding of a personality through a series of events from an idle frightened dreamer to the "only Playboy of the Western World," and concurrently the growth of fantasy in a group of minds. But it was the particulars which gave offense: the man-hunting Widow Quinn, the frankness of speech, the readiness of a community to make a hero out of a parricide. The villagers are simple people, gullible, romantic, eager to hear again and again the story of Christy's mighty deed. It is true that they turn against their hero when his "da" appears and he strikes him down again. Confronted with reality, they recognize the "great gap between a gallus story and a dirty deed." But Christy has tasted the sweets of self-realization and does not again sink down. He makes his exit the master of himself and of his fate.

The apparently simple story is told with carefully disguised art. Christy's character is illuminated not merely by his speech but by dramatic contrast with Shawn Keough, the sort of coward Christy himself was in the days before he "riz his loy," and by dramatic contrast with the widow who had killed by accident, not as an act of self-justification. The village sports which serve as a plot device to give Christy a chance to realize himself, are also a symbol of his progress. And always there is the speech, "fully flavored," to use Synge's phrase, "as a nut or apple," written by a poet who had spent long hours with his ear pressed to a crack in the floor noting the conversation of kitchen maids in a country inn. Here is Christy, making love: "If the mitered bishops seen you that time, they'd be the like of the holy prophets, I'm thinking, do be straining the bars of Paradise to lay eyes on the Lady Helen of Troy, and she abroad, pacing back and forward, with a nosegay in her golden shawl."

The same qualities of realism, simplicity, and accurately noted speech and character are to be found in Synge's one-act tragedy *Riders to the Sea* (1904). Here, however, the sense of nature, always a part of the folk spirit, becomes almost overpowering. Nature, represented by the sea, is the antagonist, acting against the protagonist, the old peasant woman.

Again it must be pointed out that the simplicity of the play is deceptive. The economy of characters and events does not imply thinness but careful selection; the few details are chosen for their richness in implication. One by one the sea has taken from old Maurya her husband and her sons; we see only the death of Bartley, her youngest. The whole tragic story is compressed into a few speeches and a bit of action. Maurya sits by the fire recalling in a rambling way the death of Patch many years before: "I was sitting here with Bartley, and he a baby lying on my two knees, and I seen two women, and three women, and four women coming in, and they crossing themselves and not saying a word. I looked out then, and there were men coming after them, and they holding a thing in the half of a red sail, and water dripping out of it—it was a dry day, Nora—and leaving a track to the door." As she pauses, the door opens and a group of old women enter, crossing themselves and kneeling at the front of the stage. A moment later men enter with the corpse of Bartley on a plank covered with a dripping sail. The repetition of the event as the old woman remembers its occurrence in the past supports the theme in a completely dramatic way, the endless struggle of human life with the forces of nature. The implications would be nearly unbearable were the scene not followed immediately by Maurya's magnificent speech of resignation and reconciliation.

In so small and so essentially poetic a play, however, realism plays a significant part, as it does in the Irish folk drama generally. For, whatever the manifestos of Yeats—and he was once forced to admit that his theater might "have to deal with passing issues until we have re-created the imaginative tradition of Ireland and filled the popular imagination with saints and heroes"—the realistic temper of the times was not to be denied, and the Abbey found itself staging the works of "the Cork Realists." Of these, the most important is Lennox Robinson whose first produced play, *The Clancy Name* (1908) probed ruthlessly into the confused and petty souls of the urban Irish as Synge had analyzed the peasants. Indeed the works of such men as Robinson, and in particular Sean O'Casey, might almost be called the folk drama of the cities. The essential simplicity is still present, and the articulate, poetic speech; for Nature, the playwright has substituted Convention or Custom, but it is Irish and national, and is observed with some objectivity, though hardly that of an anthropologist. O'Casey's own feelings, for instance, were made sufficiently plain in the almost documentary *The Plough and the Stars* to set off a disgraceful riot and drive the author in disgust from his native land.

O'Casey's plays are remarkable examples of the ability of the realist to develop general and universal themes. His two Dublin tragedies, *Juno and the Paycock* (1924) and *The Plough and the Stars* (1926), grew out of his own experience as a member of the Irish Republican Army in the Easter Uprising of 1916. In the first he concentrates on the dissection of a lower-class family, in the second he ranges over the occupants of an entire tenement.

Juno and the Paycock is a curious play and more than one member of its audience has not known whether he was expected to laugh or cry at it. O'Casey follows that departure from the well-made play first exploited by Chekhov. Instead of permitting the logic of events to make his thesis clear, he abandons the progressive structure for one of pure juxtaposition. Comedy obtrudes upon tragedy, seriousness upon farce, and the total effect of these sudden switches in tone equals the theme of the play. To take the most startling example: in the final act, Juno is informed of her son's death only a moment after she has learned that her daughter is to have an illegitimate child. She launches into a speech of the utmost pathos, lamenting the dead and crying for human pity. After her exit there is a moment's pause, and enter her husband, the Paycock, and his friend, drunk. They stagger about the stage, thickly mouthing clichés about the destiny of Ireland and the sacrifices they have made in her name, and the curtain falls.

In the same manner a scene of gaiety may be followed by a scene of pathos or bitterness, as in the interruption of the Boyles' evening party by young Tancred's funeral procession. But nothing is stable for long, and the family has barely assumed the proper solemn countenances before they are crowding for a sight of the procession with no sign of recognition that the boy in the coffin had been their neighbor. In the whole play only two things are fixed and unchanging: the suffering of Juno and the drunken worthlessness of her husband. Looking upon one picture after another, grave, joyous, pathetic, farcical, the audience becomes increasingly aware of the constant elements emphasized in the title. Juno is a kind of Mother-Image and her theme, that the living are more important than the dead, is contrasted with the romantic lying of the Paycock: "Ireland sober is Ireland free," he declares as he falls into a drunken stupor. In his way the Paycock is an image of Ireland, vainglorious, irresponsible, pious, hypocritical, and, on occasion, brutal. Perhaps there is little wonder at the resentment of Irish audiences at so ruthless a reflection of their faults and follies in a play whose atmosphere of reality permitted no questioning of the event.

The Plough and the Stars is an even broader cross-section of the life of the Dubliner, seen against the events of the most stirring week in modern Irish history, the Easter Uprising of 1916. O'Casey's attitude, as in the earlier play, is disillusion; the people for whom his comrades fought and died are not good, and are not getting any better. His despair achieves its most effective theatrical realization in the setting of the second act, a barroom through whose windows may be seen the figure of Patrick Pearsse addressing a patriotic rally. As the actual words of the great leader of the rebellion are clearly heard in the background, the saloon becomes a symbol of the inner reality of the Irish character; a prostitute plies her trade, a young patriot garbed in the uniform of the rebellion of '96 drowns his exaltation in liquor, and the Plough and the Stars itself, the flag of the Uprising, is laid on the bar while three officers drink to their future triumphs. Such juxtapositions, resulting in a kind of visual irony, are the basis of O'Casey's technique. And O'Casey has, perhaps better than any of his contemporaries, been able to achieve the ultimate purpose of the realist: to give a picture of life which will be at the same time an interpretation of life, to bring meaning out of apparent chaos without permitting the audience to become aware of the controlling presence of the artist.

4. POETIC DRAMA

For many reasons the theater of the last two centuries has not been a fortunate outlet for the poet. It is not for lack of encouragement. In the 1830's Macready was begging his poetic friends to write for him, and got for his pains Browning's *A Blot in the 'Scutcheon* and a dozen crabbed imitations of Shakespeare. Charles Kean advanced the unheard of sum of £400 to G. W. Lovell for *The Wife's Secret* in 1848, and promised J. S. Knowles £1000 for a poetic drama that never materialized. Henry Irving tried to make stageworthy vehicles out of the dramatic poems of Tennyson and treated the hack-written works of W. G. Wills as if they were genuinely poetic. In 1901, George Alexander commissioned Stephen Phillips to write *Paolo and Francesca*. Only the last of these dramatists can be said to have had any success in his own right; the others succeeded, when they succeeded, because of the superior stage-wisdom or the personalities of their leading players.

Partially they failed because they drew their models exclusively from the past, because they were—as indeed was the theater of the whole century—afflicted by Bardolatry. Only Westland Marston in *The Patrician's Daughter* (1841) attempted to reflect the life of his own time. His costumes, his setting were contemporary, his theme was the class struggle, but his solution was ladylike melodrama and his language diluted Elizabethan. A modern poetic drama could only be created by men aware not only of the spirit of their times, but of the poetic style which had been developed to give expression to that spirit.

In its creation W. B. Yeats played a major rôle. His earlier attempt, *The Land of Heart's Desire* (1894) is conventionally romantic in subject-matter and expression. The necessities of the Irish Renaissance, however, drove him to thinking more precisely on the problem of the creation of drama whose effects would endure beyond the fall of the curtain, of drama which would so move the hearts and minds of men that they would depart with a new understanding of their nature and destiny. The poetic drama must be a living, not a literary, thing; and living poetry could be found in the speech of the Irish peasant and his love of the heroic and homely in legend and daily life. The revitalizing of the poetic tradition, therefore, was to be accomplished in three ways. The diction, sensuous and musical, was to be based on a translation of the Irish vocabulary and syntax into English; the structure should be a "marshalling of the Irish fragmentary beauties into great literature"; the theme should be such as to give Ireland a constantly artistic conscience.

Yeats's earliest and most successful plays are accordingly based on folk legends, invented, as he declared, by men "who believed so much in the soul and so little in anything else." Folk legends had the additional value of remoteness, of distance from actuality and proximity to imaginative truth. Yeats's characteristics are well illustrated in his small tragedy, *On Baile's Strand* (1904) in which he recounts the final adventure of the Irish legendary hero, Cuchulain. The antiquity of the story is unquestioned, parts of it going back at least to Greek mythology, and the simplicity of its treatment allows Yeats to present the most elemental (and therefore the most universal) of human passions, uncomplicated by artificial problems of a particular society.

The interpretation Yeats wishes to put upon his action is made clear by a dramatic device of wonderful simplicity. The play is opened and closed by two grotesque characters, a fool and a blind man; the fool can see without understanding, the blind man can understand without seeing. They serve as chorus, though never in the artificial sense since they are a natural part of the locale and the situation. "Life drifts between a blind man and a fool," says one of the minor figures, and this little heroic drama is a tragic picture of the bitterness and bewilderment of existence. "Heart-mysteries there," wrote Yeats many years later of his attempt by remote stories and ancient themes, presented in the poetry and lore of the Irish peasant, to inspire the con-

temporary audience without directly attacking contemporary
society or arousing contemporary antagonisms.

Between the early work of Yeats in the first decade of the
twentieth century and the poetic revival of the thirties there is
a gap which can be filled only by the risky generalization that
the works of Laurence Binyon, Gordon Bottomley, and others,
were earnest but unsuccessful efforts largely because their authors were more skilled as poets than as playwrights. This has
been the constant problem of the poetic theater, of course, since
both poetry and drama demand technical equipment and skills
that are rarely united in a single author.

About 1935, however, a group of men headed by T. S. Eliot,
W. H. Auden, Louis MacNeice, and Stephen Spender, who had
established their reputations as poets, came to the theater with
the intention of making themselves its masters. They have not,
as yet, entirely succeeded, but at least one has very nearly done
so and the near-successes of his fellows have been the most honorable of failures. For in their work they have looked forward as
well as backward, at the present as well as the past. In seeking
a suitable dramatic form and poetic medium for the expression
of their ideas they have not thrown out the baby with the bath-
water by ceasing to imitate the panoramic form of the Elizabethans or discarding blank verse. Instead they have created their
forms out of whatever parts of the older traditions seemed useful
and have chosen to write in a half-colloquial modern verse medium free of the glaze of the antique.

T. S. Eliot's first major play, *Murder in the Cathedral,* was
produced at Canterbury in 1935 and has since had some success
in the professional theater. The form of the play is unique,
employing many elements from the classical and medieval stage
as well as certain devices better adapted to lyric poetry, but it
is well adjusted to the simple story it has to tell. Mr. Eliot re-
hearses the events by which Thomas à Becket became a martyr,
but the focus is more on the conflict within the mind and soul
of Thomas than on the external conflict by which the play gets
its whimsically sensational title.

The classical elements of the play are obvious: the chorus of
women of Canterbury, the messenger who speaks almost as if he
were translating Greek tragedy, the long speeches, and the
paucity of action. From the medieval drama come the *Everyman-*

like tone of much of the dialogue, and such characters as the
Tempters. These latter, half-allegorical, half real, are among the
most successful of Mr. Eliot's borrowings. Symbolizing as they
do worldliness, worldly power, misuse of ecclesiastical power for
temporal purposes, they summarize economically Thomas' past
history and are a dramatic realization of his spiritual struggle,
very much as Marlowe had employed the Good and Evil Angels
in *Dr. Faustus*.

Murder in the Cathedral

The device of the four knights, the murderers, is intended to
achieve precisely the opposite effect. A part of what may be
called the historical action of the play, they suddenly drop all
pretense of historicity after the killing, and address the audience
in colloquial prose and in attitudes that are recognizably contemporary. The contrast is startling, even perilously close to the
comic, but carefully handled it reminds the spectator that the
playwright is dramatizing an eternal theme, not merely the sensational conclusion of a great career.

The less successful elements of the play are largely the chorus
and the necessary anonymity of the secondary characters. The
modern audience is sufficiently unused to poetic speech; when
poetry is spoken in unison, even by small groups, the audience
is baffled. The chorus, essentially lyric, is a device with which the
poet will feel on sure ground, but the modern drama has developed means more completely dramatic for the handling of

exposition, atmosphere, and commentary. The anonymity of the characters by intention keeps the whole focus on Thomas and indeed turns the play into a kind of expression of his psychological conflict—it transpires, so to speak, in his mind. But the anonymity results in an unfortunate intellectualism. The play is cold, rather than passionate, and deliberately refuses to employ the most effective of the dramatist's tools, the humanity of the characters.

In the ironically titled, *The Family Reunion* (1939), Mr. Eliot made considerable strides in characterization, in dramatic effectiveness, and in molding a modern verse form that was fitted for the theater. He still employs a chorus, but he makes an attempt, not altogether successful, to fit his theme into what is on the surface a modern social drama set in a realistic drawing-room. Some of the dialogue is unnecessarily obscure and there are ambiguities in the diction and action which are puzzling to those trained in the literal-minded tradition of the modern theater.

For the most part, however, the play is very nearly conventional. The audience can have no difficulty in adjusting itself to the setting (which had appeared in a thousand domestic dramas) or the initial situation. The plot, too, is familiar, developing out of an unhappy triangular love-affair, and the characters are the stock types of Pinero and Jones as modified by Barker and Galsworthy. The verse form is modern and colloquial, accentually stressed, and capable of relaxation to include the reading of a telegram or a newspaper, or compression for the moments of inner revelation.

The story of the play is the reworking in terms of contemporary psychology and theology of the ancient Greek tragedy of the *Oresteia*. By so relating his action to myth Mr. Eliot achieves the kind of universality Yeats was seeking when he returned to the legends of his people. The essential conflict or contrast between Harry (the modern Orestes) and his family is the heart of the play's theme. The family is blind, and concerned only with a cozy room at the club, or the condition of the garden; haunted by a nameless fear, they are afraid to find out what it is they fear. Harry's own uneasiness about life stems from his sense also that something is present which he cannot see. He, unlike the family, penetrates to the bottom of its history, to the knot of evil (the "curse") tied by Agatha, Amy, and Lord Monchensey, and, clearly understanding the presence of the Eumenides, who are both real and symbolic—is no longer afraid, is free.

> There is more to understand; hold fast to that
> As the way to freedom.

The theme emerges as an investigation of the nature of evil in the modern world, symbolized by the Family. The Family is so spiritually impoverished, so *unconscious*, that it can not and will not perceive the evil in its own midst, the sin and guilt which are a part of its very nature, symbolized by the presence of the Eumenides in the family drawing-room. Harry, through the action of the play, becomes the "conscience of his family," the man who through spiritual awareness frees himself from the chains of ignorance, stupidity, and vulgarity. Once conscious, he can pursue the course a man must travel, without fear. In *The Family Reunion,* Mr. Eliot has faced the problem of meeting an audience on its own terms, and it is not entirely his fault if he has not completely succeeded.

W. H. Auden and Christopher Isherwood in their first poetic drama, *The Dog Beneath the Skin* (1935), met the same problem in a strikingly different way. Like Eliot they made use of familiar conventions in creating their peculiar form, but in addition they adopted some of the unfamiliar devices of expressionism. This dramatic technique, which flourished principally in Germany between the two world wars, makes great use of distortion and the grotesque; its characters are deliberately one-dimensional, almost "humours," something like the caricatures and allegorical figures of political cartoons. The expressionist seeks to present only the most quintessential "facts" about his characters or their situation, and his plays are normally filled with such abstractions as A Man in Red, A Capitalist, and so on. Auden and Isherwood make free use of this technique in such scenes as Paradise Park where Two Lovers express the essence of romantic nonsense or a Flag-Lunatic the essence of jingoism.

The more familiar devices are taken from the conventions of musical comedy and the romantic quest. The first scene is an almost perfect Gilbertian opening with its chorus of "happy villagers" singing gaily of country matters. The principal charac-

ters introduce themselves in recognizable patter songs and all is
Savoyard as can be—until the end of the play when the same
villagers do not look quite so amusing; for the authors have
not only employed the convention but used it as an instrument
of social satire. So too with the romantic plot. As in the olden
time, the hero is given a quest, a squire to accompany him, a
magic formula to recite. He meets and, through the agency of
his squire, conquers temptation. He meets and, through the agency
of his squire, conquers the "dragon." He returns home for his
promised reward, the hand of the fair lady—but the ending is
an almost obscene mockery of romanticism. Through the accidents which befall the hero on his quest, his eyes are opened to
the true nature of his society, and by intention so must the eyes
of the spectators. They are not able, by taking the comic-opera
or romantic view of life, to laugh away reality. The hero does
not get his reward, nor does the audience. This riotous con-
glomeration of music, and farce, and symbolism, and lecture,
and burlesque is actually as bitter an attack upon society as the
contemporary English theater has witnessed.

The subsequent plays of Auden and Isherwood are somewhat
more orderly in structure. *The Ascent of F6* (1936) is a Freudian
tragedy, dramatizing with considerable skill modern psychological doctrines. The plot again takes the form of a quest, the
conquest of an unclimbed mountain, and peripheral political
satire is introduced; but a fully appreciative audience must be
well acquainted with Freudian theory. *On the Frontier* (1939)
is again political satire simply and effectively organized around
the symbolic setting of a room located half in one country, half
in another. In this play, the last of their collaboration, Auden
and Isherwood attained an almost completely dramatic statement of their theme, without the use of unfamiliar because
out-moded theatrical conventions, or obscure because unfamiliar
Freudian or personal symbols.

Molière's famous Bourgeois Gentilhomme was surprised to
discover that he had been speaking prose all his life without
knowing it. It is just possible that we have had a genuine poetic
drama in the modern theater without recognizing it. In a sense,
verse is only the accidental shape in which the poet happens to
write. Far more fundamental is the completely functional nature
of the work as a whole. The poetic drama may well be defined

as that in which every aspect, the plot, the selection and arrangement of incidents, the characters, the symbols and the dialogue are concerned to the exclusion of all else with the elucidation of a theme of a certain magnitude and universal implication. When Mr. Shaw, for instance, creates Joan's famous defense of her position at her trial, he is writing "poetically." In the debate between Warwick and Cauchon, he may be writing "prosaically." But in that every element of the play, every line of dialogue, every bit of business tends finally to support his great theme, he is writing poetic drama. It is through such devotion to the completely functional relationship of form, matter, and idea that the modern drama has won its right to stand beside the great achievements of the Elizabethan and Restoration theater.

In 1747, David Garrick stepped before the curtain of Drury Lane to speak the prologue for the opening performance of the new season. Written by Samuel Johnson it is the most famous of apologies for the drama in its relation to its audience. While some of Johnson's critical judgements may today fall on disbelieving ears, the basic truth of his position is hardly open to question. As a prologue on the stage or the justification of a study of drama, it should be familiar to all those who, like Mirabel in Farquhar's *Inconstant,* could wish that their "whole life long were the first night of a new play."

> When learning's triumph o'er her barbarous foes
> First reared the stage, immortal Shakespeare rose;
> Each change of many-colored life he drew,
> Exhausted worlds and then imagined new:
> Existence saw him spurn her bounded reign,
> And panting time toiled after him in vain:
> His powerful strokes presiding truth impressed,
> And unresisted passion stormed the breast.
>   Then Jonson came, instructed from the school
> To please in method, and invent by rule;
> His studious patience and laborious art
> By regular approach essayed the heart.
> Cold approbation gave the lingering bays,
> For those who durst not censure, scarce could praise.
> A mortal born, he met the general doom,
> But left, like Egypt's kings, a lasting tomb.
>   The Wits of Charles found easier ways to fame
> Nor wished for Jonson's art, or Shakespeare's flame.

Themselves they studied; as they felt they writ,
Intrigue was plot, obscenity was wit.
Vice always found a sympathetic friend;
They pleased their age and did not aim to mend.
Yet bards like these aspired to lasting praise
And proudly hoped to pimp in future days.
Their cause was general, their supports were strong,
Their slaves were willing, and their reign was long;
Till shame regained the post that sense betrayed,
And virtue called oblivion to her aid.
   Then crushed by rules, and weakened as refined,
For years the power of tragedy declined;
From bard to bard the frigid caution crept,
Till declamation roared, while passion slept.
Yet still did virtue deign the stage to tread;
Philosophy remained, though nature fled.
But forced at length her ancient reign to quit,
She saw great Faustus lay the ghost of wit:
                              [the coming of pantomime]
Exulting folly hailed the joyful day,
And pantomime and song confirmed her sway.
   But who the coming changes can presage,
And mark the future periods of the stage?—
Perhaps if skill could distant times explore,
New Behns, new Durfeys [writers of farce] yet remain in store.
Perhaps where Lear had raved and Hamlet died,
On flying cars new sorcerers may ride.
Perhaps, for who can guess the effects of chance,
Here Hunt may box or Mahomet may dance.
   Hard is his lot, that here by fortune placed
Must watch the wild vicissitudes of taste;
With every meteor of caprice must play,
And chase the new-born bubbles of the day.
Ah! let not censure term our fate our choice,
The stage but echoes back the public voice.
The drama's laws the drama's patrons give,
For we that live to please, must please to live.
   Then prompt no more the follies you decry,
As tyrants doom their tools of guilt to die:
'Tis yours this night to bid the reign commence
Of rescued nature, and reviving sense;
To chase the charms of sound, the pomp of show,
For useful mirth, and salutary woe;
Bid scenic virtue form the rising age,
And truth diffuse her radiance from the stage.

A List of Suggested Readings

The following list of readings is divided into three parts: first, a few books on the drama and stage in general; second, books on the English drama by period; finally, individual authors, alphabetically arranged, with principal editions of and commentaries on their works. The lists are necessarily brief, but an attempt has been made to include those volumes or articles which cover the subject most completely, or which include detailed bibliographies. Mention should be made at the start of two basic tools: *The Cambridge Bibliography of English Literature,* 4 vols., Cambridge (Eng.), 1941, and the continuing bibliography published as an annual supplement to the *Publications of the Modern Language Association.* For the meaning of abbreviations, see p. 376.

I. GENERAL

BAUGH, Albert C., gen. ed., *A Literary History of England,* New York, 1948.

FERGUSSON, Francis, *The Idea of a Theatre,* Princeton, 1949.

GASSNER, John, *Masters of the Drama,* 2nd ed., New York, 1945.

GRANVILLE-BARKER, Harley, *On Dramatic Method,* London, 1931.

NICOLL, Allardyce, *British Drama,* 4th ed., London, 1947.

PRIOR, Moody E., *The Language of Tragedy,* New York, 1947.

SPRAGUE, Arthur Colby, *Shakespeare and the Actors,* Cambridge (Mass.), 1944.

II. ENGLISH DRAMA BY PERIOD

A. The Native Dramatic Tradition

1) The Folk Play

CHAMBERS, E. K., *The English Folk-Play,* Oxford, 1933.

2) Liturgical Plays

CHAMBERS, E. K., *The Medieval Stage,* 2 vols., Oxford, 1903.

YOUNG, Karl, *The Drama of the Medieval Church,* Oxford, 1933 (Texts and commentaries).

3) The Cycles

BATES, K. L., *English Religious Drama,* New York, 1904.

CADY, F. W., "The Wakefield Group in Towneley," *JEGP,* XI (1912), 244-262.

CHAMBERS, E. K., *The Medieval Stage,* 2 vols., Oxford, 1903.

—— *English Literature at the Close of the Middle Ages,* Oxford, 1945.

GAYLEY, C. M., *Plays of our Forefathers*, New York, 1907.

GREG, W. W., *Bibliographical and Textual Problems of the English Miracle Cycles*, London, 1914.

MARSHALL, M. H., "The Dramatic Tradition Established by the Liturgical Plays," *PMLA*, LVI (1941), 962-991.

POLLARD, A. W., *English Miracle Plays, Moralities, and Interludes*, Oxford, 1904 (Texts, with a noteworthy introduction).

SPENCER, M. L., *Corpus Christi Pageants in England*, New York, 1911 (Historical study of conventions of writing and production).

NOTE. Texts may be found in various volumes of the Early English Text Society. Selected plays are printed in J. Q. Adams, *Chief Pre-Shakespearean Dramas*, Boston, 1924, and J. M. Manly, *Specimens of the Pre-Shakespearean Drama*, 2 vols., Boston, 1897.

4) Moralities

FARNHAM, Willard, *The Medieval Heritage of Elizabethan Tragedy*, Berkeley, Calif., 1936.

MACKENZIE, W. Roy, *The English Moralities from the Point of View of Allegory*, Boston, 1914.

THOMPSON, E. N. S., "The English Moral Plays," *Trans. Conn. Acad. Arts and Sciences*, XIV (1910), 291-414.

See also, under The Cycles, above, the works of Adams, Chambers, Manly, and Pollard.

5) The Interlude

BASKERVILL, C. R., "Conventional Features of Medwall's *Fulgens and Lucres*," *MP*, XXIV (1926), 419-442.

BOAS, F. S., *Five Pre-Shakespearean Comedies*, London, 1934 (Text of *Fulgens and Lucres*).

—— *An Introduction to Early Tudor Drama*, London, Oxford, 1933.

BOLWELL, R. W., *The Life and Works of John Heywood*, New York, 1921.

BROOKE, Tucker, *The Tudor Drama*, Boston, 1911.

REED, A. W., *Early Tudor Drama*, London, 1926.

And see, under The Cycles and the Moralities, above, the works of Adams, Farnham, Manly, Pollard and Thompson. Texts may also be found in *Tudor Facsimile Texts* and *The Malone Society Reprints*.

B. Panoramic Drama (also called Tudor and Stuart Drama, and Elizabethan, Jacobean and Caroline Drama)

ADAMS, J. Q., *Shakespearean Playhouses*, Boston, 1917.

ADAMS, J. C., *The Globe Playhouse; Its Design and Equipment*, Cambridge (Mass.), 1942.

BALDWIN, T. W., *Organization and Personnel of the Shakespearean Company*, Princeton, 1927.

BENTLEY, G. E., *The Jacobean and Caroline Stage*, 2 vols., Oxford, 1941.

BOAS, F. S., *An Introduction to Tudor Drama*, Oxford, 1933.

BOWERS, F. T., *Elizabethan Revenge Tragedy*, Princeton, 1940.

BROOKE, Tucker, *Tudor Drama*, Boston, 1911.

BRADBROOK, M. C., *Themes and Conventions of Elizabethan Tragedy*, Cambridge (Eng.), 1935.

CHAMBERS, E. K., *The Elizabethan Stage*, 4 vols., Oxford, 1923.

ELIOT, T. S., *Elizabethan Essays*, New York, 1934.

ELLIS-FERMOR, Una, *The Jacobean Drama*, New York, 1936.

HARBAGE, Alfred, *As They Liked It*, New York, 1947.

—— *Shakespeare's Audience*, New York, 1941.

HODGES, C. W., *Shakespeare and the Players*, New York, 1949.

LAWRENCE, W. J., *Pre-Restoration Stage Studies*, Cambridge (Mass.), 1927.

MURRAY, J. T., *English Dramatic Companies, 1558-1642*, 2 vols., London, 1910.

PARROT, T. M., and BALL, R. H., *A Short View of Elizabethan Drama*, New York, 1943.

REYNOLDS, G. F., *The Staging of Elizabethan Plays at the Red Bull Theater, 1605-1625*, New York, 1940.

SCHELLING, F. E., *Elizabethan Drama*, 2 vols., New York, 1908.

—— *The English Chronicle Play*, New York, 1902.

SPENCER, Theodore, *Death and Elizabethan Tragedy*, Cambridge (Mass.), 1936.

NOTE. For texts, see under the individual authors below. Of the many anthologies, mention might be made of E. W. Parks and R. C. Beatty, *The English Drama, 900-1642*, New York, 1935; Hazelton Spencer, *Elizabethan Plays*, Boston, 1933; C. R. Baskervill, V. B. Heltzel, A. H. Nethercot, *Elizabethan and Stuart Plays*, New York, 1934.

C. Restoration Drama

BOSWELL, Eleanore, *The Restoration Court Stage*, Cambridge (Mass.), 1932.

DEANE, C. V., *Dramatic Theory and the Rhymed Heroic Play*, Oxford, 1931.

DOBRÉE, Bonamy, *Restoration Comedy*, Oxford, 1924.

—— *Restoration Tragedy*, Oxford, 1929.

ELSON, J. J., ed., *The Wits*, Ithaca, 1932 (Texts of Drolls).

GENEST, John, *Some Account of the English Stage*, 10 vols., Bath, 1832.

HARBAGE, Alfred, *Cavalier Playwrights*, Philadelphia, 1936.

HOTSON, Leslie, *The Commonwealth and Restoration Stage*, Cambridge (Mass.), 1928.

LAMB, Charles, "On the Artificial Comedy of the Last Century," *Essays of Elia*.

LYNCH, K. M., *Social Mode of Restoration Comedy*, New York, 1926.

MACAULAY, T. B., "The Dramatic Works of Wycherley, Congreve, Vanbrugh and Farquhar," *The Edinburgh Review* LXXII (1841), 490-528.

NETTLETON, G. F., *English Drama of the Restoration and Eighteenth Century*, New York, 1914.

NICOLL, Allardyce, *A History of Restoration Drama, 1660-1700*, Cambridge (Eng.), 1923, 1928.

PALMER, John, *The Comedy of Manners*, New York, 1913.

PERRY, H. T. E., *Comic Spirit In Restoration Drama*, New Haven, 1925.

SMITH, J. H., *The Gay Couple in Restoration Comedy*, Cambridge (Mass.), 1948.

SUMMERS, Montague, *The Restoration Theater*, New York, 1934.

—— *The Playhouse of Pepys*, New York, 1935.

WARD, A. W., *A History of English Dramatic Literature to the Death of Queen Anne*, 3 vols., New York, 1899.

NOTE. For texts, see under the individual authors below. Of the many anthologies, covering this period *and the eighteenth century*, mention may be made of A. E. Morgan, *English Plays, 1660-1820*, New York, 1935; Dugald Macmillan and H. M. Jones, *Plays of the Restoration and Eighteenth Century*, New York, 1931.

D. Eighteenth Century Drama

BATESON, F. W., *English Comic Drama, 1700-1750*, Oxford, 1929.

BERNBAUM, Ernest, *The Drama of Sensibility*, Boston, 1915.

Biographia Dramatica, 3 vols., London, 1812.

EVANS, Bertrand, *Gothic Drama from Walpole to Shelley*, Berkeley, 1947.

GAGEY, E. M., *Ballad Opera*, New York, 1937.

GENEST, John, *Some Account of the English Stage*, 10 vols., Bath, 1832.

GREEN, C. C., *The Neo-Classic Theory of Tragedy in England During the Eighteenth Century*, Cambridge (Mass.), 1934.

KRUTCH, J. W., *Comedy and Conscience After the Restoration*, New Ed., New York, 1949.

NETTLETON, G. F., *English Drama of the Restoration and Eighteenth Century*, New York, 1914.

NICOLL, Allardyce, *A History of Early Eighteenth Century Drama*, Cambridge (Eng.), 1925.

—— *A History of Late Eighteenth Century Drama*, Cambridge (Eng.), 1927.

NOLTE, F. O., *Early Middle Class Drama in England, 1696-1774*, Lancaster, 1935.

ODELL, G. C., *Shakespeare from Betterton to Irving*, 2 vols., New York, 1920.

SPENCER, Hazelton, *Shakespeare Improved*, Cambridge (Mass.), 1927.

THALER, A., *Shakespeare to Sheridan*, Cambridge (Mass.), 1922.

NOTE. For texts and anthologies see note under Restoration Drama, above.

E. Nineteenth and Twentieth Century Drama

ARCHER, William, *The Old Drama and the New,* Boston, 1923.
—— *Playmaking,* New York, 1929.
BALMFORTH, R., *The Problem Play and Its Influence on Modern Thought and Life,* New York, 1928.
BOYD, E. A., *The Contemporary Drama of Ireland,* Boston, 1917.
CLARK, B. H., and FREEDLEY, G., eds., *A History of Modern Drama,* New York, 1947.
CUNLIFFE, J. W., *Modern English Playwrights,* New York, 1927.
DICKINSON, T. H., *The Contemporary Drama of England,* Boston, 1931.
EATON, W. P., *The Drama in English,* New York, 1930.
ELLIS-FERMOR, Una, *The Irish Dramatic Movement,* London, 1939.
FILON, A., *The English Stage,* New York, 1907.
GREGORY, Lady, *Our Irish Theater,* New York, 1913.
HOWE, P. P., *The Repertory Theater,* New York, 1911.
JONES, H. A., *The Renascence of the English Drama,* New York, 1895.
MACARTHY, Desmond, *The Court Theater, 1904-1907,* London, 1907.
MALONE, A., *The Irish Drama,* New York, 1929.
MORGAN, A. E., *Tendencies of the Modern English Drama,* New York, 1924.
NICOLL, Allardyce, *A History of Early Nineteenth Century Drama,* 2 vols., Cambridge (Eng.), 1930.
—— *A History of Late Nineteenth Century Drama,* 2 vols., Cambridge (Eng.), 1946.
ODELL, G. C., *Shakespeare from Betterton to Irving,* 2 vols., New York, 1920.
REYNOLDS, E., *Early Victorian Drama, 1830-1870,* New York, 1936.
ROBINSON, L., *The Irish Theater,* London, 1939.
SAWYER, N. W., *The Comedy of Manners from Sheridan to Maugham,* Philadelphia, 1931.
SHAW, G. B., *Dramatic Opinions and Essays,* 2 vols., New York, 1928.
SHORT, Ernest, *Theatrical Cavalcade,* London, 1942.
THOULESS, Priscilla, *Modern Poetic Drama,* New York, 1934.
WATSON, E. B., *Sheridan to Robertson,* Cambridge (Mass.), 1926.
WEYGANDT, C., *Irish Plays and Playwrights,* Boston, 1913.
ZUCKER, Irving, *Le "Court Theatre" et l'Evolution du Théâtre Anglais Contemporain,* Paris, 1931.

NOTE. For texts see the individual playwrights below. Among the anthologies might be mentioned W. H. Durham and J. W. Dodds, *British and American Plays, 1830-1945,* New York, 1947; M. J. Moses, *Representative British Dramas, Victorian and Modern,* Boston, 1931; H. Hatcher, *Modern British Dramas,* New York, 1941; G. J. Nathan, *Five Great Modern Irish Plays,* New York, 1941.

III. INDIVIDUAL AUTHORS

[NOTE. Dates of plays are those of production, unless otherwise indicated. (pr = printed)]

ADDISON, JOSEPH (1672-1719), distinguished himself as a classical scholar during his Oxford career, and after graduation affiliated himself with the Whigs as a politician and poetical pamphleteer. A close friend of Swift and Steele, he was co-founder of the celebrated periodical, *The Tatler,* and its successor, *The Spectator.* He was variously under-secretary of state, member of parliament and chief secretary to the Lord Lieutenant of Ireland. *Cato* (1713) thus reflects his political as well as his literary experience.

PLAYS: *Cato* (1713); *The Drummer* (1715). Ed. by A. C. Guthkelch, New York, 1914.

COMMENTARY: Silas E. Summers, "Addison's Conception of Tragedy," *CE,* VIII (1947), 245-248.

AUDEN, WINSTAN HUGH (1907-   ), as an undergraduate at Oxford revealed himself as a poet exceptionally sensitive to contemporary thinking in anthropology, psychology, and politics, as well as a notable experimenter with verse forms. He has been widely influential with younger poets, although his later work has become somewhat more conventional in form and attitude. His plays were, of course, written during his most radical period, and support many attitudes which he has since abandoned.

PLAYS: *The Dance of Death* (1933); (with Christopher Isherwood) *The Dog Beneath the Skin* (1935), *The Ascent of F6* (1937), *On the Frontier* (1939).

BALE, JOHN (1495-1563), ejected from his pulpit in 1538, gathered a troupe of actors and went on a barnstorming tour of England with a repertory of plays intended to favor the cause of the Reformation.

PLAYS: *The Chief Promises of God, John Baptist's Preaching in the Wilderness, The Temptation of Our Lord by Satan, Comedy Concerning Three Laws, of Nature, Moses, and Christ . . . , King John* (all *c.* 1538). Ed. J. S. Farmer, *The Dramatic Works of John Bale,* London, 1907.

COMMENTARY: W. T. Davies, *A Bibliography of John Bale,* Oxford, 1939; J. W. Harris, *John Bale, a Study in the Minor Literature of the Reformation,* Urbana, 1940.

BARRIE, SIR JAMES MATTHEW (1860-1937), born in Scotland, began his career as a journalist and novelist, before turning to the theater.

PRINCIPAL PLAYS: *The Professor's Love Story* (1894), *The Little Minister* (1897), *Quality Street* (1901), *The Admirable Crichton* (1902), *Peter Pan* (1904), *What Every Woman Knows* (1908), *The Twelve-Pound Look* (1910), *Dear Brutus* (1917). One Volume Edition, New York, 1930.

COMMENTARY: J. A. Hammerton, *Barrie: The Story of a Genius,* New York, 1929; H. M. Walbrook, *J. M. Barrie and the Theater,* New York, 1922; W. A. Darlington, *J. M. Barrie,* New York, 1938.

BEAUMONT, FRANCIS (1584-1616), of an ancient country family, was educated at Oxford and the Inns of Court where he came under the influence of Ben Jonson, and was enrolled among the "Sons of Ben." As a member of the upper middle class and the "cavalier" writers, he reflects the tastes and talents of an urbane and accomplished school. His major talent lay in construction, and in his famous collaboration with John Fletcher, and others, his hand is chiefly to be discerned in the managing of the fable and in the creation of certain humour characters.

PRINCIPAL PLAYS: *The Woman-Hater* (1607), *The Knight of the Burning Pestle* (1608); in collaboration with Fletcher: *The Maid's Tragedy* (1610), *Philaster* (1609), *A King and No King* (1611), *The Scornful Lady* (1613). Ed: *The Works,* 10 vols., Cambridge (Eng.), 1905-1912; *Variorum,* 4 vols., New Haven, 1904-1913.

COMMENTARY: E. H. C. Oliphant, *The Plays 'of Beaumont and Fletcher,* New Haven, 1927; C. M. Gayley, *Beaumont the Dramatist,* New York, 1914; A. Mizener, "The High Design of *A King and No King*," *MP,* XXXVIII (1940), 133-154; A. H. Thorndike, *The Influence of Beaumont and Fletcher on Shakespeare,* Worcester, 1901; A. C. Sprague, *Beaumont and Fletcher on the Restoration Stage,* Cambridge (Mass.), 1926.

BOUCICAULT, DION (1820?-1890), the author of untold melodramas, is chiefly notable for the skill with which he employed the mechanical resources of the stage—lighting, scenery, machinery—as a substitute for ideas, characterization, or dialogue in the creation of drama. Much of his work is translated or adapted from the French and other continental theaters, but in his Irish melodramas he exploited a type of which he was an unchallenged master. Not a little of the success of these latter was due to his own acting of the leading rôles in a style which was a sort of bridge between the conventional Stage Irishman and that which the Abbey Theatre was later to make famous.

PRINCIPAL PLAYS: *London Assurance* (1841), *The Corsican Brothers* (1848), *The Colleen Bawn* (1859), *Arrah-Na-Pogue* (1864), *The Shaugraun* (1875), *The Octoroon* (1859), *The Streets of New York* (1857).

COMMENTARY: Townshend Walsh, *The Career of Dion Boucicault,* New York, 1915.

BULWER-LYTTON, SIR EDWARD (1803-1873), the dandaical son of an ancient and distinguished family, was one of the most prolific of nineteenth century novelists. He carried the same facility into his playwrighting, creating works which are more remarkable for their inflated and pretentious verse and melodramatic action than for any just perception of character or genuine poetic expression. His great success was due to the nice adjustment of his writing to the talents of W. C. Macready for whom he wrote his plays to order.

PRINCIPAL PLAYS: *The Duchess de LaValliere* (1837), *The Lady of Lyons* (1838), *Richelieu* (1839), *Money* (1840).

COMMENTARY: The Earl of Lytton, *The Life of Edward Bulwer, First Lord Lytton,* 2 vols., New York, 1913; E. B. Burgum, *The Literary Career of Edward Bulwer, Lord Lytton,* New York, 1924.

CHAPMAN, GEORGE (1559?-1634?), renowned as the translator of Homer, was a scholar and sonneteer, and a close friend of Ben Jonson. The influence of Chapman on Jonson, or Jonson on Chapman, was considerable; between them they established a more realistic tradition for the English comic drama, while following classical drama in structure and characterization.

PRINCIPAL PLAYS: *The Blind Beggar of Alexandria* (1596), *Comedy of Humours* (1597) (Published as *An Humorous Day's Mirth*), *All Fools* (1599), *Bussy D'Ambois* (1607?), *The Revenge of Bussy D'Ambois* (1613?), *The Conspiracy and Tragedy of Charles Duke of Byron* (1608).

COLLECTED EDITION: *Chapman's Comedies,* 1914; *Chapman's Tragedies,* 1910, ed. T. M. Parrott.

COMMENTARY: S. A. Tannenbaum, *George Chapman: A Concise Bibliography,* New York, 1938; A. S. Ferguson, "The Plays of George Chapman," *MLR,* XIII (1918), 1-24, XV (1920), 223-239; R. H. Perkinson, "Nature and the Tragic Hero in Chapman's Bussy Plays," *MLQ,* III (1942), 263-285.

CIBBER, COLLEY (1671-1757), as actor, manager, and playwright was one of the dominant figures of the early eighteenth century theater. Beginning as an actor in 1690, he wrote his first play, *Love's Last Shift,* admittedly to give himself a part suited to his particular genius for playing fops. His adaptation of *Richard III* replaced Shakespeare's original for over a century and still makes an occasional appearance. With various partners, he was co-manager of Drury Lane from 1710 to 1733, supplying the establishment with some two dozen pieces—comedies, tragedies, ballad operas—chiefly distinguished for their shrewd theater sense. In 1730 he became poet laureate and this, together with his inevitably autocratic behavior as manager, won him the enmity of Pope, Fielding, Dennis, and others. Pope substituted him for Theobald as the hero of the *Dunciad* (1743); Fielding satirized him in such plays as *The Author's Farce* (1730). To these and other attacks Cibber replied with what is justly the most famous of theatrical autobiographies, *An Apology for the Life of Mr. Colley Cibber, Comedian* (1740), a lively, if naturally prejudiced, account of the stage in his time.

PRINCIPAL PLAYS: *Love's Last Shift* (1696), *Love Makes a Man* (1700), *She Would and She Would Not* (1702), *The Careless Husband* (1705), *The Non-Juror* (from Molière's *Tartuffe*, 1717), *The Refusal* (1721).

COMMENTARY: Richard H. Barker, *Mr. Cibber of Drury Lane*, New York, 1939; Dewitt C. Croissant, *Studies in the Work of Colley Cibber*, Lawrence (Kan.), 1912.

COLMAN, GEORGE, the Elder (1732-1794), originally trained for the legal profession, was diverted to the stage by his membership in a literary club and by his friendship with David Garrick. From 1767-1774 he managed Covent Garden, from 1777-1789, the Little Theatre in the Haymarket. The author of some thirty dramatic pieces, he translated the comedies of Terence (1765) and edited the works of Beaumont and Fletcher (1778). He was the father of GEORGE COLMAN, THE YOUNGER (1762-1836), a skillful mechanic of stage-worthy farces and melodramas, on whom see, J. F. Bagster-Collins, *George Colman, the Younger*, New York, 1946.

PRINCIPAL PLAYS: *Polly Honeycombe* (1760), *The Jealous Wife* (1761), *Philaster* (adapted from Beaumont and Fletcher, 1763), *The Clandestine Marriage* (with Garrick, 1766).

COMMENTARY: George Colman, the Younger, *Random Records*, 2 vols., London, 1830; R. B. Peake, *Memoirs of the Colman Family*, 2 vols., London, 1841; E. R. Page, *George Colman, the Elder*, New York, 1935; Austin Dobson, "Polly Honeycombe," in *Eighteenth Century Vignettes*, 3rd series, London, 1896; J. M. Beatty, "Garrick, Colman, and *The Clandestine Marriage*," *MLN*, XXXVI (1921), 129-141; H. P. Vincent, "Christopher George Colman, 'Lunatick'," *RES*, XVIII (1942), 38-48.

CONGREVE, WILLIAM (1670-1729), though born in Yorkshire, was educated in Ireland, where he became a friend of Jonathan Swift. Of fairly independent means, he soon turned from the law to the more gentlemanly profession of literature, writing two comedies for Drury Lane, and two comedies and a tragedy for the company headed by Betterton at Lincoln's-Inn-Field's Theatre. The comparative failure of *The Way of the World* is reputed to have turned him from the stage in disgust, but there is little evidence to support this. As a gentleman and government official, he no doubt preferred to devote his leisure to his friends, Swift, Steele, and Pope; perhaps also the increasing sentimentalization of comedy was not to his taste.

PRINCIPAL PLAYS: *The Old Bachelor* (1693), *The Double Dealer* (1694), *Love for Love* (1695), *The Mourning Bride* (1697), *The Way of the World* (1700).

COLLECTED EDITIONS: *Comedies,* ed. Bonamy Dobrée, Oxford, 1925; *The Mourning Bride, etc.,* ed. Bonamy Dobrée, Oxford, 1728; *Works,* ed. F. W. Bateson, London, 1930.

COMMENTARY: Edmund Gosse, *A Life of William Congreve,* rev. ed., London, 1924; D. C. Taylor, *William Congreve,* Oxford, 1931; J. C. Hodges, *William Congreve the Man,* New York, 1941; George Meredith, *An Essay on Comedy,* London, 1897; L. C. Knights, *Explorations,* New York, 1947.

CROWNE, JOHN (1640?-1712?), an industrious but imitative hack, wrote eleven tragedies and five comedies so completely in the prevailing modes that in plot, characterization, and dialogue they may almost be considered as textbooks of late Restoration playwriting. His *Sir Courtly Nice,* in the comedy of that name, is a not unworthy member of the gallery of theatrical fops, and his *Calisto, or the Chaste Nymph* acquires a kind of significance for the virtue which it untypically celebrates.

PRINCIPAL PLAYS: *Calisto* (1674), *The Country Wit* (1675), *City Politics* (1683), *Sir Courtly Nice* (1685), *Thyestes* (1681), *The English Friar* (1690), *The Married Beau* (1694).

COLLECTED EDITION: *The Dramatic Works of John Crowne,* 4 vols., London, 1873-1874.

COMMENTARY: A. F. White, *John Crowne,* Cleveland, 1922.

CUMBERLAND, RICHARD (1732-1811), a graduate of Cambridge, was a professional man of letters, novelist, and playwright. By nature a sentimentalist, he took particular delight in choosing for his heroes men who hitherto had been treated as villains or comic stereotypes, or had been ignored as unworthy of theatrical attention. He was satirized as Sir Fretful Plagiary in Sheridan's *The Critic;* for his own view of his character, see his *Memoirs* (2 vols., London, 1806-1807), which though hardly free of evidence of self-satisfaction, are filled with vivid glimpses of the late eighteenth century theater in action.

PRINCIPAL PLAYS: *The Brothers* (1769), *The West Indian* (1771), *The Fashionable Lovers* (1782), *The Mysterious Husband* (1783), *The Jew* (1794), *The Wheel of Fortune* (1795), *The Days of Yore* (1796).

COMMENTARY: Stanley T. Williams, *Richard Cumberland*, New Haven, 1917.

DAVENANT, SIR WILLIAM (1606-1668), though a minor poet and dramatist, is of first importance in the history of the stage [see within, pp. 191, 215]. Succeeding Ben Jonson as Poet Laureate in 1638, he shared little of Jonson's classical tastes but devoted himself to the themes and styles then fashionable with the court. His "Entertainments" in the latter half of the Commonwealth period anticipated the direction which the new drama of the Restoration would take in subject matter, verse form, and production techniques.

PRINCIPAL PLAYS: *Love and Honour* (1634), *The Platonic Lovers* (1636), *The Wits* (1636), *The Siege of Rhodes* (1656), *The Tempest* (with Dryden, an adaptation of Shakespeare, 1667).

COLLECTED EDITIONS: *Dramatic Works,* ed. Maidment and Logan, 5 vols., Edinburgh, 1872-1874; *Love and Honour and The Siege of Rhodes,* ed. J. W. Tupper, Boston, 1909.

COMMENTARY: Alfred Harbage, *Sir William Davenant*, Philadelphia, 1935; A. H. Nethercot, *Sir William D'Avenant,* Chicago, 1938; H. Spencer, *Shakespeare Improved,* Cambridge (Mass.), 1927.

DEKKER, THOMAS (1572?-1632), as a member of Henslowe's stable of writers between 1598 and 1602, was the sole author of ten and part author of some thirty plays. Among his collaborators was Ben Jonson who later satirized him in *The Poetaster* (1601) in the character of Demetrius "a dresser of plays about the town." Dekker replied by patching up an unfinished tragedy by one William Rufus, adding to it a farcical subplot in which the characters of *The Poetaster* return to the stage to attack Ben Jonson as Horace, the "humourous poet"; this play was entitled *Satiromastix* (1602). Dekker appears to have been an easy-going, romantic Londoner and his affection for the city is evident in his best plays. He was a notable pamphleteer, and the chapter "How a Gallant Should Behave Himself in a Playhouse," in his *Gull's Horn-book* (1609) gives a vivid glimpse of a Jacobean theatrical performance.

PRINCIPAL PLAYS: *The Shoemaker's Holiday* (1599), *Old Fortunatus* (1599), *Satiromastix* (1602), *Patient Grissel* (with Chettle and Haughton, 1600), *Westward Ho* and *Northward Ho* (with Webster, 1604), *The Honest Whore, Part I* (with Middleton, 1604), *Part II* (*c.* 1608), *Sir Thomas Wyatt* (with Webster, 1607), *The Roaring Girl* (with Middleton, 1611), *The Virgin Martyr* (with Massinger, *c.* 1620), *The Witch of Edmonton* (with Ford and Rowley, 1622), *Match Me in London* (1631).

COLLECTED EDITION: *The Dramatic Works of Thomas Dekker,* ed.
R. H. Shepherd, 4 vols., London, 1873.

COMMENTARY: S. A. Tannenbaum, *Thomas Dekker: A Concise
Bibliography,* New York, 1939; M. L. Hunt, *Thomas Dekker,* New
York, 1911; K. L. Gregg, *Thomas Dekker, a Study in Economic and
Social Backgrounds,* Seattle, 1924; W. E. Halstead, "What 'War of the
Theaters'?," *CE,* IX (1948), 424-426 (and see comment by R. Withing-
ton in *CE,* X, 163-164); R. A. Law, *"The Shoemaker's Holiday* and
Romeo and Juliet," SP, XXI (1924), 356-361; L. J. Teagarden, "The
Dekker-Middleton Problem in *Michaelmas Term,"* University of Texas
Studies in English, 1947, pp. 49-58; J. Gerald, "Dekker's Part in *The
Familie of Love,"* in *J. Q. Adams Memorial Studies,* Washington, 1948,
pp. 723-738; G. F. Reynolds, "Aims of a Popular Elizabethan Drama-
tist," *PQ,* XX (1941), 340-344.

DRYDEN, JOHN (1631-1700), the literary arbiter of the Restoration as dramatist, poet, and critic, reflected and supported the views
of the court. As a reward he was made Poet Laureate in 1668, a post
which he held for twenty years until his conversion to Roman Catholi-
cism prevented his taking oaths of allegiance to William and Mary.
He was a prolific writer by nature and by necessity, averaging about
a play a year from 1663-1678 in addition to a steady stream of poems,
prefaces, miscellaneous prose works, and translations. Dryden's dramatic theories, as outlined in *An Essay of Dramatic Poesy* (1668), "Of
Heroic Plays," prefacing *The Conquest of Granada* (1670), "Defense
of the Epilogue" affixed to *The Conquest of Granada, Part II* (1671),
"The Grounds of Criticism in Tragedy," prefacing *Troilus and Cressida* (1679), and the Preface to *All for Love* (1678), not only explain
and justify his own changing practice but are full of suggestion and
more or less original thinking upon the subject of the drama. Through
Aurengzebe (1676) his serious plays are in heroic couplets, thereafter
chiefly in blank verse.

PRINCIPAL PLAYS: *The Wild Gallant* (1663), *The Indian Queen*
(with Sir Robert Howard, 1665), *The Indian Emperor* (1665), *Sir Martin Mar-all* (1668), *Tyrannic Love* (1669), *Tempest* (from Shakespeare,
with Davenant, 1670), *Almanzor and Almahide, or The Conquest of
Granada* (Two Parts, 1670, 1671), *Marriage à la Mode* (1673), *Amboyna*
(1673), *Aurengzebe* (1676), *The State of Innocence* (from *Paradise Lost,*
1677), *All for Love* (1678), *Troilus and Cressida* (1679), *Oedipus* (with
Lee, 1679), *The Spanish Friar* (1681).

COLLECTED EDITIONS: *Works,* ed. W. Scott and G. Saintsbury, 18 vols.,
Edinburgh, 1888-1892; *Essays,* ed. W. P. Ker, 2 vols., Oxford, 1926;
Dramatic Works, ed. Montague Summers, 6 vols., London, 1931-1932.

COMMENTARY: Hugh MacDonald, *John Dryden: A Bibliography,*
Oxford, 1939; J. M. Osborn, *John Dryden, Some Bibliographical Facts*

and Problems, New York, 1940; Mark Van Doren, *The Poetry of John Dryden,* rev. ed., New York, 1945; T. S. Eliot, *John Dryden,* London, 1932; L. I. Bredvold, *The Intellectual Milieu of John Dryden,* Ann Arbor, 1934; M. Sherwood, *Dryden's Dramatic Theory and Practice,* Boston, 1898; A. Nicoll, *Dryden as an Adapter of Shakespeare,* London, 1922; B. J. Pendlebury, *Dryden's Heroic Plays,* New York, 1923; N. B. Allen, *The Sources of Dryden's Comedies,* Ann Arbor, 1935; T. W. Russell, *Voltaire, Dryden, and Heroic Tragedy,* New York, 1946.

EDWARDS, RICHARD (1524-1566), graduate of Oxford and widely admired by his contemporaries as a lyric poet, was master of the children of the Chapel Royal, 1561-1567. Developing the practice established by his predecessors, of employing the "Children" for interludes or entertainments at court, he composed for their use *Damon and Pithias* (1564), his only surviving play, "a tragical comedy." In 1566, his lost play *Palamon and Arcite* was presented with great splendor before Queen Elizabeth on her state visit to Oxford.

COMMENTARY: L. Bradner, *The Life and Poems of Richard Edwards,* New Haven, 1927.

ELIOT, THOMAS STEARNS (1888-   ), though born and educated in America, became an English citizen before his first plays were produced. In them he has sought and proposed solutions to the problem of the desperation of modern life as described in his celebrated poem, *The Wasteland* (1922). In his critical discussion of Elizabethan and other playwrights, and in his "Dialogue on Dramatic Poesy," Mr. Eliot has raised the questions which confront the poet in the theater and attempted answers based on the practice of earlier writers. His own plays draw freely upon all dramatic conventions—Greek, Elizabethan, Classical French, and the well-made play—not omitting the pageant and the music hall.

PRINCIPAL PLAYS: *Sweeney Agonistes* (fragment, 1932), *The Rock* (1934), *Murder in the Cathedral* (1935), *The Family Reunion* (1939), *The Cocktail Party* (1949).

COMMENTARY: F. O. Matthiessen, *The Achievement of T. S. Eliot,* 2nd ed., New York, 1947; L. Unger, ed., *T. S. Eliot, a Selected Critique,* New York, 1948; Francis Fergusson, "Action as Passion: *Tristan and Murder in the Cathedral,*" *Kenyon Review,* IV (1947), 201-221.

ETHEREDGE, SIR GEORGE (1634?-1691), a widely traveled and well-educated man-about-town, devoted his life to genteel behavior. He studied law without becoming a lawyer, and wrote three plays without becoming a playwright. In 1685 he entered the diplomatic service as a thoroughly gentlemanly occupation. In 1685, James II sent him as envoy to Ratisbon, but his career was cut short by the Revolution. As a loyal Jacobite he went into exile in Paris, where he died.

PRINCIPAL PLAYS: *The Comical Revenge, or Love in a Tub* (1664), *She Would if She Could* (1668), *The Man of Mode* (1676).

COLLECTED EDITION: Ed. H. F. Brett-Smith, 2 vols., Oxford, 1927 (includes both biographical details and critical commentary).

FARQUHAR, GEORGE (1678-1707), the son of an Irish clergyman, spent a year in Trinity College, Dublin, and a few years in the army before turning to the stage as an actor. After accidentally wounding one of his fellows, he abandoned acting in favor of playwrighting, where his practical experience stood him in good stead in contriving situations best described as "good theater." His plays are written with an eye to stage effectiveness rather than literary merit. In spite of the success of his last plays, he died penniless, just after learning of the triumph of *The Beaux' Stratagem.*

PRINCIPAL PLAYS: *Love and a Bottle* (1699), *The Constant Couple, or a Trip to the Jubilee* (1700), *Sir Harry Wildair* (1701), *The Inconstant* (1702), *The Twin Rivals* (1702), *The Stage-Coach* (with Motteux, 1704), *The Recruiting Officer* (1706), *The Beaux' Stratagem* (1707).

COLLECTED EDITION: *Complete Works,* ed. C. A. Stonehill, 2 vols., London, 1930.

FIELDING, HENRY (1707-1754), best known as the creator of *Tom Jones,* before turning to prose fiction supported himself by playwrighting and by managing the Haymarket Theatre. However, the thinly disguised satire of his productions (in particular, *The Historical Register for 1736*) provoked the passing of the Licensing Act of 1737 and deprived him of his livelihood. He then wrote his famous series of novels and became Justice of the Peace for Westminster. He died in Lisbon, where he had gone for his health.

PRINCIPAL PLAYS: *Love in Several Masques* (1728), *The Tragedy of Tragedies or the Life and Death of Tom Thumb the Great* (1730), *The Temple Beau* (1730), *The Author's Farce* (1730), *The Welsh Opera* (1731), *The Mock Doctor* (from Molière, 1732), *The Modern Husband* (1732), *The Miser* (from Molière, 1733), *Don Quixote in England* (1734), *The Universal Gallant* (1735), *Pasquin* (1736), *Tumble-Down Dick* (1736), *The Historical Register for 1736* (1737), *Eurydice* (1737).

COLLECTED EDITION: *Works,* ed. W. E. Henly, 16 vols., London, 1903.

COMMENTARY: W. L. Cross, *The History of Henry Fielding,* 3 vols., New Haven, 1918; W. H. Rogers, "Fielding's Early Aesthetic and

Technique," *SP*, XL (1943), 529-551; F. Cordasco, *Henry Fielding, A List of Critical Studies Published from 1895 to 1946*, Brooklyn, 1947.

FLETCHER, JOHN (1579-1625), of a family of notable poets, began writing plays for the Children's companies. He early manifested a remarkable sense of the changing theatrical taste of his age and, alone and in collaboration with a half dozen other men, became the chief supplier of plays to the Globe-Blackfriars-Kings' Men Company. The greatest number of his collaborations were with Massinger, though the most famous were with Beaumont. He worked with Shakespeare on his last plays and seems to have inherited his position as Company Playwright. For twelve years before his death in the Plague he produced some four plays annually, a record for both indefatigability and facility. His easy, diffuse verse is well suited to such vast productivity; his play structure is the careless result of haste, unless put in order by his team-mate-of-the-moment.

PRINCIPAL PLAYS: *The Faithful Shepherdess* (c. 1610), *Wit Without Money* (pr. 1639), *Valentinian* (ante 1619), *The Loyal Subject* (c. 1618), *The Mad Lover* (c. 1619), *The Humourous Lieutenant* (c. 1619), *The Wild Goose Chase* (1621), *The Pilgrim* (1621), *The Island Princess* (1621), *Monsieur Thomas* (1619), *The Woman's Prize, or the Tamer Tamed* (a sequel to Shakespeare's *Taming of the Shrew*, c. 1625), *A Wife for a Month* (1624), *Rule a Wife and Have a Wife* (c. 1624), *The Chances* (1620); with Beaumont: *Four Plays in One* (c. 1608), *Philaster* (1609), *The Maid's Tragedy* (1610), *A King and No King* (1611), *Bonduca* (1614); with Massinger: *Sir John Van Olden Barnavelt* (c. 1619), *The Little French Lawyer* (pr. 1647), *The Spanish Curate* (1622), *The Beggar's Bush* (1622); *The Maid in the Mill* (with Rowley, 1623), *The Fair Maid of the Inn* (with Massinger, Jonson, Rowley, pr. 1647), *The Nice Valour* (with Middleton, pr. 1647), *The Bloody Brother* (with Jonson and others, c. 1616), *The Two Noble Kinsmen* (with Shakespeare, pr. 1634), *Henry VIII* (with Shakespeare, 1613).

COLLECTED EDITION: See Beaumont, Francis, above.

COMMENTARY: See Beaumont, Francis, above; W. W. Greg, *Pastoral Poetry and Pastoral Drama*, London, 1906; F. H. Ristine, *English Tragicomedy*, London, 1910; L. B. Wallis, *Fletcher, Beaumont and Company, Entertainers to the Jacobean Gentry*, New York, 1946.

FOOTE, SAMUEL (1720-1777), "The English Aristophanes," began his career as an actor after he had dissipated his fortunes at Oxford. An astounding gift for mimicry and an impudent spirit combined to win him the admiration of his audiences and the hatred of his victims. No one was safe from him: George Whitefield was burlesqued as Dr. Squintum in *The Minor;* Squire Long, the superannuated lover of the future Mrs. R. B. Sheridan, in *The Maid of Bath;* the Duchess of

Kingston in *A Trip to Calais*. When his leg was amputated in 1766, he promptly wrote a farce exploiting his new condition. As compensation for his injury, he received a patent and built the Little Theatre in the Haymarket in 1767. During the third quarter of the century he supplied himself and his company with a continuous run of boisterous farces, skits, and topical pieces which kept alive the traditions of laughing comedy in the prevailing gloom of sentiment.

PRINCIPAL PLAYS: *The Diversions of the Morning* (1747), *Taste* (1752), *The Minor* (1760), *The Liar* (1762), *The Mayor of Garret* (1764), *The Maid of Bath* (1771), *The Nabob* (1772), *A Trip to Calais* (1776).

COMMENTARY: M. Belden, *The Dramatic Work of Samuel Foote*, New Haven, 1929.

FORD, JOHN (1586-1655?), although the leading tragic playwright of his era, is almost totally unknown as a man. A member of the Inner Temple as early as 1602, his earliest surviving play is dated 1624. He seems to have begun as a collaborator of Dekker. Later, under the influence of Burton's *Anatomy of Melancholy*, he wrote the unique tragedies for which he is best known. Several of his comedies have survived to confirm his right to the title of The Melancholy Poet.

PRINCIPAL PLAYS: *The Sun's Darling* (with Dekker, 1624), *The Lover's Melancholy* (1629), *Love's Sacrifice* (1633), *'Tis Pity She's a Whore* (1633), *The Broken Heart* (1633), *Perkin Warbeck* (1634), *The Ladies' Trial* (1638), *The Queen* (pr. 1653).

COLLECTED EDITION: *Dramatic Works*, Gifford-Dyce, London, 1869.

COMMENTARY: M. J. Sargeaunt, *John Ford*, Oxford, 1935; G. T. Sensabaugh, *The Tragic Muse of John Ford*, New York, 1945; S. B. Ewing, *Burtonian Melancholy in the Plays of John Ford*, Princeton, 1940; W. A. Bacon, "The Literary Reputation of John Ford," *HLQ*, XI (1947), 181-199.

GALSWORTHY, JOHN (1867-1933), the well-educated son of an upper-middle-class country family, had already gained some reputation as a novelist when he submitted his first play to Granville-Barker at the Court Theatre in 1906. It is as a novelist and recorder of the life of the mercantile classes of the turn of the century that he will doubtless be remembered. His plays reflect his serious, sympathetic observation of his fellow men, and he does not escape the sentimentality which seems inseparable from domestic drama generally. He was perhaps more conscious of classes and groups of men than of individuals, and in his strongest plays the leading rôles are usually embodiments of class characteristics, and the conflicts become those of class against class.

PRINCIPAL PLAYS: *The Silver Box* (1906), *Strife* (1909), *Justice* (1910), *The Pigeon* (1913), *The Skin Game* (1920), *Loyalties* (1922), *Old English* (1924), *Escape* (1926).

COLLECTED EDITION: *Novels, Tales, and Plays*, 22 vols., New York, 1926-1929.

COMMENTARY: H. V. Marrot, *The Life and Letters of John Galsworthy*, New York, 1936; Galsworthy, "Some Platitudes Concerning the Drama," in *The Inn of Tranquillity*, New York, 1912.

GARRICK, DAVID (1717-1779), fellow townsman and pupil of Samuel Johnson at Litchfield, came to London with his master in 1737 to become the leading figure of the eighteenth century theater and one of the greatest actors in the history of the stage. He made his debut, anonymously, at Goodman's-Fields with sensational success. From 1747 he was part-manager of Drury Lane where he established himself as an interpreter of Shakespeare and something of an innovator in staging, introducing the new lighting methods of the French theater, and encouraging the mechanical ingenuities of his Dutch scene designer and production master, De Loutherbourg. As an actor he was "natural," that is to say, less formal than his eighteenth century predecessors, but not at all averse to theatrical effects. His plays are lively but negligible farces, but his adaptations of Shakespeare (*Catharine and Petruchio* (1756), and *Romeo and Juliet*, (1748)) are early manifestations of the spirit of "Bardolatry." The former is not unknown on the modern stage; the latter, in which Romeo is given a foolish dying speech, left the stage before its adapter.

PRINCIPAL PLAYS: *The Lying Valet* (1741), *Miss in Her Teens* (1747), *The Clandestine Marriage* (with Colman the Elder, 1766), *Bon Ton, or High Life Above Stairs* (1775).

COMMENTARY: Thomas Davies, *Memoirs of David Garrick*, 2 vols., London, 1780; E. P. Stein, *David Garrick, Dramatist* (1938); A. S. Downer, "Nature to Advantage Dressed: Eighteenth Century Acting," *PMLA*, LVIII (1943), 1002-37; W. J. Laurence, "The Pioneers of Modern English Stage Mounting: De Loutherbourg," *The Magazine of Art*, March 1895; G. C. O'Dell, *Shakespeare from Betterton to Irving*, 2 vols., New York, 1920; Hazelton Spencer, *Shakespeare Improved*, Cambridge, (Mass.), 1827; A. C. Sprague, *Shakespeare and the Actors*, Cambridge (Mass.), 1940; D. Macmillan, "David Garrick, Manager: Notes on the theater as a cultural institution in England in the eighteenth century," *SP*, XLV (1948), 630-646; G. W. Stone, Jr., "Garrick's Production of *King Lear*: a Study in the Temper of the Eighteenth Century Mind," *SP*, XLV (1948), 89-103; G. W. Stone, Jr., "The God of His Idolatry: Garrick's Theory of Acting and Dramatic Composition with Especial Reference to Shakespeare," *J. Q. Adams Memorial Studies*, Washington, 1948.

GASCOIGNE, GEORGE (1539?-1577), poet and a member of Gray's Inn, wrote for that Nest of Lawyers (and witty gentlemen) *The Supposes* (1566), the earliest English prose comedy. This was an adaptation, with additional complications, from Ariosto's Italian comedy, *I Suppositi* (1509), which was in turn a patchwork from Roman comedies by Plautus and Terence. From Gascoigne's piece Shakespeare took the subject matter for the sub-plot of *The Taming of the Shrew.* Gascoigne was generally a pioneer and experimenter. In addition to writing the first English prose comedy, he translated an Italian version of Euripides' *Phoenissae* as *Jocasta* (1566), employing the new medium of blank verse, but retaining much Senecan tragic machinery. In 1577, he treated the "prodigal son" formula in his "tragicomedy," *The Glass of Government.* His plays were quickly forgotten in the rapid development of the drama in the next generation, but he is of considerable importance as a forerunner.

PRINCIPAL PLAYS: *The Supposes* (1566), *Jocasta* (1566), *The Glass of Government* (1576).

COLLECTED EDITIONS: R. W. Bond, *Early Plays from the Italian,* Oxford, 1911; J. W. Cunliffe, *The Works of George Gascoigne,* 2 vols., Cambridge (Eng.), 1907-1910.

COMMENTARY: S. A. Tannenbaum, *George Gascoigne: A Concise Bibliography,* New York, 1942; C. T. Prouty, *George Gascoigne, Elizabethan Courtier, Soldier, and Poet,* London, 1942.

GAY, JOHN (1685-1732), the intimate friend of Pope and Swift, a successful writer of occasional verse, may be considered the inventor of comic opera or musical comedy in English. His *Beggar's Opera,* supposedly suggested by Swift's hinting that a "Newgate pastoral" would be a pretty kind of burlesque, is the obvious ancestor of Sheridan's *The Duenna,* and the works of Gilbert and Sullivan. Its success brought a flood of "ballad operas" on the stage, which were in turn succeeded by the more conventional "comic operas" with especially composed scores. *The Beggar's Opera* further established as suitable subject-matter a unique combination of young love or sentimentality and political or social satire.

PRINCIPAL PLAYS: *What d'ye Call It?* (1715), *Three Hours after Marriage* (with Pope and Arbuthnot, 1717), *The Beggar's Opera* (1728), *Polly* (1729).

COMMENTARY: Lewis Melville, *Life and Letters of John Gay,* New York, 1921; W. E. Schultz, *Gay's Beggar's Opera: Its Content, History, Influence,* New Haven, 1923; W. H. Irving, *John Gay,* Durham, 1940; George Sherburne, "The Fortunes and Misfortunes of *Three Hours after Marriage,*" MP XXIV (1926), 91-109; William Empson, *Some Versions of Pastoral,* London, 1935.

GILBERT, SIR WILLIAM SCHWENCK (1836-1911), began his career, like many of his predecessors, in an unsuccessful attempt to establish himself as a lawyer. Turning to light verse in his plentiful spare time, he became a regular contributor to *Fun,* a rival of *Punch.* These poems, the famous *Bab Ballads,* contain the kernels of the later Savoy operas and are completely typical of Gilbert's whimsical topsy-turvy attitude. After considerable success as a playwright and author of burlesques, he joined with the composer Arthur Sullivan in writing the famous comic operas, called Savoy Operas after the theater built (in 1882) for their especial use.

PRINCIPAL PLAYS: *Dulcamara* (1866), *The Palace of Truth* (1870), *Pygmalion and Galatea* (1871), *The Wicked World* (1873), *Engaged* (1877); The Savoy Operas (with Sir Arthur Sullivan): *Trial by Jury* (1875), *The Sorcerer* (1877), *H. M. S. Pinafore* (1878), *The Pirates of Penzance* (1879), *Patience* (1881), *Iolanthe* (1882), *Princess Ida* (1884), *The Mikado* (1885), *Ruddigore* (1887), *The Yeoman of the Guard* (1888), *The Gondoliers* (1889), *Utopia, Ltd.* (1893), *The Grand Duke* (1896).

COMMENTARY: Hesketh Pearson, *Gilbert and Sullivan, A Biography,* New York, 1935; Isaac Goldberg, *The Story of Gilbert and Sullivan,* New York, 1929; C. L. Purdy, *Gilbert and Sullivan, Masters of Mirth and Melody,* New York, 1946.

GOLDSMITH, OLIVER (1730-1774), an Irishman, a graduate of Trinity College, Dublin, came to London in 1756 to establish himself as a physician. To supplement his meager earnings, he turned hack writer, gradually became acquainted with the foremost men of Dr. Johnson's circle, and developed from the writing of occasional essays and reviews to the writing of plays, poems, and a novel which stand high among the achievements of his immediate circle of eminent men of letters. He attacked managerial cupidity in his essay "Of the Stage" in an *Enquiry into the Present State of Polite Learning in Europe* (1759). When he offered Garrick his first play, *The Good Natur'd Man,* Garrick not only rejected it but brought out Hugh Kelley's *False Delicacy* on the night of its first performance at Covent Garden. As a consequence the play was only a modest success. *She Stoops to Conquer* (1773) was, on the other hand, an instant and continuing triumph, a fitting close for the career of a good-natured writer-of-all-trades.

PRINCIPAL PLAYS: *The Good Natur'd Man* (1768), *She Stoops to Conquer* (1773), *The Grumbler* (adapted from Sedley, 1773).

COLLECTED EDITION: *Plays,* ed. Austin Dobson, London, 1901.

COMMENTARY: Sir James Prior, *The Life of Oliver Goldsmith,* 2 vols., London, 1837; Austin Dobson, *The Life of Oliver Goldsmith,* London, 1888.

GRANVILLE-BARKER, HARLEY (1877-1946), after gaining experience as an actor in provincial stock companies, associated himself with the New Theater Movement by writing *The Marrying of Ann Leete* for The Stage Society, by acting with that group and with William Poel's Elizabethan Stage Society. Poel totally reformed the production of Shakespeare and awakened critics to a new understanding of his plays. Granville-Barker continued Poel's experiments, though along his own lines, in famous productions of *The Winter's Tale, A Midsummer Night's Dream,* and *Twelfth Night.* In addition to his experiments at the Court with the New Drama, and with new interpretations of the Old, he toured American college stadia with revivals of Greek tragedy, and wrote widely on the art of the drama, most influentially in his *Prefaces to Shakespeare,* 2 vols., Princeton, 1947.

PLAYS: *The Marrying of Ann Leete* (1901), *The Voysey Inheritance* (1905), *Waste* (1907), *The Madras House* (1910), *The Secret Life* (1923).

COMMENTARY: A. S. Downer, "Harley Granville-Barker," *The Sewanee Review,* LV (1947), 627-645.

GREENE, ROBERT (1560?-1592), educated at Oxford and Cambridge, a Bohemian wit, turned his pen to romances, pamphlets, poems, plays, anything that was likely to catch a penny. He supplied highly popular plays to the various companies of professional actors and is supposed to have been Shakespeare's guide in his earliest dramatic venture *(Henry VI).* His final pamphlet, *Greene's Groatsworth of Wit* (1592), written on his death bed, contains a direct admonition to his fellows to beware of Shakespeare whom he accuses of plagiarism. His prose narrative, *Francesco's Fortune,* contains a vivid, and possibly autobiographical scene between a young poet-playwright and a company of actors.

PRINCIPAL PLAYS: *Friar Bacon and Friar Bungay (c.* 1589), *James IV* (1590), *Orlando Furioso (ante* 1591); *A Looking Glass for London and England* (with Lodge, 1590); attributed to Greene: *George à Greene (ante* 1593), *Fair Em (c.* 1590), *The Famous Victories of Henry V (ante* 1588).

COLLECTED EDITIONS: *The Life and Complete Works of Robert Greene,* ed. A. B. Grosart, 15 vols., London, 1881-1886; *Plays and Poems,* ed. J. C. Collins, 2 vols., Oxford, 1905.

COMMENTARY: See collected ed., above; S. A. Tannenbaum, *Robert Greene: A Concise Bibliography,* New York, 1939; P. Z. Round, "Greene's Materials for *Friar Bacon and Friar Bungay," MLR,* XXI (1926), 19-23; R. Hudson, "Greene's *James IV* and Contemporary Illusions to Scotland," *PMLA,* XLVII (1932), 652-667; W. F. MacNair, "Traditional Elements in the Character of Greene's Friar Bacon," *SP,* XLV (1948), 172-179.

GREGORY, LADY AUGUSTA (1852-1932), chiefly noted as a dramatist, began her literary work as a collector of folk legends and a translator of ancient Irish tales. When she joined with Yeats and Martyn in the founding of the Irish National Theater she brought not only intense patriotism and knowledge of the cultural heritage but industry, enthusiasm, and discipline. She acted first as secretary to Yeats and later as his adviser and collaborator, assisting him in the hard work of reducing poetic fancy to workable drama. She was indefatigable and unshakable in her purpose; when the Abbey Theatre toured the United States (1911, 1913), Lady Gregory bravely outfaced riots and threats of riots, and refused to be turned aside by the ignorance of public censors or oversensitive Irish expatriates. In her modesty she felt she was only serving Yeats and the cultural revival, but it was Yeats who said, with complete truth, "The Irish Theater was hers, and she made it."

PRINCIPAL PLAYS: *Spreading the News, Hyacinth Halevy, The Rising of the Moon, The Workhouse Ward, The Goal Gate* (all in *Seven Short Plays*, New York, 1908); *The Kiltartan Molière* (translations from three French classics), New York, 1910.

COMMENTARY: See her *Our Irish Theater*, New York, 1912; and *Journals*, ed. Lennox Robinson, New York, 1946.

HANKIN, ST. JOHN (1860-1909), after graduation from Oxford, began a journalistic career by writing successively for *The Saturday Review*, the Calcutta *Indian Daily News* and the London *Times*. His dramatic criticisms for the last inspired him to write "Mr. Punch's Dramatic Sequels" (1901) a series of supplementary acts to great masterpieces, which quite possibly were responsible for his attempts at playwrighting. In 1905 he retired to the country and devoted himself to writing for the stage, translating and adapting works from the French "New Theater" as well as creating his own ironic and shrewd analyses of middle class English culture.

PRINCIPAL PLAYS: *The Return of the Prodigal* (1905), *The Cassilis Engagement* (1905), *The Last of the De Mullins* (1908).

COLLECTED EDITION: *Plays*, 2 vols., London, 1923 (includes Hankin's essays on dramatic subjects).

COMMENTARY: See John Drinkwater's memoir prefacing the collected *Plays* above.

HAUGHTON, WILLIAM (*fl.* 1598), one of Henslowe's staff of writers, provided the Lord Admiral's Company with the "first full-length comedy of London life," *Englishmen for My Money, or a Woman Will Have Her Will* (1598). He is known also to have collaborated with Chettle and Dekker on *Patient Grissel* (1600).

PRINCIPAL PLAYS: *Englishmen for My Money* (1598), ed. A. C. Baugh, Philadelphia, 1917.

HEYWOOD, JOHN (1497?-1580?), a member of Sir Thomas More's circle and married to his niece, the daughter of John Rastell, was court musician to Henry VIII and Queen Mary.

PRINCIPAL PLAYS: *Witty and Witless, Gentleness and Nobility, The Four P's, The Play of the Weather, A Play of Love;* attributed: *The Pardoner and the Frere; John John, Tyb his wife, and Sir John the Priest* (all 1522-1532).

COLLECTED EDITION: *The Dramatic Writings of John Heywood*, ed. J. S. Farmer, London, 1905.

COMMENTARY: R. de la Bere, *John Heywood, Entertainer*, New York, 1937; R. W. Bolwell, *The Life and Works of John Heywood*, New York, 1921; H. N. Hillebrand, "On the Authorship of the Interludes attributed to John Heywood," *MP*, XIII (1915), 267-280; K. W. Cameron, *The Background of John Heywood's Witty and Witless*, Raleigh, 1941; K. Young, "The Influence of French Farce upon the Plays of John Heywood," *MP*, II (1904), 97-124; W. Phy, "The Chronology of John Heywood's Plays," *ESt* LXXIV (1940), 27-41.

HEYWOOD, THOMAS (1570?-1641), one of the most phenomenally productive of Elizabethan playwrights, by his own statement composed or collaborated on some 220 plays of which about twenty survive. He was especially given to the popularization of history and classical story, and, in his romances, to making pleasant use of the jingoism of the naïve but true-born Englishmen who frequented the Red Bull and other lower-class theaters.

PRINCIPAL PLAYS: *The Four Prentices of London* (c. 1600), *Edward IV* (Two Parts, 1599), *A Woman Killed with Kindness* (1603), *The Fair Maid of the West* (pr. 1631), *The English Traveller* (pr. 1637), *The Age Plays* (Five Parts, 1611+), *Fortune by Land and Sea* (with Rowley, pr. 1655).

COLLECTED EDITION: *The Dramatic Works of Thomas Heywood*, ed. R. H. Shepherd, 6 vols., London, 1874.

COMMENTARY: S. A. Tannenbaum, *T. Heywood: A Concise Bibliography*, New York, 1939; A. M. Clark, *Thomas Heywood, Playwright and Miscellanist*, Oxford, 1931; O. Cromwell, *Thomas Heywood, A Study in the Elizabethan Drama of Everyday Life*, New Haven, 1928; R. G. Martin, "Notes on Thomas Heywood's *Ages*," *MLN*, XXXIII (1918), 23-29; J. Q. Adams, "Shakespeare, Heywood, and the Classics," *MLN*, XXXIV (1919), 336-339; L. B. Wright, "Heywood and the Popularizing of History," *MLN*, XLIII (1928), 287-293; H. D. Smith, "*A Woman Killed with Kindness*," *PMLA*, LIII (1938), 138-147.

HOME, JOHN (1722-1808), a Scots minister, political figure, and nationalist. As part of the mid-century revival of interest in the folk and the romantic past, William Collins urged Home to collect the highland legends out of which came his one successful tragedy, *Douglas* (1756). Based on the ballad of *Child Maurice*, the play managed to capture enough of that sense of nature which was to lead to the Romantic Revival of the turn of the century to hold the stage in spite of occasionally turgid poetry and structural defects. The other dramatic works of "The Scots Shakespeare" were failures.

PRINCIPAL PLAY: *Douglas* (1756).

COMMENTARY: Alice E. Gipson, *John Home,* Caldwell (Idaho), 1917; W. J. Bate, *From Classic to Romantic: Premises of Taste in Eighteenth-Century England,* New York, 1946.

HOWARD, SIR ROBERT (1626-1698), brother-in-law of Dryden, the "Crites" of the latter's *Essay of Dramatic Poesy,* was his collaborator in the writing of *The Indian Queen* (1664), the first heroic play produced in London.

PRINCIPAL PLAYS: *The Committee* (1662), *The Indian Queen* (with Dryden, 1664), *The Great Favorite, or the Duke of Lerma* (1668).

COMMENTARY: F. R. Scott, "Teg—the Stage Irishman," *MLR,* XLII (1947), 314-320.

JERROLD, DOUGLAS (1803-1857), a facile contributor of topical essays and character sketches to *Punch,* was a man of notoriously crabbed disposition. In his plays little of his sarcasm or wit is evident, since they are mostly written to the public taste for melodrama. His attempts to revive the old style of comedy (of Sheridan, etc.) were fore-doomed, the audience preferring melodrama and domesticity. He was among the first to exploit the most popular subjects of early Victorian melodrama: the sailor, the drunkard, and the poor but honest farmer.

PRINCIPAL PLAYS: *Black-ey'd Susan* (1829), *The Rent Day* (1832), *Fifteen Years of a Drunkard's Life* (1828), *Bubbles of a Day* (1842).

COLLECTED EDITION: *Works,* ed. W. B. Jerrold, 4 vols., London, no date.

JONES, HENRY ARTHUR (1851-1929), the author of nearly one hundred plays and many essays propagandizing the "Renascence of the English Drama," began his career with a melodrama (*The Silver King*) and a version of *A Doll's House* (*Breaking a Butterfly,* 1884), but soon sensed the changing temper of the times. His later plays show a progressive attempt to record life-as-a-whole, though he never completely lost the touch of "good theater" which was a *sine qua non* of the drama of the eighties. Only with the realization of the "renascence" in the first years of the twentieth century did Jones's sentimentality and frequent begging of his own questions become apparent. In the light of his own day (except to Bernard Shaw) he was radical, and not altogether proper.

PRINCIPAL PLAYS: *The Silver King* (with Henry Herman, 1882), *Saints and Sinners* (1884), *The Dancing Girl* (1891), *The Masqueraders* (1894), *The Case of Rebellious Susan* (1894), *Michael and His Lost Angel* (1896), *The Liars* (1897), *Mrs. Dane's Defense* (1900).

COLLECTED EDITION: *Representative Plays of H. A. Jones*, ed. Clayton Hamilton, 4 vols., New York, 1926.

COMMENTARY: D. A. Jones, *Life and Letters of Henry Arthur Jones*, London, 1930; R. A. Cordell, *Henry Arthur Jones and the Modern Drama*, New York, 1932; M. Northend, "Henry Arthur Jones and the Development of Modern English Drama," RES, XVIII (1942), 448-463.

JONSON, BEN (1572-1637), educated at Westminster School, the son of a bricklayer, became the arbiter of Elizabethan literary matters, the center of a cult (The Sons of Ben), and the first of the playwrights to demand a place among men of letters. He enrolled in Henslowe's company in 1597, and changed to the King's Men in 1599-1600 for whom his great comedies were composed. Scholarly by instinct and classical in taste, he attempted to regularize the panoramic drama and developed the humour-theory of characterization. Alone of his contemporaries he edited and published his own works with great care in a folio volume of 1616.

PRINCIPAL PLAYS: *The Case Is Altered* (1598), *Everyman in His Humour* (1598), *Everyman out of His Humour* (1599), *Cynthia's Revels* (1600), *Poetaster* (1601), *Sejanus* (1603), *Volpone* (1606), *The Silent Woman* (1609), *The Alchemist* (1610), *Catiline* (1611), *Bartholomew Fair* (1614), *The Devil Is an Ass* (1616), *The Staple of News* (1626), *The New Inn* (1629), *The Sad Shepherd* (frag., no date) (For his Masques, see vol. 7 of Herford and Simpson, below).

COLLECTED EDITION: *Poems and Plays*, ed. Herford and Simpson, 8 vols., Oxford, 1925-1947.

COMMENTARY: S. A. Tannenbaum, *Ben Jonson: A Concise Bibliography*, New York, 1938; [*Supplement*, 1947]; John Palmer, *Ben Jonson*, New York, 1934; E. C. Dunn, *Ben Jonson's Art*, Northampton, Mass., 1925; H. W. Baum, *The Satiric and Didactic in Ben Jonson's Comedy*, Chapel Hill, 1947; F. L. Townshend, *Apologie for Bartholomew Fayre: The Art of Jonson's Comedies*, New York, 1947; A. H. Sackton, *Rhetoric as a Dramatic Language in Ben Jonson*, New York, 1948; H. Levin, "Jonson's Metempsychosis," PQ XXII (1943), 231-239; G. E. Bentley, *Shakespeare and Jonson*, 2 vols., Chicago, 1945; F. T.

Bowers, "Ben Jonson the Actor," *SP, XXXIV* (1937), 392-406 (and see above, under Dekker).

KILLIGREW, THOMAS (1612-1683), a favorite in the courts of both Charles I and Charles II, began writing romantic tragicomedies in the Love-and-Honor mode before the closing of the theaters. With the Restoration he was granted one of the two royal patents for establishing a dramatic company and founded the theater later to be known as Drury Lane.

PRINCIPAL PLAYS: *The Parson's Wedding* (*ante* 1642), *The Prisoners, Claricilla, The Princess* (all 1635-1636), *Cecilia and Clorinda* (*post* 1660).

COMMENTARY: A. Harbage, *Thomas Killigrew, Cavalier Dramatist,* Philadelphia, 1930; W. Van Lennep, "Thomas Killigrew Prepares His Plays ●for Production," *J. Q. Adams Memorial Studies,* Washington, 1948.

KNOWLES, JAMES SHERIDAN (1784-1862), an impoverished schoolmaster, tried playwrighting in a desperate attempt to eke out his salary. Designing his plays after the models of Shakespeare and tailoring them to the talents of particular stars—Edmund Kean, Macready—he was sensationally successful. His plays are rhetorical in speech but exciting in action; his blank verse is generally shabby, but with a touch of colloquialism most appealing to audiences influenced by the Romantic Revival.

PRINCIPAL PLAYS: *Virginius* (1820), *William Tell* (1825), *The Hunchback* (1832), *The Wife* (1833), *The Love Chase* (1837).

COMMENTARY: L. H. Meeks, *Sheridan Knowles and the Theater of His Time,* Bloomington (Ind.), 1933.

KYD, THOMAS (1558-1594), a "university wit," was educated at the Merchant Taylors' School in London. By profession a scrivener, he furnished an occasional play for Edward Alleyn and his company. His *Spanish Tragedy* is a bustling melodrama which had great effect on Elizabethan dramatic structure and technique. He is generally accepted as the author of the *"Ur-Hamlet,"* the lost version of the story which preceded Shakespeare's.

PRINCIPAL PLAYS: *The Spanish Tragedy* (*c.* 1585), *Soliman and Perseda* (pr. 1599), *Cornelia* (1594).

COLLECTED EDITION: *The Works of Thomas Kyd,* ed. F. S. Boas, Oxford, 1901.

COMMENTARY: T. W. Baldwin, "On the Chronology of Thomas Kyd's Work," *MLN, XL* (1925), 343-349; "Thomas Kyd's Early Company Connections," *PQ*, VI (1927), 311-313; C. M. Lewis, *The Genesis of Hamlet*, London, 1907; H. D. Gray, "Reconstruction of a Lost Play," *PQ*, VII (1928), 254-274.

LEE, NATHANIEL (1649?-1692), a graduate of Trinity College, Cambridge, failing to make his mark as an actor, turned to the writing of tragedies. His plays draw their subject-matter largely from the classics (occasionally from the classics as strained through French romances) and their verse style from the more extravagant of the Elizabethans.

PRINCIPAL PLAYS: *Nero* (1675), *Sophonisba* (1675), *The Rival Queens* (1677), *Oedipus* (with Dryden, 1679), *Lucius Junius Brutus* (1681), *The Princess of Cleve* (1689), *The Massacre of Paris* (1689).

COMMENTARY: R. G. Ham, *Otway and Lee*, New Haven, 1931.

LILLO, GEORGE (1693-1739), a somewhat mysterious figure, seems to have been of Flemish descent and a jeweller by profession. As a playwright he was interested in the older Elizabethan domestic drama and attempted to revive it on the eighteenth century stage. Two of his plays had some success, *The London Merchant* holding the boards for a century, but his influence was felt more largely on the continent in the works of Lessing and Diderot.

PRINCIPAL PLAYS: *The London Merchant, or The History of George Barnwell* (1731), *The Christian Hero* (1735), *Fatal Curiosity* (1736), *Arden of Feversham* (adapted from the Elizabethan version, 1736).

COLLECTED EDITION: *The London Merchant and Fatal Curiosity*, ed. A. W. Ward, Boston, 1906.

COMMENTARY: D. B. Pallette, "Notes for a Biography of George Lillo," *PQ*, XIX (1940), 261-267.

LYLY, JOHN (1554?-1606), educated at Oxford and Cambridge, attached himself to Elizabeth's court as a kind of preceptor in elegant behavior and speech. His famous novel *Euphues* (1579) introduced the prose style named after it "Euphuism," elaborate, antithetical, allusive, alliterative, so burlesqued in Falstaff's mock-heroic advice to Hal to shun pitch (I *Henry IV*, II, 4). Lyly carried this prose style over into his romantic comedies, thereby freeing comic dialogue from the shambling verse which had hitherto been its medium. His plays were written for the court, presented before Elizabeth, and acted not by the professional troupes but by companies of boys, the Children of the Chapel, who had acquired great repute for their skill in elaborate speech and graceful action. Lyly provided them with ample opportunities to display their especial qualities.

PRINCIPAL PLAYS: *Alexander and Campaspe* (1584), *Endimion* (1591), *Midas* (1592), *Mother Bombie* (1594), *The Woman in the Moon* (1597).

COLLECTED EDITION: *Works,* ed. R. W. Bond, Oxford, 1902.

COMMENTARY: S. A. Tannenbaum, *John Lyly: A Concise Bibliography,* New York, 1940; A. Feuillerat, *John Lyly,* Cambridge (Eng.), 1910; V. M. Jeffrey, *John Lyly and the Italian Renaissance,* Paris, 1929; G. W. Knight, "Lyly," *RES* XV (1939), 146-163; B. F. Huppé, "Allegory of Love in Lyly's Court Comedies," *ELH,* XIV (1947), 93-113.

MARLOWE, CHRISTOPHER (1564-1593), the first major English dramatic poet, was born in Canterbury and educated at Corpus Christi, Cambridge. The details of his career have been partially clarified only by the scholarly researches of the last few decades. It is believed that he was a government agent, which may have had something to do with the warrant issued for his arrest as an atheist in 1593 and with his murder, ostensibly over a tavern reckoning, in the same year. His four great tragedies *(I, II Tamburlaine, Dr. Faustus, The Jew of Malta)* were tailored to the measure of Edward Alleyn; he may have had a hand in the three parts of *Henry VI,* later revised by Shakespeare. His major contribution was, of course, his "mighty line," but he had also a gift for theatrical effect (as a substitute for mere rhetoric) and an ability to capture dramatically the aspiring temper of the Renaissance.

PRINCIPAL PLAYS: *Dido, Queen of Carthage* (with Nashe, pr. 1594), *Tamburlaine* (Two Parts, 1587, 1588), *Dr. Faustus* (pr. 1604), *The Jew of Malta* (c. 1588), *Edward II* (c. 1591), *Massacre at Paris* (c. 1593).

COLLECTED EDITION: *The Works and Life of Christopher Marlowe,* gen. ed. R. H. Case, 6 vols., Oxford, 1930-1933.

COMMENTARY: S. A. Tannenbaum, *Christopher Marlowe: A Concise Bibliography,* New York, 1937; [*Supplement,* 1947]; John Bakeless, *The Tragical History of Christopher Marlowe,* 2 vols., Cambridge (Mass.), 1942; P. H. Kocher, *Christopher Marlowe: A Study of His Thought, Learning and Character,* New York, 1946; J. L. Hotson, *The Death of Christopher Marlowe,* New York, 1925; T. Brooke, "Marlowe's Versification and Style," *SP* XIX (1922), 186-205; W. Thorp, "The Ethical Problem in Marlowe's *Tamburlaine,*" *JEGP,* XXIX (1930), 385-389; H. L. Gardner, "The Second Part of *Tamburlaine the Great,*" *MLR,* XXXVII (1942), 18-24; B. D. Brown, "Marlowe, Faustus, and Simon Magus," *PMLA,* LIV (1939), 82-121; P. H. Kocher, "Nashe's Authorship of the Prose Scenes in *Faustus,*" *MLQ,* III (1942), 17-40; L. J. Mills, "The Meaning of *Edward II,*" *MP,* XXXII (1934), 11-31; R. B. Heilman, "The Tragedy of Knowledge: Marlowe's Treatment of Faustus," *QRL,* II (1946), 316-332.

MARSTON, JOHN (1576-1634), educated at Oxford and admitted to the Middle Temple, preferred the writing of verse to studying law. A friend, an enemy, and an imitator of Ben Jonson, he briefly turned playwright before settling upon the Church as his career. His plays are fashionable, more imitative than original, and make effective use of such conventions as the Malcontent and the Revenger; he was notorious for the exuberance of his dialogue and the violence of his imagery; during their celebrated quarrel (recorded in *Poetaster*, etc.) it is these qualities which Jonson most effectively ridiculed. Their differences were composed, however, in time for a collaboration on *Eastward Ho*, a lively bourgeois comedy, which led to a brief period of imprisonment for the authors for political reasons.

PRINCIPAL PLAYS: *Jack Drum's Entertainment* (1600), *Antonio and Mellida, Antonio's Revenge* (both pr. 1602), *The Malcontent* (1604), *Eastward Ho* (with Chapman and Jonson, 1605), *Dutch Courtesan* (1605), *Parasitaster* (1606), *The Wonder of Women, or The Tragedy of Sophonisba* (1606).

COLLECTED EDITION: *The Plays of John Marston*, ed. H. H. Wood, 3 vols., Edinburgh, 1934-1938.

COMMENTARY: T. Spencer, "John Marston," *Criterion*, XIII (1934), 581-599; L. Lockert, "Marston, Webster, and the Decline of the Elizabethan Drama," *Sewanee Rev.*, XXVII (1919), 62-81; E. E. Stoll, "Shakespeare, Marston, and the Malcontent Type," *MP* III (1906), 281-303.

MASSINGER, PHILIP (1583-1640), born of a country family closely allied to the aristocracy, was educated at Oxford and became for his contemporaries the most famous of the latter-day Elizabethan playwrights. His serious plays reflect both his aristocratic connections and his Roman Catholic faith, but while mechanically competent they are generally drab. His comedies are somewhat more colorful; he seems (in *A New Way* and *The City Madam*) to have had at least a partial purpose of regularizing the excessive exuberance of earlier comic dramatists, and generally finds his theme in a sound middle-class moral. *A New Way to Pay Old Debts*, largely because of the possibilities for sensational acting in its central figure, has had the longest stage-history of any non-Shakespearean seventeenth century play.

PRINCIPAL PLAYS: *The Bondman* (1623), *The Roman Actor* (1626), *A New Way to Pay Old Debts* (1626), *The City Madam* (1632), *The Virgin-Martyr* (with Dekker, 1622), *The Fatal Dowry* (with Field, 1632); *The False One, The Elder Brother, The Custom of the Country* (all with Fletcher, *q.v.*).

COLLECTED EDITION: *Works*, ed. Gifford-Cunningham, London, 1868.

COMMENTARY: S. A. Tannenbaum, *Philip Massinger: A Concise Bibliography*, New York, 1938; A. H. Cruickshank, *Philip Massinger*, Oxford, 1920; R. H. Ball, *The Amazing Career of Sir Giles Overreach*, Princeton, 1939.

MEDWALL, HENRY (*fl.* 1486), chaplain to Cardinal Morton, was the author of *Fulgens and Lucres* and the first English dramatist whose name has been recorded. For the nature of his contribution to the drama, see within, p. 38.

PLAYS: *Nature* (c. 1495), *Fulgens and Lucres* (1497).

COMMENTARY: F. S. Boas and A. W. Reed, *Fulgens and Lucres,* Oxford, 1926 (text with introduction); J. K. Lowers, "High Comedy Elements in Medwall's *Fulgens and Lucres,*" *ELH* VII (1941), 103-106.

MIDDLETON, THOMAS (1580-1627), began his career as a member of Henslowe's staff and continued until his death to compose comedies and tragedies of unfailing attractiveness to Jacobean audiences. He wrote for any and all companies and aimed at the tastes of the general audience rather than of the court. By nature a realist, in his comedies he portrays London life with the same unsparing clarity as his analysis of the motives of the protagonists of his romantic tragedies (esp. *The Changeling*). *A Game at Chess* (1624) is a kind of documentary, treating a notorious contemporary international situation as an allegory: it was the greatest dramatic attraction of its time, playing before eight consecutive crowded audiences at the Globe until the interference of the Spanish Ambassador forced its abandonment. Middleton is the reputed author of certain additions to the witch scenes of *Macbeth*.

PRINCIPAL PLAYS: *Michaelmas Term* (1607), *A Trick to Catch the Old One* (1608), *A Mad World, My Masters* (1608), *The Roaring Girl* (with Dekker, 1611), *A Fair Quarrel* (with Rowley, 1617), *The Changeling* (with Rowley, 1623), *A Chaste Maid in Cheapside* (pr. 1630), *A Game at Chess* (1624).

COLLECTED EDITION: *Works,* ed. A. H. Bullen, 8 vols., London, 1885-1886.

COMMENTARY: M. Eccles, "Middleton's Birth and Education," *RES,* VII (1931), 431-441. R. C. Bald, "The Chronology of Middleton's Plays," *MLR,* XXXII (1937), 33-43; H. B. Bullock, "Thomas Middleton and the Fashion in Playmaking," *PMLA* (1927), 766-776; W. D. Dunkel, *The Dramatic Technique of Thomas Middleton in His Comedies of London Life,* Chicago, 1925; R. C. Bald, "The Sources of Middleton's City Comedies," *JEGP,* XXXIII (1934), 373-387; R. C. Bald (ed.) *A Game at Chess,* Cambridge (Eng.), 1929; J. R. Moore, "The Contemporary Significance of Middleton's *Game at Chess,*" *PMLA,* L (1935), 761-768.

O'CASEY, SEAN (1884-), the greatest of the "Second Generation" of the Abbey Theatre dramatists, came into prominence with realistic tragedies of Dublin life written after the First World War. A child of the slums, he wrote out of his experience of poverty and revolution drawing vivid pictures which are supplemented by the sketches in his equally revealing autobiographical volumes. Now a communist and resident of England, O'Casey has turned to expressionism in his latest plays, attempting with some success to make primary the universal ideas which were somewhat submerged under the humor and realism of his earlier works.

PRINCIPAL PLAYS: *The Shadow of a Gunman* (1923), *Juno and the Paycock* (1924), *The Plough and the Stars* (1926), *The Silver Tassie* (1928), *Within the Gates* (1933), *Red Roses for Me* (1943), *Oak Leaves and Lavender* (1947), *Cock-a-Doodle-Dandy* (1949).

COMMENTARY: See his (continuing) autobiography, beginning with *I Knock at the Door* (1939), and esp. *Inishfallen Fare Thee Well* (1949).

ORRERY, EARL OF [ROGER BOYLE] (1621-1679), was one of the earliest writers of heroic tragedy. In several of his plays he makes use of English historical materials but casts them into the familiar love-and-honor struggle and adopts the rhyming verse form of dialogue.

PRINCIPAL PLAYS: *Henry V* (1664), *The General* (1664), *Mustapha* (1665), *The Black Prince* (1667).

COLLECTED EDITION: *The Dramatic Works of Roger Boyle,* ed. W. S. Clark, 2 vols., Cambridge (Mass.), 1937.

COMMENTARY: See the ed. by W. S. Clark, above; C. W. Miller, "A Source Note on Boyle's *The General,*" *MLQ* VIII (1947), 146-150.

OTWAY, THOMAS (1652-1685), a graduate of Oxford, first essayed the stage as an actor, without success. Turning to playwrighting he wrote several heroic plays in rhyme, then shifted to blank verse for his greatest successes, *The Orphan* and *Venice Preserved*. His most notable characteristic is his domestic pathos which ensured his hold on the stage during the eighteenth and nineteenth centuries.

PRINCIPAL PLAYS: *Alcibiades* (1675), *Don Carlos* (1676), *Titus and Berenice* (from Racine, 1677), *The Cheats of Scapin* (from Molière, 1677), *Caius Marius* (1680), *The Orphan* (1680), *Venice Preserved* (1682).

COLLECTED EDITION: *Works,* ed. J. C. Ghosh, 2 vols., Oxford, 1932.

COMMENTARY: R. G. Ham, *Otway and Lee,* New Haven, 1931; A. Mackenzie, "Venice Preserved," *Tulane University Studies in English,* 1949, pp. 81-118.

PEELE, GEORGE (1556-1596), a Londoner by birth, educated at Oxford, has been called the Francois Villon of the seventeenth century.

Shortly after his early death, a volume of his *Merry Conceited Jests* was published depicting him as generally a scoundrel and sometimes a criminal. His works, inspired by contemporary events and the importunities of creditors, are facile, jingoistic, and flattering. For all that, however, he was a considerable poet; his lyric gift places him in the top rank of Elizabethans, and his blank verse is often suggestive of Marlowe's. Much of his dramatic writing is devoted to pageants and festival occasions. Only *The Old Wives' Tale* and *David and Bethsabe* demonstrate his genuine skill as a playwright.

PRINCIPAL PLAYS: *The Arraignment of Paris* (c. 1581), *The Battle of Alcazar* (pr. 1594), *The Old Wives' Tale* (pr. 1595), *David and Bethsabe* (pr. 1599).

COLLECTED EDITION: *Works,* ed. A. H. Bullen, 2 vols., London, 1888.

COMMENTARY: S. A. Tannenbaum, *George Peele: A Concise Bibliography,* New York, 1940; H. M. Dowling, "The Date and Order of Peele's Plays," *N&Q,* CLXIV (1933), 164-168, 183-185; S. L. C. Clapp. "Peele's Use of Folklore in *The Old Wives' Tale,*" *Univ. of Texas Studies in English* (1926), pp. 146-156; G. Jones, "The Intention of Peele's *Old Wives' Tale,*" *Aberstwyth Studies,* VII (1925), 79-93.

PINERO, SIR ARTHUR WING (1855-1934), beginning his theatrical career as an actor, about 1880 produced the first of a series of comedies which display the actor's sure knowledge of stage effect. Under the influence of Scribe he practiced the technique of well-made playwrighting; under the later influence of Dumas *fils* (with just a touch of Ibsen) he turned to "serious" social themes and problems. But, perhaps due to his training in the older theater which he memorialized in *Trelawney of "The Wells,"* he was never willing to dissociate problem and stage effect.

PRINCIPAL PLAYS: *The Magistrate* (1885), *The Second Mrs. Tanqueray* (1893), *The Notorious Mrs. Ebbsmith* (1895), *Trelawney of "The Wells"* (1898), *The Gay Lord Quex* (1899), *Iris* (1901), *The Thunderbolt* (1908), *Mid-Channel* (1909).

COLLECTED EDITION: *Social Plays,* ed. Clayton Hamilton, 4 vols., New York, 1917-1922.

COMMENTARY: H. Fyfe, *Sir Arthur Wing Pinero's Plays and Players,* London, 1930; W. D. Dunkel, *Sir Arthur Pinero: A Critical Biography with Letters,* Chicago, 1941.

PORTER, HENRY (d. 1599), is known for a single play, the realistic comedy, *Two Angry Women of Abingdon.* According to Henslowe's *Diary,* upon the success of this play payment was advanced for a sequel, *The Two Merry Women of Abingdon,* but the author's death effectively prevented its completion.

EDITION: C. M. Gayley, *Representative English Comedies*, New York, 1912, vol. I.

COMMENTARY: R. E. Shear, "New Facts about Henry Porter," *PMLA* XLII (1927), 641-655; E. H. C. Oliphant, "Who was Henry Porter?," *PMLA* XLIII (1928), 572-575; L. Hotson, "The Adventure of the Single Rapier," *Atlantic Monthly*, CXLVIII (1931), 26-31; J. M. Nosworthy, "Notes on Henry Porter," *MLR*, XXXV (1940), 517-521; R. H. Bowers, "Notes on 'The Two Angry Women of Abingdon,'" *N&Q* CXCIII, 311-314.

PRESTON, THOMAS (1537-1598), known author of only one play, the ranting and bombastic *Cambises,* was a graduate of Cambridge and for a year vice-chancellor of that university.

PLAY: *A Lamentable Tragedy mixed full of Pleasant Mirth containing the Life of Cambises, King of Persia* (pr. 1569).

RASTELL, JOHN (1475?-1536), brother-in-law of Thomas More and father-in-law of John Heywood, was a lawyer by profession and a printer and playwright by avocation. He seems to have been thoroughly stage-struck: surviving from his press are several early plays and among the court records of the time is a suit brought against him by a carpenter for the construction of a stage at his home.

PLAY: *The Nature of the Four Elements* (c. 1518).

COMMENTARY: M. E. Borish, "The Source and Intention of *The Four Elements,*" *SP*, XXXV (1938), 149-163; E. M. Nugent, "Sources of John Rastell's *The Nature of the Four Elements,*" *PMLA*, LVII (1942), 74-88; J. Parr, "John Rastell's Geographical Knowledge of America," *PQ*, XXVII (1948), 229-240.

ROBERTSON, THOMAS WILLIAM (1829-1871), was born into a family of provincial actors, spent many years touring their theatrical circuit as actor, prompter, and general handyman. Coming to London, he began supplying plays for the minor houses and adapting French successes for the theatrical publisher, T. H. Lacy. Associating himself with Marie Wilton (Lady Bancroft) in her managerial venture at the Prince of Wales's Theatre—known for good reasons as "The Dust Hole"—he made the tentative experiments with realism which earned him the title of pioneer in the modern drama.

PRINCIPAL PLAYS: *David Garrick* (1864), *Society* (1865), *Ours* (1866), *Caste* (1867), *Play* (1868), *School* (1869), *M. P.* (1870).

COLLECTED EDITION: *Principal Dramatic Works,* 2 vols., London, 1889.

COMMENTARY: T. E. Pemberton, *The Life and Writings of T. W. Robertson*, London, 1893; A. W. Pinero, "The Theatre of the 'Seventies," in *The Eighteen-Seventies*, ed. H. Granville-Barker, London, 1929, pp. 135-163 [and see also Pinero's play, *Trelawney of "The Wells"*].

ROBINSON, LENNOX (1886-   ), brought to the Abbey Theatre the kind of realism Galsworthy and Granville-Barker were developing at the Court Theatre in London. Known as one of "The Cork Realists," he shows little of the expected interest in folklore and legend but devotes himself to pictures of urban life, sometimes comic, sometimes tragic, and not always free of sentimentality. For many years stage-director at the Abbey, he is now on the board of management and its official historian.

PRINCIPAL PLAYS: *The Clancy Name* (pr. 1911), *The Whiteheaded Boy* (1916), *The Cross-Roads* (1909), *The Round Table* (1922), *Drama at Innish* (1933).

ROWE, NICHOLAS (1674-1718), yet another lawyer turned playwright and poet, marks a return to dramatic traditions earlier than those of the Restoration. In 1709 he prepared an edition of Shakespeare's works, dividing them into acts and scenes and supplying stage directions which demonstrated how imperfectly the Elizabethan traditions were understood a century later. After this task of editing, Rowe's own work became less "classical" in structure and diction, however, and his characters moving through their somewhat melodramatic plots display human emotions rather than superhuman attitudinizing. *The Fair Penitent* and *Jane Shore,* his "she-tragedies," long held the stage because of the opportunities they offered to strongly emotional actresses like Mrs. Siddons.

PRINCIPAL PLAYS: *The Ambitious Stepmother* (1700), *Tamerlane* (1701), *The Fair Penitent* (from Massinger's *The Fatal Dowry*, 1703), *Jane Shore* (1714), *Lady Jane Grey* (1715).

COLLECTED EDITION: *Three Plays*, ed. J. R. Sutherland, London, 1929.

COMMENTARY: A. Jackson, "Rowe's Historical Tragedies," *Anglia* LIV (1930), 307-330.

ROWLEY, WILLIAM (1585?-1626), actor and playwright, was most successful in his collaborations, his unassisted compositions being marked by coarseness and sensation. One of his famous rôles was The Fat Bishop in Middleton's *A Game at Chess;* as a fat clown he was extremely popular. Wise in the ways of pleasing audiences, he was of great service to a number of playwrights, especially Thomas Middleton with whom he wrote several distinguished tragedies.

PRINCIPAL PLAYS: *A New Wonder* (1632), *All's Lost by Lust* (1633), *A Match at Midnight* (1633), *A Shoemaker a Gentleman* (1638); with Middleton: *A Fair Quarrel* (1617), *The Changeling* (1622), *The Spanish Gypsy* (1622); *The Travels of the Three English Brothers* (with Day and Wilkins, 1607), *Fortune by Land and Sea* (with Heywood, pr. 1655), *The Witch of Edmonton* (with Dekker and Ford, c. 1622).

COMMENTARY: R. G. Wiggin, *An Inquiry into the Authorship of the Middleton-Rowley Plays*, Boston, 1897; W. D. Dunkel, "Did Not Rowley Merely Revise Middleton?," *PMLA*, XLVIII (1933), 799-805.

MR. S., M. A. The author of *Gammer Gurton's Needle* has been variously identified as John Still, later Bishop of Bath and Wells, and as William Stevenson. There is nothing genuinely conclusive about either identification. See C. M. Gayley, *Representative English Comedies*, New York, 1912, I, 197-202; C. W. Roberts, "The Authorship of *Gammer Gurton's Needle*," *PQ* XIX (1940), 97-113.

SETTLE, ELKANAH (1648-1724) was a prolific and popular playwright in the heroic and heroic-sentimental modes. His fame today rests on his quarrel with Dryden resulting from the latter's pique at the success of Settle's *Empress of Morocco*. Dryden with the aid of Crowne and Shadwell wrote a critical attack on the play, to which Settle replied with an attack on *The Conquest of Granada*. This earned him a kind of immortality as the satirized Doeg in "Absalom and Achitophel."

PRINCIPAL PLAYS: *Cambyses* (1671), *The Empress of Morocco* (1673), *The Conquest of China by the Tartars* (1675), *Ibrahim the Illustrious Bassa* (1676), *Distressed Innocence, or the Princess of Persia* (1690), *The World in the Moon* (1691), *The City Ramble* (1711).

COMMENTARY: F. C. Brown, *Elkanah Settle*, Chicago, 1910; R. G. Ham, "Dryden vs. Settle," *MP*, XXV (1928), 409-416.

SHADWELL, THOMAS (1642?-1692), after graduation from Cambridge, became a professional writer and, after 1668, produced a play annually for nearly fifteen years. A devotee of Ben Jonson, Shadwell attempted to revive his comic structure of contrasted humour characters. This led to a quarrel with Dryden and an exchange of satires, including Shadwell's "The Medal of John Bayes" and Dryden's "MacFlecknoe." In 1688 Shadwell succeeded Dryden as poet laureate.

PRINCIPAL PLAYS: *The Sullen Lovers* (from Molière, 1668), *Epsom Wells* (1672), *The Virtuoso* (1676), *The Squire of Alsatia* (1688), *Bury Fair* (1689), *The Enchanted Island* (from Shakespeare's *The Tempest*, 1673).

COLLECTED EDITION: *Complete Works*, ed. Montague Summers, 5 vols., London, 1927.

COMMENTARY: A. S. Borgman, *Thomas Shadwell*, New York, 1928; W. M. Milton, "Tempest in a Teapot," *ELH*, XIV (1947), 207-218; J. H. Smith, "Shadwell, The Ladies, and the Change in Comedy," *MP*, XLVI (1948), 22-33.

SHAKESPEARE, WILLIAM (1564-1616), the son of a merchant and minor civic official of Stratford-on-Avon, educated in the Stratford school, came to London about 1586 and associated himself with the Lord Chamberlain's (later the King's) Men as actor and playwright. He rapidly became a leading member of the company and a principal shareholder and was recognized by many of his contemporaries as the leading playwright of the day. His reputation was somewhat diminished after his death, and it was not until the middle of the eighteenth century that actor-managers and critics began to recognize again his true position. By the end of the century a veritable cult had developed, partially attributable to the attraction his great central figures had for such star players as Garrick and Kemble. In the nineteenth century the cult continued to develop, fostered by such actors as Kean, Macready, Phelps and Irving, and such critics and commentators as Lamb, Coleridge, Hazlitt, Cowden-Clarke, until the entire theater was afflicted with "Bardolatry." The rise of the New Drama and a less romantic and emotional school of criticism has resulted in a more realistic analysis of Shakespeare's art without in any way denying his claim to the title of England's, and the modern world's, greatest playwright.

COMMENTARY: W. Ebisch and L. L. Schücking, *A Shakespeare Bibliography*, Oxford, 1931, [*Supplement*, 1937]; E. K. Chambers, *William Shakespeare*, 2 vols., Oxford, 1930; H. Granville-Barker, *et al.*, *A Companion to Shakespeare Studies*, New York, 1934; Ann Bradby, *Shakespeare Criticism*, Oxford, 1936 [a sampling of contemporary critical approaches].

SHAW, GEORGE BERNARD (1856-   ), an expatriate from Dublin, began his literary career in London as a novelist and columnist, and his political career as a debater for the Fabian [socialist] Society. His brilliant attack on the drama of his day appeared in his weekly columns in *The Saturday Review* (1895+) and was collected in *Dramatic Opinions and Essays*, 2 vols., 1907 (a later complete edition in 3 vols., as *Our Theaters in the Nineties*). His first plays were written for the Independent Stage Society (1892+), his first great popular successes scored at the Court Theatre (1904+).

PRINCIPAL PLAYS: *Widowers' Houses* (1892), *The Philanderer* (1893), *Mrs. Warren's Profession* (1894), *Arms and the Man* (1894), *Candida* (1895), *The Devil's Disciple* (1897), *Caesar and Cleopatra* (1899), *Man and Superman* (1903), *John Bull's Other Island* (1907), *Major Barbara*

(1907), *Getting Married* (1908), *The Doctor's Dilemma* (1911), *Androcles and the Lion* (1913), *Pygmalion* (1913), *Heartbreak House* (1917), *Back to Methuselah* (1921), *Saint Joan* (1923), *The Apple Cart* (1930), *Too True to Be Good* (1932), *Geneva* (1938), *"In Good King Charles' Golden Days"* (1939), *Buoyant Billions* (1949).

COMMENTARY: A. Henderson, *Bernard Shaw, Playboy and Prophet,* New York, 1932; G. K. Chesterton, *George Bernard Shaw,* New York, 1909; Hesketh Pearson, *G. B. S.: A Full Length Portrait,* New York, 1942; E. R. Bentley, *Bernard Shaw,* Norfolk (Conn.), 1947, William Ervine, *The Universe of GBS,* New York, 1949.

SHERIDAN, RICHARD BRINSLEY (1751-1816), son of the actor Thomas Sheridan and his novelist-playwright wife Frances, wrote his first successful comedy (*The Rivals*) when he was 24. With equal ease he turned out a comic opera (*The Duenna*), a revision of Vanbrugh, a satire on the contemporary theater, and the most famous comedy of the eighteenth century. In 1776 he purchased Garrick's share in Drury Lane and became manager—at first brilliantly, later carelessly as the fascination of politics grew upon him. After 1780 he was much in the House of Commons and seldom in the Green Room at Drury. He was a celebrated wit and as facile a speaker and *bon vivant* as writer of comedy.

PRINCIPAL PLAYS: *The Rivals* (1775), *The Duenna* (1775), *A Trip to Scarborough* (rev. from Vanbrugh, *The Relapse,* 1777), *The School for Scandal* (1777), *The Critic* (1779), *Pizarro* (tr. from Kotzebue, *The Spaniards in Peru,* 1799).

COLLECTED EDITION: *The Plays and Poems of Sheridan,* ed. R. C. Rhodes, 3 vols., Oxford, 1928.

COMMENTARY: R. C. Rhodes, *Harlequin Sheridan,* London, 1933; T. Moore, *Memoirs of The Life of Richard Brinsley Sheridan,* London, 1825.

SHEIL, RICHARD LALOR (1791-1851), known as "Orator Sheil" for his impassioned parliamentary speeches, came to London from Ireland with the intention of setting up as a barrister. When success eluded him, he took refuge in literature, writing a series of bombastic and melodramatic plays for his Irish compatriot, Eliza O'Neill. When she left the stage to become Lady Boothby, Sheil's inspiration failed and he gave up the theater for politics. His plays are actors' vehicles, full of claptrapping sentiment and horrendous situations modeled on the most violent of the Jacobeans, and his success was largely dependent upon the skill with which he outfitted the talents of his stars—Miss O'Neill, Charles Kemble, and W. C. Macready.

PRINCIPAL PLAYS: *The Apostate* (1817), *Evadne* (from Shirley, *The*

Traitor, and Massinger, *The Fatal Dowry,* 1819), *Bellamira, or the Fall of Tunis* (1818), *The Huguenot* (1822).

COMMENTARY: W. T. McCullagh, *Memoirs of Richard Lalor Sheil,* 2 vols., London, 1855.

SHIRLEY, JAMES (1596-1666), educated at the Merchant Taylors' School, at Oxford and at Cambridge, was headmaster of a grammar school before commencing as a playwright in 1625. He wrote some forty plays in all the popular types: romantic comedy, comedy of manners, revenge tragedy, tragicomedy. He wrote also masques and poems of greater freshness and originality than his plays which are full of echoes of the great dramatists who had preceded him. Such works as *Hyde Park* and *The Lady of Pleasure* display him at his best as a kind of bridge (with Fletcher) between Caroline and Restoration comedy.

PRINCIPAL PLAYS: *The Maid's Revenge* (1626), *The Witty Fair One* (1628), *The Traitor* (1631), *Love's Cruelty* (1631), *The Changes* (1632), *Hyde Park* (1632), *The Gamester* (1633), *The Coronation* (1635), *The Lady of Pleasure* (1635), *The Cardinal* (1641), *The Sisters* (1642).

COLLECTED EDITION: *Dramatic Works and Poems,* ed. A. Dyce, 6 vols., London, 1833.

COMMENTARY: A. H. Nason, *James Shirley, Dramatist: a Biographical and Critical Study,* New York, 1915; A. C. Baugh, "Some New Facts about Shirley," *MLR,* XVII (1922), 228-235, and "Further Facts about James Shirley," *RES,* VII (1931), 62-66; A. H. Stevenson, "James Shirley and the Actors at the First Irish Theater," *MP,* XL (1942), 147-160. H. T. Parlin, *A Study in Shirley's Comedies of London Life,* Austin, 1914; R. S. Forsythe, *The Relation of Shirley's Plays to the Elizabethan Drama,* New York, 1914.

SOUTHERNE, THOMAS (1660-1746), born and educated in Dublin, went to London as a barrister but turned to the theater about 1682, perhaps under the influence of his friend, Dryden. His works may be distinguished from those of his greater contemporaries by their disregard of French neo-classical rules, their direct appeal to an increasingly bourgeois audience in subordinating theme and character-portrayal to minutely analyzed scenes of passion and emotion, and by their development of the female as the central tragic figure. He is thus a transitional figure, looking towards the sentimental and domestic drama of the eighteenth and nineteenth centuries.

PRINCIPAL PLAYS: *The Loyal Brother* (1682), *The Disappointment* (1684), *Sir Anthony Love* (1691), *The Maid's Last Prayer* (1693), *The Fatal Marriage* (from a story by A. Behn, 1694), *Oroonoko* (from a story by A. Behn, 1696), *The Fate of Capua* (1700).

COMMENTARY: J. W. Dodds, *Thomas Southerne, Dramatist,* New Haven, 1933.

STEELE, SIR RICHARD (1672-1729), Dublin born, the friend and associate of Joseph Addison, wrote his first comedy in 1701 with the intention of restoring morality to the stage. Though neither this nor its immediate successors (including *The Tender Husband,* which applies the techniques of Restoration comedy to a serious domestic situation) was particularly pleasing to the audiences, the great success of *The Conscious Lovers* two decades later indicates that Steele was ahead of his audiences and had anticipated the change in their tastes. In 1715, urging that he would direct the theater into useful channels, Steele obtained a life-patent to Drury Lane and for seven years participated more or less actively in the management.

PRINCIPAL PLAYS: *The Funeral* (1701), *The Lying Lover* (1703), *The Tender Husband* (1705), *The Conscious Lovers* (1722).

COLLECTED EDITION: *Dramatic Works,* ed. G. A. Aitken, New York, 1903.

COMMENTARY: G. A. Aitken, *Life of Richard Steele,* 2 vols., London, 1889.

SYNGE, [pronounced SING] JOHN MILLINGTON (1871-1909), at the urging of W. B. Yeats, returned from Paris to his native Ireland to participate in the Irish Renaissance. After a series of annual visits to the Aran Islands he began the writing of peasant plays which, resented at first, later won him recognition as the major dramatist of the "First Generation" of the Abbey Theatre. His plays are deceptively simple, his themes and motifs going back through folk-legend to remotest antiquity, and his dialogue, based on the speech of the Aran Islanders as recorded by himself, is poetic in its rich imagery and singular rhythms.

PRINCIPAL PLAYS: *The Shadow of the Glen* (1903), *Riders to the Sea* (1904), *The Well of the Saints* (1905), *The Playboy of the Western World* (1907), *The Tinker's Wedding* (1907), *Deirdre of the Sorrows* (posthumous, 1910).

COLLECTED EDITION: *Complete Works,* 4 vols., London, 1935.

COMMENTARY: M. Bourgeois, *John Millington Synge and the Irish Theater,* London, 1913; A. D. Estill, *The Sources of Synge,* Philadelphia, 1931; D. H. Greene, "Synge's Unfinished Deirdre," *PMLA,* LXIII (1948), 1314-1321, and "*The Shadow of the Glen* and *The Widow of Ephesus,*" *PMLA* (1947), 233-238, and "*The Tinker's Wedding,* a Revaluation," *PMLA,* LXII (1947), 824-827, and "*The Playboy* and Irish Nationalism," *JEGP,* XLVI (1947), 199-201; R. L. Collins,

"The Distinction of *Riders to the Sea,*" *Univ. of Kansas City Rev.* XIII (1947), 278-284.

TAYLOR, TOM (1817-1880), professional journalist and editor of *Punch,* was one of the more successful carpenters of plays for the mid-Victorian theater. Melodrama, farce, and romanticized history were his forte, and in such works as *Still Waters Run Deep* and *The Ticket-of-Leave Man* there is the barest suggestion of the domestic problem play which was to dominate the stage of the eighties and nineties. The latter play also introduces an early model of the stage detective, the immortal Hawkshaw.

PRINCIPAL PLAYS: *To Parents and Guardians* (1845), *Still Waters Run Deep* (1855), *Our American Cousin* (1858), *The Fool's Revenge* (from Victor Hugo, 1859), *The Ticket-of-Leave Man* (1863).

COMMENTARY: W. Tolles, *Tom Taylor and the Victorian Drama,* New York, 1940.

TOURNEUR, CYRIL (1580?-1626), is a very nearly anonymous poet and playwright. Little is known of his life or his contemporary reputation. *The Revenger's Tragedy* seems to have been acted by the King's (Globe-Blackfriars') Company; *The Atheist's Tragedy,* according to its title page, was "often" acted in "divers places." There have been several rather futile attempts to ascribe the first play to another author. If his works are, as has been said, melodramas, few contemporaries found richer expression for the dramatic anatomizing of melancholy.

PLAYS: *The Revenger's Tragedy* (pr. 1607), *The Atheist's Tragedy* (pr. 1611).

COLLECTED EDITION: *Works of Cyril Tourneur,* ed. A. Nicoll, London, 1929.

COMMENTARY: L. Lockert, "The Greatest of Elizabethan Melodramas," *Parrott Presentation Vol.,* Princeton, 1935, pp. 103-126; E. M. Waith, "The Ascription of Speeches in *The Revenger's Tragedy,*" *MLN,* LVII (1942), 119-121; U. M. Ellis-Fermor, "The Imagery of *The Revenger's Tragedy* and *The Atheist's Tragedy,*" *MLR,* XXX (1935), 289-301.

UDALL, NICHOLAS (1505-1556), headmaster of Eton and Westminster, translated and arranged portions of the works of Terence into a grammar-school text of rhetoric: *Flowers for Latin-Speaking, Selected and Gathered out of Terence and the Same Translated into English* (1533). In 1553 he wrote a political interlude *Respublica,* and about the same time one of the two first fully developed English comedies in the vernacular. *Roister Doister* may or may not precede *Gammer Gur-*

ton's Needle, but the two plays share the distinction of introducing to the English theater the five-act structure and complex intrigue of Roman comedy. *Roister Doister* is somewhat closer to the classical tradition in its characteristic parasite, Merrygreek, and its braggart warrior, Ralph.

PLAYS: *Respublica* (1553), *Ralph Roister Doister* (*c.* 1553).

COMMENTARY: See *Roister Doister,* ed. by G. C. Child, Boston, 1912; T. W. Baldwin and M. C. Linthicum, "The Date of *Ralph Roister Doister,*" *PQ,* VI (1927), 379-395; W. Peery, "The Prayer for the Queen in *Roister Doister,*" *Univ. of Texas Studies in English,* XVII (1948), 222-233; L. Bradner, "A Test for Udall's Authorship [of *Respublica*]," *MLN,* XLII (1927), 378-380.

VANBRUGH [pronounced VANBROOK], SIR JOHN (1664-1726), soldier and architect, was provoked into playwriting by his objections to the outcome of Cibber's *Love's Last Shift.* Aside from *The Relapse* and *The Provoked Wife* his plays are adaptations from the French, carelessly written but with a certain verve and eye for stage-effect. He designed and managed for two years the New Theatre in the Haymarket, an ornate neo-classical structure which proved totally unsuitable for the production of plays and became the King's Theatre, the later home of opera and pantomime.

PRINCIPAL PLAYS: *The Relapse* (1696), *The Provoked Wife* (1697), *Aesop* (from Boursalt, 1696-7), *The False Friend* (from Le Sage, 1702), *The Confederacy* (from Dancourt, 1705), *The Mistake* (from Molière, 1705), *The Cuckold in Conceit* (from Molière, 1707), *Journey to London* (uncompleted; finished by Cibber as *The Provoked Husband,* 1728).

COLLECTED EDITION: *Complete Works,* ed. B. Dobrée and G. Webb, 4 vols., London, 1927-1928.

COMMENTARY: Laurence Whistler, *Sir John Vanbrugh,* London, 1938; G. H. Lovegrove, *The Life, Works, and Influence of Sir John Vanbrugh,* London, 1902; P. Mueschke and J. Fleisher, "A Re-Evaluation of Vanbrugh," *PMLA,* XLIX (1934), 848-889; R. C. Boys, "The Architect Vanbrugh and the Wits," *College Art Jour.,* VI (1947), 283-290.

WEBSTER, JOHN (1580?-1638), son of a London tailor, first appears in Henslowe's accounts in 1602 as author and collaborator on various plays. Although his contemporary reputation was great, almost nothing is known of his life or his theatrical career beyond the record of his plays. As a tragic writer he must be ranked close to Shakespeare; his comedies, except those written in collaboration with Dekker, and his tragicomedies, are less successful.

PRINCIPAL PLAYS: *Westward Ho* (with Dekker, 1603), Induction to *The Malcontent* (1604), *Northward Ho* (with Dekker, 1604), *Sir Thomas Wyatt* (with Dekker, 1607), *The White Devil* (1608), *The Duchess of Malfi* (1613), *The Devil's Law Case* (1623), *Appius and Virginia* (with Heywood, pr. 1654), *A Cure for a Cuckold* (with Rowley, pr. 1661).

COLLECTED EDITION: *The Complete Works of John Webster*, ed. F. L. Lucas, 4 vols., London, 1927.

COMMENTARY: E. E. Stoll, *John Webster*, Cambridge (Mass.), 1905; R. Brooke, *John Webster and the Elizabethan Drama*, London, 1916; F. E. Pierce, *The Collaboration of Webster and Dekker*, New York, 1909.

WILDE, OSCAR (1854-1900), born in Ireland and educated at Trinity, Dublin, and Oxford, became a disciple of Ruskin and Pater and a founder of the cult of aestheticism and art-for-art's-sake mocked by W. S. Gilbert in *Patience*. His comedies, beginning with *Lady Windermere's Fan* in 1892, brought him wide popular renown. He was acclaimed more for his wit than his drama, which, except in *The Importance of Being Earnest*, is perfunctory and mechanical.

PRINCIPAL PLAYS: *The Duchess of Padua* (1891), *Lady Windermere's Fan* (1892), *A Woman of No Importance* (1893), *Salome* (in French, produced in Paris, 1894), *The Ideal Husband* (1895), *The Importance of Being Earnest* (1895).

COLLECTED EDITIONS: *Complete Works*, 14 vols., London, 1908; *Plays*, New York, Modern Library (no date).

COMMENTARY: Frances Winwar, *Oscar Wilde and the Yellow Nineties*, New York, 1940; A. H. Nethercot, "Oscar Wilde and the Devil's Advocate," *PMLA*, LIX (1944), 833-850; E. Roditi, *Oscar Wilde*, Norfolk (Conn.), 1947.

WYCHERLEY, WILLIAM (1641-1716), born in Shropshire, was educated in France and, briefly, at Oxford. Shortly after 1660 he was enrolled in the Inner Temple in London. In 1671 his first comedy was performed and won him the favor of the court. His subsequent plays are noted for their sardonic and sometimes brutally comic picture of London life; a comparison of his *The Plain Dealer* with its "source" in Molière's *Le Misanthrope* indicates his savage disposition and explains the prudish nose-holding of such nineteenth century critics as Macaulay who thought him merely licentious and indecent.

PRINCIPAL PLAYS: *Love in a Wood* (1671), *The Gentleman Dancing-Master* (1672), *The Country Wife* (1675), *The Plain Dealer* (in part from Racine and Molière, 1676).

COLLECTED EDITION: *Complete Works,* ed. Montague Summers, 4 vols., London, 1924.

COMMENTARY: W. Connely, *Brawny Wycherley,* New York, 1930; H. P. Vincent, "The Death of William Wycherley," *Harvard Studies and Notes in Phil. and Lit.,* XV, (1933), 219-242.

YEATS, WILLIAM BUTLER (1865-1939), son of an Irish painter, spent his early years in London. He was, nonetheless, intensely interested in the revival of Irish culture, and became a leader in the Literary Renaissance that led to the founding of the Abbey Theatre. Although his enduring reputation is likely to be that of one of the greatest modern poets, his plays are not without significance in the development of the folk-play and the revitalizing of poetic drama. His theories and pronouncements on dramatic and theatrical matters are of great interest and will be found principally in *The Cutting of an Agate,* 1912.

PRINCIPAL PLAYS: *The Countess Cathleen* (1892), *The Land of Heart's Desire* (1894), *Cathleen ni Houlihan* (1902), *The Pot of Broth* (1904), *The King's Threshold* (1904), *On Baile's Strand* (1904), *Deirdre* (1907), *Four Plays for Dancers* (Irish materials treated in Japanese Noh style, 1921), *Words upon the Windowpane* (1930).

COLLECTED EDITION: *Collected Plays,* New York, 1935.

COMMENTARY: A. J. A. Symonds, *Bibliography,* London, 1924; J. Hone, *W. B. Yeats,* New York, 1943.

ABBREVIATIONS

CE	*College English*
ELH	*English Literary History*
E St	*Englische Studien*
HLQ	*Huntington Library Quarterly*
JEGP	*Journal of English and Germanic Philology*
MLN	*Modern Language Notes*
MLQ	*Modern Language Quarterly*
MLR	*Modern Language Review*
MP	*Modern Philology*
N & Q	*Notes and Queries*
PMLA	*Publications of the Modern Language Association*
PQ	*Philological Quarterly*
QRL	*Quarterly Review of Literature*
RES	*Review of English Studies*
SP	*Studies in Philology*

Index

This index lists under a single alphabet play-titles (in *italics*), authors, actors, theaters, characters in plays, and such subjects as staging, characterization, and so forth. The principal treatment of any entry is indicated by **bold-face** numerals, an illustration by *italic* numerals.

(1)